JEAN FOUQUET

THE MELUN DIPTYCH

JEAN FOUQUET

The Melun Diptych

For the Gemäldegalerie, Staatliche Museen zu Berlin,
edited by Stephan Kemperdick

Gemäldegalerie
Staatliche Museen zu Berlin

MICHAEL IMHOF VERLAG

IMPRINT

This publication accompanies the exhibition
JEAN FOUQUET. THE MELUN DIPTYCH
Gemäldegalerie der Staatlichen Museen – Preußischer Kulturbesitz
September 15, 2017 to January 7, 2018

EXHIBITION
Stephan Kemperdick

CONSERVATION
Georg Josef Dietz, Sandra Stelzig

FRAMING AND EXHIBITION INSTALLATION
Christine Exler, Peter Scheel, Rainer Wendler

EXHIBITION ARCHITECTURE
Hansjörg Hartung

PHOTOGRAPHY
Christoph Schmidt

EXHIBITION SECRETARY
Julie Rowlins

FINANCES
Maren Eichhorn-Johannsen

COMMUNICATION
Fabian Fröhlich

EDUCATIONAL SERVICES
Ines Bellin

MUSEUM PUBLICATIONS MANAGEMENT
Sigrid Wollmeiner

DESIGN AND REPRODUCTIONS
Patricia Koch, Michael Imhof Verlag

TRANSLATIONS
Melissa M. Thorson: Essays by Kemperdick, Seidel, König,
Kurmann-Schwarz, Kurmann, von Fircks, Dyballa, Schrijvers
and all catalogue entries
Svea Janzen: Preface, Introduction, and essay by Klein

PROOFREADING
David Sánchez Cano, Svea Janzen, Stephan Kemperdick

PUBLISHED BY
Michael Imhof Verlag GmbH & Co. KG
Stettiner Str. 25
D-36100 Petersberg
Tel. 0661/29 19 16 6-0
Fax 0661/29 19 16 6-9
info@imhof-verlag.de
www.imhof-verlag.com

PRINT
Gutenberg Beuys Feindruckerei GmbH, Langenhagen

© 2018 Staatliche Museen zu Berlin – Preußischer Kulturbesitz
© 2018 Michael Imhof Verlag, Petersberg

www.smb.museum
www.imhof-verlag.com

ISBN 978-3-7319-0620-9

COVER ILLUSTRATIONS
Front: Jean Fouquet, Madonna, Antwerp, Koninklijke Museum voor
Schone Kunsten
Back: Jean Fouquet, Self-Portrait, Paris, Louvre

CONTENTS

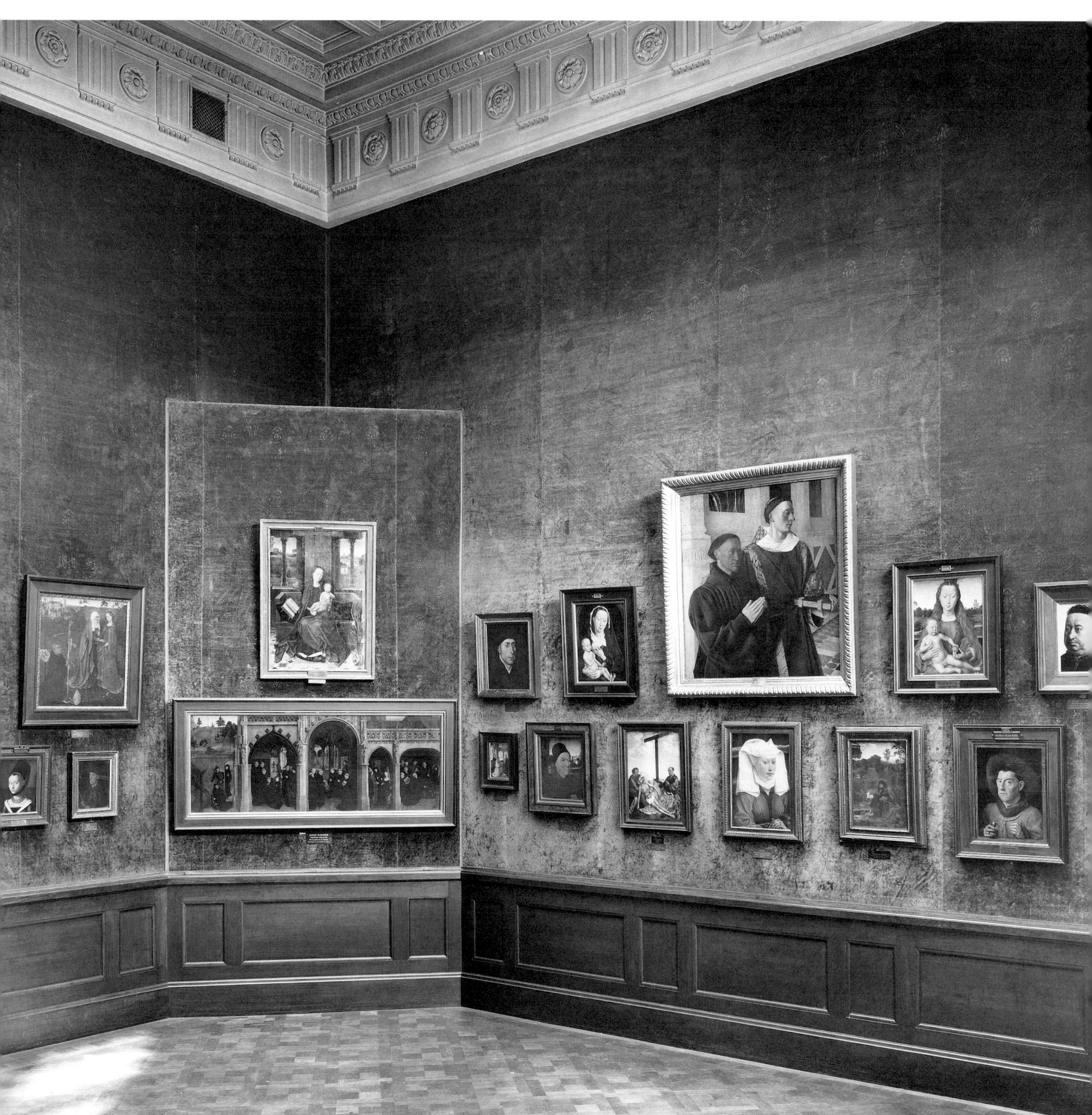

Kaiser-Friedrich-Museum Berlin, Room 70, in 1917

PREFACE

Jean Fouquet ranks among the most important artists of the 15th century. His work unites in an unparalleled fashion the French pictorial tradition with elements derived from both Netherlandish painting and the Italian Renaissance. The unique charm of his works has enchanted and challenged experts and museum visitors until today.

The *Diptych of Melun*, which is regarded as his *chef d'œuvre*, is at the center of this small and exquisite exhibition. The two panels of the diptych were separated around 1775 and are now, after exactly 80 years, reunited for the first time since the Paris 1937 World Fair. This and the fact that they will likely not be exhibited together for a long time to come, will attract art lovers and connoisseurs to the Gemäldegalerie. The show is complemented by other important paintings from the Gemäldegalerie's own collection as well as by several ravishing and, due to their light sensibility, rarely exhibited drawings from the neighboring Kupferstichkabinett, which illustrates the richness and the outstanding quality of the collections of the Staatliche Museen zu Berlin, in this case particularly of the museums located at the Kulturforum.

We are very delighted and grateful for the fact that alongside the Koninklijk Museum voor Schone Kunsten Antwerp—whose loan of the wing with the Madonna was of course the *conditio sine qua non* for the whole undertaking—several other important museums have contributed to this project with top-level loans. Thus, the portrait of the Court Jester Gonella from the Kunsthistorisches Museum in Vienna attributed to Fouquet can now for the first time be studied together with the painter's undisputed works. An incunabula of European portrait painting, Jean Fouquet's enamel self-portrait from the collections of the Musée du Louvre, complements the exhibition. This medallion once adorned the frame of the diptych, and thus all of the diptych's preserved parts are, albeit for only a short time, united again.

From the beginning the exhibition project was blessed with lively interest from the scholarly community. This resulted in the present catalogue, which has ended up being much more than just a simple companion volume to the exhibition. In their essays, sixteen internationally renowned scholars illuminate various facets of Fouquet's oeuvre, the complexity of which is mirrored in their sometimes controversial opinions.

I owe my gratitude to Stephan Kemperdick, who curated the exhibition and edited the catalogue, and to our research assistants Katrin Dyballa and Christine Seidel. This exhibition would not have been possible without the outstanding generosity of the lenders. Thanks are due to Manfred Sellink, director of the Koninklijk Museum voor Schone Kunsten Antwerp, to Jannic Durand, director of the Département des objets d'art at the Musée du Louvre, and to the responsible curator, Élisabeth Antoine. I would also like to express my gratitude to Stefan Weppelmann, director of the Gemäldegalerie of the Kunsthistorisches Museum in Vienna, and to the curator Sabine Penot; further to Eike Schmidt, director of the Gallerie degli Uffizi in Florence; and finally to Holm Bevers, acting director of the Kupferstichkabinett of the Staatliche Museen zu Berlin, as well as to its curator Dagmar Korbacher and its chief conservator Georg Josef Dietz. At the Gemäldegalerie thanks are also due to Rainer Wendler, who made a wonderful new frame for the Berlin panel which is modeled after the lost original frame in such a way that it also matches the frame of the Antwerp panel. Sandra Stelzig was responsible for the conservation of the Berlin painting. Sarah Salomon, Christoph Schmidt, Peter Scheel and Julie Rowlins contributed largely to the realization of the exhibition. Hansjörg Hartung created a most appropriate exhibition architecture. Special thanks are finally also due to all the contributors to the catalogue as well as to the publisher Michael Imhof and the layout designer Patricia Koch, who in well-established cooperation created this appealing volume.

Michael Eissenhauer
Director General of the Staatliche Museen zu Berlin
Director of the Gemäldegalerie and the
Skulpturensammlung

Christine Seidel and Stephan Kemperdick

1415-1483
FRANCE IN THE TIMES OF JEAN FOUQUET

Jean Fouquet lived in a period that was marked by profound social changes and political upheaval. France, which at the beginning of the century had been politically weakened and territorially divided, emerged from around 1430 on as a powerful state ruled by an undisputed king. Fouquet was born probably in the years before or around 1420 in Tours, a town on the Loire that had belonged to the crown land since the times of Louis IX of France (1214-1270), but which only rose to greater importance under Charles VII (1403-1461) and his successors. Fouquet's childhood and youth coincide with the final phase of the Hundred Years' War between England and France, which had lasted since 1337 and which seemed to take a catastrophic turn in 1415 when French troops were defeated by Henry V at Agincourt in Normandy. The territories north of the Loire were occupied by the English, Burgundian and English troops marched into Paris, while the royalist Armagnacs fled the capital. The French king Charles VI, who reigned for over forty years despite suffering from mental illness, and his queen Isabeau of Bavaria, whose negative reputation has lasted until today, gave in to the English claim for the French crown. On May 21, 1420 the king signed the corresponding Treaty of Troyes and the unity of both crowns was manifested in the wedding of Charles' daughter Catherine of France to the English king Henry V. This not only turned Henry into Charles's adoptive son as it were, but also made him his successor.[1] According to the agreement the French crown should go over to the English king and his successors after the death of Charles VI. The dauphin Charles, who in 1418 had precipitously fled to Bourges, was wrongfully denounced as a bastard and excluded from the succession to the throne.[2]

It had only been after the deaths of all of his brothers, the last of whom had passed away in 1417, that Charles had become dauphin and as such successor to the throne. In 1413 he was engaged to Marie d'Anjou, daughter of duke Louis II d'Anjou and sister of René d'Anjou (1409-1480). The latter was one of the most extraordinary rulers of the period and King of Naples from 1435 to 1442, who wrote poetry and employed the exquisite painter Barthélemy d'Eyck (cat. 9). Having spent parts of his youth between 1415 and 1416 at the Angevin court in Tarascon in Provence and in Anjou, Charles must have known René, who was younger by six years. It was only in 1422, living in exile in Bourges, when Charles married his fiancée Marie d'Anjou.

At first it seemed as if the crown was lost for Charles. But in 1422, Henry V died and only a few months later Charles VI followed him to the grave. The English king left behind an infant son, Henry VI (1421-1471), who was proclaimed King of England and France in Paris, while almost simultaneously in Bourges, the dauphin was proclaimed the legitimate French King Charles VII by his followers. For seven years, he held court in the central territories of the French crown, mocked as "King of Bourges", until the tide turned with Joan of Arc. The Maid of Orleans and Charles VII met in 1429 in Chinon on the Loire, where she succeeded in convincing him of her mission. When shortly thereafter she was able to free the city of Orleans from the English siege, the path to Reims and thus to the ceremonial crowning was open. Joan of Arc accompanied Charles VII to the cathedral of Reims, where on July 17, 1429 he was anointed as King of France.[3] In the rush, a simple crown had to be manufactured for the ceremony, since the French regalia were kept in the traditional burial place of the kings in St. Denis, hence out of reach in the occupied territories.[4] Paris, where the duke of Bedford (1389-1435) acted as regent for his underage nephew Henry VI, initially remained under English and Burgundian rule. Charles VII, on the other hand, was to betray Joan of Arc only a short time afterwards when she was taken captive by the Burgundians, sold to the English and burnt in 1431 in Rouen; not until 1456 was she vindicated in official proceedings. Changing political alliances marked the king's regency from its onset.[5] In a full-page miniature in the Munich Boccaccio (Bayerische Staatsbibliothek, cod. Gall. 6) Fouquet recorded the famous *Lit de justice de Vendôme*, the trial for treason against Jean II d'Alençon presided by Charles in 1458. It was probably meant as an allegory for the ever-changing destinies that seemed to be mirrored in Boccaccio's *On the Fates of Famous Men*.

The political climate changed decisively with the Congress of Arras in 1435, when the Duke of Burgundy, Philip the Good, acknowledged Charles VII as legitimate ruler, which set an end to the Hundred Years' War. In 1437 the king finally found himself able to enter Paris; the townspeople, who could not necessarily count on the benignity of a king whom they had repudiated for so long, greeted him with "all due honors and humbleness"[6] and presented him with the keys to the city.[7] From the 1430s to the 1450s, Charles VII led numerous military campaigns, in the course of which large parts of the territories occupied by the English were re-conquered for the crown: by 1453 Champagne, Normandy, and Guyenne had been recuperated as French territories. These triumphs earned Charles the title of "most victorious king" (fig. 11).

During the years of the re-conquest, young Fouquet lived in Rome; probably by the end of the 1440s he returned to what had become an almost entirely united France. When Charles VII died in 1461 in Mehun-sur-Yèvre near Bourges, a large funeral cortège set off for Paris. The king's body lay in state in Notre-Dame and his effigy was carried through the streets, accompanied by a funeral procession.[8] Around this time Fouquet stayed in Paris, where the painter Pierre Hennes from Tours was supposed to meet him in connection with the preparations for the obsequies, possibly concerning the painting of Charles' death mask. However, Pierre Hennes could not find Fouquet.[9] Charles VII, father of countless children with his queen and several mistresses—among them the famous Agnès Sorel (cat.

5)—left behind a consolidated state. Long forgotten were the insecurities of the "roi de Bourges"; the king had become an assertive and victorious monarch who had strengthened the crown territorially and administratively.[10] His son Louis (1423-1483), who in his youth had rebelled against his father, mounted the throne as Louis XI. In his service Fouquet rose to the position of court painter, a position occupied since the times of Charles VII by Jacob de Littemont, who died in 1474. Yet even before this, Fouquet had received commissions from Charles (fig. 11) as well as from Louis.[11] At first the distrustful new king removed his father's stalwarts from all higher functionary positions, but soon afterwards took them back in his service. Among them were some of Fouquet's clients, such as Étienne Chevalier and Guillaume Jouvenel des Ursins. Before Louis XI's death in 1483 he had successfully continued the expansion of royal power begun under his father as well as the strengthening of France, which in the following years was to expand its military and political engagement outside its own territories, especially in Italy. Jean Fouquet died a few years before the king; in 1481 a document mentions his widow. He established a school of manuscript illumination in Tours and left behind two sons who were active as illuminators, Louis and François.

1   Potin 2017, p. 230.

2   Contamine 2017, pp. 70-71.

3   Ibid., pp. 178–181. The most detailed description can be found in a letter of three Angevin noblemen to Marie d'Anjou and her mother Yolande both of whom were not attendant in Reims; du Fresne de Beaucourt 1882, pp. 228-229.

4   Vallet de Viriville 1863, Vol. 2, pp. 96–97.

5   After the Duke of Brittany and Connétable of France, Arthur III de Richemont, fell into disgrace in 1427, his successor Georges de la Trémoille, who had been successful in Orléans and the following campaigns, only stayed in office until 1433. When Richemont had him jailed, the king did not intervene. La Trémoille was part of those aristocrats who in 1440 led the uprising known under the name *Praguerie*; Contamine 2017, pp. 251-255.

6   Contamine 2017, p. 234.

7   Vale 1974, p. 199.

8   Ibid., pp. 210-211; Contamine 2017, pp. 397-400.

9   Cat. Paris 2003, p. 418, doc. 2; Schaefer 1994, pp. 197, 346ff.

10   This is further illustrated by posthumous praise of the king such as the *Épitaphe pour Charles VII* by Simon Grebon and the *Vigiles de la mort de Charles VII*, composed in 1483 by Martial d'Auvergne (Paris, BnF, Ms. Fr. 5054).

11   Schaefer 1994, p. 349; Cat. Paris 2003, p. 420, doc 12. Fouquet painted the frontispiece of the statutes of the Order of Saint Michael founded by Louis XI in 1469; Paris, BnF, Ms. fr. 19819; Cat. Paris 2003, no. 29.

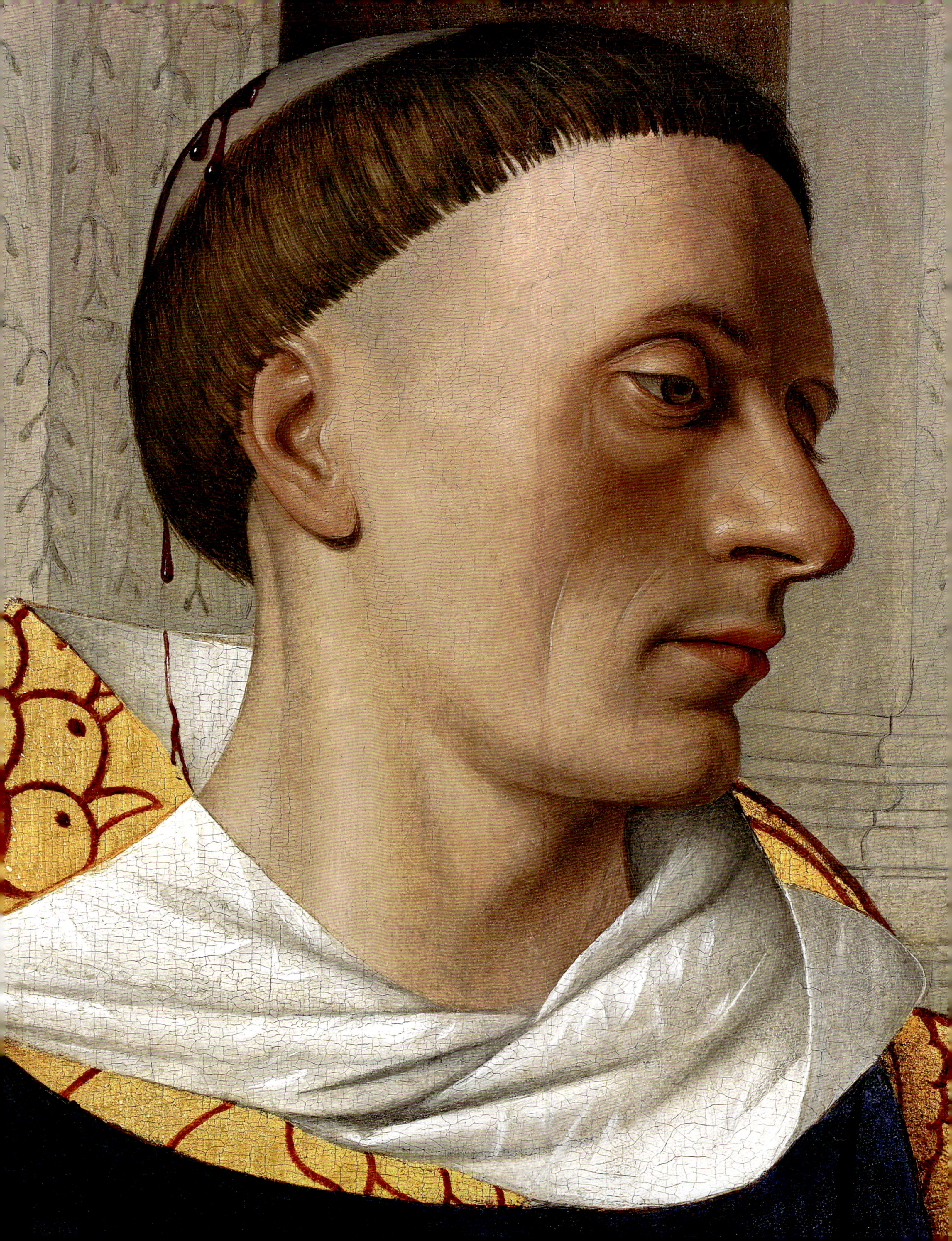

Stephan Kemperdick

FOULQUET LE PEINTRE.
THE PANEL PAINTER JEAN FOUQUET
AND THE *MELUN DIPTYCH*

The Madonna with her bare breast, round as a billiard ball, and her snow-white skin glowing against a background of red and blue angels is astonishing to the modern viewer. Today this panel, one of the most remarkable works of 15th-century painting, is far better known than its creator, and has also proven its usefulness as a motif for book covers and a challenge to artists of our time. This *Virgin and Child* once formed the right wing of a diptych (figs. 93, 94, cat. 1) painted by Jean Fouquet not long after 1452 for Étienne Chevalier, treasurer of King Charles VII of France. Its counterpart, the original left wing of the diptych, shows the donor himself presented to the Mother of God and her Son by St. Stephen, his patron saint. In a shockingly off-handed way, blood drips from the back of the tonsured head of St. Stephen, the first Christian martyr, in thin, dark-red threads that echo the red brocade pattern on the trim of Stephen's dalmatic.

All three adults are shown in half figure and are nearly life-size. Depicted at close range, they fill most of the area of the panels, which measure nearly one meter in height. The robust, almost square format of the paintings and the monumentality of the figures set these two panels apart from the Early Netherlandish works among which they usually hang in their respective museums in Berlin and Antwerp. Yet the play of light and shade and the realism of detail also betray a connection to the art of the Low Countries, while the dominant triad of white, red, and blue in the image of the Virgin is familiar from

French manuscript illumination of the early 15th century. At the same time, the architecture depicted in the patron's wing is taken straight from the Italian Renaissance and recedes into depth according to the rules of linear perspective. This dynamic spatiality contrasts with the relief-like arrangement of the *Virgin and Child*, and Fouquet further intensifies the disparity between the two panels by using differing degrees of abstraction—for example in the rendering of gold, using glistening gold leaf on the left wing and brownish paint on the right. Yet the painter also confidently unifies the two very different panels of the diptych: while the Mother of God appears in shimmering white and light gray against a red-blue background, in the patron's wing blue and red figures are placed before light gray architecture. Black, heavily veined squares of polished marble adorn both the wall in the left panel and the throne in the right one. In this singular masterpiece, as in his other panel paintings and manuscript illuminations, Fouquet has woven strands of French artistic tradition together with inspirations from the North and the South.

When Jean Fouquet was born around 1420 in Tours on the river Loire, many of the most notable representatives of the courtly International Style in France, like the Limbourg Brothers († 1416), had already disappeared, and the first generation of great innovators in Netherlandish painting had entered the stage. In 1422, Jan van Eyck began his career as a court painter, which in 1425 was to take him from the court of Holland in The Hague to Lille and Bruges in the services of the Duke of Burgundy; meanwhile, Rogier van der Weyden, born in 1399, was finishing his training and working as a journeyman in

Fig. 1. Melun Diptych, Donor's wing, detail: St. Stephen, scale 1:1

Tournai. In 1432, when Fouquet may have been a young apprentice, Jan van Eyck completed his most important work, the famous *Ghent Altarpiece*; the same year, Rogier became an independent master in his home town. The same period also saw the rise of the great protagonists of Early Renaissance art in Italy. Since 1418, Fra Angelico had been working as a painter in Tuscany, and in Florence in the 1420s, Masaccio executed the pioneering murals of the Brancacci Chapel in Santa Maria del Carmine as well as the perspectively correct fresco of the *Holy Trinity* in Santa Maria Novella.

When Fouquet died around 1480, Jan van Eyck had been deceased for 40 years, Fra Angelico for 25 years, and Rogier van der Weyden for 15 years. In the meantime, book printing and engraving had been invented and had spread from the upper and middle Rhineland to all of Europe. Jean Clouet, who was to become court painter to King François I of France, was born in Brussels, Perugino and Botticelli accomplished the first frescoes of the Sistine Chapel, and Albrecht Dürer was almost ten years old.

Panel Painting

In Northern Europe, panel painting was the medium in which the masters of the generation born around 1400 developed their pioneering pictorial language, their approach to the representation of reality, and their artistic technique. Panel painting, especially in the now fully developed oil technique, became the leading medium of artistic innovations for generations to come. Jean Fouquet, too, achieved impeccable mastery in this demanding, highly valued technique. Panel paintings, the *Portrait of King Charles VII* (fig. 11) and the *Melun Diptych* presented here (cat. 1), belong to his earliest known works, while his earliest documented piece, long since lost, was the *Portrait of Pope Eugene IV and Two Retainers*, a painting on canvas which Fouquet executed in Rome around 1446.[1] It was probably this portrait not least of all that inspired the Italian architect and sculptor Filarete, who had met Fouquet in the Eternal City, to refer to him as a "buon maestro, massime de ritrarre al naturale" ("a good master, the best at drawing from nature") in his architectural treatise of around 1465.[2] The attribution of the *Por-*

trait of the Court Jester Gonella (cat. 4) to Fouquet is debated; if it is indeed an authentic work we would possess even earlier evidence of his activity as a panel painter: a completed, thoroughly Netherlandish oil painting on wood, dating from before his journey to Italy.

Later in his career, Fouquet likewise received multiple commissions for panel paintings. The *Portrait of Guillaume Jouvenel des Ursins* (1401-1472), probably painted in the 1460s (fig. 123; cat. 3), depicts the chancellor of France on a panel of approximately the same size and half-figure composition as the wings of the *Melun Diptych*.[3] Like Chevalier, Jouvenel turns to the right in prayer, probably facing a Madonna in a once-adjacent picture. His portrait may likewise have been part of a diptych; however, the panel's format is somewhat more vertical than the portraits of *Chevalier* and *Charles VII*, and the Renaissance architecture in the background runs parallel to the picture plane instead of receding into depth as in Chevalier's painting. It is thus conceivable that the panel originally belonged to a triptych, with Geneviève Héron, the chancellor's wife, occupying the right-hand wing.[4]

Around the same time as the portrait of Jouvenel, during the fiscal year 1465-66, Fouquet received a commission from Jean Bernard, archbishop of Tours, for a panel with the *Assumption of the Virgin* for the considerable sum of 70 *écus*;[5] it was intended for the church in Candes on the Loire that had been built over the death house of St. Martin of Tours. At the same time, the archbishop also commissioned Fouquet to paint an image of the Virgin for 25 *livre tournois* as a gift for the cathedral of Tours. In 1471, Fouquet received the sum of 55 *livres tournois* from King Louis XI for "certains tableaux", possibly coats of arms for the knights of the Order of St. Michael, newly founded by the king in 1469.[6] Around 1470, the Dominican monk Francesco Florio, an Italian living in Tours, viewed paintings by Jean Fouquet in the church of Notre-Dame-la-Riche and compared them with older pictures likewise present there; he concluded that Fouquet surpassed the painters of all other centuries, indeed that he was even superior to Polykleitos and Apelles, and that words could hardly be found to describe his mastery.[7] In 1517, the collection of Margaret of Austria in Mechelen, which included such works as Jan van Eyck's famous *Arnolfini Portrait*, also boasted "un petit tableau de Nostre-Dame, bien vieulx, de la main de Foucquet".[8]

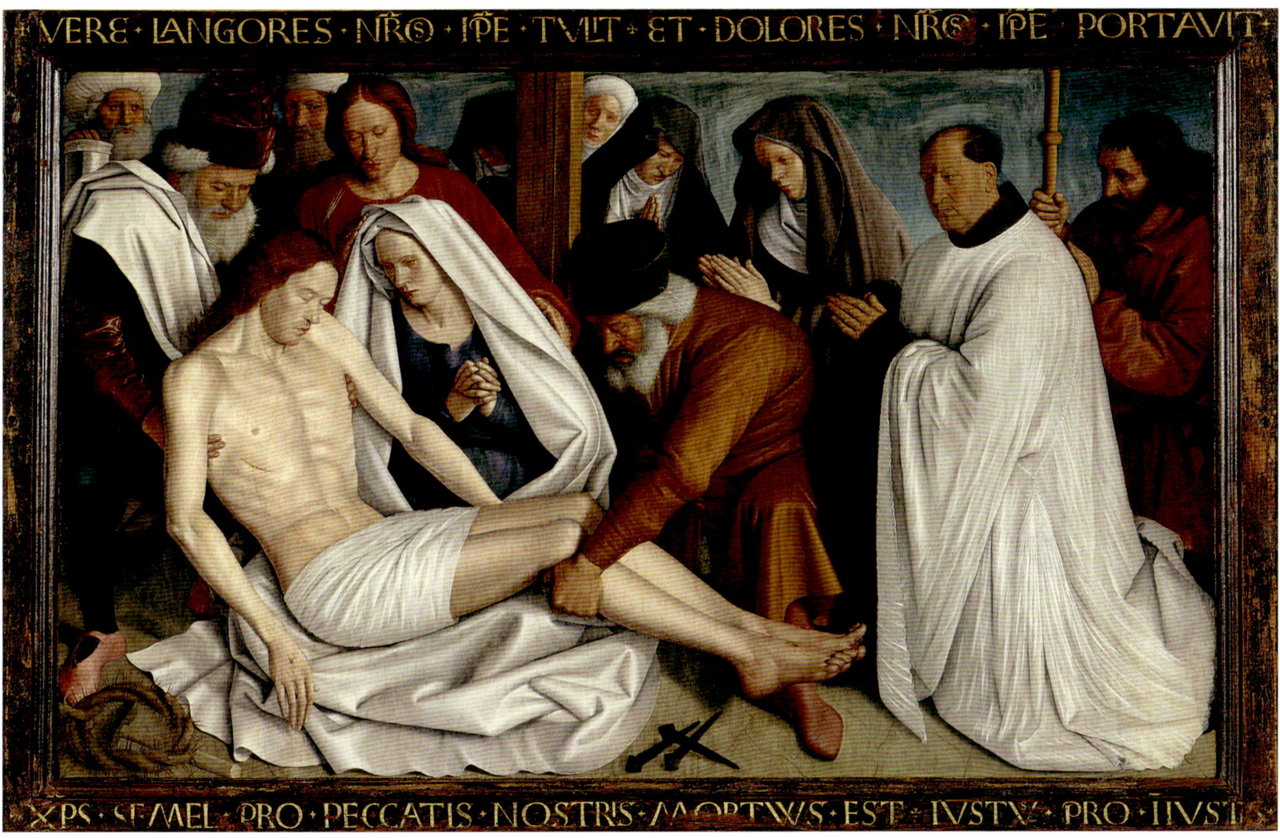

Fig. 2. Jean Fouquet, Pietà, ca. 1470/80(?), walnut, 168 x 259 cm incl. original frame, Nouans, Church

None of these panels has survived. However, a *Lamentation (Pietà)* (fig. 2) now held in the small parish church of Nouans-les-Fontaines (Indre-et-Loire) is generally attributed to Fouquet and was commissioned for an unknown church by an unknown canon, who is represented on the same scale as the holy figures in the scene.[9] With its nearly life-size figures and a painted surface measuring 146 x 237 cm, the *Pietà* of Nouans is comparable in size to two of the largest surviving Netherlandish panels of the 15th century—namely the central panels of the *Ghent Altarpiece* by the van Eyck brothers (138 x 243 cm) and of the *Monforte Altarpiece* by Hugo van der Goes, painted around 1470 (147 x 242 cm)[10]—but far surpasses them both in the scale of the figures.

Fouquet's Training and French Painting

However, panel painting only forms the minor portion of Fouquet's surviving oeuvre, while a much larger number of miniatures attributed to his hand have come down to us, the earliest of which are also dated to the time around 1450.[11] The patron of his most splendid miniatures was again Étienne Chevalier, whose lavishly illustrated book of hours (figs. 7, 10, 43, 77, 81) was made between ca. 1452 and 1460 and thus more or less at the same time as his Diptych.[12] These miniatures, measuring an average 20 to 14 cm, seem like small panel paintings, and show robust figures and naturalistic optical effects— such as shining armor (fig. 81)—and they are characterized by marked Italian inspirations. In contrast to all known panels by the master, his miniatures, in Chevalier's book of hours as well as in later manuscripts, regularly present narratives set in elaborate scenes of landscapes, towns, and interiors. These works show Fouquet as a master of storytelling who is clearly indebted to the French tradition of book illumination. No doubt, Fouquet knew earlier miniatures like, for example, the works of the outstanding Boucicaut-Master (fig. 44), active in Paris at the beginning of the 15th century, and he also collaborated with other miniature painters (fig. 22).[13] However, it remains questionable if he had trained with one of them.

Jean Fouquet's *jeunesse* has been the subject of much speculation. Aside from Otto Pächt's attribution of *Gonella* (cat. 4), early works by Fouquet have always been sought among the numerous manuscript illuminations that survive from mid-15th-century France; none of these suggestions, however, has proven convincing.[14] No manuscript illumination clearly prior to 1450 and securely attributable to Fouquet has yet been found.

The reason for this absence, however, could be that such a work does not exist. There is no indication that Fouquet's beginnings lay in manuscript illumination; as we have seen, he appears early on as a panel painter and worked in that craft his entire life. Furthermore, contemporary sources mostly refer to him as "peintre" and only occasionally as "enlumineur"; the very earliest documentary mention of the artist, in connection with the funeral celebration of King Charles VII in 1461, identifies him as "Foulquet le peintre".[15] Of the two terms, "peintre" was likely the more high-ranking and comprehensive designation.

Certainly panel painting, especially in oil, was a more complex and technically demanding art than manuscript illumination. In Tournai in the southern Netherlands, for example, the painter Jacques Daret took on a certain Eleuthère Dupret as an apprentice for manuscript illumination in June 1436; by July 1438, Eleuthère had already completed his apprenticeship, since the course of training for illuminators lasted only two years instead of the four years required for panel painters.[16] In contrast, some of the leading panel painters of the 15th century did also occasionally work as manuscript illuminators. Around 1425 (or perhaps not until 1435?), Jan van Eyck, the "roy de peintres" as Jean Lemaire de Belges called him in 1505,[17] created what are probably the most breathtaking illuminations of the time in the so-called *Turin-Milan Hours*, images that seem like miniature panel paintings of the richest atmospheric density and spatial breadth.[18] Similarly, the dedication page of the *Hainaut Chronicle*, painted in 1448 for Duke Philip the Good of Burgundy, is the work of Rogier van der Weyden[19] and the only manuscript illumination attributed to him. Compared to the other miniatures in the volume, it too seems like a book-sized panel painting and depicts the figures' physiognomies as realistic portraits. A little further to the east, in Cologne, the best miniatures—once again, quite reminiscent of paintings—come from the hand of the panel painter Stefan Lochner.[20]

Painters in France may have worked in both media more regularly and frequently than in the Netherlands or Germany. Illuminations as well as panels are attributed to Enguerrand Quarton, who is documented as a panel painter in Aix-en-Provence and Avignon beginning in the 1440s, or to the Master of the Aix Annunciation, who was likewise active in Provence by 1443 at the latest and who may be identical with Barthélemy d'Eyck, one of the best and most unusual manuscript illuminators of the 15th century (cf. cat. 9).[21] Both Enguerrand and Barthélemy arguably came from northern France or even from the Netherlands, and thus it is likely that they, just like the Flemish masters mentioned above, were trained primarily as panel painters and only worked as book illuminators on occasion, not the other way round. Simon Marmion (ca. 1425-1489), an artist of the same generation as Fouquet from the border area between the Netherlands and France, is securely documented as both a panel painter and a manuscript illuminator.[22] Simon, too, started out as a painter of large scale panels, having trained with his father Jean Marmion, a panel and polychrome painter in Amiens.[23]

Thus it seems beyond doubt that Jean Fouquet, a brilliant master at a large scale, was trained as a panel painter.[24] However, there still remains the difficult question of when and where. According to Francesco Florio, the Touronese painter had produced the *Portrait of Pope Eugene IV*, executed in Rome around 1445, in his youth; but such a designation could refer to an age of 18 as well as 38. In any case, Fouquet must have already enjoyed an outstanding reputation, and likely also connections to the social elite, for the pontiff to have agreed to sit for him. It seems likely that Fouquet's portrait painting met with enthusiasm in Rome because it exemplified Netherlandish verism, a style that, although quite new at the time, was much sought after in Italy. Yet even with suitable training under his belt, a foreign journeyman painter would hardly have gained access to the curia with no further ado; perhaps, therefore, Fouquet was recommended by an important personage or was traveling as part of a

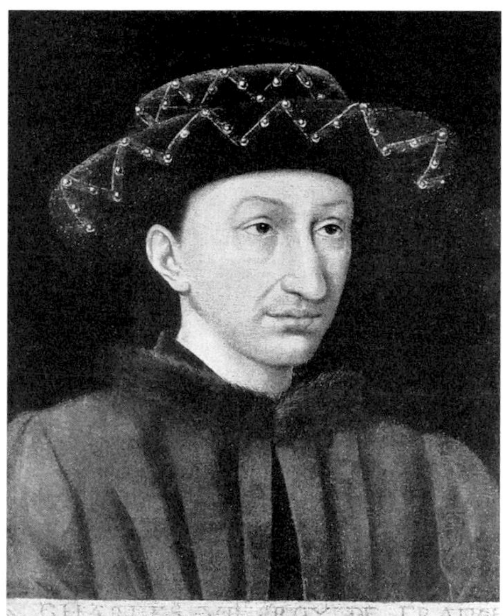

Fig. 3. After Jean Fouquet (?), Portrait of Charles VII, copy from the 16[th](?) century, whereabouts unknown

legation.[25] Charles Sterling and Nicole Reynaud have suggested that the painter may have taken a portrait of the French king Charles VII with him to Rome: apparently, shortly before his demise, Eugene IV commissioned a now-lost series of frescoes with portraits of important contemporaries, works that were still admired in the 16th century, and which included a representation of Charles VII.[26] The latter's portrait in the Vatican could thus have been derived from a work brought to Rome by the young French painter. This hypothetical portrait of Charles VII would not have been the same as the panel now preserved in the Louvre (fig. 11), which most certainly was not painted until after Fouquet's return from Italy; however, copies do exist of a smaller picture of the king, showing only head and shoulders (fig. 3), in which the monarch seems significantly younger than on the panel in the Louvre. According to Dominique Thiébaut's plausible assessment, the lost prototype was also a work by Fouquet,[27] who therefore must have been working for the king already before his departure for Italy, i.e., around 1440.

And so with all due caution, we may assume that at the time of his visit to Rome, Jean Fouquet was about 30 years old, plus or minus five years at the most. Since he lived until around 1480, the year of his birth likely fell between ca. 1410/15 and 1420, which means that the boy Jean would have begun his apprenticeship sometime between the early 1420s and the early 1430s. His training could have occurred in his hometown of Tours or in a neighboring town such as Bourges or Angers.

Fouquet's familiarity with both the Italian art of the Quattrocento and the new way of representing reality exemplified by Jan van Eyck and Rogier van der Weyden is evident, and was already noted by pioneering researchers in the field. In 1822, in what seems to be the first art historical statement on the painter, Carl von Rumohr remarked on the "exquisite miniatures" of the *Hours of Étienne Chevalier*, asserting that they were painted "in the Netherlands, but probably by an Italian"; ten years later, Johann David Passavant attributed one of these miniatures to the "early Flemish school".[28] But where might Fouquet have acquired his knowledge of Netherlandish art? The possibility of a local artist acting as an intermediary has been proposed multiple times, such as the painter Jacob de Littemont, active in Bourges,[29] who is documented from 1451 to 1474 as court painter in the service of Charles VII and Louis XI. However, not a single documented work survives from Littemont's hand, and since he died hardly more than five years before Fouquet, it is highly questionable whether he was even older than the Touronese painter.[30] In the 1430s, when Fouquet was likely becoming acquainted with the new art from the northwest, it had only just begun to spread within the Netherlands itself and from there to the rest of Europe. Among its earliest practitioners beyond the borders of Flanders and Brabant were Konrad Witz, active in Basel after 1434, and Luís Dalmau, who lived and was trained in Valencia but who was sent to Bruges from 1431 to 1436 by King Alfonso V of Aragon to study with Jan van Eyck.[31] To assume a hypothetical French intermediary for Netherlandish elements in Fouquet is thus unlikely in terms of chronology. Although individual French painters in the 1430s did adopt features of the new Netherlandish way of painting, these elements essentially remained set pieces.[32] They can be seen, for instance, in the isolated panel painting *The Priesthood of the Virgin*, painted in 1438 in Amiens,[33] where pearls and jewels sparkle naturalistically and individual objects cast shadows. However a new conception of the picture as a whole and a comprehensive transformation in the rendering of the visible world would not happen in

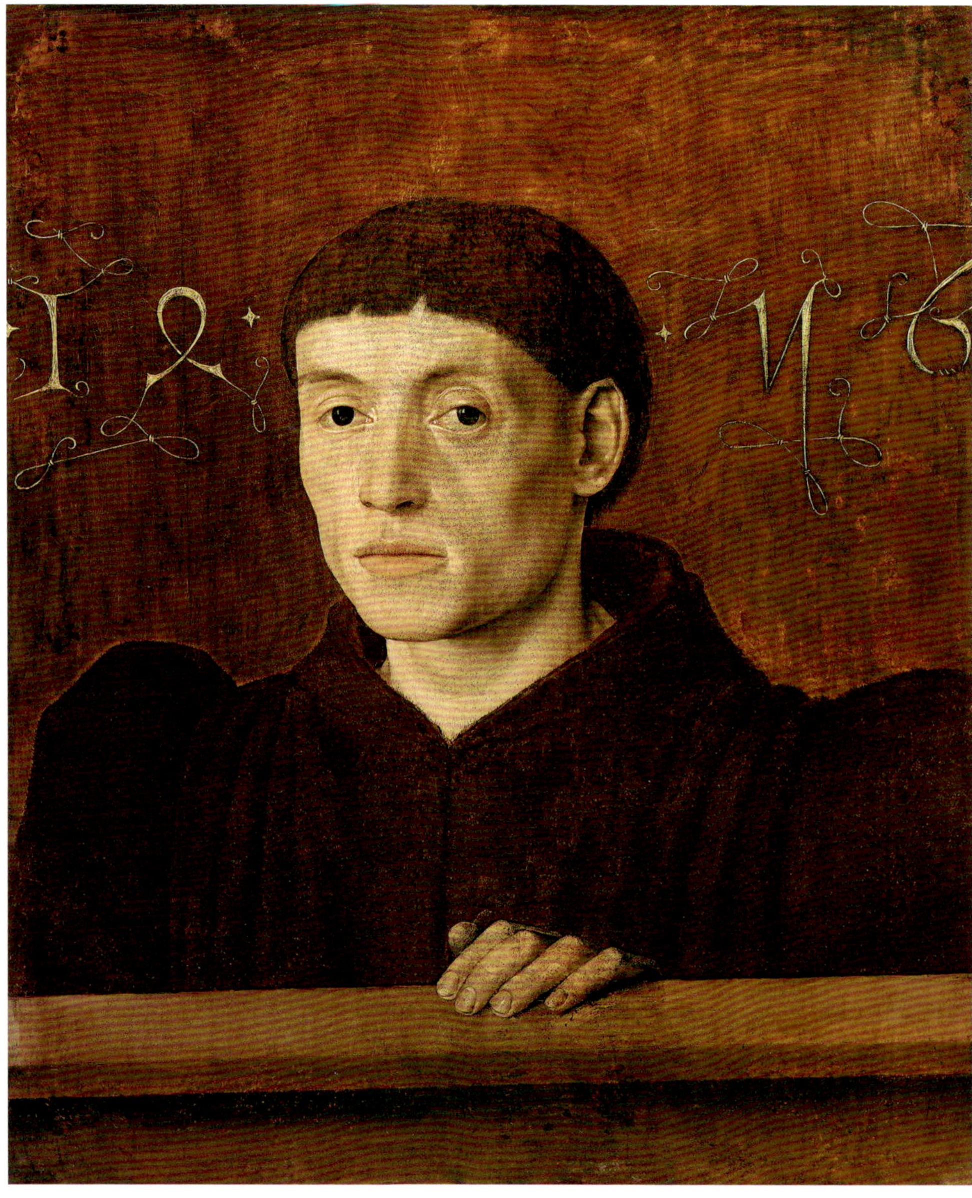

Fig. 4. French Painter (Barthélemy d'Eyck?), Portrait of a Man, 1456, parchment glued on coniferous panel, 50.9 x 41.7 cm, Vaduz, Collections of the Prince of Liechtenstein

France until the work of painters such as Enguerrand Quarton, the Master of the Aix Annunciation, the Master of Dreux Budé (André d'Ypres ?), and of course Fouquet, all of whom appeared on the scene beginning in the 1440s.[34]

A number of works by these painters who were active in France in the mid-15th century show striking similarities that cannot be explained in terms of the common influence of Netherlandish (or even Italian) painting. In the *Portrait of a Man* of 1456 (fig. 4), for example, which is almost exactly contemporary with the *Melun Diptych* and is definitely French, the influence of Jan van Eyck

(cat. 6) is evident in the subtle modeling of the features in light and half-tones;[35] at the same time, however, it is much more closely related to the work of Jean Fouquet than to Netherlandish paintings, and in fact the portrait was formerly attributed to the Touronese painter himself.[36] The similarity essentially resides in the angular, sculpturally rendered features and the marked presence of the subject, who, like Fouquet's *Charles VII*, turns his broad shoulders almost frontally to the viewer. Amazingly, despite the considerably smaller size of the painting, the head of the unknown man from 1456 is almost exactly as large as the head of Chevalier in his donor panel.

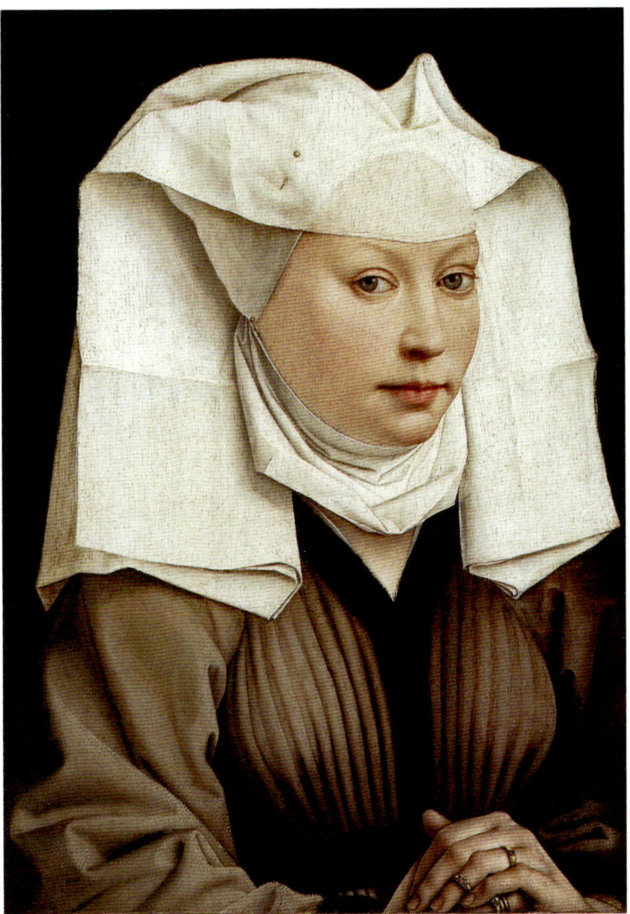

Fig. 5. Rogier van der Weyden, Portrait of a Young Woman, ca. 1440, oak, 47 x 32 cm, Berlin, Gemäldegalerie

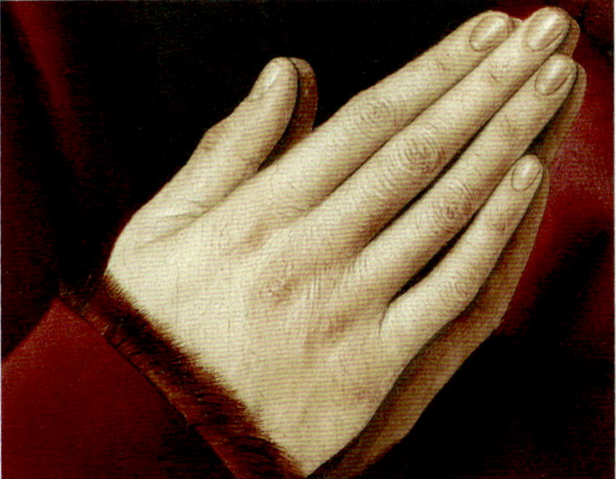

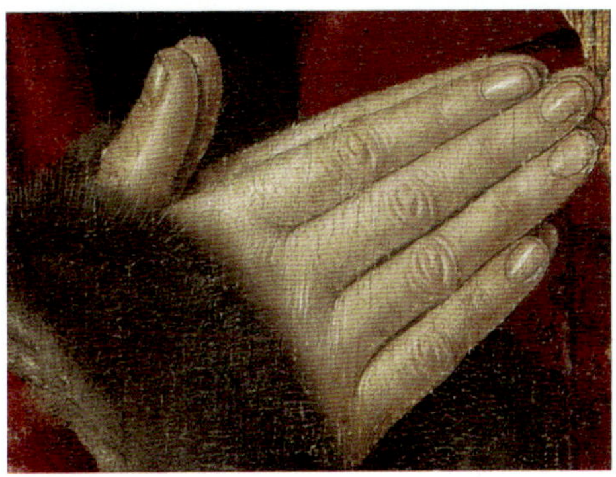

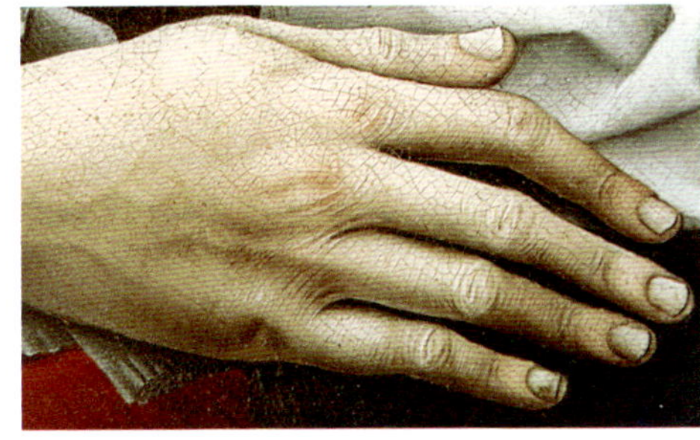

Fig. 6. Jean Fouquet, Hands of a. Étienne Chevalier. b. Guillaume Jouvenel; c. Rogier van der Weyden, Hand of St. John from the *Large Descent from the Cross*, Madrid, Prado, ca. 1440

Whether this parallel reveals a common standard for formal portraits in French crown lands, or whether there was in fact a direct connection between the two works or between their two creators, is a question for another time. Here the situation becomes particularly puzzling: if the painter of the 1456 portrait were identical with the manuscript illuminator Barthélemy d'Eyck,[37] who is documented in the service of René d'Anjou, a number of geographical points of connection to Fouquet would immediately be established, for Barthélemy was active in Angers in the 1450s and thus was not far from Tours. Moreover, in the 1440s—in other words, exactly at the time of Fouquet's visit to Italy—he is thought to have accompanied his master to Naples and there to have executed the drawings for the *Cockerell Chronicle* (cat. 9), the series that was sometimes, recently by Mark Evans, considered as a possible early work by Jean Fouquet.[38]

Barthélemy d'Eyck would appear as a somewhat more Eyckian double of Fouquet.

Netherlandish Inspirations

Jean Fouquet assimilated the inventions and achievements of contemporaneous Netherlandish painting and transformed them into his own mode of expression. The rendering of lighting effects and cast shadows, and the convincing description of a variety of materials are unmistakable Netherlandish features. This applies for instance to the rendering of the soft velvet of Chevalier's

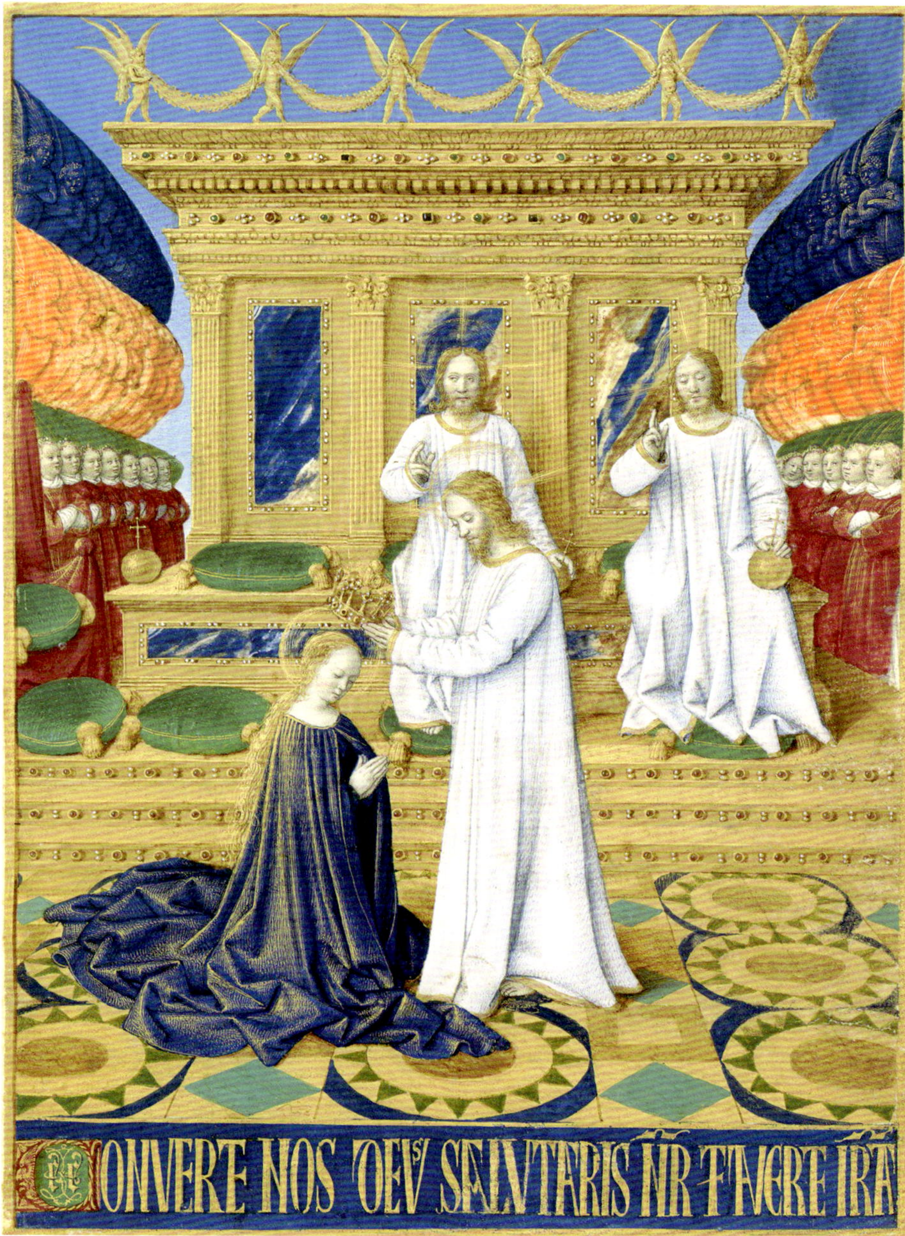

Fig. 7. Jean Fouquet, Coronation of the Virgin, from the Book of Hours of Étienne Chevalier, ca. 1455, 17 x 12.5 cm, Chantilly, Musée Condé

robe on the Melun donor's wing. Similarly, the semi-matt highlights on the bodies of the red putti in the Virgin's panel give the little angels a rich, plump surface like lacquered wood, contrasting sharply with the glassy highlights that lend their eyes such a strangely unreal vitality.

Scholars have identified Jan van Eyck, the pioneer of a hitherto unprecedented mimetic art, as the most important source of inspiration for Fouquet. Philipp Lorentz has pointed to the similarity of reflections of painted water surfaces in Fouquet's illuminations to the works of Jan, and has also uncovered clear allusions to motifs in the middle- and background of the latter's *Virgin of Chancellor Rolin*.[39] On the other hand, there are no reminiscences of the *Ghent Altarpiece* in Fouquet's oeuvre,[40] the most influential work of Van Eyck that also provided numerous inspirations for the stained glass windows of the chapel of Jacques Cœur in Bourges Cathedral which are tentatively attributed to Jacob de Littemont.[41]

On the whole, Fouquet's creations do not seem particularly Eyckian, much less so than, for example, the *Portrait of a Man* of 1456 (fig. 4). Fouquet's forms appear more generalized; facial wrinkles such as those on the forehead of Étienne Chevalier or Guillaume Jouvenel (fig. 123) are systematized as parallel, ornamental lines. Instead of focusing attention on a myriad of surface details, Fouquet uses a greater degree of abstraction to give the entire head a powerful, clearly defined sculptural form, as is obvious in the donor wing of the *Melun Diptych*.[42] In Jan van Eyck, the heads of portrait subjects are individualized down to the tiniest wrinkles and are typically very large in relation to their busts (cat. 6), which remain undeveloped and basically function only as pedestals for the heads. In Fouquet, on the other hand, the bodies are bulky and broad—greatly emphasized, to be sure, by mid-century fashions in clothing—with somewhat smaller heads that seem to pop out of them. In this way, representative clothing and accessories as indicators of social standing are foregrounded all the more, a device on which the *Portrait of Charles VII* essentially depends for its effect (fig. 11).[43] In comparison to Jan van Eyck, Fouquet is less meticulous in his rendering of the varying appearance of surfaces under the influence of light, resulting in greater emphasis on color in and of itself. The angels that surround the Virgin of the *Melun Diptych* verge on pure local color. Thus the powerful effect of Fouquet's large, cohesive areas of color is achieved.

Fouquet's pictorial design with its tendency toward abstraction and geometry certainly manifests his own personal artistic sensibility. At the same time, a surprisingly similar approach is also visible in the work of Rogier van der Weyden, who likewise constructs his heads as clear, rounded overall forms and abstracts the features and wrinkles of his faces. Also reminiscent of portraits by Rogier is the distinctive rendering of the rear eye in the Berlin *Chevalier*. Barely foreshortened, it seems folded out onto the picture plane, a feature that seems typical for portraits from Rogier's circle (fig. 5; cat. 7).[44] The hands in Fouquet's portraits are also worth noting in this regard. Comparison of *Étienne Chevalier* with *Guillaume Jouvenel des Ursins* reveals hands that are largely identical (fig. 6a, b): the painter has not produced portraits of individual hands, but has adopted a schema for the overall form, fingernails, and wrinkles around the joints; in the painting of Jouvenel, the fingers are simply somewhat foreshortened and pressed together to harmonize with the massive body. This formula approximates the one

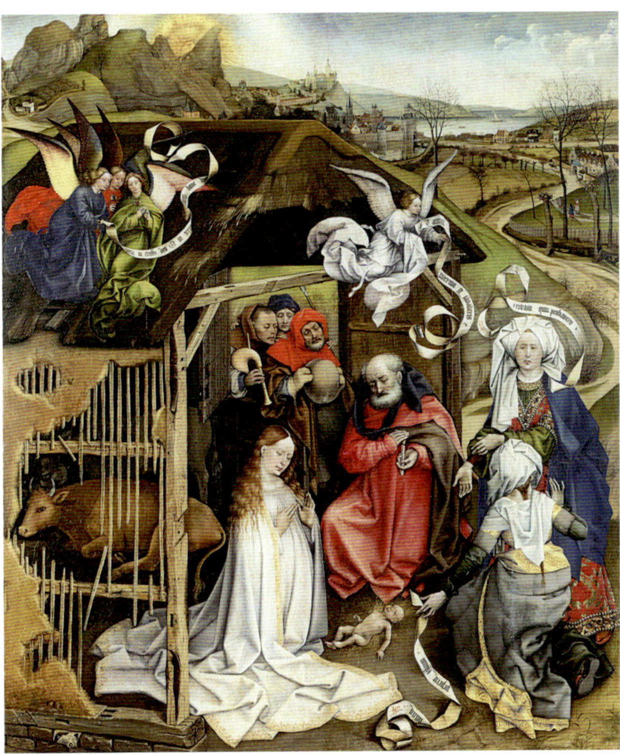

Fig. 8. Master of Flémalle, Nativity, before 1432, oak, 84 x 69.9 cm, Dijon, Musée des Beaux-Arts

employed by Rogier van der Weyden: in particular, the right hand of St. John (fig. 6c) in Rogier's magnum opus, the large *Decent from the Cross* painted before 1443,[45] shows a very similar configuration of parallel wrinkles pulled diagonally between the knuckles and ring-shaped folds around the finger joints.

To a certain extent, the portrait of the "most victorious King of France" (fig. 11) conveys a somewhat stronger Eyckian impression, at least more so than *Étienne Chevalier*. This is due to the play of light and shade, and to some minute details of the face like the fine white stubble on the chin. However, these qualities are also found in some early works by Rogier van der Weyden, especially *St. Luke Drawing the Virgin* from around 1435-40 (fig. 12),[46] which certainly seems equally lifelike with its subtle shading, fine white beard stubble, and glistening eyes. Thus Fouquet could easily have become acquainted with the new approach to portraiture with its emphasis on detailed naturalism in the work of Rogier van der Weyden. Other similarities to Fouquet can be observed in the milieu of both Rogier van der Weyden and the so-called

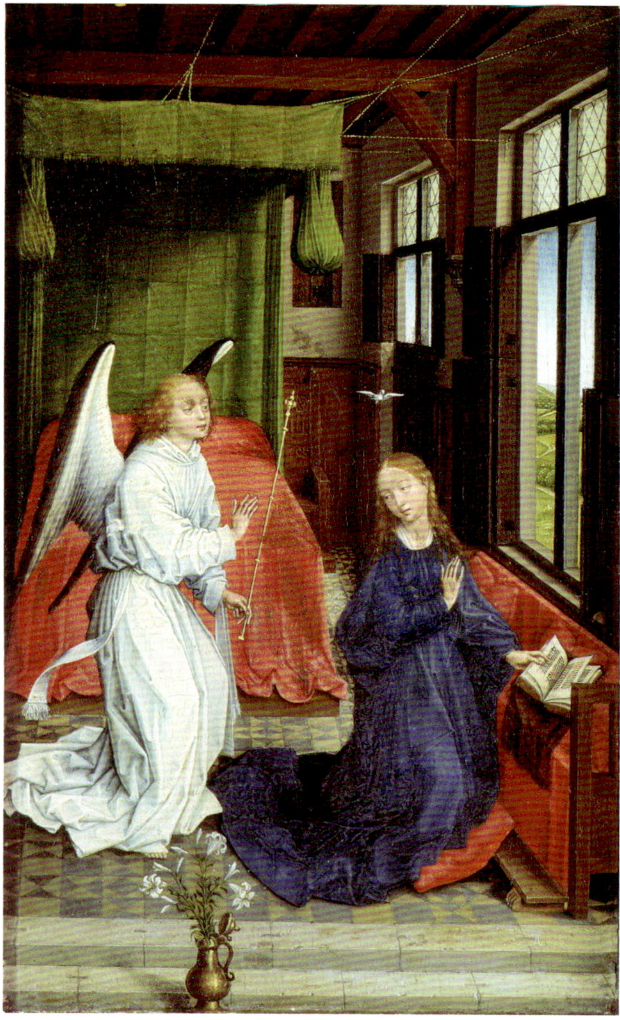

Fig. 9. Rogier van der Weyden, Workshop, Annunciation, ca. 1450, oak, 20 x 12 cm, Antwerp, Koninklijk Museum voor Schone Kunsten

Master of Flémalle.[47] The relationship is apparent in various miniatures from the *Hours of Étienne Chevalier*, where we often see artfully arranged folds of drapery piled up on the ground, spreading luxuriantly around the figures and forming repeating patterns of elongated cones and triangles that converge to a point (fig. 7).[48] Such configurations occur regularly in both the Flémalle and the Rogier group, for example in the Flémallesque *Nativity* in Dijon (fig. 8).[49] In the latter painting, the figure of the Virgin in its entirety so resembles the Mother of God in Fouquet's *Coronation of the Virgin* (fig. 7) that a chance parallel hardly seems plausible. Both images show an upright, kneeling woman of very similar proportions, bowing her head slightly and lifting her hands

in prayer; an improbably large mantle falls from her shoulders, cascading down the figure in long folds and spreading out on the ground around her in a broad circle of looping forms and gracefully undulating curves. Also characteristic are the pointed edges of some garments, which lie flat on the ground in a form resembling a linden leaf. Fouquet used this elegant motif in numerous miniatures, for example in the presentation scene from the *Hours of Étienne Chevalier* (fig. 43) for the corner of St. Stephen's dalmatic, turned out to show its green lining, and the end of the black band hanging down from the donor's *chaperon*. This type of fold is quite characteristic of the drapery in Rogier's paintings and is found in the large *Deposition* or the roughly contemporary *Durán Madonna* and many other paintings.[50]

Finally, mention should be made of a rather direct borrowing from Rogier van der Weyden in the work of Jean Fouquet. In Fouquet's miniature of the *Annunciation of the Death of the Virgin* (fig. 10) from the *Hours of Étienne Chevalier*, we see what at first appears to be a surprisingly Renaissance-inspired interior, with walls articulated by pilasters and marble incrustation. In actuality, however, this interior with the corner of a room is anything but an Italian composition; rather, all of its structural elements are modeled closely on an *Annunciation* (fig. 9) that survives in a small panel from Rogier's workshop, probably made around the middle of the century but likely preceded by earlier versions.[51] There we see the same corner of a room with the right wall precipitously receding from outside of the pictorial field. The floor as well as the beamed ceiling are visible, and in both images a large canopied bed stands in the background, its curtain gathered up in the customary way; it may or may not be a coincidence that in both pictures the bed is green. More significant, however, are the parallels in the articulation of the space: where Rogier paints windows, Fouquet has mounted marble panels, and the pilaster between them at the center takes the place of a wooden supporting structure in the Netherlandish picture. On the rear wall to the right of the bed, Rogier shows an armchair in front of paneling, and above it a shuttered window. Again, Fouquet has transformed this window into a marble panel in exactly the same position on the rear wall, while the paneling becomes a passageway. This example shines a spotlight, as it were, on Fouquet's work-

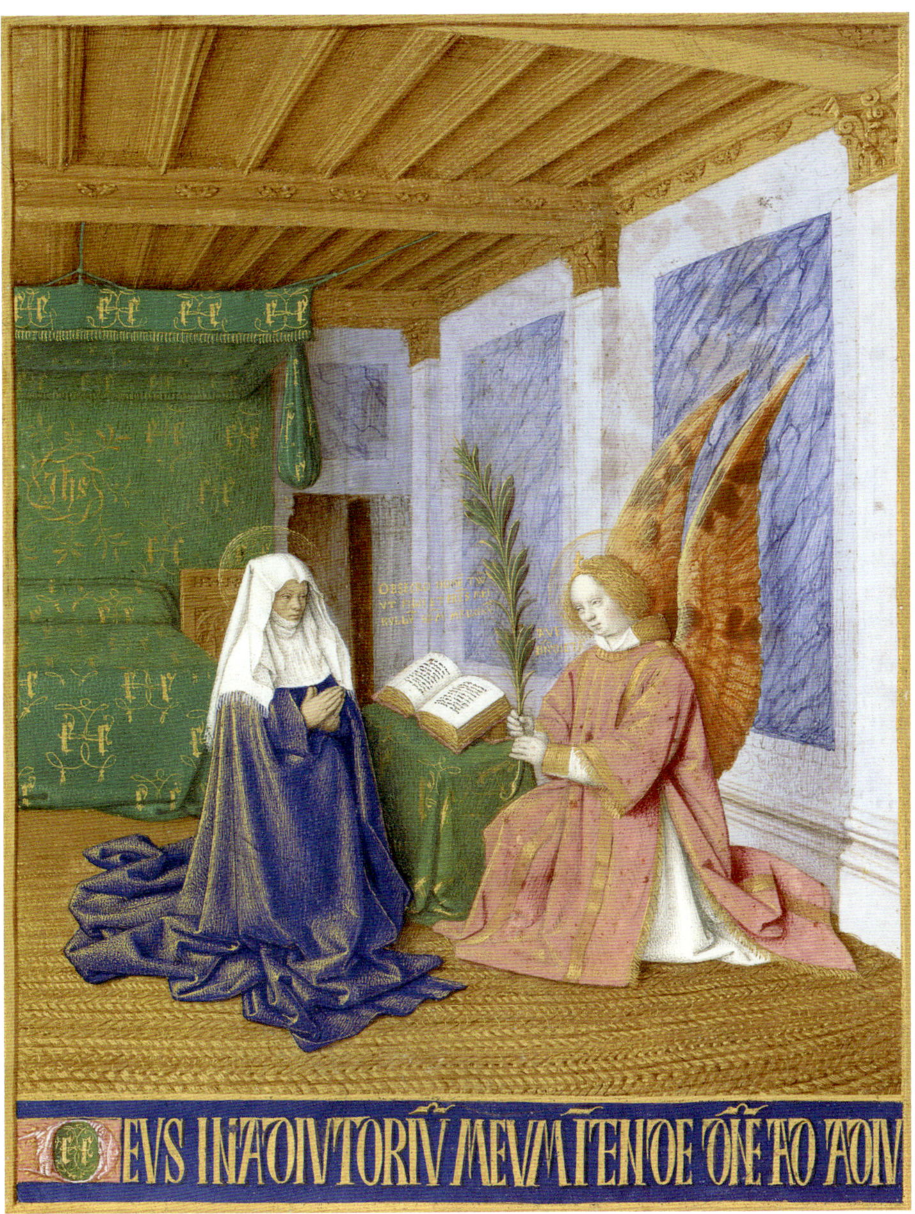

Fig. 10. Jean Fouquet, Annunciation of the Death of the Virgin, from the Book of Hours of Étienne Chevalier, ca. 1455, 16.5 x 12.2 cm, Chantilly, Musée Condé

ing method and his ability to achieve synthesis: he begins with a Northern prototype—in this case a Rogieresque one—but redecorates the Gothic interior with classical Italian elements and corrects the perspective in keeping with Early Renaissance discoveries, making the space seem wider and deeper.

In this case, therefore, we may assume that Fouquet was directly inspired by the Netherlandish composition, even if he reinterpreted it stylistically. This influence could have occurred in a number of ways, none of which would necessarily have required direct contact with Rogier's workshop; however, the factors we have just discussed significantly increase the likelihood of such contact. Above all, the closely related schemata for the representation of hands and the very similar elaboration of drapery folds—which never involve literal copying, but always a playful reinvention in the spirit of the prototype—speak, in my opinion, for contact between Fouquet and the workshop of Rogier or the Master of Flémalle. Given the historical circumstances, interaction with them would indeed have been more probable than with Jan van Eyck. The latter lived in Flemish-speaking Bruges, whereas Tournai, where Rogier van der Weyden was active until the mid-1430s, was francophone, and even afterwards, a

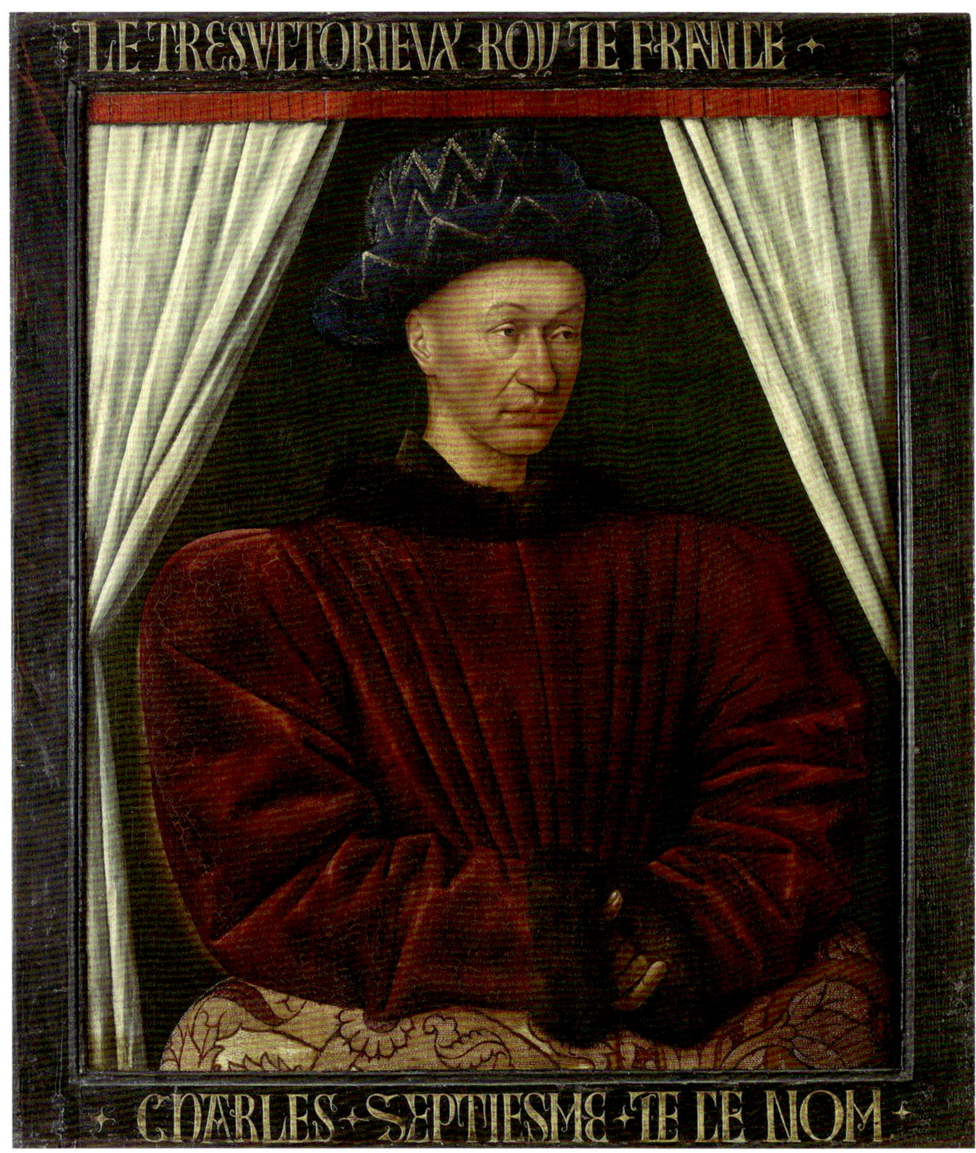

Fig. 11. Jean Fouquet, King Charles VII of France, ca. 1450, oak, 98.8 x 84.5 cm incl. original frame, Paris, Musée du Louvre

French-speaking young painter certainly would have felt more at home in Rogier's workshop in bi-lingual Brussels. Thus if Fouquet acquired his wide-ranging and fundamental knowledge of the new art of painting in the Netherlands at the source itself, it was most probably in the workshop of Campin or Rogier van der Weyden; in view of Fouquet's reconstructed biography, however, the latter seems more likely.

If the so-called *Gonella* (cat. 4) should indeed be a youthful work of Jean Fouquet, it would give us a further clue for a sojourn of the French painter in the Netherlands: for while the panels of his "mature" works (figs. 11, 123, cat. 1) are constructed of oak wood from local, French trees, the panel of *Gonella* consists of Baltic oak,[52] the standard material for panels in the Netherlands. Thus it is highly likely that the image of the jester was made in the Netherlands or perhaps in a neighboring region in the north of France. Since the wood's youngest growth ring dates to 1411, the panel could have been cut around 1426 and used as early as the late 1420s, although the middle of the following decade is more likely. These dates would certainly fit well with a presumed Netherlandish sojourn by the young Touronese painter in the mid-1430s. However, as the attribution itself is highly problematic, these speculations remain hypothetic.

Charles VII, Étienne Chevalier, and the *Melun Diptych*

The *Portrait of Charles VII* (fig. 11) is not dated, and older scholarship was divided as to whether it should be assigned to the period before or after Fouquet's journey to Italy.[53] Based on the physiognomy of the subject as well as his completely white beard hairs, however, it seems likely that the painting was created around 1450,[54] when the king, who was born in 1403, was approaching the age of fifty. Furthermore, the classicizing Capitalis lettering used for the inscription—also seen in the *Hours of Étienne Chevalier*—suggests an Italian experience.[55] The date of the royal portrait is also highly significant for reconstructing the genesis of the *Melun Diptych*: an X-ray image of the *Portrait of Charles VII* reveals a partially completed, but subsequently partially erased depiction of the Madonna under the visible layer of paint, an image whose contours and size exactly match those of the *Virgin and Child* on the Antwerp panel (fig. 13).[56] Though visible only as a schematic form, the diagonal edge of the white ermine mantle on the left is still recognizable and apparently had already been painted in lead white. The flesh areas of mother and child, on the other hand, appear as dark shapes and had thus remained untouched, while the robes all around them received at least an initial underpainting. In all probability, the Antwerp *Virgin and Child* is a later version of the design of the panel in the Louvre. First of all, the diptych is usually dated later than the royal portrait—though admittedly there is no actual proof of this. Secondly, it is clear that the design for the figure was not developed on the panel executed for Chevalier, for the underdrawing of the figures of the Virgin and Child (fig. 97) shows few deviations or corrections, quite unlike what we find on the left wing of the diptych (fig. 96).[57] The composition must therefore have been laid out with the help of a full-size cartoon, probably drawn on paper, which was transferred to the prepared panel by means of a stylus or some other mechanical procedure. The cartoon used by Fouquet was derived either from the *Virgin* beneath the *Portrait of Charles VII*—whether as a preliminary design or a tracing afterwards—or from another, lost variation of the figure.

One can only speculate as to why the earlier painting of the Madonna was rejected during the course of the work-

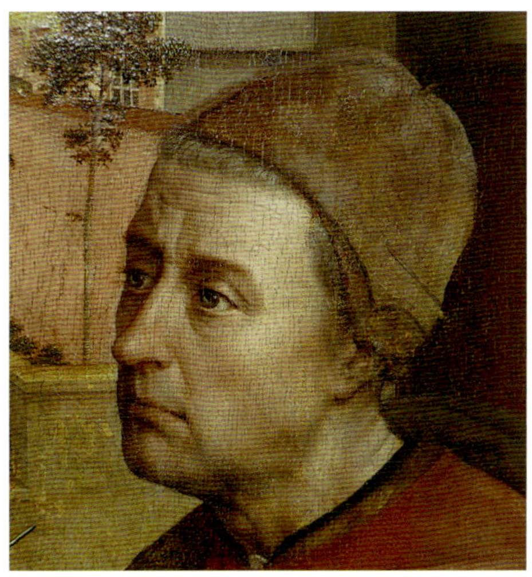

Fig. 12. Rogier van der Weyden, St. Luke drawing the Virgin, ca. 1435/40, oak, Boston, Museum of Art, detail: Luke (ca. 18 x 16 cm)

ing process. Reynaud suggests that after the painting had been started and was already quite advanced, Fouquet received an urgent portrait commission from the king and, lacking another suitable panel, unceremoniously scraped off the image of the Virgin and covered it with lead white in order to paint on top of it.[58] However, this explanation is unsatisfactory, for a medium-sized wooden panel would certainly have been readily available in Tours or its environs. In addition, the painter would have had to allow the layer of white paint on top of the previous picture to dry before he could begin the portrait, to say nothing of the waste of effort and paint.

On the other hand, it is quite conceivable that the patron of the *Madonna* simply withdrew his commission. Or, Fouquet himself could have rejected the half-finished picture for artistic reasons, if he were dissatisfied with the result he had obtained up to that point. The key difference between the abandoned composition and the version later realized in the diptych lies in the size of the support: while the painted surface of the Antwerp painting measures ca. 91.6 x 83 cm, the earlier version, beneath the present-day royal portrait, was only 86 x 71 cm. In other words, there the Virgin was depicted within a significantly smaller space; at the bottom, the feet of the Christ Child rested directly on the frame. It is possible that the painter—or his patron—viewed this composition as too crowded and therefore decided to transfer it to a somewhat larger support and use the old panel for another purpose.

If the Madonna beneath the *Portrait of Charles VII* was created some time before that of the *Melun Diptych*, it was probably also intended for a different patron—possibly the king himself, if in fact the portrait subsequently painted on top of it was the king's own commission, as is usually assumed.[59] If this were so, it would permit the plausible hypothesis that the king ordered a *Virgin*, which Fouquet began but then rejected during the painting process. The design for the figure, which he apparently considered successful, was preserved in a cartoon. Assuming the original patron did not withdraw his order entirely, the painter might have used the cartoon to transfer the design onto another, presumably larger panel. Some time later, he definitely reused the cartoon for the *Virgin and Child* of Étienne Chevalier.

When Chevalier commissioned his diptych, he was probably aware that his *Virgin and Child* was not a new invention. In fact, repetition of the earlier version was probably his intention, which would be even more plausible if the original had been created for Charles VII: the imitation of the king's Madonna picture would have constituted an act of homage. Such an attitude would accord exceptionally well with the strange iconography of the miniature of the *Adoration of the Magi* from the *Hours of Étienne Chevalier* (fig. 81).[60] Here, in place of the oldest, traditionally bearded magus, we see Charles VII himself, portrayed in contemporary clothing, kneeling on a carpet with French lilies before the divine Child; the other two magi, young men wearing *robes longues* and crowned hats, clearly represent Charles's sons. A heavily-armed escort in the king's personal colors of red, white, and green is arrayed behind him, while the French army overpowers a castle in the background. The patron's loyalty to the king and his embodiment of sacred kingship could not be more clearly expressed. Similarly, in his diptych Chevalier prays to a Madonna who, in a manner of speaking, was King Charles's own Virgin Mary.

This observation leads directly to one of the most interesting aspects of the diptych and one that has been discussed for centuries: the question of whether the Mother of God was modeled after Charles's famous mistress Agnès Sorel, reputed to have been so proud of her flawless white complexion.[61] In the earliest surviving description of the work from 1661, Denis Godefroy noted: "Aucuns veulent dire que cette image est peinte sous la figure d'Agnes Sorel, amie de Charles VII."[62] By that point the identification must already have been long-standing, since as early as 1608 the Madonna panel was described quite matter-of-factly as a picture of the "belle Agnès".[63] In addition, imaginary portraits of Agnès Sorel from the 16th and early 17th centuries (fig. 57) are obviously modeled after this Madonna, though it is unclear whether they ultimately derive from the Antwerp panel itself or perhaps rather from the presumed prototype. In any case, in 1640 the royal councilor and historian Charles Sorel, a later descendant of Agnès' family, already objected to her improper and titillating depiction with bared breast.[64]

Support for the rumor circulated by Godefroy may be found above all in the Virgin's highly fashionable costume,[65] which is completely unprecedented in representations of the Madonna. Even Fouquet himself, in the *Hours of Étienne Chevalier*, had clothed the nursing Queen of Heaven (fig. 43) and the Virgin of the *Adoration of the Magi* (fig. 81) in traditional dress. These *Virgins*, too, have fashionably high foreheads and white skin, but the forehead of the woman in the diptych is blatantly shaved, and the black fillet under the crown further emphasizes the stylish, erotic aspect of her appearance. Such ribbons, placed beneath a headdress, were part of the adornment of noble women and are frequently seen in representations of noble ladies (cf. cat. 8)—also in the portrait drawing of Agnès (cat. 5) and on her tomb sculpture (fig. 58)—but never of the Virgin Mary. In 1717, the Madonna's utterly uncanonical costume completely misled a certain Abbé Bertin into noting, while viewing the diptych in Melun, that the locals called the woman on the right wing the "reine blanche", but in reality she must be the wife of the gentleman on the left panel.[66] While religious conceptions certainly had changed since the 15th century, it is still remarkable that a Catholic clergyman of the *ancien regime* did not even recognize the crowned figure surrounded by angels as the Mother of God.

Jean Fouquet likely knew Agnès Sorel, who died young in February 1450 and who had often been with the king in Tours. Fouquet had probably even made her portrait; in any case, the lost original of a portrait that survives in three drawn copies from the 16th century (cat. 5) is attributed to him. The features of the young woman in

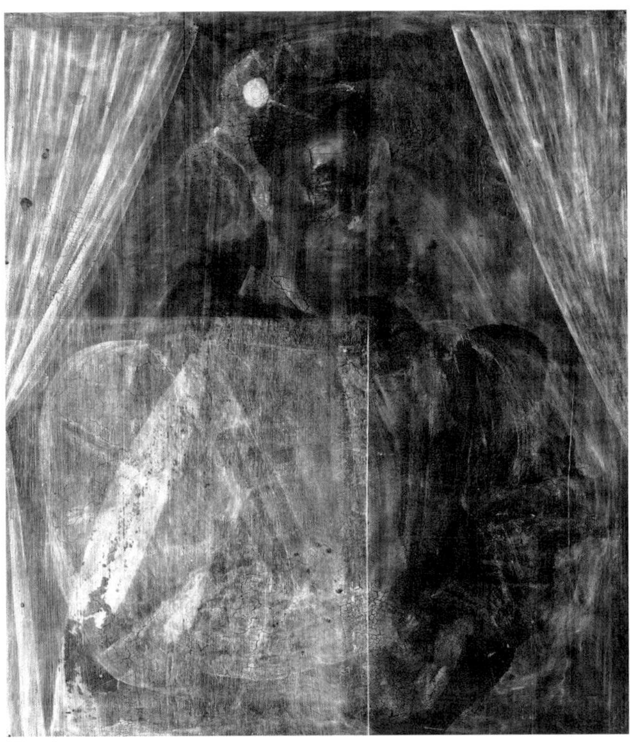
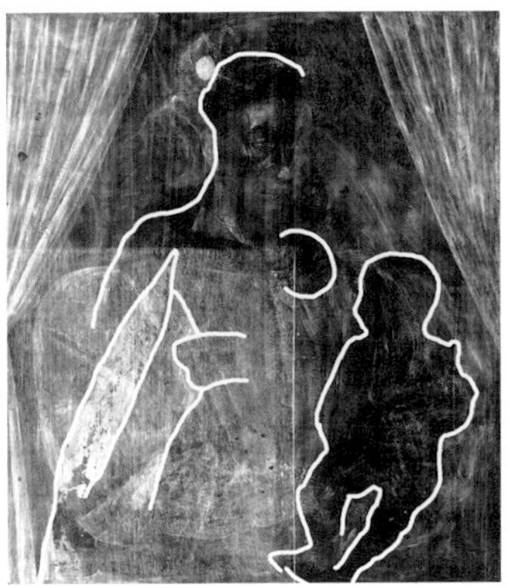

Fig. 13. Radiography of the Portrait of Charles VII (Fig. 11), and tracing of the overpainted figure

this work are similar to those of the Madonna on the Antwerp panel, especially with respect to the slightly curved nose, although the painted *Virgin* appears more idealized. The same is true of the face of Agnès' tomb figure in Loches (fig. 58), which bears a clear resemblance to the Antwerp Madonna.[67] To be sure, identification on the basis of facial features can be problematic, especially with women's portraits of this era, which were usually standardized in accord with current ideals of beauty. To mention just one example, a *Portrait of a Young Girl* by Petrus Christus (cat. 8) was painted ten to fifteen years after Fouquet's *Virgin and Child* and has no connection to it, but nonetheless treats the facial features in a very similar way, idealizing and perfecting them into clear, stereometric forms and rendering the skin in flawless white.

Despite these qualifications with respect to physiognomy, in my opinion it is likely that here, the Madonna was in fact depicted as Agnès Sorel, for otherwise her fashionable appearance would be nearly inexplicable. Even a small detail such as the bag attached to the woman's waist by a braided strap gains meaning through this identification: it appears to be an *aumonière*, an alms purse, which would be out of place for the Queen of Heaven, but

could well be a reference to Agnès' Christian charity, which is mentioned in one of her epitaphs and also left its mark on the stipulations of her will.[68] As Claude Schaefer has shown, Agnès Sorel's three epitaphs invoke ideas strikingly similar to the representation on the *Melun Diptych*: in one of them, she is addressed as "mitis simplexque columba/ Candidior cignis, flamma rubicumdior ignis", that is, as a "gentle and simple dove, whiter than a swan, redder than flame", who at the same time deserves to be clothed in ducal robes.[69] To call Agnès a dove clearly is an allusion to the Virgin Mary, referred to as a dove in hymns or in the line "una est columba mea" of the Canticles (cant. 6.8).[70] In the *Virgin* panel, the colors as well as the clothing, pearl-studded crown, and above all the ermine mantle agree perfectly with the ideas of the said epitaph. Another Latin epitaph evokes the image of the deceased woman ascending to heaven amidst saints, there to delight God with her presence— the parallel with the Assumption of the Virgin is unmistakable.[71]

Thus as the essentially beatified mistress of King Charles VII, the deceased Agnès Sorel could by all means play the role of the Virgin Mary on the right panel of the *Melun Diptych*. The objection has been raised that it would hardly have been proper for Chevalier, himself a widower since 1452, to have a strange woman depicted, much less the former lover of the king, in the role of the Virgin on the diptych. This concern, however, is probably not justified; on the contrary, the considerations presented here suggest that such a representation would have functioned not only as an homage to Agnès Sorel—of whose last will Étienne Chevalier was an executor—but as an homage to the king himself. This would be all the more true if, as suggested above, the Antwerp version of the Madonna is in fact modeled on an earlier version prepared for the king himself. Chevalier would thus have had repeated a figure that was, in a double sense, the Madonna of his king.

Finally, in this connection we should once again recall the *Adoration of the Magi* (fig. 81) from the *Hours of Étienne Chevalier*. Crowned heads had occasionally been depicted in role portraits as one of the Three Magi at least since the time of Emperor Charles IV (r. 1355-1378).[72] Yet these representations never went as far as this illumination, where Charles VII and his sons are not even slightly disguised as biblical figures and their military might is overtly displayed. This mixture of sacred and profane, of worldly splendor and religious devotion, makes the conflation of mistress and Queen of Heaven on the Antwerp panel seem less surprising. By no means is it as absurd or even shocking as Johann Huizinga and other writers of the 19th and 20th centuries perceived it to be.[73]

The reference to Agnès Sorel in the *Melun Diptych* did not contradict its religious function any more than the role portrait of Charles VII devalued the sacredness of the Three Magi or the pervasive presence of Chevalier's monogram profaned the chambers of the Virgin Mary in the *Hours of Étienne Chevalier* (fig. 10). There is no doubt that Chevalier relied in earnest upon the intercession of the Virgin as anticipated in the diptych, where the displaying of the breast that nourished her divine Son, the future Judge of the World, was a theologically relevant motif.[74] Nonetheless, modern viewers are probably not alone in also seeing the representation as erotically charged. The highly abstracted rendering of Mary's upper body, the unnaturally wide spacing of her breasts, the extreme wasp waist, and the smooth, perfectly spherical form of the naked white breast do not weaken the erotic element, but rather emphasize it. And the highly

demonstrative way in which the plump, naked breast emerges from the bodice only theoretically brings maternal nourishment to mind. Later in the Reformation era, the powerful sensual quality that could emanate from images of female saints was articulated and sharply criticized,[75] but was probably not a new phenomenon. It seems at least conceivable that the Antwerp *Virgin and Child* was intended to allude to the physical beauty and fashionable extravagance of Agnès Sorel, whose plunging necklines were mocked by the Burgundian chronicler Georges Chastellain.[76]

Jean Fouquet's use of a previous version of the *Virgin and Child* for the *Melun Diptych*, as discussed above, may also help explain another peculiarity of the Antwerp panel. Mary's pose is strangely ambiguous: it is unclear whether she is standing in front of the throne or seated on it. At the lower edge of the picture, her white mantle projects outward as if resting on the knee of a seated figure, but her hips and the vertical folds of the left edge of her garment look like those of a standing figure. The position of the Christ Child is likewise unclear: although at first glance he seems to be securely seated, the loose folds of Mary's mantle beneath him do not betray any underlying hip or thigh as a support. The X-ray image does not indicate whether the configuration was different in the earlier version; if one imagines her as a seated figure, the child could be resting on her left leg, although a composition that cut off a seated figure exactly at the knees would be exceedingly strange. Hence it is more likely that the earlier version showed a standing Madonna. The X-ray shows no trace of the throne or the angels. Perhaps they had not yet been started, but then again perhaps they were not intended at all; certainly on the left side there would not have been enough room for the angels who carry the throne in the Antwerp painting. If the throne and angels were not planned, the first version of Fouquet's elegant Madonna would have shown the Virgin in half-figure before a more or less neutral background—in other words, it would have corresponded to a common 15th-century type.[77]

Thus when Fouquet painted this figure again in exactly the same size, but on a somewhat larger panel—at the latest in Chevalier's diptych—he lengthened her by a number of centimeters at the bottom and gave her more room on each side. Perhaps the idea of providing the

Queen of Heaven with a throne arose at that point. This explanation would account for the ambiguity of the figure's pose: planned as a standing Madonna, she was given a seat after the fact. In any case, the placement of the throne is quite remarkable: rather than being positioned axially behind the Mother of God, it is shifted farther to the left. Combined with the unusual motif of angels carrying the throne, a sequence of action seems to be suggested: the red angels are approaching with the throne so that the Mother of God can lower herself onto it, and she appears in the very act of taking a seat on the splendid throne, thereby becoming the *Sedes sapientiae*.[78] Thus an unusual moment of action and a temporal sequence is woven into the inherently timeless image of the Virgin. Perhaps it is a reference to the transition from the earthly to the heavenly existence of the Virgin and Child; perhaps Mary is being presented on the one hand as a human mother—quite in accord with the display of her breast—and at the same time as the transcendent Queen of Heaven.

As has often been noted with surprise, Fouquet designed the two panels of the diptych very differently;[79] yet there is no doubt that they were created at the same time.[80] The sharply receding architecture of the left panel is completely absent on the right; however, its function is not merely to identify the earthly sphere of the donor, but also to significantly strengthen the orientation of the entire composition toward the figure of the Madonna. As mentioned at the beginning, the dominant color chord of red, white, and blue, inherited from French painting of around 1400, is skillfully varied between the two panels. Nevertheless, both the red and the whitish-gray tones are different on the right and on the left—Fouquet has avoided the easy solution to work with identical colors on both panels. Moreover, the realistic rendering of surfaces in the Netherlandish manner and the greater tactility of materials on the donor panel once again makes visible the distinction between the earthly and the heavenly. By contrast, the golden throne of the Madonna, though sumptuously adorned with gems and pearls, is represented in a comparatively less elaborated way, and parts of it are positively simplified—such as the almost cursory, schematic treatment of the tassels and gem settings (fig. 47). Its brownish tone, which has nothing of the brilliance of the gold on the other wing,

unites it with the red angels into a tonal background, setting off the whitish and highly plastic figure of the Mother of God. The same brown color also indicated the strands of hair on both sides of the Virgin's neck; surprisingly, these strands of hair as well as a portion of the throne with its pearls have been left in an unfinished state of underpainting (fig. 56). The generally much more abstracted representation of the Virgin has already been discussed; this approach is manifested even in details such as her hands, which resemble the indistinct surfaces of the angels' bodies more than human skin and thus fundamentally differ from the "Rogieresque" hands of the donor.

While the architecture of the left wing is overtly classical, the right wing reveals Italian influence in other ways. Reynaud has observed that the crowded company of angels behind the Virgin is prefigured in the great Madonna panels of the Trecento.[81] Albert Châtelet in turn has pointed out some Florentine reliefs of the Virgin Mary in half figure with angels, like for instance those by Antonio Rosselino or Luca della Robbia;[82] accordingly, he understands Fouquet's Virgin as the representation of a sculpture in front of which Chevalier is praying—this, however, does neither go along with the presence of the "real" St. Stephen next to him nor with the lack of perspective and space on the Virgin's panel. Yet a much closer relationship is apparent in a work that has never before been discussed in this connection: a panel by Benozzo Gozzoli (ca. 1420-1497) (fig. 14).[83] Here, too, angels vividly painted in red and blue form a dense background for a Madonna in half figure. These angels are likewise rendered as highly plastic, almost sculptural forms; their expressive, childlike faces are also very similar to those of Fouquet's angels. Finally, even the faces of the Virgin and her child in each instance are comparable, which at the very least shows how much Fouquet had learned from Italian painting in regard to the three-dimensional, sculptural development of heads.

Admittedly, Gozzoli's painting cannot have been the actual model for Fouquet's *Virgin and Child*, since it was probably created at about the same time as the latter. Gozzoli, however, had been a pupil and assistant of Fra Angelico, the Italian painter with whom Fouquet is most closely associated and in whose workshop he may have worked for a time.[84] Gozzoli's *Virgin* may possibly reflect an older composition by Fra Angelico or his workshop, which may likewise have inspired Fouquet; the existence of such clear parallels between the two panels makes the notion of pure coincidence highly implausible.

In contrast to Gozzoli, however, Fouquet shows completely nude putti with visible thighs and bellies and only one pair of wings each. Aside from the color these are the same childlike angels that carry the shields with the patron's "e&e"-device in the presentation miniature of the *Hours of Étienne Chevalier* (fig. 43). In the mid-15th century, nude putti of this sort were not yet common north of the Alps; Memling was probably the first to use them in the Netherlands around 1480. Fouquet would certainly have brought these putti back from Italy, in fact from the circle of Fra Angelico and Benozzo Gozzoli: The Berlin drawing by the latter's hand (cat. 10) shows putti with fruit garlands almost exactly like the ones in the aforementioned illumination.[85] The *Virgin and Child* of the *Melun Diptych* is every bit as Italianizing as the donor panel, albeit in a different way.

Fig. 14. Benozzo Gozzoli, Virgin with Angels, ca. 1455, poplar, 65.4 x 50.5 cm, Detroit, The Detroit Institute of Art

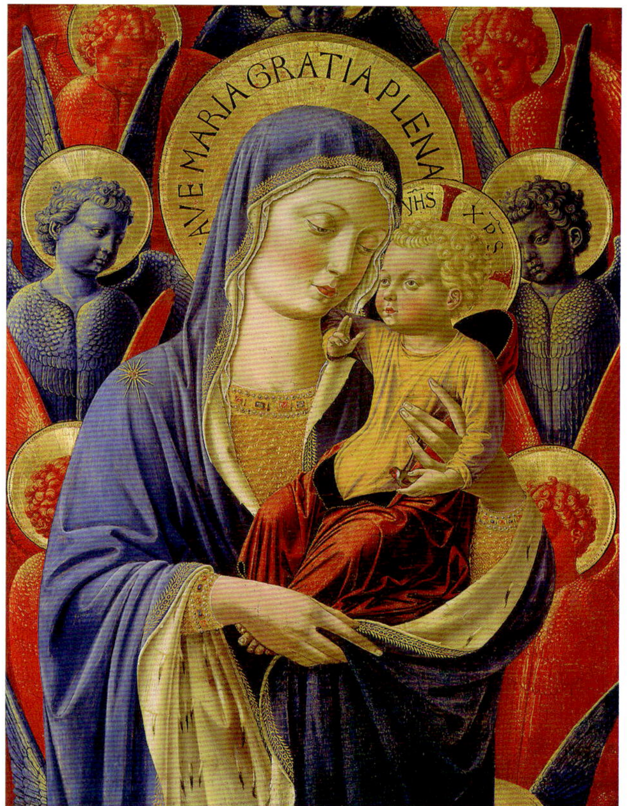

A Reconstruction

The *Melun Diptych* originally consisted of more than just the two surviving panel paintings. According to Godefroy's well-known description of 1661, it also boasted elaborate frames adorned with figural golden medallions:

"les bordures desdits tableaux sont couvertes en dedans de velours bleu, orné et enrichy tout autour de quantité de grands lacs d'amour à l'antique, separés d'une esgale distance l'un de l'autre; et tissus d'une petite broderie d'or et d'argent; dans chaque costé desquels lacs, est un grand E (Estienne) aussi à l'antique, tout couvert de petites perles fines; et entre ces lacs d'amour, sont les médailles d'argent doré, de moyenne grandeur, représentans quelque histoire saincte, dont les personnages sont peints admirablement bien."[86]

According to general assumption, two of these medallions have survived or are photographically documented, though they do not consist of "gilt silver" but of a kind of enamel.[87] One was formerly held in Berlin, but was lost in 1945; it is quite certain that it belonged to the frame of the donor panel for it shows the *Choosing of the Seven Deacons*,[88] the first episode of the legend of St. Stephen. The large photograph from the pre-war period (fig. 15), published here for the first time, enables us to see not only the mastery and monumentality that Fouquet achieved on the smallest possible scale, but also the iconographically significant halo of the foremost deacon, which identifies him as Stephen himself. The other, justly famous medallion (cat. 2) constitutes the earliest securely identified self-portrait by any French painter, indeed by any painter north of the Alps. As it is inscribed with the artist's name, there can be no doubt as to the identity of the subject, and since its size corresponds to that of the medallion of St. Stephen, it might have come from the same ensemble. Admittedly, it cannot be ruled out that this self-portrait once adorned the frame of another work by Fouquet: The mastery of the execution does not suggest that these enamels were a one-time, ad-hoc work. On the other hand, a self-portrait of the painter would seem especially fitting for a work for Étienne Chevalier, the patron of Fouquet's most beautiful creations. Be that as it may, the idea for a small self-portrait with signature, integrated into a larger work, may have been inspired by Italian examples such as the bronze doors of Lorenzo Ghiberti in

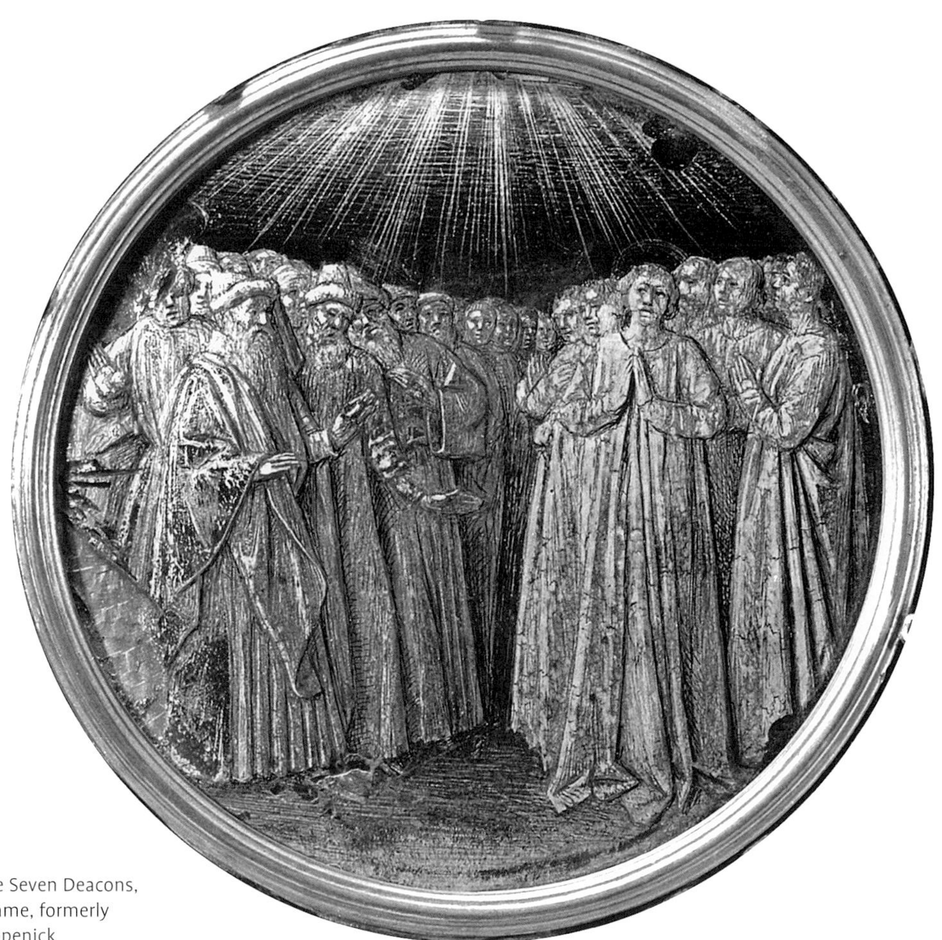

Fig. 15. Jean Fouquet, The Choosing of the Seven Deacons, ca. 1452-60, enamel, Ø 6.9 cm without frame, formerly Berlin, Kunstgewerbemuseum Schloss Köpenick

Florence or of Filarete in Rome.[89] The frontal bust, however, occurs in western and central Europe already around 1400 and before, on roundels with images of prophets that adorned picture frames.[90] Frames decorated with narrative medallions are likewise known from these regions; four precious, individually preserved examples in enamel with scenes from the Passion, Parisian works of ca. 1420-25, may originally have been fastened to a picture frame or other object.[91] It is remarkable that these earlier enamels have exactly the same diameter, 6.9 cm, as the pictorial field of Fouquet's two medallions, and thus it might have been a standard measurement for enamel roundels in France.

The frames described by Godefroy with their velvet covering, embroidery, and enamel work may be considered unusual, even extravagant. No other velvet-covered frames for panel paintings seem to have survived or be documented from either the late Middle Ages or the early modern period. On the other hand, precious fabrics were frequently used for book bindings and sometimes also for small, book-like diptychs. The estate of the Duke of Bedford, former regent of Paris, inventoried in London in July 1433, included a small diptych with painted scenes from the martyrdom of St. George under glass on the inside; on the outside was the saint with his cross "assise sur satin vermeil", or "sitting on red satin". The whole thing could be closed like a book and secured with clasps.[92] And in 1516, Margaret of Austria owned a small painted diptych of the Virgin that could be closed like a book; it was described as "couvert de satin brouché gris, et ayant fermaulx d'argent doré et bordé de velours vert. Fait de la main de Johannes [van Eyck]".[93]

Presumably Chevalier himself requested the unusual decoration of the frames, which combined costly, ostentatious materials and whose meaning would have consisted above all in the display of extravagance and splendor. The velvet most likely had the same deep blue color we see in countless painted textiles in Fouquet's illuminations and also in the dalmatic of St. Stephen; at the same time, the texture of the velvet also echoed the donor's garment on the left wing of the diptych, connecting the frame to the image in a double sense. The colored fabric also provided an ideal ground for Chevalier's monogram: his silver-golden "e&e" on dark blue[94] must have resembled the fabric with the *fleur-de-lys* of the French crown that Fouquet depicted again and again in his illuminations (figs. 80, 81), and such resemblance to the heraldic colors of the monarchy would certainly have been amenable to the donor. In any case, this design gave the frame a heraldic character and probably recalled the aesthetic of heraldic tapestries or garments decorated with devices and coats of arms.

The original frames can be reconstructed to a certain extent, based on the old description. The perspective of the left wing, with its focal point exactly on the central axis of the right one, indicates that the distance between the two pictures measured ca. 20 cm, and thus each of the frames was 9-10 cm in width; their inner edges were gilded.[95] The outer edges of the frames were probably finished in the same way, so that the area covered in velvet was enclosed by two narrow golden strips which, for reasons of protection of the enamels, must have been slightly higher than the medallions. The enamel medallions, ca. 7.5 cm in diameter including the setting, were placed on top of the fabric. Godefroy tells us nothing about their number, iconography, or distribution on the frames; certainly the medallions with the legend of St. Stephen surrounded the donor panel, while those of the Madonna panel could have shown scenes from the Life of Christ and the Virgin. In the hierarchy of this decorative scheme, the enamels with depictions of the saints would doubtlessly have ranked higher than the embroidered monograms, and would therefore have been mounted in the corners and on the central axes of the two frames, making a count of eight medallions per frame seem plausible.[96] Designed in this way, the frames not only intensified the splendor of the object in a precious, jewel-like way, but also enriched the vivid color composition of the painting with yet another variation on blue and gold (fig. 16).

Yet the reconstruction of Chevalier's diptych may go beyond even the splendid frames. As Godefroy reports, the two wings were connected with hinges and could be folded together, "se fermans l'un dans l'autre". The recent examination of the Berlin panel has shown that it was split with a saw, and the purpose of this technically difficult and risky procedure could only have been to make two pictures out of a panel that was painted on both sides.[97] Thus we can assume that originally, the back of the donor's wing was painted as well. The cradle that was subsequently glued onto the back does not match what was normally used in the Berlin museum, and therefore must have been attached before the panel was acquired in 1896. Visitors to the Brentano collection in Frankfurt, where the piece had been held since about 1820, say nothing about an image on the back side; accordingly, the panel had probably already been split by that time. It is likely that this occurred when the diptych was dismantled around 1773 and its fragments sold in order to raise funds for the renovation of the church of Notre-Dame in Melun.[98] More money could be gained from the sale of three instead of only two paintings, and the splitting and cradling of painted panels was an already common practice by the time.[99] The back of the Virgin's panel, on the other hand, was never painted; the original wooden surface bears an inscription dated 1775 in which a lawyer by the name of Gaulthier identifies the painting as a donation by Chevalier and a role portrait of Agnès Sorel (fig. 95). Doubtless this certified identification of illustrious persons was intended to increase the painting's value. We can do no more than speculate as to the image on the outer side of the donor wing which is lost without a trace. It must have been a figural representation, to justify splitting the panel, and perhaps showed saints or the Crucifixion of Christ.

The reconstruction thus yields a foldable diptych, also painted on the outside of the left wing, with panels measuring about 115 x 105 cm each including their extraordinary and magnificent frames. There is no doubt that from the beginning, the work was intended for the place where it would be documented beginning in the 17th century: The donor's private chapel in the collegiate church of Notre-Dame in Melun, home town of Étienne Chevalier (ca. 1400-1474).[100] His wife Catherine Budé died young in 1452 and was buried in the chapel where Chevalier, too, would find his final resting place 22 years later. His chapel was located behind the high altar to the east, and encompassed the 12th-century apse (figs. 17,

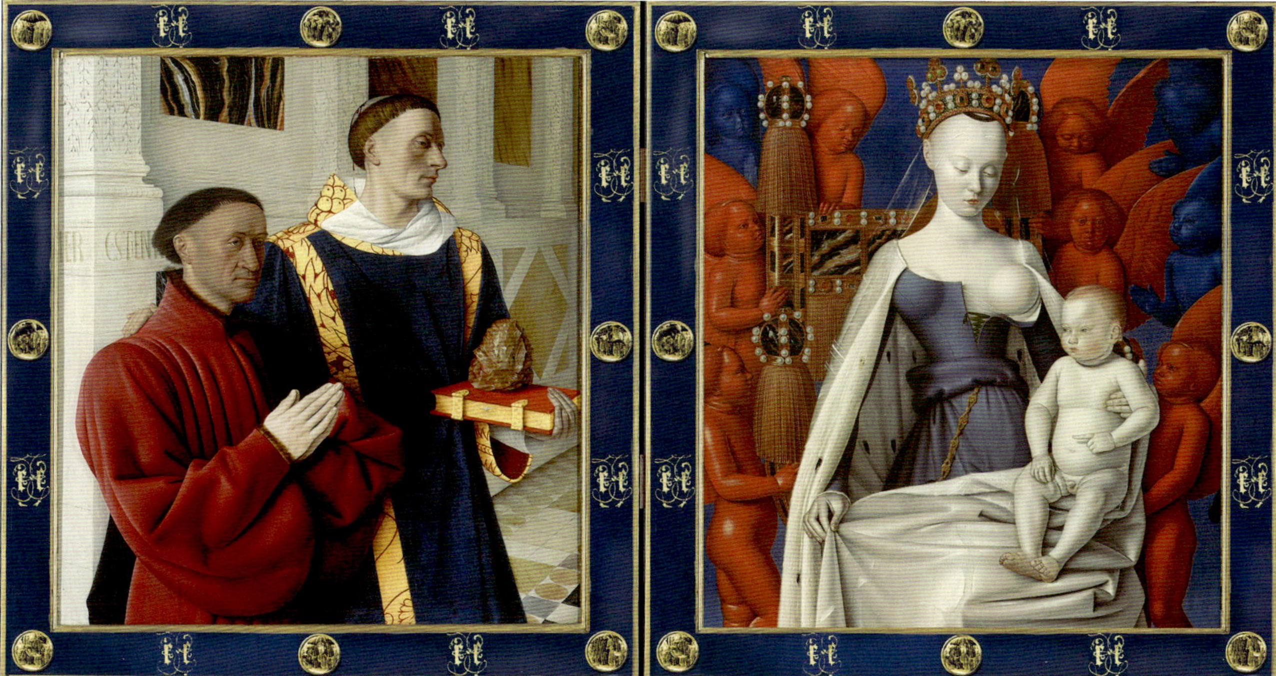

Fig. 16. Reconstruction of the Frames of the Melun Diptych

18). This space "derrière le chœur" was 6.55 m wide and about 14 m deep;[101] it thus included the apse and the two adjacent bays. This was the site of Chevalier's flat brass tomb slab with figural decoration; recorded only in an engraving of the 17th century, it showed Étienne and his wife, with their four children below on a smaller scale (fig. 52).[102] According to Godefroy, an altar stood in the chapel "derrière le chœur, vis à vis des sépultures susdites" (i.e., Chevalier's), in other words, on the east wall of the apse.[103] Chevalier had endowed a daily mass at this altar; by Godefroy's time, however, it had to be celebrated at another altar, since the number of people attending exceeded the limited space behind the choir.[104] This area behind the high altar is also where the diptych was located. Godefroy describes it as hanging at medium height on the wall on the sacristy side (i.e., on the south); at that time the lower edges of the panels must have been about 3 m above the floor.[105] Yet the diptych was not meant to be viewed from so far below. For one thing, the horizon line of the perspective is on the same level as the back of the Virgin's throne, only slightly above the donor's line of sight. Above all, however, the small, finely executed scenes on the medallions would no longer have been legible at three or four meters in height. According to Gode-

froy, some of these medallions were already missing in 1661, and so it seems logical to assume that in order to protect them from further theft, the panels were hung high enough that they could not be reached without a ladder.

The construction of the work as a large, non-portable diptych with one painted exterior side fundamentally speaks against any intention of hanging it high up on a wall somewhere. Few large diptychs of this kind have survived, but there are at least two Netherlandish examples, made by Gerard David around 1502 and Adriaan Isenbrant around 1530;[106] there is also the little-known diptych from the cathedral of Lübeck, destroyed in 1942, which Hermen Rode created for Heinrich Greverade in 1494 and whose wings each measured a sizeable 164 x 188 cm.[107] All of these works had three painted surfaces, and all were altarpieces. The foldable structure of the *Melun Diptych* would likewise correspond to this function, but would have made little sense for an epitaph mounted on a wall, as the work has usually been understood; the concealing of the donor in the interior would defeat the entire purpose of an epitaph, which was to cause passersby to remember the deceased. The simple circumstance that the deceased Catherine Budé is not

31

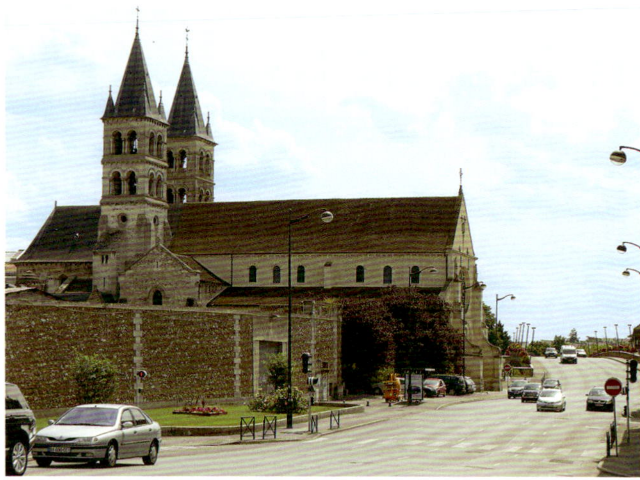
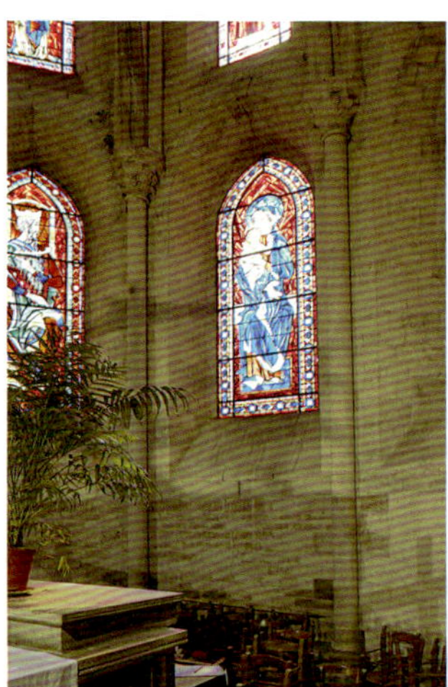

Fig. 17. Collegiate Church Notre-Dame, Melun, and interior of the eastern apse

Fig. 18. Collegiate Church Notre-Dame, Melun, Ground Plan, 1837, Musée municipal de Melun

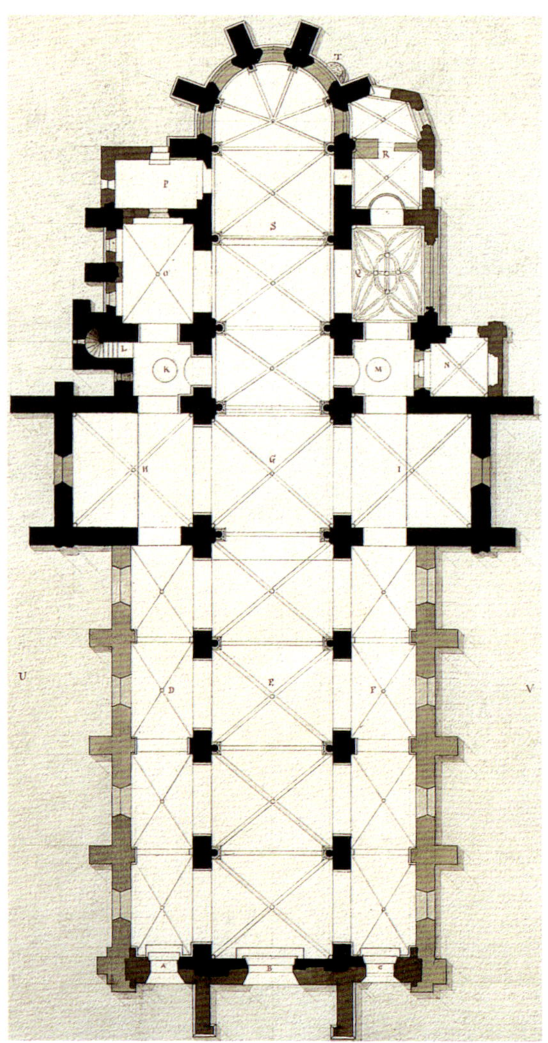

shown together with her husband also speaks against the identification of the piece as an epitaph; epitaphs usually commemorated not merely one person, but family members as well. Chevalier's chapel did in fact include an "épitaphe escrite aussi en lettres gothiques sur une grande table de cuivre jaune cramponnée contre la muraille",[108] a large brass panel with Gothic script which was fastened to the wall. Significantly, the material of this panel echoed the brass of the married couple's tomb slab—the two objects thus were related to each other.

To me, therefore, it seems undeniable that the *Melun Diptych* was meant to function as an altarpiece.[109] Consequently, it can only have been placed on the altar of the Chevalier chapel, and in fact its measurements perfectly fit that location. If we assume that the now-lost altar, with a step beneath it, was ca. 1 to 1.1 m high, and we add ca. 1.15 m for the diptych with frame, its upper edge would have reached to a height of ca. 2.2 to 2.3 m. The distance from the floor to the lower edge of the embrasure of the window in the apse measures 2.3 m; thus the diptych, standing on the altar, would have perfectly filled this space. The middle section of the apse where the altar must have stood is framed on either side by shafts positioned ca. 2.2 m apart from each other; if we imagine an altar of approximately the same width as the framed Madonna panel or a little wider (ca. 1.10-1.30 m), there would still be approximately 50 cm from the mensa to the shafts on either side. In this position, the left wing of the diptych would not be able to open completely to 180 degrees, but would stand slightly at an angle, extending beyond the

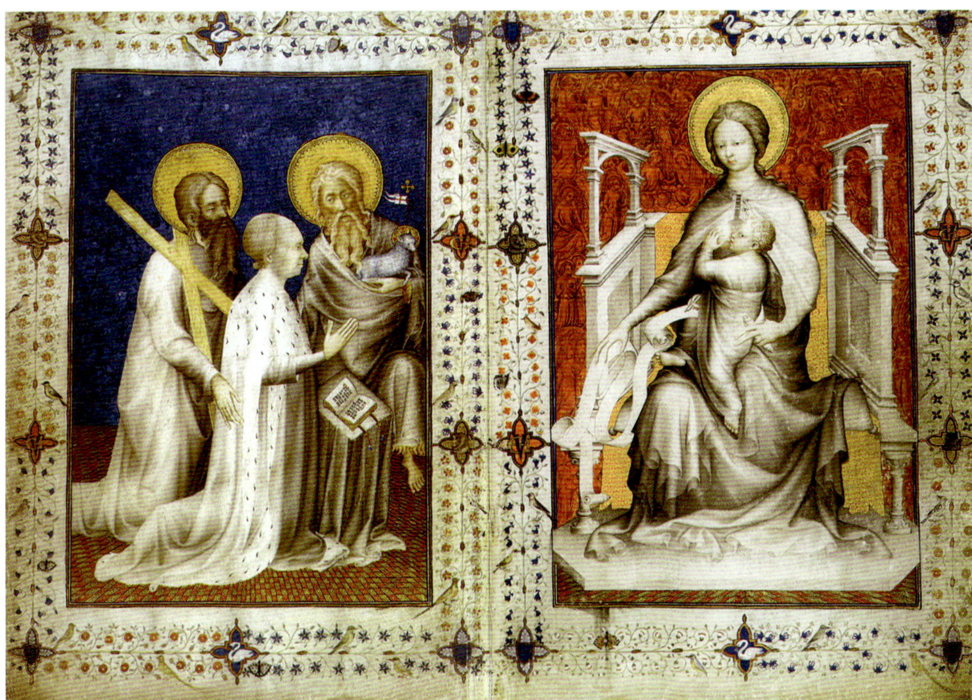

Fig. 19. The Duc de Berry with his Patron Saints and Virgin Enthroned, double page from the Très Belles Heures (Heures de Bruxelles), ca. 1400, Brussels, Bibliothèque Royale, ms. 11060-1, S. 10, 11

shaft to the left. As Hugo van der Velden has demonstrated, such a display, opened at a flat angle, would have been appropriate for a large diptych functioning as an altarpiece.[110]

In his altarpiece, as in his private book of hours (fig. 43), Étienne Chevalier had himself represented alone before the Mother of God as the still-living donor. His position on the left wing, which in heraldic terms is the superior, dexter position, suggested to Erwin Panofsky and others that in accord with the rules of hierarchy, a third panel depicting the donor's wife would also have to have been present,[111] making the *Virgin and Child* the central panel of a triptych. Godefroy's description, however, very clearly rules out an additional wing. Yet in a certain sense, the Madonna did indeed occupy the central position in the diptych: she stood firm and immutable on the altar, while the donor wing was opened and closed, clearly marking it as the subordinate element.[112]

In essence, Chevalier was depicted here according to a time-honored scheme, one that occurs in works such as the well-known double-page illumination in the *Brussels Hours* of Duke Jean de Berry, painted around 1400 (fig. 19): the donor is shown in the left-hand image, kneeling with his patron saint (or saints) and turning toward the enthroned Virgin and Child on the opposite page. But

what makes Fouquet's solution so innovative and pioneering is his approach to composition: the painter shows the figures at close range, as a "dramatic close-up" in Sixten Ringbom's terms,[113] transforming the full figures usually seen on altarpiece wings into half figures. As such, they seem more monumental and their postures and gestures appear more striking. Although the half-figure Virgin had numerous predecessors, fewer existed for the donor; for what Fouquet created here was not a more or less autonomous portrait of the type that had existed since the 14th century, showing the subject's shoulders or even half the body. Rather, he transformed the donor panel of an altarpiece into a half figure portrait, thereby rendering the patron saint, too, as a portrait-like figure. In effect, he shortened the presentation diptych in the above-mentioned Berry book of hours by the lower one-third of the picture. Fouquet thus invented a type of altarpiece which, ten years later, must also have appealed to the chancellor Jouvenel des Ursins (fig. 123) and which was revisited around 1500 by the Master of Moulins, Jean Hey.[114] Thus in the mid-1450s, Étienne Chevalier's ambitious commissions gave the painter Jean Fouquet the opportunity to create his best and most innovative works, in both manuscript illumination and panel painting.

1 Schwager 1970; Schäfer 1994, pp. 24ff., 289ff.; Cat. Paris 2003, cat. 2, 3.
2 Cat. Paris 2003, p. 420.
3 Paris, Musée du Louvre; Reynaud 1981, pp. 28-31, 82ff.; Schaefer 1994, pp. 199-203, 297ff.; Cat. Paris 2003, no. 5 (Dominique Thiébaut).
4 Since Jouvenel's wife, unlike Chevalier's, did not die before him, this possibility was considered by Reynaud 1981, p. 31; Schaefer 1994, p. 201.
5 Schaefer 1994, p. 419, doc. I.6.
6 Ibid., pp. 419ff., doc. I.8; Reynaud 1981, p. 78, n. 8.
7 Schaefer 1994, p. 421, doc. II.2.
8 Le Glay 1839, vol. 2, p. 481.
9 Cat. Paris 2003, cat. 17 (François Avril); Reynaud 1981, cat. 13.
10 For the *Ghent Altarpiece*, see Cat. Berlin 2014; for the *Monforte Altarpiece*, Berlin, Gemäldegalerie, Dhanens 1998, pp. 187-212.
11 See the essay by Seidel in this volume.
12 40 miniatures from the book that was dismembered in the 18th century are in the Musée Condé, Chantilly, six are in other collections, see Schaefer 1994, pp. 40-137; Reynaud 2006; Cat. Paris 2003, no. 24.
13 See the essay by Seidel in this volume.
14 Durrieu 1904, and Pächt 1940, for example, identified the illuminations in Frontinus, *Livre des stratagèmes*, Brussels, Bibliothèque Royal, ms. 10475, as youthful works by Fouquet; however, they were executed not around 1435, but after 1471, as demonstrated by König 1982, pp. 10-14 and passim; Cat. Paris 1993, cat. 58 (François Avril). The same is true for works now attributed to the Jouvenel Master, an artist who was probably somewhat older than Fouquet and had contact with him; see König 1982, pp. 27-41, 213-221; Cat. Paris 2003, cat. 59.
15 Cat. Paris 2003, p. 418, doc. 2. Fouquet appears as "peintre" twice in 1461, once each in 1465/66, 1471, 1472, 1474, 1475, and 1481, as "enlumineur" in 1465, and as "paintre et enlumineur" in 1488/1503; see the documents in Cat. Paris 2003, pp. 418-420.
16 Houtard 1906, p. 36.
17 In his *Couronne margaritique*, written for Margaret of Austria; see Cat. Paris 2003, doc. 6b, p. 422.
18 See most recently Cat. Rotterdam 2012, cat. 80.
19 Brussels, Bibliothèque Royale, ms. 9242, fol. 1r; de Vos 1999, cat. 16; Cat. Brussels/Paris 2011/12, cat. 19.
20 Chapuis 2004.
21 On the Master of Aix or Cœur-Master or Barthélemy d'Eyck respectively, see Reynaud 1989; König 1996; Dominique Thiébaut in Cat. Paris 2004, pp. 123-141.
22 Grosshans 1991; Kemperdick 2014.
23 Cat. Los Angeles 2003, p. 98.
24 As already suggested by Schaefer 1994, p. 23; Reynaud, 2006, p. 242.
25 Evans 1998, pp. 168-169, suggests the French General of the Dominicans, Barthélemy Texier, who lived in the monastery of Santa Maria sopra Minerva, as a possible liaison.
26 Sterling 1987, p. 39; Sterling 1988, p. 22; Reynaud 1981, p. 80, n. 44; Thiébaut 2003, pp. 30-31.
27 Sterling 1987, p. 39; Thiébaut 2003, pp. 30-31; Thiébaut in: Cat. Paris 2003, pp. 104-106.
28 Rumohr 1822, p. 377, with reference to Brentano's miniatures in Frankfurt; Passavant 1833, p. 87, referring to the page with *David at Prayer*, which at the time was in the possession of Rogers, but is now in London, British Library, add. ms. 37421; Reynaud 2006, no. 25.
29 Schaefer 1994, pp. 21, 277-281; cf. Lorentz 2003, pp. 48ff.
30 As noted already by Lorentz 2003, p. 49.
31 Cf. e.g. Cat. Berlin 2014, pp. 29-33.
32 For example in the miniatures of the *Salisbury Breviary* by the Bedford Master, ca. 1432- 35(?), Paris, BN, ms. lat. 17294; Sterling 1987, cat. 60, pp. 436-437, 444.
33 Paris, Louvre; it is the first panel of the so-called "Puy d'Amiens", the annual donation of a painting by a confraternity in Amiens.
34 The Master of Dreux Budé, known for both manuscript and panel painting, might be identical with André d'Ypres, as suggested by Nicole Reynaud in Cat. Paris 1993, p. 53. André d'Ypres is documented already in

35 1428 as a free master in Tournai and died in 1450 in Paris. Even so, however, his "modern" panels, such as the *Altarpiece of the Parliament of Paris*, date to the later 1440s; Lorentz 2004, pp. 92-96.
35 Liechtenstein, Collections of the Prince of Liechtenstein; see Cat. Basel 2006, cat. 1.
36 Friedländer 1896, p. 213 (as a self-portrait by Fouquet!); Leprieur 1897, pp. 347ff.; Cat. Paris 1904, no. 51 (Henri Bouchot); Künstler 1975, pp. 32-35.
37 The portrait is not attributed to Fouquet by Hulin de Loo 1904, pp. 30-34, and Ring 1943, no. 143. It is called Master of Aix or Barthélemy d'Eyck by Wescher 1947, pp. 61-62; Reynaud 1989, n. 88; Cat. Bruges 2002, no. 66 (Till-Holger Borchert); Thiébaut in Cat. Paris 2004, pp. 130-131. In the present author's view, the formulas and understanding of faces in particular differ in this portrait and the Aix-panels, cf. Cat. Basel 2006, cat. 1.
38 Evans 1998, p. 169.
39 Paris, Louvre. Lorentz 2003, pp. 39-42, fig. III.4, III.5.
40 On its long-lasting influence see Cat. Berlin 2014.
41 Kurmann-Schwarz 1988, pp. 17-19, 30-33; Kurmann-Schwarz 1999, pp. 13-149; Lorentz 2003, pp. 47-49.
42 Cf. the characterization in Pächt 1974, p. 55 and passim.
43 Cf. the essay by von Fircks in this volume.
44 Cat. Frankfurt/Berlin 2008/09, no. 20.
45 Madrid, Prado; de Vos 1999, no. 4.
46 Boston, Museum of Fine Arts; de Vos 1999, no. 8.
47 The works grouped together under this conventional name are certainly heterogeneous and should not be understood as the work of a single artist. Whether any of these works is attributable to the painter Robert Campin (ca. 1375-1444), and if so, which, can hardly be resolved; hence the "Flémalle" designation will continue to be used here. For discussion of the problem, see Cat. Frankfurt/Berlin 2008/09. Campin's workshop, however, was doubtless the place where most of the works in question were made, at least until 1432, when Rogier van der Weyden, Jacques Daret, and two other journeymen attained the rank of master.
48 Chantilly, Musée Condé; Reynaud 2006, no. 1, 21.
49 Dijon, Musée des Beaux-Arts; Cat. Frankfurt/Berlin 2008/09, no. 5.
50 In the *Deposition*, it appears on the right-hand corner of Mary's mantle and the fluttering tip of the white robe of the man on the ladder. The *Durán Madonna* in Madrid, Prado, see de Vos 1999, cat. 5.
51 Cat. Frankfurt/Berlin 2008/09, cat. 44.
52 Cf. the contribution by Klein in the present volume.
53 Cf. Cat. Paris 1981, no. 3, pp. 12-18, 80-81; Schaefer 1994, pp. 152-155, 293; Cat. Paris 2003, no. 4 (D. Thiébaut), especially pp. 107-109.
54 Dendrochronological analysis also suggests this date; see Klein in the present volume.
55 Thiébaut in Cat. Paris 2003, pp. 107-110, with reference to François Avril.
56 Reynaud 1981, p. 14; Reynaud 1983.
57 See the essay by Stelzig in the present volume.
58 Reynaud 1981, p. 14; Reynaud 1983.
59 Cat. Paris 1981, no. 3; Cat. Paris 2003, no. 4 (D. Thiébaud); Schäfer 1994, pp. 152-155, 293. The portrait was intended for the Sainte-Chapelle in Bourges, an important royal residence. Nash 2008, p. 288, assumes a royal commission for the discarded version.
60 Schäfer 1994, p. 44, Cat. Paris 2003, 198; Reynaud 2006, no. 2.
61 See the essays by Kurmann-Schwarz, Kren, and von Fircks in the present volume.
62 Godefroy 1661, quoted in Schäfer 1975, p. 98: "Some claim that this picture was painted from the figure of Agnes Sorel, mistress of Charles VII".
63 Jean Héroard accompanied the Dauphin Louis XIII to Melun on March 10, 1608: "on lui [Louis] montre le tableau de la belle Agnès et ce-lui d'E-tienne Chevalier, qui le donna en ce temps-la; il semble tout frais, pour avoir été bien conservé", Héroard 1868, p. 323.
64 Charles Sorel, *La Solitude et l'Amour philosophique de Cléomède, premier sujet des exercices moraux*, Paris 1640, p. 331, quoted in Curmer 1864, pp. 88ff.
65 See the essay by von Fircks in the present volume.

66 Curmer 1864, p. 88.

67 Châtelet 1975, however, noted that the figure was heavily restored in the 19th century.

68 Schaefer 1975, p. 24 (epitaph), p. 20 (testament). An 18th-century transcription in the Archives municipales de Melun, GG d 108, pièce 3, quotes one of the stipulations of Agnès Sorel's will as bequeathing 40 *ècus d'or* for the maintenance of the church St. Aspais in Melun; the executors of the will were Étienne Chevalier and Jacques Cœur.

69 Schaefer 1975, p. 24.

70 Salzer 1898, pp. 134-140 (lemma „Taube").

71 Schaefer 1975, pp. 27-29.

72 Cf. Cat. Prague 2006, no. 15, diptych with the Adoration of the Magi and the Death of the Virgin, ca. 1360, New York, Pierpont Morgan Library. Among others, the Hapsburg emperors Frederick III and Maximilian I were also portrayed in the role of worshiping Magi.

73 See the quotation in Kurmann-Schwarz, n. 39, in the present volume.

74 See the essay by Kurmann-Schwarz in the present volume.

75 In the *Neu-Karsthans*, for example, printed in 1520 in Strasbourg, we read: "Hett auch offt böse gedancken in anschauwung der fräwlichen bildungen auff den altären" ("evil thoughts often came to my mind when viewing the images of women on the altars"); and in Huldrych Zwingli's opinion, "die säligen wyber gstaltet man so hürisch, so glat und ußgestrichen [herausgeputzt] (...) das die man an inen gereitzt werdind zu uppigkeit [Wollust]" ("the saintly women are depicted in such a whorish way, so fancy and tarted up (...) that they tempt one to lust"); quoted in Baxandall 1984, p. 100.

76 See the essay by Kurmann-Schwarz in the present volume, who points out that Chastellain was not amicably disposed toward the French crown.

77 It was already wide-spread in the early 15th century in Germany and France, e.g. Cat. Paris 2004, nos. 187, 113; Cat. Rotterdam 2012, no. 12, 13; Kemperdick 2010, no. 31, fig. 224.

78 See the essay by Kurmann-Schwarz in the present volume.

79 Durrieu 1911, pp. 728, 731 even wanted to attribute the *Virgin and Child* to a different painter.

80 The use of boards from the same tree in both panels provides incontrovertible evidence; see Klein in the present volume.

81 Reynaud 1981, pp. 21, 90.

82 Châtelet 1975, pp. 128-133, his idea of a painted sculpture was convincingly refuted by Lombardi 1978, pp. 4-5.

83 Detroit Institute of Arts; Cat. New York 2005, no. 60 (Pia Palladina).

84 See the essay by Rowley in the present volume.

85 As noted already in Schaefer 1994, p. 31; Sricchia Santoro 2003, p. 61.

86 Quoted in Schaefer 1975, p. 98: "The frames of the paintings mentioned are covered with blue velvet on the inside, ornamented and enriched all over with a quantity of large antique love knots, evenly spaced and executed in fine gold and silver embroidery. On each side of these knots is a large E (Estienne), likewise antique and covered entirely with small pearls. And between these love knots are medium-sized medallions of gilt silver, which represent a sacred story with admirably well-painted figures".

87 An anonymous source from the late 17th century says that "la bordure est d'emaille", doubtless referring to the medallions mentioned by Godefroy; ibid., p. 11; de Laborde 1855, vol. 1, p. 709. See the essay by Antoine and Beillart in the present volume.

88 Gauthier 1972, no. 252; Reynaud 1981, pp. 23-24; Legenda Aurea 1978, p. 59.

89 Schaefer 1994, pp. 26-27; Cat. Paris 2003, pp. 135-136; cf. the essay by Rowley in the present volume.

90 In France and the Netherlands, almost none of these are preserved, since almost all original frames have been lost. There are examples from western Germany, however, including the frame of the high altar retable of the Wiesenkirche in Soest of ca. 1340, Berlin, Gemäldegalerie (see Kemperdick 2010, no. 6) or the frame of the *Tempziner Altar* produced in Wismar around 1400, Güstrow, Museum (Hegner 2015, pp. 59-63).

91 Louvre; Cat. Paris 2004, cat. 224. A mirror frame with attached medallions showing scenes from the Passion is famously depicted in Jan van Eyck's so-called *Arnolfini Portrait* of 1434 in London.

92 Stratford 1993, pp. 199, 307-308, B 112.

93 Le Glay 1839, p. 480, "covered in gray broché satin and with clasps of gilded silver, edged with green velvet. By the hand of Johannes".

94 On the meaning of "e&e" see the essay by König in the present volume.

95 Cf. the essay by Stelzig in the present volume; Avril 2003, p. 127.

96 Already suggested by Thiébaut in Cat. Paris 2003, p. 134. Twice this number of medallions could also be distributed equally well on the frames, but the resulting number of scenes—a total of 32—would be improbably high. On the other hand, fewer medallions—four per frame, assuming a symmetrical distribution—could hardly be described as alternating with the monograms, as indicated by Godefroy. He also states that a number of medallions had already been stolen; with so few to begin with, hardly any would be left over.

97 Cf. the essay by Stelzig in the present volume.

98 This plausible reason for the sale is suggested by Schaefer 1994, p. 291; Avril 2003, p. 125.

99 Many thanks to Ute Stehr, Berlin, for information; cf. Stehr 2014.

100 Cf. the essay by König in the present volume. On the church also Förstel 2008.

101 As indicated in Fortelle 1843, p. 87. The space between the modern high altar, which is located much further to the east, and the apse wall now amounts to only ca. 3.5 m.

102 The material is mentioned by Abbé Bertin in 1717; he speaks of a "tombe platte de cuivre", but it was probably brass, not copper, like in other tomb slabs of the time; see Schaefer 1975, p. 13.

103 Godefroy 1661; quoted in Schaefer 1975, p. 98.

104 Godefroy's manuscript, ibid., p. 99.

105 Schaefer 1975, p. 98; Schaefer 1994, pp. 290-291.

106 David's diptych of Bernardijn Salviati (London und Berlin) and Isenbrant's Van de Velde diptych (Brussels) are discussed extensively in Van der Velden 2006.

107 Stange, KV 1, no. 658.

108 Godefroy, in the manuscript for the publication of 1661, Paris, Institut de France, Ms. fond Godefroy 241, fol. 385r, quoted in Schaefer 1975, p. 99.

109 As suggested already by Van der Velden 2006, pp. 146-147, followed by Nash 2008, pp. 286-287.

110 Van der Velden 2006, pp. 146-147.

111 Panofsky 1953, p. 480. Wescher 1947, p. 55, also suggests a triptych, for aesthetic reasons.

112 Van der Velden 2006 maintains that the heraldic principle of the superiority of right over left does not apply to diptychs, since the donor wing on the heraldic right stands diagonally, positioning the supplicant across from the saint rather than directly to the side. In my opinion, however, the subordinate status of the movable wing per se seems a better explanation.

113 Ringbom 1964.

114 Cat. Paris 2004, fig. 22.

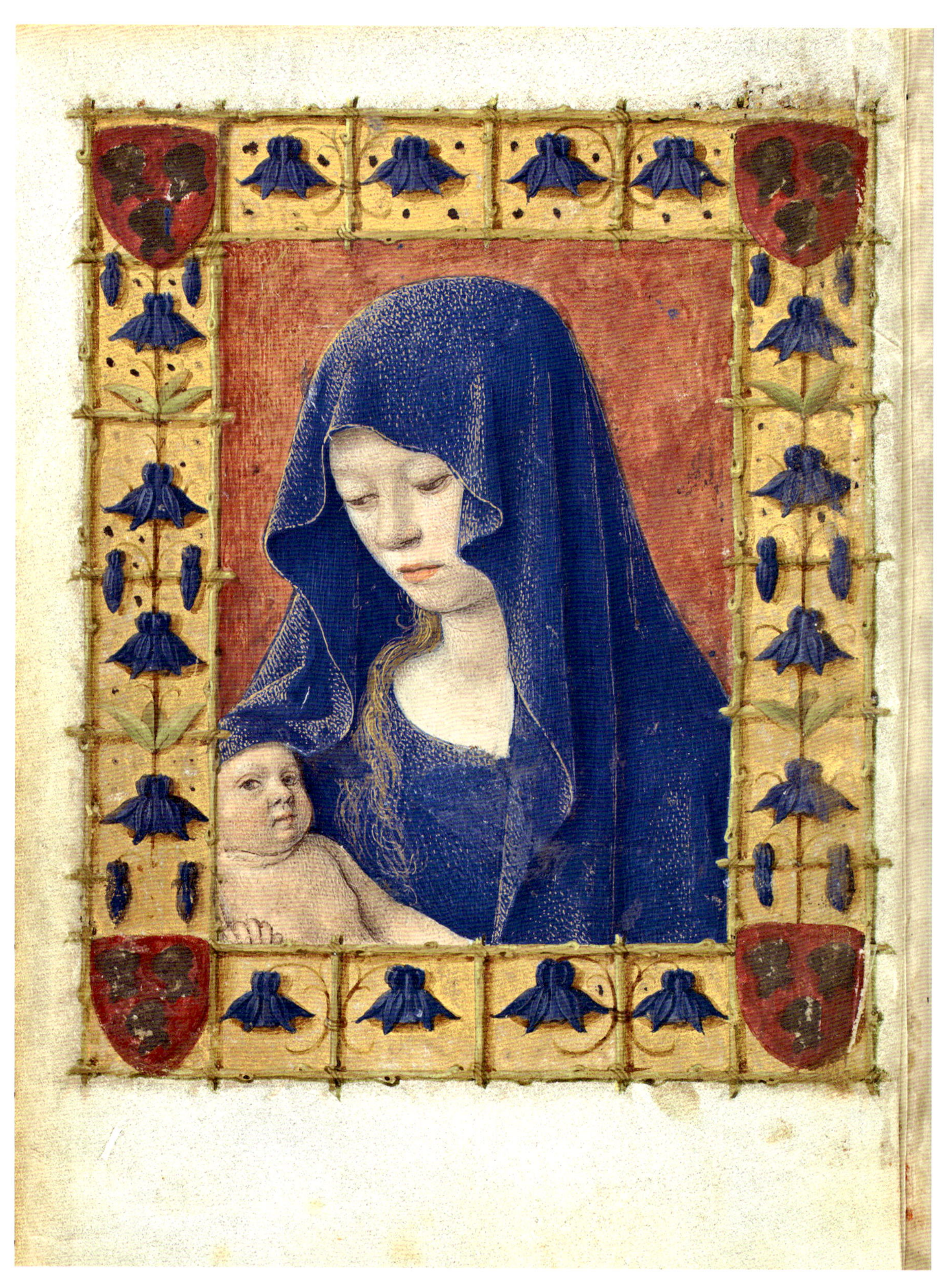

Christine Seidel

(MANUSCRIPT-)PAINTING:
THE ART OF JEAN FOUQUET
IN THE WORK OF HIS CONTEMPORARIES

In the late 15th century, François Robertet wrote the following note on the final page of the first volume of the *Antiquités judaïques*, now in the Bibliothèque nationale in Paris: "This book has twelve miniatures, the first three by the illuminator of Jean, Duke of Berry, and nine by the hand of the *bon peintre* and illuminator of King Louis XI, Jehan Foucquet of Tours."[1] In the margin, a later writer corrected the numbers to indicate that fourteen miniatures adorned the manuscript, eleven of which were by Jean Fouquet. The manuscript belonged to Pierre II, Duke of Bourbon and the Auvergne from 1488 on, who received it from the estate of Jacques d'Armagnac, Duke of Nemours, who was executed for high treason in 1477; the latter had commissioned the completion of the two-volume manuscript, begun before 1416.[2] The note by the Bourbon duke's secretary at the end of the first volume, stating that the first illuminations were made for the Duke of Berry and the subsequent ones were painted by Jean Fouquet, is probably unique for the late 15th century: while in France it was not uncommon for the names of illuminators to be recorded by contemporaries, such references would be found in account books and inventories rather than the *ex libris* of a manuscript. The note was made after 1488, by which time both Fouquet and Louis XI had already been dead for a number of years. Yet this recollection of both artist's and patron's names, even after their death, does not bear witness to an admiration for art akin to that of a modern connoisseur, for Robertet says

nothing of the fact that not one, but two painters created the first three miniatures for the Duke of Berry. Rather, the emphasis lies on the status of "painter and illuminator of the king," an interest that reflects the manuscript owner's ambition to be numbered among a circle of illustrious patrons whose works would later constitute the foundation of the royal library at Blois: the wife of the Bourbon duke, Anne de Beaujeu, was not only the daughter of Louis XI, but also regent of France until 1491 for her younger brother, the later Charles VIII.[3] Jean Fouquet continued to be praised alongside the great painters of Northern Europe by writers and scholars into the 16th century, and after a long period of obscurity, interest in his remarkable artistic personality was revived once again by means of this Parisian manuscript and Robertet's note at the end of the volume.

Beginning in the 19th century, the illuminations of the *Antiquités judaïques* (fig. 79) served as the point of departure for the reconstruction of the oeuvre of probably the most influential French artist of the mid-15th century. Gustav Friedrich Waagen, who had the advantage of being familiar with the illuminations from the *Hours of Étienne Chevalier* as well as the portrait of the latter in the collection of Georg Brentano in Frankfurt, associated these works with the name of Jean Fouquet on the strength of the note in the *Antiquités judaïques*. He wrote: "These 11 pictures show so much artistic insight, such a sense of style, such refined taste, primarily in the compositions, that from this alone one could already conclude that the author must also have worked on a larger scale."[4] In 1851, in a review of Léon de Laborde's *La Renaissance des arts à la cour de France* of 1850, Waagen also credited Fouquet

Fig. 20. Jean Fouquet, Virgin and Child, c. 1450-55, The Hague, Koninklijke Bibliotheek, 74 G 37a, fol. 1v (enlarged)

with the illuminations in a copy of Boccaccio's *Des cas des nobles hommes et femmes* in the Bayerische Staatsbibliothek in Munich (cod. gall. 6),[5] even before the pages from the *Hours of Étienne Chevalier* were published in a monograph, making them accessible to a broader audience. At the beginning of the last century, Paul Durrieu, a brilliant French scholar from the École des Chartes and one of the first to establish the importance of the art historical perspective in manuscript studies, not only astutely recounted the history of the painter's rediscovery, but also ingeniously identified the patron of the Munich Boccaccio when he recognized the motto RIEN SUR LY N'A REGARD as an anagram for the name of Laurens Gyrard, the notary, secretary, and financial officer of the French king.[6]

Today, the illuminations of the *Hours of Étienne Chevalier* hang in large frames on the walls of the Santuario at the Musée Condé in Chantilly. In 1891, the Duke of Aumale acquired them from Louis Brentano. Not one of them has ever been loaned in accordance with the will of their former owner, not even for the major Fouquet exhibition in Paris in 2003, which presented almost all the drawings, manuscripts, and paintings attributed to or associated with the painter and his immediate milieu.[7] Alongside the works that have been considered evidence of Fouquet's activity for nearly 200 years, the exhibition also investigated the painter's sphere of influence and addressed the question of which of the surviving works should be attributed to Fouquet himself, and which betray the hand of other artists, indeed other personalities. Today, five or six panel paintings are attributed to Fouquet (cat. 1, 3, fig. 2, 11, 123). Illuminated manuscripts, preserved in large numbers, paint a more diverse picture. François Avril characterized the Master of the Munich Boccaccio as an artist who must have worked almost parallel to Fouquet. In 1982, Nicole Reynaud had already expressed doubt as to the traditional attribution of the *Antiquités judaïques*, and most recently Avril has credited the Master of the Munich Boccaccio[8] with the very work that, on the basis of Robertet's note from the late 15th century, had provided Waagen with a point of departure for the identification of Fouquet's oeuvre, a standpoint which Friedländer had likewise embraced in 1896 when the portrait of Étienne Chevalier was acquired for the Gemäldegalerie in Berlin.[9] Avril's hypothesis, however, presents the Master of the Munich Boccaccio solely as an illuminator, whose color choice and application of paint differs fundamentally from "the other Fouquet," alongside whom he worked in the Munich Boccaccio of 1458.[10] In this view, Robertet's note is interpreted as attributing the completion of the manuscript ordered by the Duke of Nemours to Fouquet's workshop in Tours, but not as definitive proof of the latter's authorship. This interpretation once again opens up the possibility of a larger workshop, most recently called into question by Clancy,[11] and at the same time further refines the picture of artistic production in Tours as compared to a center like Angers. Some of the miniatures in the two-volume book begun for the Duke of Berry—which, in addition to the *Antiquités judaïques* (Paris, BnF, Ms. fr. 247), also includes the *Guerres des juifs* (Paris, BnF, Ms. NAF 21013)—are now attributed to Jean Bourdichon, Fouquet's most important successor in Tours around the turn of the century.[12] If this large illumination project is removed from Jean Fouquet's oeuvre, there remains the self-portrait in the Louvre and its association with the patronage of Étienne Chevalier, since it probably belonged to the frame of the *Melun Diptych*.[13] The contours of both artist and oeuvre become more sharply defined—and the number of potential manuscript illuminators grows in order to be able to appropriately divide up the work.[14]

As early as the 1460s, very exact repetitions of compositions from the *Hours of Étienne Chevalier* appear in manuscript illuminations from Tours. The monumental effect of its figures, along with its recession in depth, complex spatial motifs, and perspective constructions in small format, were imitated by contemporaries, often in partial copies.[15] Illuminators in Tours replicated the famous miniature of St. Martin down to the very lines in a number of manuscripts, while in the *Hours of Mary Stuart* entire compositions are copied from the New York *Hours of Jean Robertet*, in which Fouquet had paraphrased his own compositions from the *Hours of Étienne Chevalier*.[16] Fouquet's miniatures appear like small panel paintings in books—an effect that is primarily caused by the artist's neglect of the obligatory guidelines of the manuscript layout. He rather tends to paint full-page miniatures, which can be observed in another case. The remarkable *Hours of Simon de Varie*, now bound in three parts, was richly illuminated by the Dunois Master and the Master of Jean Rolin, probably around the middle of the century.[17] Both

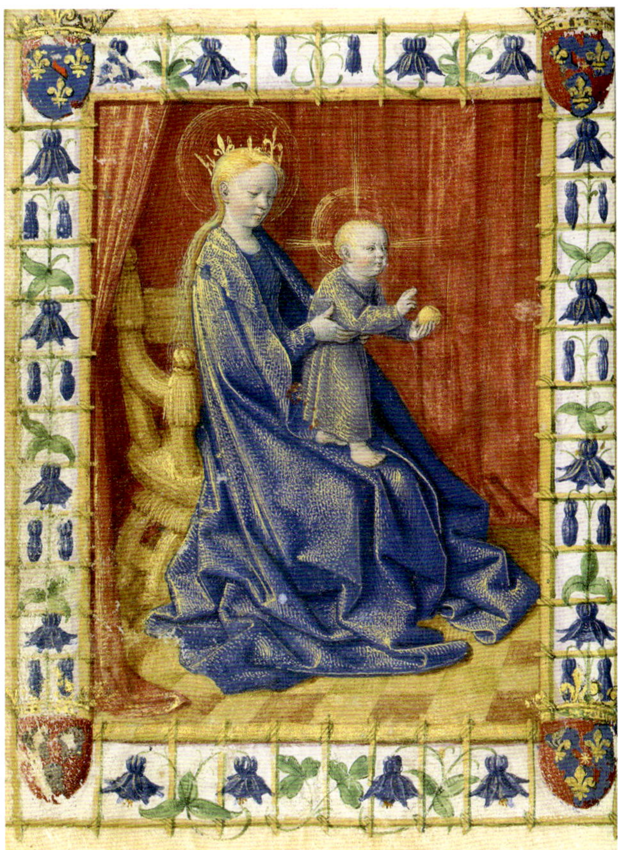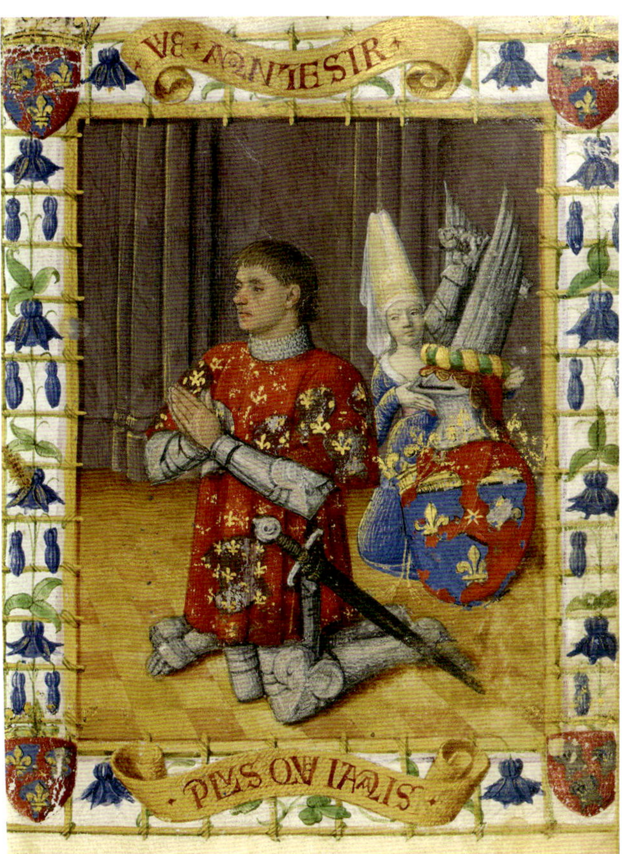

Fig. 21. Jean Fouquet, Simon de Varie in Prayer in Front of the Virgin, Book of Hours of Simon de Varie, Los Angeles, J. Paul Getty Museum, ms. 7, fol. 1v, 2

of these artists were among the leading illuminators in Paris at the time. Very little is known about Simon de Varie; he came from Bourges and was an official at the court of Charles VII.[18] For him, Fouquet painted a double page and a half-figure image of the Virgin, a full-page miniature causing the effect of a small panel painting (fig. 20). The double page shows Simon de Varie praying before the Mother of God in two full-page illuminations framed by trellises decorated with columbine and the patron's coat of arms, which was later overpainted (fig. 21). Now placed at the beginning of the manuscript, it opens like a diptych; full-page coats of arms on the backs of the pages are likewise framed by trellises with flowers, fruits, and the patron's motto. The design of this double page adopts a format used in panel painting and applies it to manuscript illumination, contrasting markedly with the aesthetic of the original book, which was created at almost the same time. Moreover, the painting technique of these additions differs notably; greyish blue hatchings are used

for shading to create a sculptural, cool color effect.[19] This technique can, slightly adapted, also be seen in the application of bluish-grey color brushed onto skin tones in Fouquet's panel paintings – such as for example the shaded areas of the Virgin and Child's skin in the Antwerp panel and on the face of St. Stephen in the Berlin portrait.

A book of hours for the use of Angers (Paris, BnF, ms. NAL 3211) is considered one of the earliest examples of Fouquet's work after his return from Italy, and was produced in conjunction with those illuminators whom scholars of a previous generation identified as the early Fouquet: the Jouvenel Master and the Master of the Geneva Boccaccio.[20] The miniature showing the stigmatization of St. Francis diverges sharply from the overall concept of the book (fig. 22). The saint, kneeling in a landscape, appears before a jagged, towering cliff; the contours of his shoulders and the back of his head show traces of reworking in a meticulous stippling technique, a rare example of intensive reworking and alteration in manuscript painting, which is often executed only in thin glazes. The border was painted by an artist from Angers, although it too departs from the dominant mode of border decoration in its inclusion of colorful decorative bands. Both the script and the design of the picture, which expands beyond the prescribed frame for an illumination, differ from the rest of the book. Fouquet's contribution thus appears as an independent one, operating outside the specifications for the project and his fellow illuminators. Considering such a debut, it seems fitting that the artist who painted outside the lines, as it were, was also the one tasked with rendering the praying clergyman, the patron of the miniature, in a recognizably lifelike manner. This Angevin book of hours has been dated to around 1450 and thus stands as one of the earliest examples of Fouquet's art after his return from Italy. Was Fouquet, then, a panel painter who illuminated books?

In light of the meager evidence for French panel painting in the first half of the 15th century, scholars have long wondered about Fouquet's origins. The question of his early work has been discussed since Durrieu, and has been sought in the milieu of Angevin painters who worked at the court of Anjou in the mid-15th century.[21] Eberhard König's work on French manuscript illumination around 1450 established that not only the Jouvenel Master, but also various other artists in Angers worked alongside Fouquet until the late 1460s.[22] Fouquet may have been trained in this environment before his trip to Italy—except that no works exist to prove any "pre-Italian" activity at all. Recently the so-called *Hours of Jeanne de France* has emerged from a private collection (now Paris, BnF, ms. NAL 3244).[23] There we find two scenes from the Passion set before barren, hilly landscapes, with elongated figures in a color chord of red, blue, and gold camaïeu in a wide pictorial space otherwise unknown in France at this time (fig. 23). The manuscript must have been made before 1452, when the coat of arms of Jeanne de France was painted over that of another female owner. As Marie-Hélène Tesnière has recently shown, the latter may have been Madeleine de Bretagne, a daughter of Marguerite d'Orléans and Richard d'Étampes. Since 1448 the mother of the original owner—like the latter's brother, Charles d'Orléans, two years earlier—had worn the viper of the Visconti in her coat of arms, an allusion to the Milanese origin of her mother, Valentina Visconti.[24] The manuscript

was then painted over for the young Jeanne de France, who was espoused to the count of Clermont, Jean II of Bourbon, as early as 1447, but joined him in Moulins only in 1452.[25] Could these have been the first miniatures painted by Fouquet after his return from Italy, as König, and more recently Avril, have suggested?[26] The color scheme may seem anomalous, but in fact it accords well with the less developed areas in the *Hours of Étienne Chevalier*, particularly in the background design. A miniature cut out of the latter book, now in the Louvre, shows St. Margaret as a shepherdess (fig. 24); like the picture of St. Stephen, it numbers among the earliest images in the prayer book from the perspective of book design.[27] The procession of horsemen in the middle ground has been interpreted as a contemporary reference akin to the one in the Adoration of the Magi: it shows the seven-year-old Charles of France, the second son of the king, out on a ride.[28] The color harmony—bright, glowing blue on delicate green and yellow, with figures in warm red and brown tones heightened with gold—corresponds to the warm coloration of the miniatures in the *Hours of Jeanne de France*. In the image of St. Margaret, the use of washes and glazes to model the forms is confined to the background, while in the Crucifixion it characterizes the entire illumination. On the basis of this comparison, might we be justified in permitting the artist a certain latitude in the development and execution of his images?[29]

Another manuscript, the so-called *Hours of the Cardinal of Bourbon* (Copenhagen, Gl. Kgl. Saml. 1610, 4°), shows features completely unusual in France: large historiated initials as well as majuscules for emphasis at the beginning of the Little Office of the Blessed Virgin Mary, of a kind that we otherwise find only in Italy in the late Middle Ages.[30] This format, which was prepared on individual folios without text, bears witness to the Italian experience of its painter. The first border decoration is typical of western France in the mid-15th century, and was added after the initials and the decorative script.[31] Might this indicate that Fouquet introduced himself to the workshop of the Jouvenel Master with folios of this kind? The masterpieces both small and large that he created for Étienne Chevalier, which do not bear authentic dates, suggest to us today that such an extraordinary artist would surely have altered his contemporaries' visual sensibilities at a single stroke. It is not until 1461 that Fouquet is men-

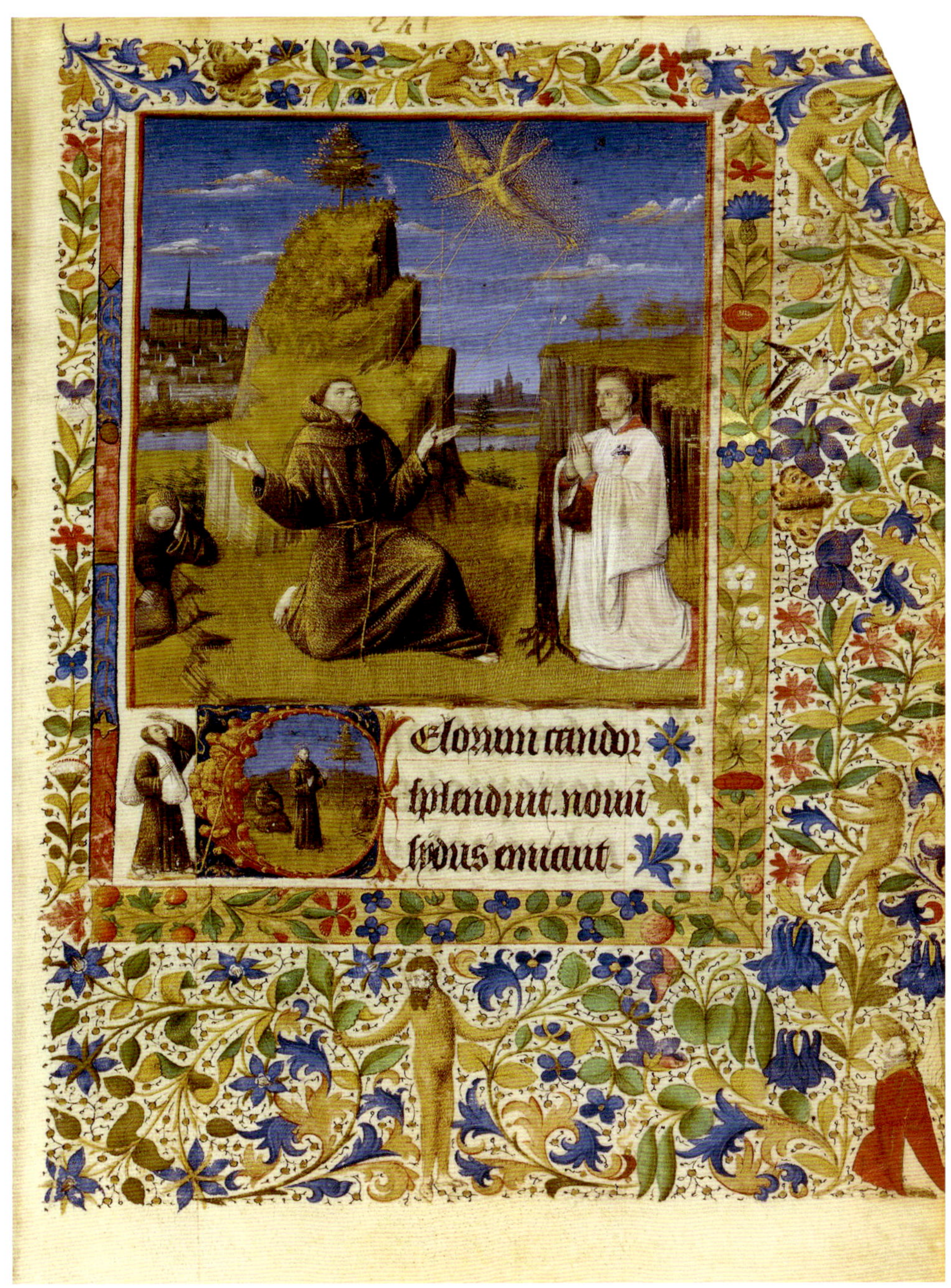

Fig. 22. Jean Fouquet, The Stigmatization of Saint Francis, c. 1455?, Paris, Bibliothèque nationale de France, ms. NAL 3211, fol. 241

tioned in connection with Charles VII: Pierre Hennes, who brings the king's death mask to Paris, is also supposed to meet Fouquet there; why, we do not know. The death mask was prepared by Jacob de Littemont and Colin d'Amiens as well as Pierre Hennes, who is mentioned multiple times together with Fouquet and, as Schaefer suspected, worked with the latter in Tours.[32]

It is entirely conceivable that Fouquet, having just returned from Italy, did not immediately find a position at court and perhaps did not establish his position as royal painter until the reign of Louis XI. The earliest manuscripts from Angers and Tours show that he did not work independently of regional workshops, but rather participated in larger decoration projects, and—if indeed the miniatures in the *Hours of Jeanne de France*, lat. 1417, and the so-called *Hours of the Cardinal of Bourbon* in Copenhagen are by his hand—that he submitted to convention as circumstances required. Even the *Hours of Étienne Chevalier*,

41

which may be considered a genuine picture book with its surviving full-page miniatures, showed Angevin acanthus decoration on its text pages.[33]

While it is fair to say that with regard to manuscript illumination, no painter left as lasting an impression on the art of the second half of the 15th century as Fouquet, when it comes to panel painting he has virtually no immediate followers. This state of affairs certainly also arises from the fact that very little French panel painting survives from before the 17th century, though there is more from the 16th century. Jean Bourdichon and Jean Poyer, both

members of Fouquet's workshop, were also active as panel painters toward the end of the 15th century.[34] A few notable panel paintings from Paris and the north are known from the mid-15th century, and in the south of France large-scale artistic projects had been produced almost continuously since the time of the popes. Manuscript illuminations are almost always attributed to these painters as well.[35] Moreover, significant stained glass commissions since the late 14th century have been convincingly associated with manuscript illuminators; the most famous may have been created in the workshop of André Beauneveu

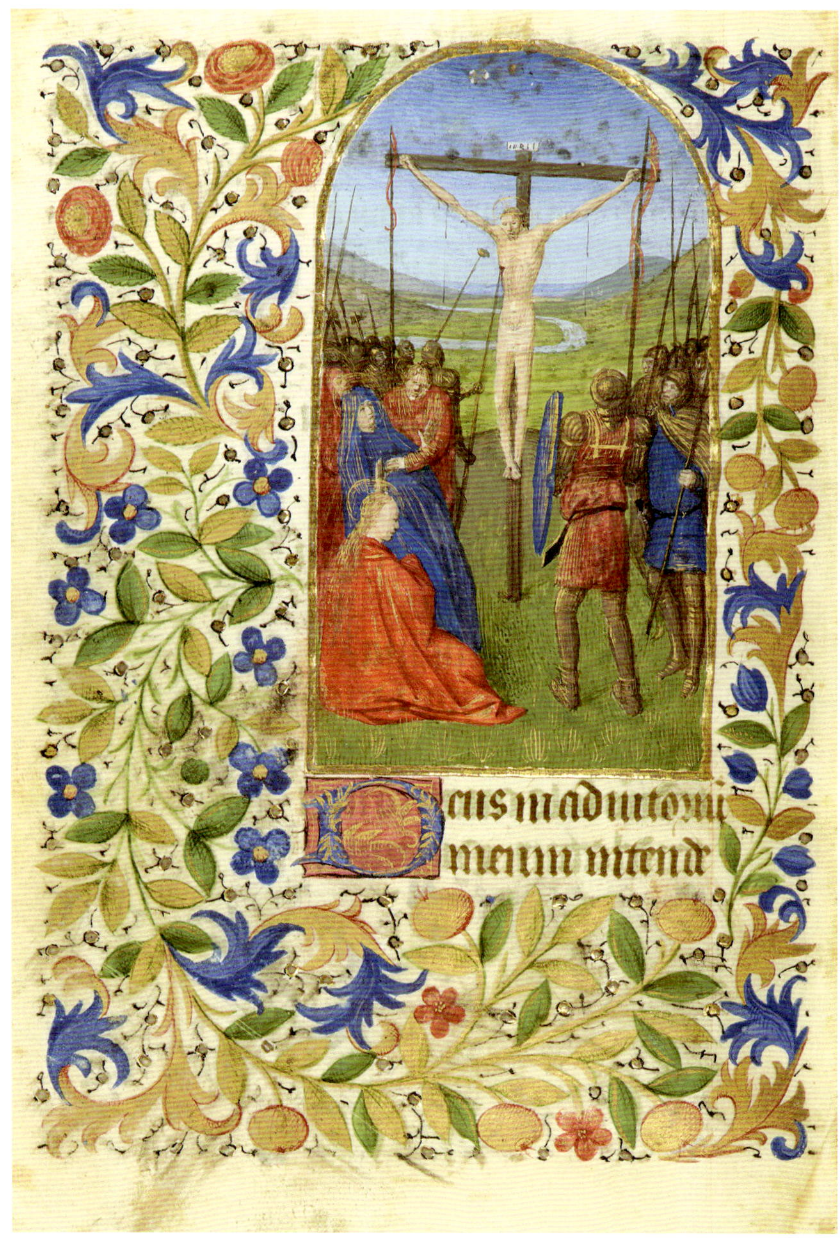

Fig. 23. Jean Fouquet (?), Crucifixion, before 1452, Paris, Bibliothèque nationale de France, ms. NAL 3244, fol. 270v

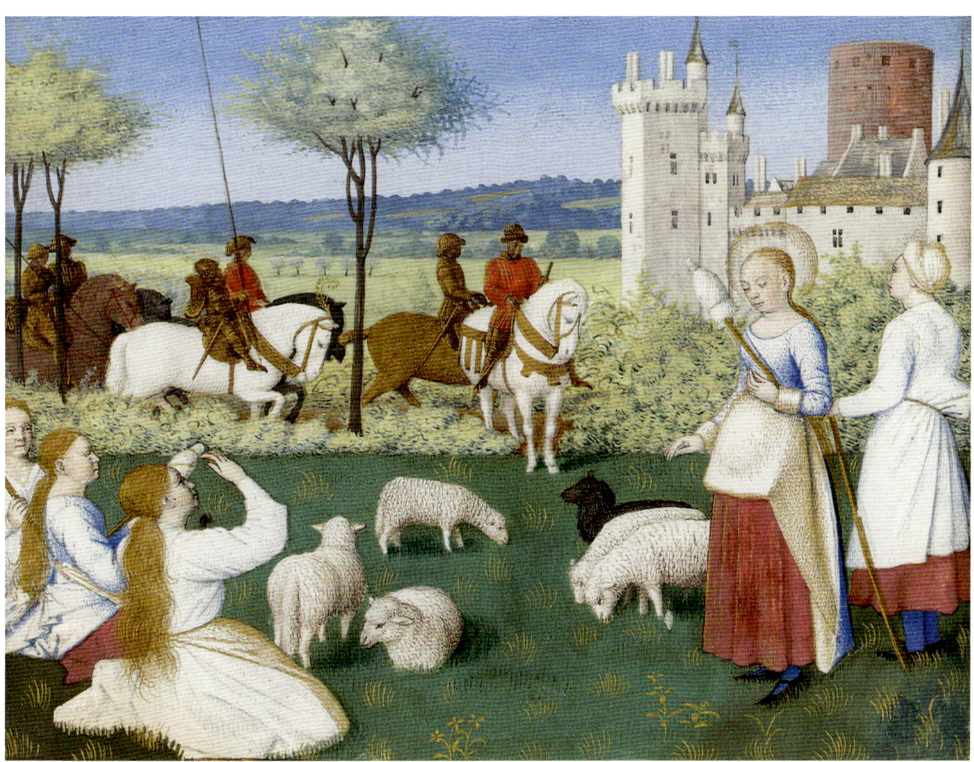

Fig. 24. Jean Fouquet, Saint Margaret as Shepherdess, Paris, Musée du Louvre, dép. des Arts graphiques, M.I. 1093

and are now located in the crypt of the cathedral of Bourges. Our information on artistic production in 15th-century France, however, is nowhere as extensive as our knowledge of the Netherlands, German-speaking Europe, and of course Italy.

Thus as far as works on a larger scale are concerned, there are no noteworthy successors to the known paintings of Fouquet. His masterful portraiture leaves virtually no traces; a *Romuléon* for Charles de France, the king's younger son and until 1465 the Duke of Berry, includes an imitation of the famous *Portrait of Charles VII* in the Louvre (fig. 11),[36] on which there was debate as to whether the surviving version dates to around 1450 or was painted only after the king's death in 1461.[37] The same image appears as a thoroughly symbolic allusion in a manuscript of Virgil probably made for Jacques Coeur, the financier of Charles VII and until 1451 one of the most influential men in the French kingdom (fig. 25).[38] In both examples, the king is clothed in a red doublet with a blue beaver hat, clearly echoing the prototype of Fouquet's portrait; in the Virgil, he even appears in the heavens leading a host of riders that will lend divine aid to Aeneas and give him victory over the Latins.[39]

The question also arises as to whether the extraordinary *Virgin and Child* in Antwerp had an effect on manuscript illumination. Although after the painting was made it was installed in the collegiate church at Melun, far from Tours, it seems to have been known among the Touronese illuminators of Fouquet's milieu. The composition for the Antwerp painting was not developed on the panel itself, but was based on a finished cartoon which likewise served as the point of departure for an image found beneath the portrait of Charles VII in the Louvre before the latter panel was used for the royal portrait. A prototype must have been known to contemporaries, therefore, indicating that the *Melun Diptych* was not necessarily the only source for this particular image.

Perhaps the most remarkable echo of the Antwerp Madonna is found in the *Belleville Hours* (Austin, University of Texas, HRC, ms. 8). Marie de Belleville was a lady-in-waiting to Queen Marie d'Anjou from 1452 to 1462, and a member of the queen's household by 1447.[40] In 1453, she married Bertrand Larchevêque, Seigneur de Soubise, and since books of hours for noble ladies were frequently commissioned for such occasions, we may assume that the manuscript was made at this time, perhaps even before the wedding, and probably in Angers rather than Tours.

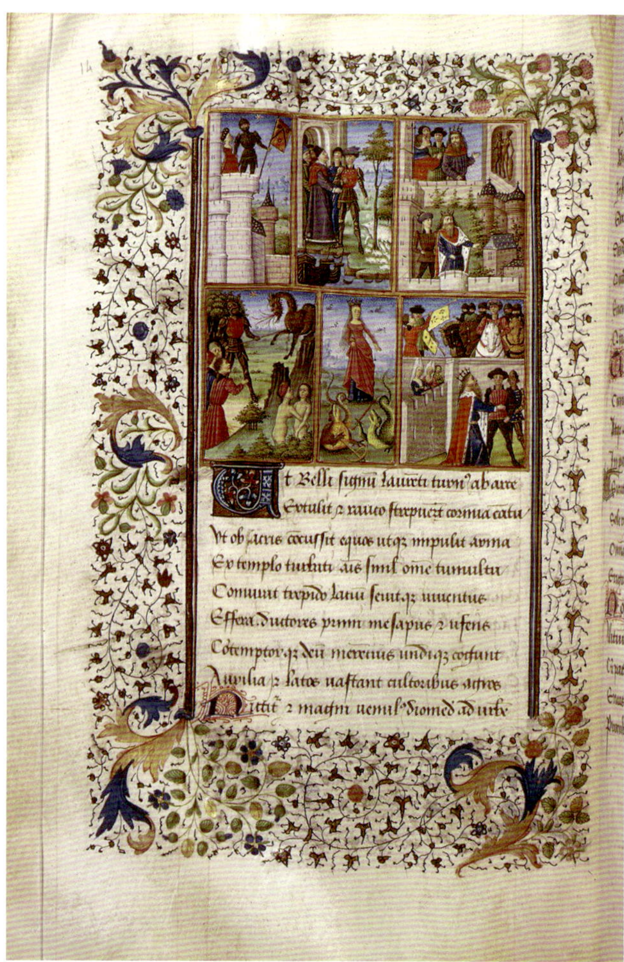

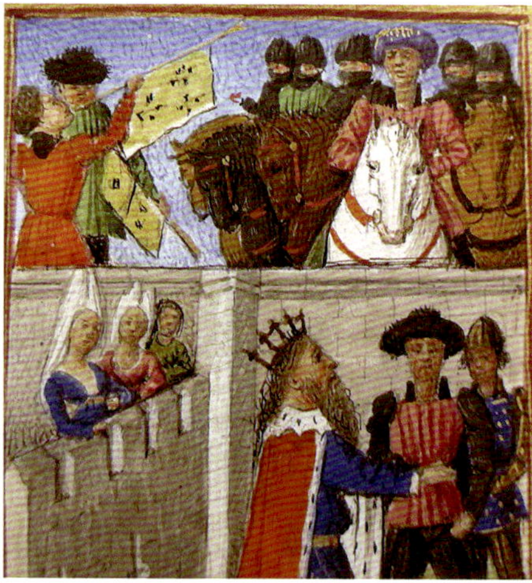

Fig. 25. Painter of Bourges 594 (?), Virgil, Opening of the 8th book of the Aeneid, Cambridge (Mass.), Harvard University, Houghton Library, ms. Richardson 38, fol. 216v

The French Marian prayer *A toy royne de hault parage dame du ciel et de la terre* ("To you, Queen of noble blood, Lady of heaven and earth"), likely composed by the Norman Benedictine monk Guillaume Alexis,[41] is introduced by a large miniature showing the Madonna as a half figure on a crescent moon borne aloft by red seraphim (fig. 26). She holds the naked Christ Child in her arm and nurses him: here, at the moment of her coronation, Mary is shown not only as the Queen of Heaven, but also as *Maria lactans*, a mother. Her head is covered with a fine veil which falls over her left shoulder and enshrouds the Christ Child, while her wide blue mantle generously encompasses the contours of her figure and falls over the crescent moon. Her outspread arms reveal a view of her small, high-bound waist. While the image is not an exact replica of the Antwerp composition, a number of elements connect the basic concept of the miniature with the painting, beyond mere formal similarity. First of all, the classic image of the Virgin and Child, expanded to include the motif of the nursing mother, is here combined with the very familiar representation of the Madonna on the crescent moon, this time in accord with the iconographically older, half-figure type that appears in France shortly after 1400. The seraphim, who bear her aloft and place the heavenly crown on her head, are an element that was likewise widespread in France a generation before. In Fouquet's Antwerp painting, Mary is already crowned and the angels carry her throne—which, echoing the form of the *faldistorium*, a symbol of spiritual (and, in 15th-century France, secular) power, calls to mind her heavenly throne. The *Belleville Hours* also contains another allusion to the association of heavenly power and secular rule inherent in the Antwerp image of the Virgin: in the border of the page, a fashionably dressed nobleman in a short red doublet and black hose leads a lady by the hand, while her train is carried by a lady-in-waiting. This "lady of the world" can be read as a visual allusion to the text of the prayer, which is almost never illustrated.[42] These manuscript illuminations, probably painted in Angers, thus not only reflect the life of the queen's lady-in-waiting, but also show how strongly Fouquet's pictorial inventions were anchored in local tradition.[43]

A strange peculiarity of the Antwerp *Virgin and Child* is the ambiguity of Mary's pose: as has long been noted, it is unclear whether she is standing or sitting. The highly

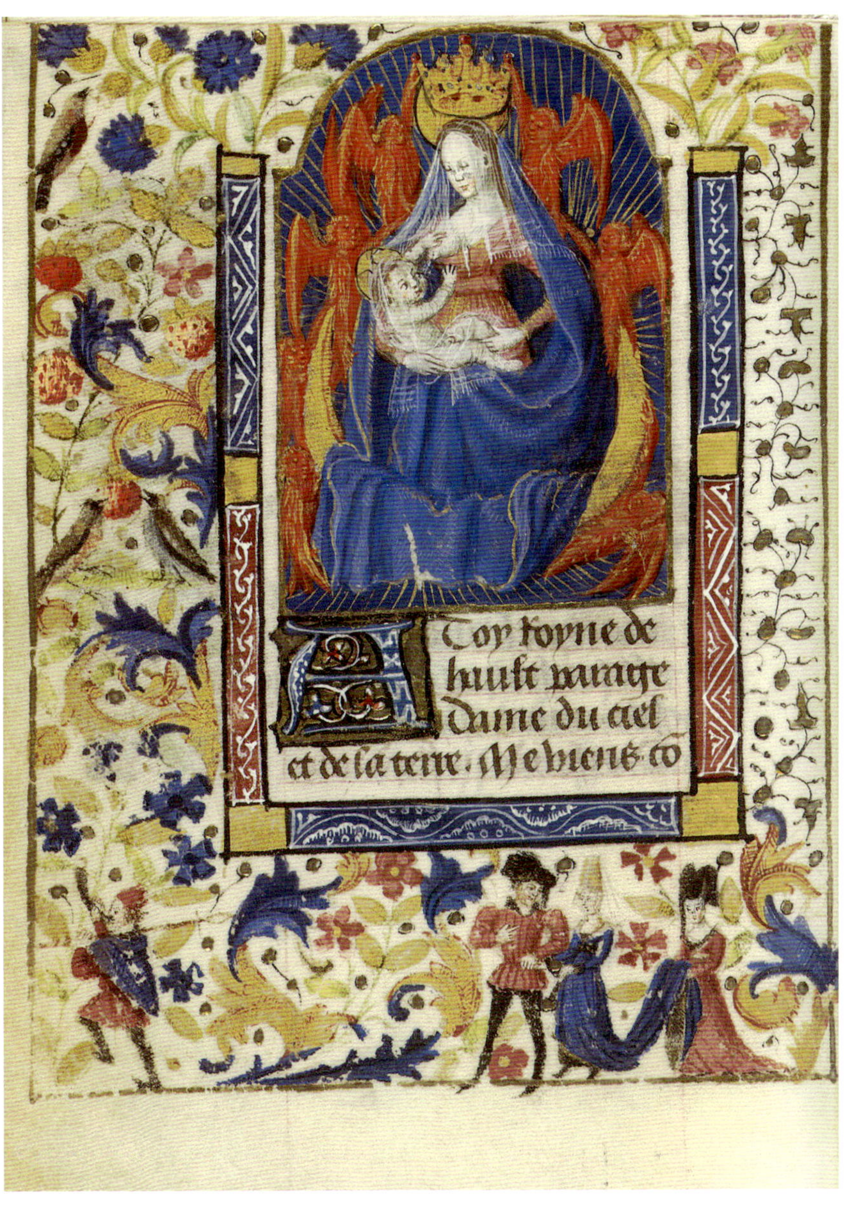

Fig. 26. Painter of the arbre des batailles (Arsenal 2695), Virgin and Child, Austin, University Library, Harry Ransom Center, ms. 8, fol. 186v

unusual arrangement of the Virgin's mantle—stretched tautly in front of her abdomen with its compressed folds forming a seat for her Son, who actually sits to her left— does not appear in any other work. Rather, the position of the Child, who points to the viewer's left and therewith directly toward the donor on the left wing, seems to have been a unique solution devised for the special demands of this diptych.

Another variant based on a more traditional type of standing Madonna and Child was common among Fouquet's contemporaries in Angers and Tours between 1460 and 1480: the standing Virgin in half figure, holding the naked Child in her arms and gathering her mantle in gen-

erous folds in front of her abdomen. This image of the crowned Queen of Heaven is found in the *Hours of Louis de Laval* (Paris, BnF, ms. lat. 920), which was begun before 1469[44] and which shows the same version of the Madonna on the crescent moon as a book of hours made in Tours around the same time, in the milieu of Jean Fouquet (Paris, BnF, ms. lat. 13305). This composition was still being used around 1480 by a manuscript illuminator known to have had direct contact with Jean Fouquet: the Master of Christophe de Champagne, alias Guillaume Piqueau, who was probably assigned to the same patrol as Fouquet in the town watch of Tours in 1464.[45] In his rendering of the subject, found in a book of hours in Epinal (ms. 100, fol. 98v, fig. 27), the Virgin's crown is pushed far back on her head in a manner even more obviously reminiscent of the actual prototype: the Madonna on the Antwerp wing.

This same painter, however, also created a second version of the Madonna influenced by Fouquet, this time a seated one. In a book of hours in Bloomington (Indiana University, Lilly Library, Medieval and Renaissance 29), the *Obsecro te* ("I beseech thee"), one of the most important Marian prayers in a book of hours, is introduced by an enthroned Virgin and Child. The abraded miniature shows a peculiar stone throne with a wooden baldachin standing in front of a cloth of honor from behind which red seraphim, discernable only in outline, look out (fig. 28). Although the posture and iconography of the Virgin and therewith the content of the figure are quite different from the Antwerp picture, the enthroned Mother of God in the Lilly Library still shows compositional peculiarities

that can likely be traced back to Fouquet's Virgin. First of all, the Christ Child, clad only in a white loincloth, sits on Mary's hand nearly at a right angle and turns to the left, pointing with both hands—even though the page across from him is a verso with no text, providing no point of reference for the gesture. The blue mantle of the Virgin, draped over her lap around the crossed legs of the Christ Child, reveals a view of her high waist. The figure could also be interpreted as standing, for the mantle falls over a low-placed knee, suggested in gold.[46]

The examples cited above, however, seem to react not to this version, but to the compositional peculiarities found in the Antwerp *Virgin and Child*. If we once again consider the *Hours of Jeanne de France*, created in Angers during the years after Fouquet had returned from Italy, we find a standing *Maria lactans* on fol. 27 for the Marian prayer *O intemerata* ("O undefiled one"), painted by the Jouvenel Master (fig. 29). The Virgin, standing in front of a cloth

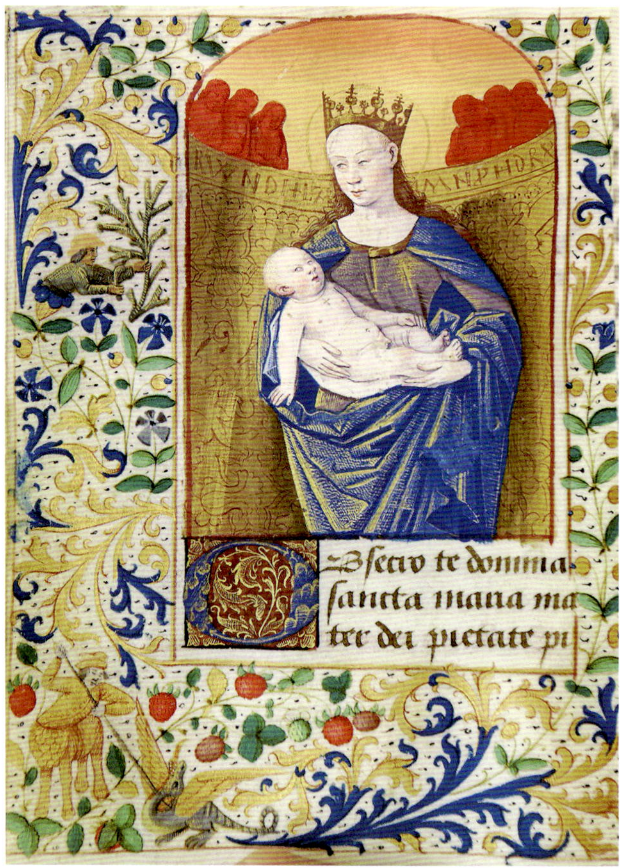

Fig. 27. Master of Christophe de Champagne, Virgin and Child, Épinal, Bibliothèque municipale, ms. 100, fol. 98v

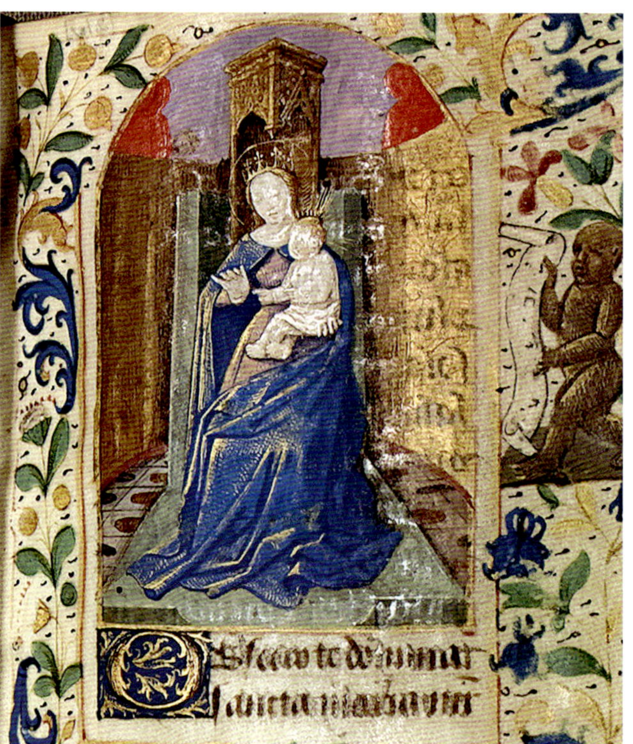

Fig. 28. Master of Christophe de Champagne (?), Virgin and Child, Bloomington, Indiana University, Lilly Library, Medieval and Renaissance 29

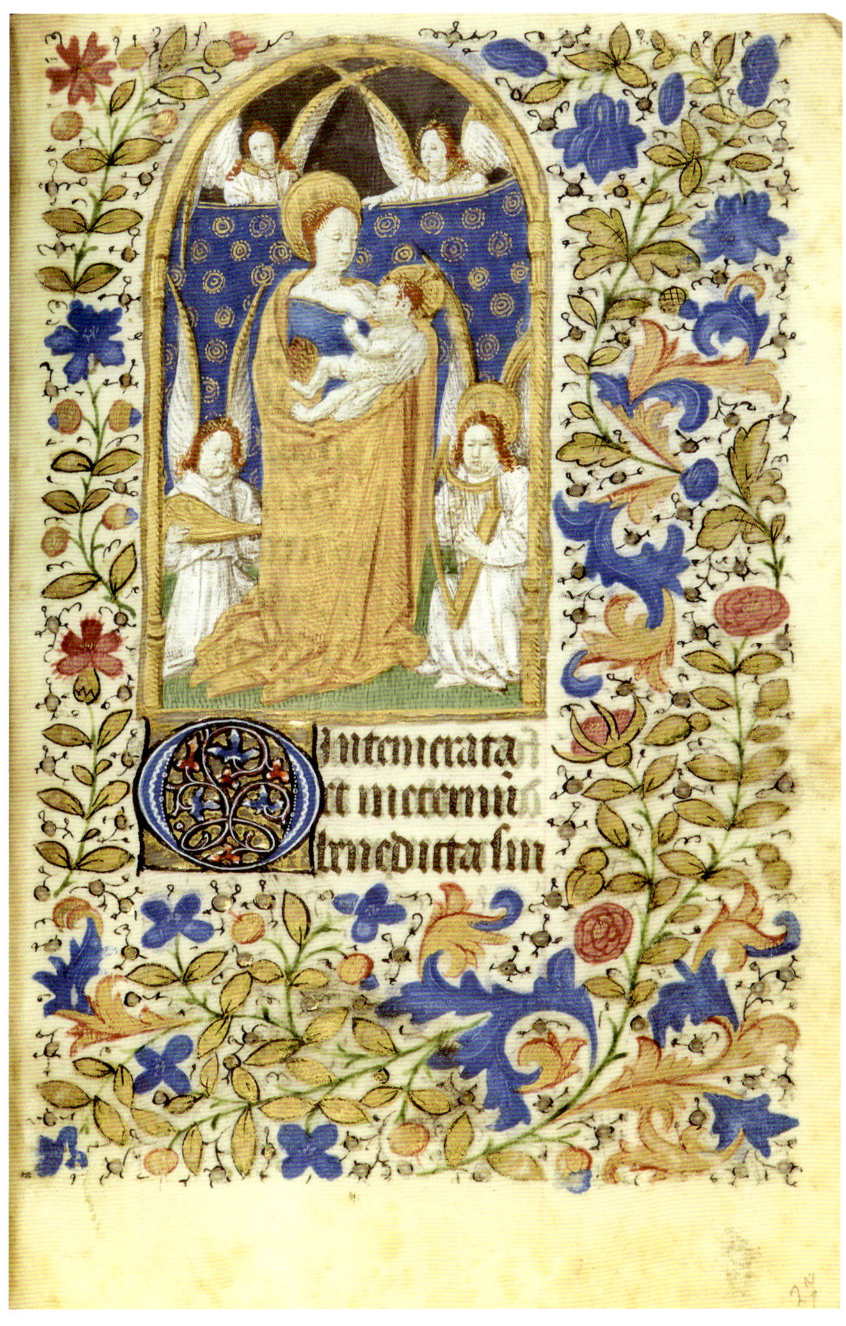

Fig. 29. Jouvenel Master, Virgin and Child, before 1452, Paris, Bibliothèque nationale de France, ms. NAL 3244, fol. 27

of honor, is surrounded by music-making angels in albs, echoing a type of Madonna image widespread in France. Her dress opens just above her high, narrow waist to expose the breast on which the naked Christ Child sucks. Her left arm supports the reclining Child in front of her abdomen, while her golden mantle falls in a wide curve, revealing her arched back and protruding belly. This elegant Gothic S-curve is unusual for the Jouvenel Master, who is otherwise known for his block-like and somewhat stiff figures, and Tesnière has compared this curving form with that of the Antwerp Madonna.[47] Might this Virgin and Child by the Jouvenel Master constitute the earliest known reflection of Fouquet's extraordinary composition? Or rather, if in fact this manuscript was already begun in 1447, did the work of an older painter, inspired by new impressions, serve as the model for his younger counterpart? The *Hours of Jeanne de France* not only show refinement in the Jouvenel Master's brushwork, but also bear witness to the influence of Parisian pictorial models from the workshop of the Dunois Master. This influence is apparent both in the borders of the images and in iconographic innovations such as the *Seven Deadly Sins* riding on animals in the company of the penitent David (NAL 3244, fol. 127). In the *Dunois Hours* (London, BL, Yates Thompson MS 3), a book made for Jean Dunois, Bastard of Orléans and comrade of Joan of Arc in the defense of Orléans, these figures occupy entire miniatures.[48] The Jouvenel Master's contact with manuscripts from Paris was not only implicit, but quite direct: in the recently discovered *Hachette Hours*, he painted the heads of Mary and other main figures into miniatures by the Master of the Munich Golden Legend, much like Fouquet in the *Hours of Simon de Varie*.[49]

If in fact the two Passion images in the *Hours of Jeanne de France* are the earliest known works by Fouquet after his return from Italy, the possibility of an intermediary relationship becomes likely; continued investigation will show whether the concept of a (manuscript-)painter who worked quickly and employed Italian motifs for the first time in one of his most important commissions, the *Hours of Étienne Chevalier*, is tenable. Certainly this understanding would not only connect Fouquet to the local milieu of Angevin painters who worked for the royal and ducal courts and were also influenced by experiences in Paris; it would also demonstrate that for all their technical differences, the integral relationship between manuscript illumination and panel painting—particularly in French art of the 15th century ("when painting was in books"[50])—extended even to the use of the same pictorial models.

1 Paris, BnF, ms. fr. 247, fol. 311v: "En ce livre a douze ystoires les troys premières de l'enlumineur du duc Jehan de Berry et les neuf de la main du bon peintre et enlumineur du Roy Loys XI, Jehan Foucquet natif de tours."

2 The second volume (Paris, BnF, ms. NAF 21013) contains the *Guerres des juifs* of Flavius Josephus; the young Jean Bourdichon also worked on the illuminations: Cat. Paris 2003, no. 34.

3 In general, cf. Pélicier 1882; Pradel 1986; see also Adams 2013, pp. 138-146.

4 Waagen 1839, pp. 371f.

5 Waagen 1851, p. 92.

6 Durrieu 1907, pp. 123f.; most recently, Cat. Paris 2003, no. 32.

7 Cat. Paris 2003. Widowed and without any heirs, the duc d'Aumale left his estate to the Institut de France and decreed in his testament in 1884 that the Castle of Chantilly should be preserved in its entirety.

8 Cat. Paris 2003, pp. 18-28.

9 Friedländer 1896, pp. 208f.

10 Avril in Cat. Paris 2003, pp. 18f.

11 Through codicological analysis, Clancy has attempted to show that Fouquet's activity as an illuminator occurred outside the context of a major workshop; see Clancy 1993a, pp. 208f.

12 Most recently, Cat. Paris 2003, no. 34.

13 Friedländer 1896, pp. 212f., surmised that the medallions must have measured about 15 cm in diameter and was not necessarily convinced that they had belonged to the frame of the *Melun Diptych*. Furthermore, despite occasional references to the contrary in more recent literature, he did not discuss the Berlin medallion (acquired in 1891). Since it is reported that the medallions on the frame showed scenes from the life of St. Stephen, and the lost Berlin medallion (formerly in the Kunstgewerbemuseum) was the same size as the one in the Louvre, it was assumed that the probable origin of both works was the *Melun Diptych*, initially by Marquet de Vasselot 1904, p. 145; cf. also Schaefer 1975, pp. 55-57; most recently, Cat. Paris 2003, no. 9.

14 Avril, for example, dates the illuminations of the *Histoire ancienne jusqu'à César* and the *Faits des Romains* Paris, Musée du Louvre, dép. des Arts graphiques, R.F. 4143, R.F. 5271, R.F. 29493, R.F. 29494 and Amsterdam, Rijksmuseum, Prentenkabinet, RP-T-1889-A-1943, to the same time as the *Antiquités judaïques*, and in Cat. Paris 2003, no. 30, attributes them to "Fouquet or an affiliated coworker," where they seem to stand on the same stylistic level as the miniatures of the *Antiquités judaïques*.

15 See Clancy's thesis of a "selective model book." Although he assumed that this book would have been located with Jean Colombe in Bourges, in fact it would have to have been in the Touronese milieu of the Master of the Vienna Mamerot; see Clancy 1988, pp. 158-163.

16 Paris, Musée du Louvre, dép. des Arts graphiques, R.F. 1679; for various repetitions in the milieu of the Master of the Vienna Mamerot, see Cat. Paris 1993, pp. 152-155, Reynaud 2006, pp. 182-187; Gras 2015; Seidel 2017, pp. 70-75. In 2016, Samuel Gras completed an as yet unpublished dissertation on the painter. On the *Hours of Mary Stuart* (Paris, BnF, ms. lat. 1405 and private collection), see also Cat. Paris 2003, no. 56 and König 2013, vol. 2, no. 24; on the *Hours of Jean Robertet* (New York, PML, M. 834), see Cat. Paris 2003, no. 28, with comprehensive bibliography.

17 The Hague, Koninklijke Bibliotheek, Ms. 74 G 37 and 74 G 37a, Los Angeles, J. Paul Getty Museum, Ms. 7; see Marrow 1985, especially for the identification of the patron; Marrow/Avril 1994 and most recently also Cat. Paris 2003, no. 23.

18 The original coats of arms, which the collector and later owner Philippe de Béthune had overpainted (in his time the manuscript was also bound in three parts), are identified in Avril 1985, who also gathered the scant information on the owner.

19 On the painting technique in the *Hours of Simon de Varie* cf. Turner 2005, p. 68. I would like to thank Nancy Turner and Elizabeth Morrison for the opportunity to study the part in the J. Paul Getty Museum with regard to this aspect.

20 Most recently, Cat. Paris 2003, no. 20.

21 Durrieu 1904; Pächt 1941 identifies the Jouvenel Master's most important work, the London book of hours for the use of Nantes (BL, Add MS 28785), as an early work by Fouquet.

22 König 1982; Cat. Paris 1993, pp. 105-127.

23 Acquired in 2013 for the Bibliothèque nationale; cf. Avril 2013. König 1982, pp. 80-82, who knew the manuscript only from a description in an auction catalogue and from illustrations, had already tentatively dated the book to 1447 and suggested that these miniatures might be Fouquet's earliest work after his return from Italy.

24 Tesnière 2015, p. 13.

25 Contamine/Tesnière 2013, pp. 10, 13.

26 König 1982, pp. 81f.; Avril 2013, pp. 18f.

27 Paris, Musée du Louvre, dép. des Arts graphiques, M.I. 1093; cf. Reynaud 2006, pp. 208-211. For the dating of the miniature format within the manuscript, see König 1974.

28 Cat. Paris 2003, p. 198; Reynaud 2006, p. 210.

29 A book of hours for the use of Paris (Paris, BnF, ms. lat. 1417) already shows all the characteristic features of Fouquet's style, although no Italian motifs appear: Durrieu 1906, p. 257, who dated it rather late. König 1982, pp. 109f., assumed that this work could have been one of the earliest works by Fouquet; most recently Cat. Paris 2003, no. 21.

30 Cat. Paris 2003, no. 22, with illustrations.

31 Angevin acanthus borders are painted on fol. 1, fol. 4, and fol. 20; the decorations on fol. 3 and fol. 10 belong to the additions of the period around 1500; for the codicology, see Clancy 1993 and most recently also Cat. Paris, no. 22.

32 Schaefer 1994, Doc. 4, pp. 346f.

33 Now in the De Kesel collection; see Schaefer/de Hamel 1981 and most recently Reynaud 2006, pp. 230f., with illustration.

34 Hofmann 2004; Hofmann 2007 and Herman 2014, who has also written a dissertation on Jean Bourdichon.

35 Avril 1977; Reynaud 1982; Laclotte/Thiebaut 1983.

36 As already pointed out in Reynaud 1981, pp. 17f. The manuscript is now in the Bodmer collection in Geneva, Ms. 143; for the most recent discussion, see Schindler 2016, pp. 93-95, who has published a monograph on the Piccolomini Master and the library of Charles de France.

37 This thesis is advanced by Vale 1968. In response to the historian's argument that the designation *très victorieux* is documented only after the king's death (in the epitaph of Charles VII), it should be noted that the inscription on the contemporaneous frame could have been added later; there is no further evidence to help answer this question (Cat. Paris 2003, pp. 106f.). Vale's case is disproven by Schaefer 1994, p. 293, on the basis of the inscription on the marble panel of the tomb monument of Jean de Berry, where the words "Charles VII roi de France, son nepveu et héritier, prince très xrian et très victorieux fist faire ceste sepulture" ("Charles VII king of France, nephew and heir [of Jean de Berry], most Christian and most victorious prince, had this sepulcher made") appear as an addition to the actual tomb inscription, which is already documented in 1757; cf. Champeaux/Gauchery 1894, pp. 42-44; Béatrice Chancel-Bardelot in Cat. Bourges 2004, p. 137.

38 Cambridge (Mass.), Houghton Library, MS Richardson 38: most recently, Cat. Boston 2016, no. 190.

39 Aeneid, Book 8, 518-529; the arrival of the 200 Arcadian riders is followed by the heavenly sign of Cytherea (Venus, the mother of Aeneas), accompanied by the Tyrrhenian trumpets. Both moments seem to be depicted in the miniature.

40 *Nouvelle biographie* 1866, p. 256; Beaucourt 1891, p. 426; Hirschbiegel 2003, p. 91.

41 Cf. Sonet 1956, pp. 4f., no. 24; Piaget/Picot 1908, p. 195.

42 Sonet 1956, p. 4, lists 14 manuscripts from the 15th and early 16th century, not including the *Belleville Hours* and the Provençal book of hours with miniatures by Enguerrand Quarton in the Huntington Library, HM 1129. In the Touronese portion of the *Hours of Marie de Rieux* (ms. 217, fol. 1), the prayer is preceded by an image of the crowned, nursing Madonna enthroned in the *hortus conclusus*.

43 For a more detailed description of the manuscript, which was probably made by a painter from the milieu of the Master of Marguerite d'Orléans in Angers, see Seidel 2017, pp. 182-185.

44 For the possible relevance of sculptural precedents, since Colombe was the son and brother of two important sculptors, see Seidel 2014, pp. 156-161.

45 Schaefer 1994, p. 348 (Doc. 7) and p. 359 n. 16. Also see above all Gras 2015.

46 This proportional peculiarity also occurs in the three-quarter-view Madonna of the *Hours of Simon de Varie* and the additional folio in the *Hours of Adelaïde de Savoie* (Chantilly, Musée Condé, ms. 76, fol. 21), attributed to a "Fouquetesque painter" in Cat. Paris 2003, no. 54.

47 Tesnière 2015, pp. 8f.

48 The decorative border of the Annunciation (fol. 35) and the drinking shepherds in the border for Prime (fol. 83) also come from the Bedford milieu in Paris; cf. Avril 2013, pp. 15-18. In the so-called *Hours of Louis d'Anjou*, created in the 1440s (Cambridge, Fitzwilliam Museum, Ms. 39-1950), the landscape in the miniature of the Virgin and Child for the Marian prayer *Doulce dame* (fol. 263) is a variation of the landscape from Jan van Eyck's *Madonna of Chancellor Rolin*; motifs from this work also recur in works by the Dunois Master. Cf. König in Cat. Angers 2009, no. 51. For the *Dunois Hours*, see Châtelet 2008.

49 Offered for sale by Millon in the Hôtel Drouot, April 27, 2012, lot 147. The borders of all the text pages, as well, were extended into four-sided borders, possibly by the Master of the Bartholomaeus Anglicus, who repeated the miniature for the Office of the Dead in a book of hours executed entirely by his own hand, now in the Rosenberg Collection (ms. 4): Cat. New York 1982, no. 35.

50 From the title of the exhibition by François Avril and Nicole Reynaud in Paris in 1993, *Quand la peinture était dans les livres*: Cat. Paris 1993.

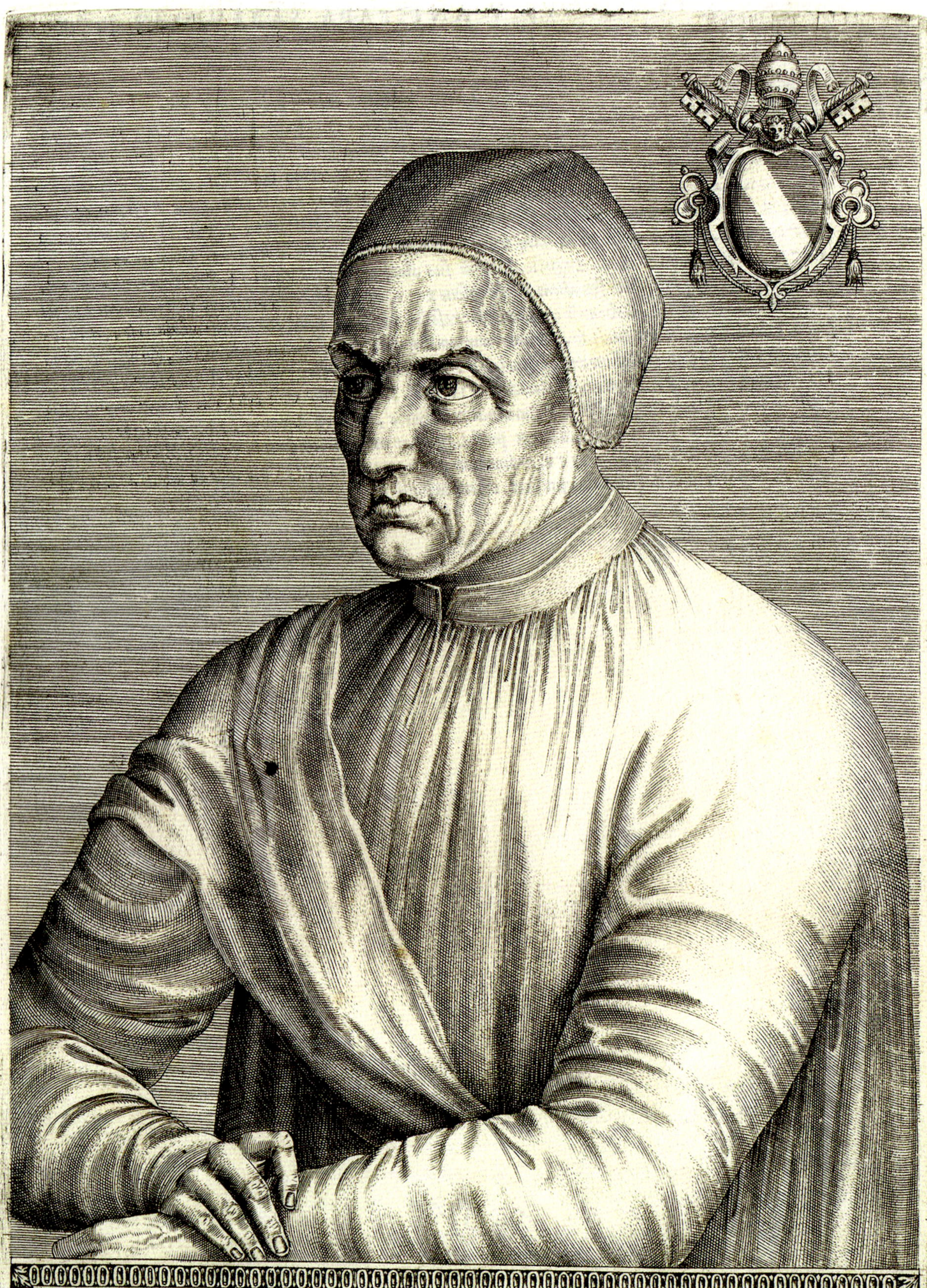

EVGENIVS . IIII . PAPA . VENETVS

Neville Rowley

SEARCHING FOR FOUQUET IN ITALY

"In the Berlin Museum, *Étienne Chevalier and St Stephen* hangs among the Flemish Primitives but it looks like a Tuscan work; in the Uffizi [in Florence], the painting would seem Flemish": in 1967, the French art historian Michel Laclotte encapsulated in an expressive dichotomy the stylistic features of the famous portrait by Jean Fouquet, then preserved in the Gemäldegalerie of West Berlin, in Dahlem (cat. 1).[1] Such a paired characterization was not new in the historiography of Fouquet; in the Berlin portrait, the minute realism had long been seen as inherited from Jan van Eyck or Rogier van der Weyden, while the use of mathematical perspective, classical pilasters, and colored-marble decoration are clear signs of Italian influence. Since his rediscovery in the 19th century, Jean Fouquet has been interpreted as one of the rare painters capable of a personal alchemy between the more advanced artistic tendencies of European art in the mid-15th century, those North and South of the Alps, in a manner that Michel Laclotte, then at the beginning of an extraordinary career at the service of the public museums of his country, was not unpleased to name "French".[2]

The Italian flavor in Fouquet's art is not only perceptible in the *Portrait of Étienne Chevalier*; its pendant from the ensemble known as the *Melun Diptych*, the *Virgin and Child with Cherubs* now in the Koninklijk Museum voor Schone Kunsten in Antwerp, exhibits a sense of geometry closely associated with Italian art, especially in the anatomy of the Virgin, while the cherubs around the mother and her child recall the *putti* or *spiritelli* of Roman inspi-

ration that haunted sculptures and paintings in Italy from the early 15th century. Many miniatures by Fouquet, especially those in the *Hours of Étienne Chevalier* (now in the Musée Condé, Chantilly), made for the same patron of the *Melun Diptych*, further testify to this affinity: the rendering of space makes occasional use of the one-point perspective invented in Florence around 1415 by Filippo Brunelleschi, while many architectural details are directly copied from Roman monuments such as the Arch of Septimius Severus, or at least contain numerous *spiritelli* (figs. 7, 43). That this deep knowledge of Italian art reflects a sojourn of Fouquet in Italy is beyond reasonable doubt; one cannot see how a sedentary French artist would have been so aware of a culture that had not yet been massively imported to France, as would be the case from the start of the Italian wars in 1494.

The presence of Fouquet in Italy is confirmed by two 15th-century sources stating that the painter completed in Rome a portrait of Pope Eugene IV together with "two of his relatives", a work on canvas once set in the sacristy of the Dominican convent of Santa Maria sopra Minerva. In the 16th or 17th century, the painting ended up in the collections of the Farnese family; it is now lost and known only through an engraving published in 1568, where the two "relatives" around the pope are missing (fig. 30).[3] What little information we have is still valuable: it can be deduced that Fouquet went to Rome sometime between September 1443, when Pope Eugene IV came back to the city after a decade in exile, and February 1447, when the pontiff died. Painting the pope's portrait was a great honor; Fouquet must have already achieved a certain reputation by this time. Beyond this, many questions remain, from how the French painter entered the papal court to why there is a mysterious absence of other works by him in Rome or else-

Fig. 30. Philippe Soye, Portrait of Eugene IV (probably after Fouquet), in Onofrio Panvinio, Onuphrii Panvinii Veronensis Fratis Eremitae Augustiniani XXVII Pontificum (…), Rome 1568

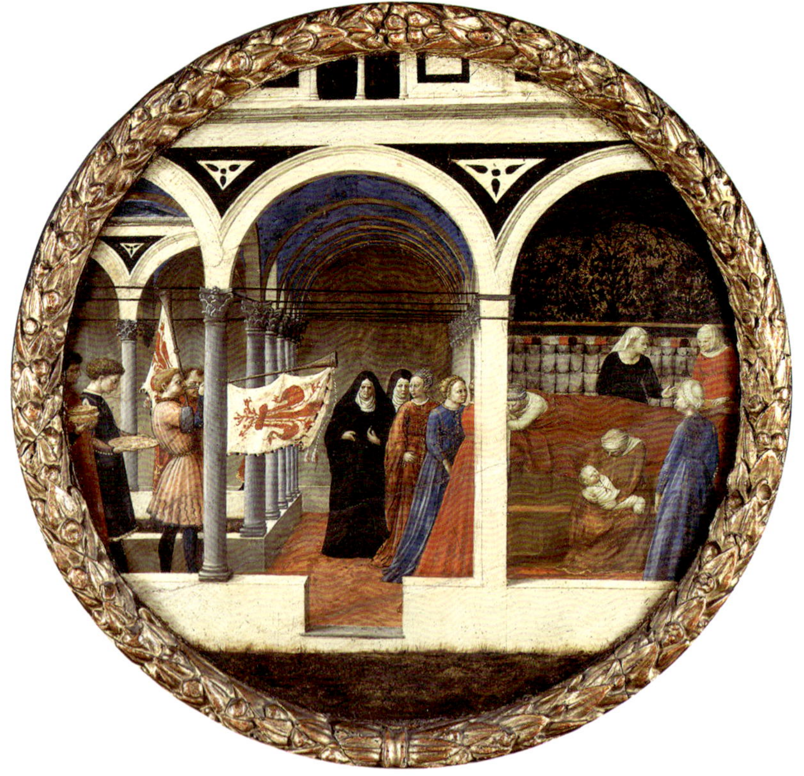

Fig. 31. Masaccio, A Scene of Birth, (desco da parto) c. 1423/25, Berlin, Gemäldegalerie

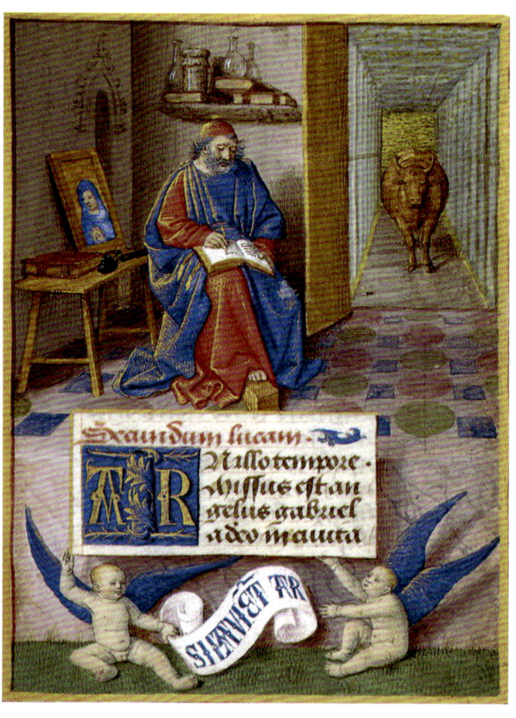

Fig. 32. Jean Fouquet, St Luke, c. 1460/65, Hours of Antoine Raguier (?) and Jean Robertet, New York, Pierpont Morgan Library, ms. M. 834, fol. 15

where in Italy. Even if documents are silent on that matter, art historians did not hesitate to propose narratives to account for how Fouquet could have assimilated so much of Italian art, while leaving such scant traces behind him.

Since the mid-20th century, several scholars have postulated the presence of Fouquet not only in Rome, but also in other Italian cities. The main reason for this supposition is the relative dearth of what Fouquet could have seen in the Eternal City: if the ruins of antique monuments were certainly more visible there than anywhere, Rome in the 1440s had not yet become the artistic center it would be from the last quarter of the 15th century onwards, the symbolic turning point being the first decoration campaign in the Sistine Chapel, completed in 1481/82 by a team of famous painters, from Perugino to Botticelli. Fouquet's knowledge of Renaissance art, the argument goes, could only be explained by an extended stay in the city that had been the cradle of the new discoveries: Florence. The article cited

at the beginning of this essay is a good example of this tendency: Michel Laclotte affirmed that Fouquet remained at least three or four years in Florence, long enough to shape his "Tuscan" style. Among other arguments, Laclotte drew a suggestive comparison between the earliest-preserved painting using the technique of linear perspective, a birth tray created by Masaccio in the early 1420s (fig. 31),[4] and a miniature by Fouquet from the manuscript known as the *Hours of Jean Robertet* (fig. 32).[5] In the birth tray, certainly made for a Florentine patron (as demonstrated by the red lily—the heraldic emblem of Florence—preeminently shown on a banner), the view into the cloister allowed the painter to show his skill in the new art, especially in the central colonnade, in the middle of which a nun dressed in black emerges towards the viewer; Fouquet would have reused the colonnade, just transforming the nun into the Christian symbol of St Luke: an ox. The conclusion was logical: Jean Fouquet must have come to Florence and carefully studied the work of Masaccio.[6]

In the same publication, Michel Laclotte also hypothesized the presence of Fouquet in another Italian city: Naples.[7] As with the sojourn of the French artist in Florence, this was not an isolated proposition: since the early 1950s, converging attempts had been made in that sense, following an attribution to Fouquet of two miniatures from the codex known as the *Manuscript of the Confraternity of St Martha* preserved in the National Archives in Naples (fig. 33), which would imply the painter's presence in the city around the middle of the century—a time when Naples was disputed between Kings René d'Anjou and Alfonso of Aragon.[8] A significant number of miniatures and paintings created in Naples were added to the corpus of Fouquet by various art historians; it was even suggested that the portrait of Alfonso of Aragon, carved on the triumphal arch of Castel Nuovo, was designed by Fouquet himself.[9] According to this theory, Fouquet had not only visited Naples, he also played an important role in the artistic life of the city.[10]

In 2003, another attribution to Fouquet was presented as an explanation for the artist's presence in Italy—this time in Florence. Fiorella Sricchia Santoro, who has discussed earlier the formal affinities between Fouquet and Fra Angelico, now argued for a direct participation of the French painter in the decoration of the Florentine convent of San Marco, which was painted under the direction of Fra Angelico from the late 1430s until the mid-1440s.[11] She extensively compared the portrait-like face of St Francis in the monumental *Crucifixion* of the chapter room (fig. 34), finished by August 1442, to the St Stephen of the Berlin panel of the *Melun Diptych*, in order to affirm that both had been painted by the same artist: Jean Fouquet.[12] After this collaboration, the French painter would have followed Fra Angelico to Rome, working with him again in the Vatican in two chapels that were destroyed during the 16th century. The numerous portraits Fouquet made then would have facilitated his access to Pope Eugene IV. After the latter's death, Fra Angelico and his workshop went to Orvieto to decorate the chapel of San Brice, whose vault bears faces seen in a subtle lateral light with such mastery that "they seem to tolerate only the name of Fouquet".[13] By the end of summer 1447, Fra Angelico returned to Rome to work for the new pope, Nicholas V, leaving the Orvieto chapel incomplete (the frescoes would be finished by Luca Sig-

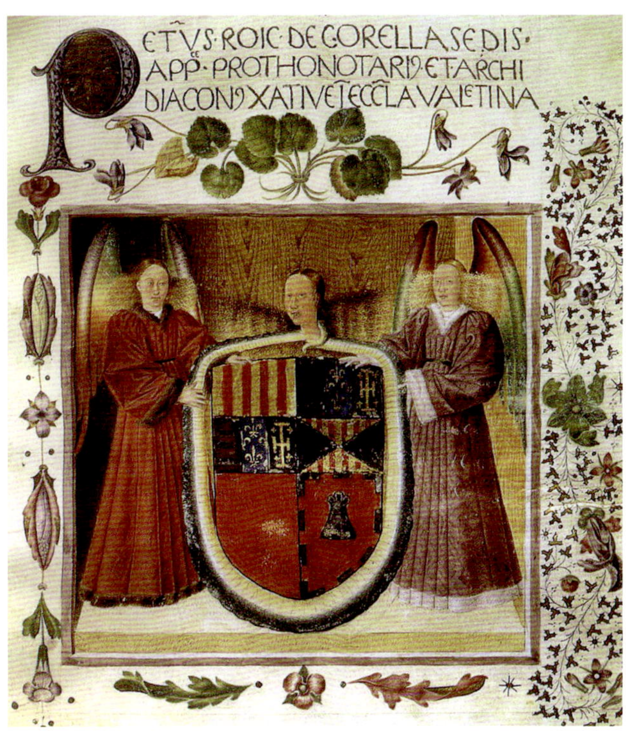

Fig. 33. Neapolitan or Valencian painter, Arms of Ximenez Perez Ruiz de Corella, Manuscript of the Confraternity of St Martha, Naples, Archivio di Stato, Museo Storico, ms. 99C 1, fol. 43

norelli half a century later); Fouquet returned to France and resumed his brilliant career.

The efforts of many specialists to find Fouquet's trace in cities where there is no record of his presence have to be seen in a historiographical context. From the 1950s, scholars were especially keen to demonstrate that many artistic phenomena could be explained by mechanisms other than seeing them through the traditional prism of the "schools", which isolated artistic developments from one another. Works, models, but also artists of the past had travelled more than one had thought; this was the case for Jan van Eyck, whose stay in Italy was debated at the same time, or for other French artists, besides Fouquet, whose hybrid style have captivated art historians, from Enguerrand Quarton to a long-time anonymous painter and miniaturist now identified as Barthélemy d'Eyck (cf. cat. 9).[14]

These interpretations of Fouquet's Italian journey cannot be dissociated from the magisterium of one of the most important art historians of the past century, Roberto Longhi (1889-1970). From early in his career, Longhi's ambition had been no less than to rewrite almost entirely the history of Italian painting. In this gigantic project, Longhi reserved a central place for two artists he conceived as unsurpassable, Piero della Francesca for the 15th century and Caravaggio for the 17th. In 1911, the young scholar completed his Ph.D. thesis on Caravaggio, giving to the Lombard painter an importance that has now become commonplace but that was extremely audacious at the time.[15] In 1914, Longhi assigned to Piero della Francesca a crucial role in the development of the art of Antonello da Messina, Giovanni Bellini and 16th-century Venetian painting, a judgment he would invariably repeat over the years and that has also become widely accepted, even if it lacks a firm basis.[16] In a celebrated monograph on Piero della Francesca published in 1927, Longhi enlarged the artist's influence to the most modern tendencies of European painting; the synthetic style of Jean Fouquet was presented as unthinkable without the example of Piero.[17] As Fouquet was mentioned only in Rome, where Piero was not to be found at least before the mid-1450s, Fouquet therefore had to have come to Florence during the early 1440s.[18] Longhi was also one of the first art historians to insist on the presence of Fouquet in Naples, attributing to him the miniatures of the *Manuscript of St Martha* (fig. 33), and supporting other attempts to enlarge Fouquet's Neapolitan corpus.[19] The propositions of Michel Laclotte and Fiorella Sricchia Santoro cited above cannot be understood without the example of Longhi, a figure who was for them an undisputed master.[20]

Even if the prodigious talent of Roberto Longhi is not to be questioned, one cannot but regret the influence he exerted on scholarship in the specific case of Jean Fouquet's Italian journey. Of the attributions proposed by this historiographic tradition over the years, not a single one has reached consensus, beginning with the Neapolitan works: one could only wonder why Fouquet would have added one or two pages of the *Manuscript of the Confraternity of St Martha* before disappearing into the void.[21] A methodological problem is also at the center of the thesis of Fiorella Sricchia Santoro, who imagined Fouquet as an undocumented "outsider" working with Fra Angelico in a fresco technique he would never use again.[22] Since 2003, the attribution to Fouquet of the San Marco and Orvieto frescoes has never been

accepted by specialists of both Fouquet and Fra Angelico. The single work related to Italy whose attribution to Fouquet has gained consensus, the portrait known as *Gonella* in the Kunsthistorisches Museum in Vienna (cat. 4), comes not from the same tradition and also represents a difficult case: if Gonella was a court jester in Ferrara, we are not even sure that the Vienna painting actually represents his portrait, or that it had been painted in Italy.[23]

The affinities between Florentine art and the work of Fouquet are also problematic—first and foremost because one cannot find in Fouquet's oeuvre direct, indisputable borrowings from works known to have been in Florence. The parallel made by Michel Laclotte between the birth tray by Masaccio and the miniature with *St Luke* (figs. 31, 32) is certainly suggestive, but it is impossible to establish that Fouquet ever saw the tray,

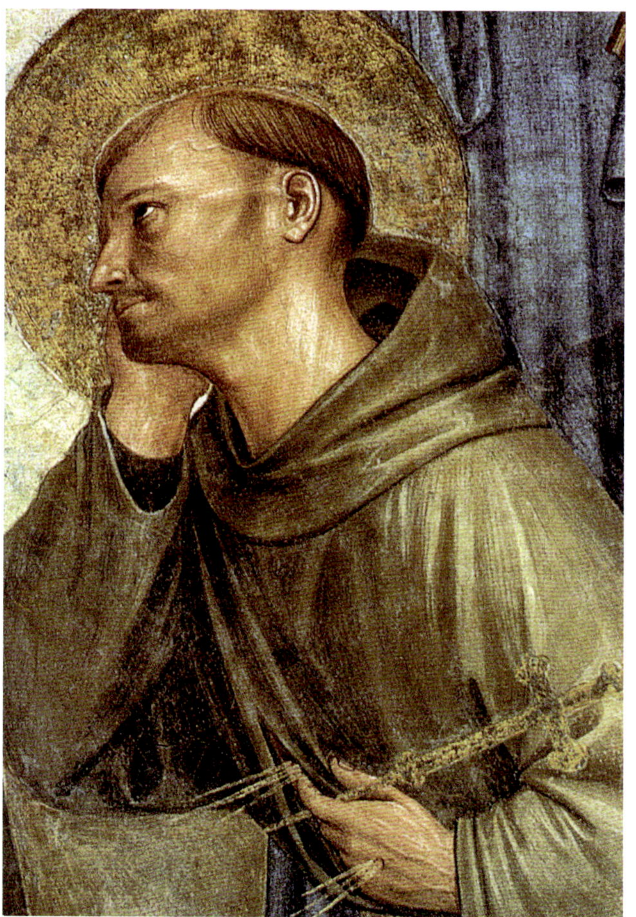

Fig. 34. Fra Angelico, Crucifixion, detail: St. Francis, 1442, Florence, convent of San Marco

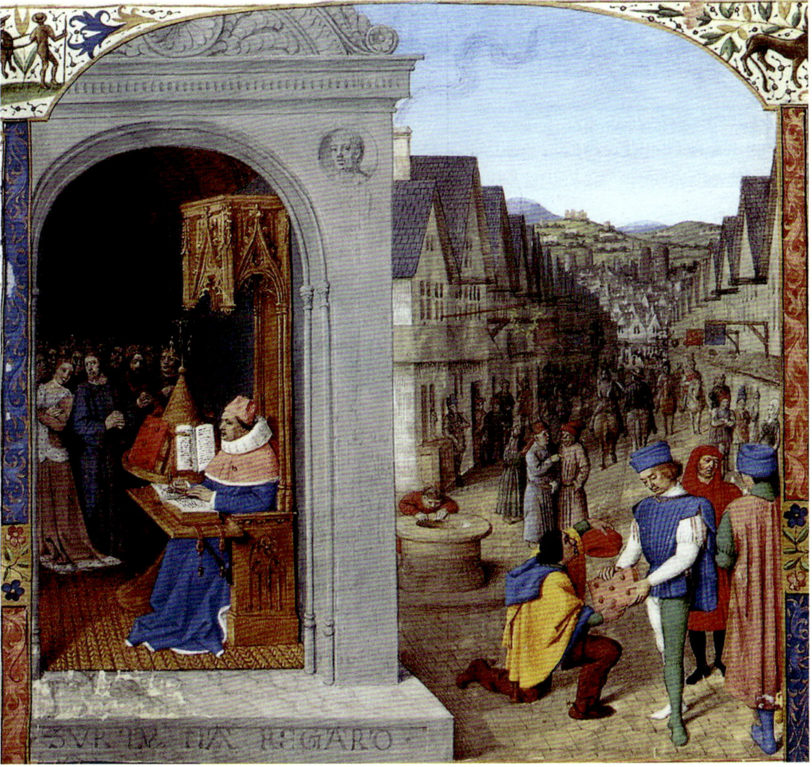

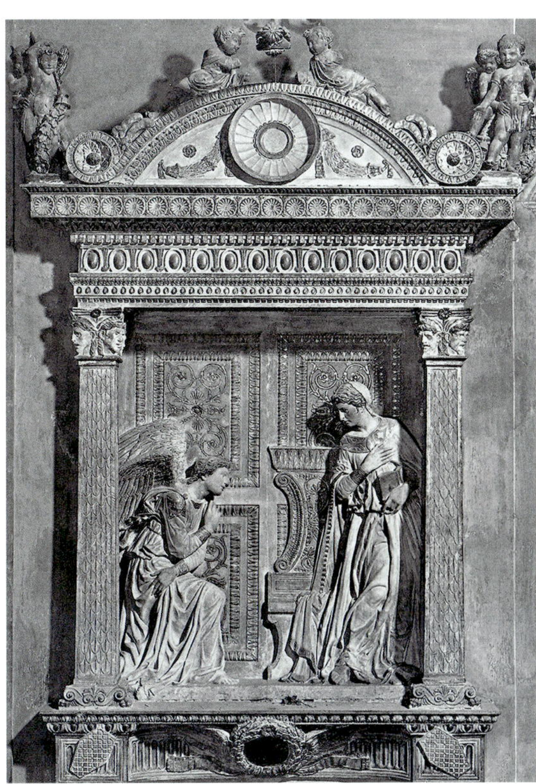

Fig. 35. Jean Fouquet or the Master of the Munich Boccaccio, A messenger giving the manuscript of Boccaccio to Meinardo de' Cavalcanti (Munich Boccaccio), Munich, Bayerische Staatsbibliothek, Cod Gall. 6, fol. 10

Fig. 36. Donatello, Cavalcanti Annunciation, ca. 1435, Florence, Santa Croce

which was privately owned, or created a similar composition. As for the tabernacle of San Miniato al Monte by Michelozzo, which seems to turn up unchanged in a miniature closely associated with Fouquet (the manuscript known as the *Munich Boccaccio*, fol. 207 r.), its creation after 1448 has led scholars to imagine a second journey to Italy that would have left no trace at all.[24] Another miniature of the *Munich Boccaccio* (fig. 35) has been compared with a Florentine work, namely the frame of the *Cavalcanti Annunciation* made by Donatello for the church of Santa Croce (fig. 36), a comparison that could seem especially pertinent as the patron of the manuscript in question was a member of the Cavalcanti family.[25] The resemblance between the frame and the painted arch of the miniature does exist; however, if Fouquet had been asked to copy the *Cavalcanti Annunciation*, one wonders why he departed from his model.[26] One after another, the speculations surrounding the journey of Fouquet in Florence seem to fall like a house of cards.

This uncertainty does not preclude Fouquet from having visited Florence, Naples or others Italian cities.[27] However, this should lead scholars to concentrate on what little information there is, stating that the painter was in Rome between September 1443 and February 1447. It has been mentioned, it is true, that the portrait of Eugene IV could had been made earlier, when the pope was still living in Florence, or even after his death; however, there is no reason to doubt the account by the sculptor and theoretician Filarete that the portrait was painted when he was in Rome himself.[28] The importance of the acquaintance of Fouquet and Filarete has long been underscored; besides the written testimonies (including the one by Giorgio Vasari), the major work of the latter artist, a bronze set of doors made for the basilica of St Peter and finished in 1445, is filled with antique references, such as *putti* and garlands, but also includes a self-portrait in a roundel—a device that would be used by Fouquet in the frame of the *Melun Diptych* (cat. 2).[29] The intimate knowledge of antique architecture that one perceives in

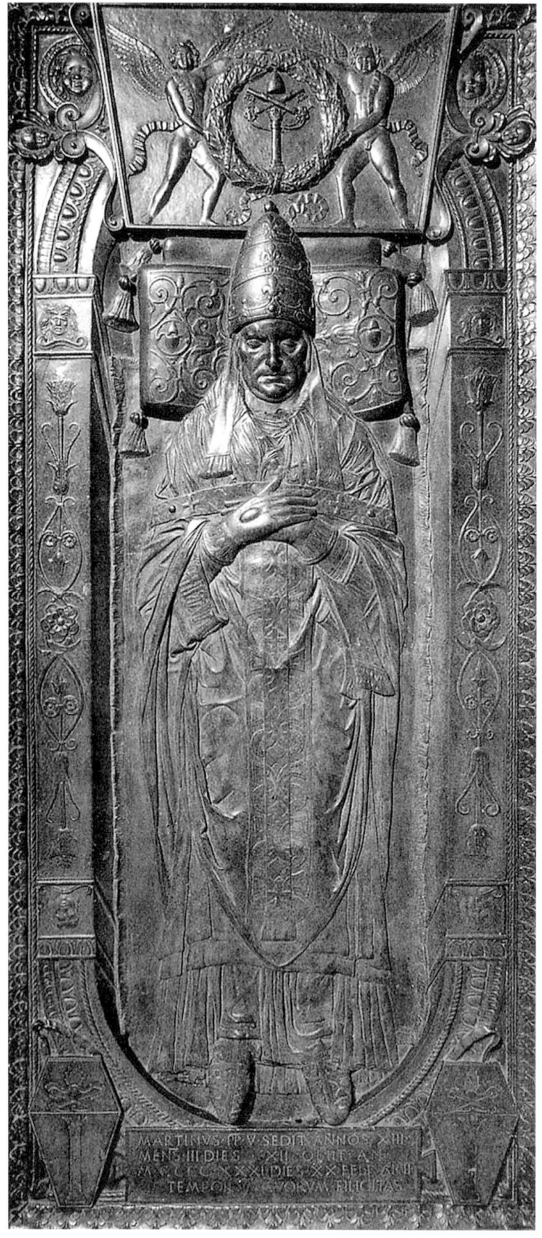

Fig. 37. Donatello and workshop, Tomb Slab of Pope Martin V, finished by 1445, Rome, St John in Lateran

ument was also visible in Rome, in the central nave of the basilica of St John in Lateran: the tomb slab of Pope Martin V, designed by Donatello and executed by the sculptor in a collaboration with his workshop (fig. 37).[30] Even if it is certainly not one of the best masterpieces of Donatello, some details are of great quality, to the point that it is a good candidate to have served as a direct model for the young Fouquet, who could have been interested in the niche framing the pope, following the grammar of antique architecture and the visual rules of perspective, but also in the baby faces in the roundels in the upper corners, and in a couple of *putti* holding the pope's shield. In the church of St Peter, a marble tabernacle by Donatello, this time entirely autograph, also used extensively the reference to antique architecture and numerous *putti*.[31] In St John in Lateran, again, the French artist could have seen portraits of popes which could have inspired him for his *Portrait of Eugene IV between two of his relatives*: a late 13th-century fresco of *Pope Boniface VIII Blessing*, showing the pontiff between two of his advisers, and the *Portrait of Pope Martin V and ten counselors* painted by Gentile da Fabriano in 1426.[32]

In Rome, Fouquet was also able to get a direct appreciation of more recent Florentine painting. During the late 1420s, Masolino and Masaccio had been working for Martin V, leaving creations that testified to the revolution of light and space that Masaccio initiated in Florence on the walls of the Brancacci chapel in the church of Santa Maria del Carmine. As had been the case at the Brancacci chapel, Masaccio and Masolino collaborated on a polyptych, now dismantled, for the church of Santa Maria Maggiore; they probably planned to fresco together the chapel of St Catherine in the church of San Clemente, but Masaccio's sudden death explains why the frescoes were painted by Masolino alone. The magnificent *Annunciation* over the entrance arch of the chapel (fig. 38) demonstrates that there was no need to go to Florence to learn the new art of light and space.[33]

But Fouquet's greatest model during his stay in Rome was certainly Fra Angelico. An Observant Dominican friar, Fra Angelico had been the first painter in the mid-1420s to understand the importance of the revolution instigated by Masaccio. The death of the latter had made him the most praised artist in Florence, closely linked with the Medici family after they took over power in

the portraits and miniatures by Fouquet certainly benefitted from his contact with Filarete, who later wrote a complete treatise on the subject.

For Fouquet, Filarete was certainly more attractive in his intellectual and artistic ambitions than in his actual craftsmanship; the bronze doors for St Peter are, stylistically but also technically speaking, way behind Lorenzo Ghiberti's achievements in Florence, in the rightly celebrated doors of the Baptistery. From 1445, another bronze mon-

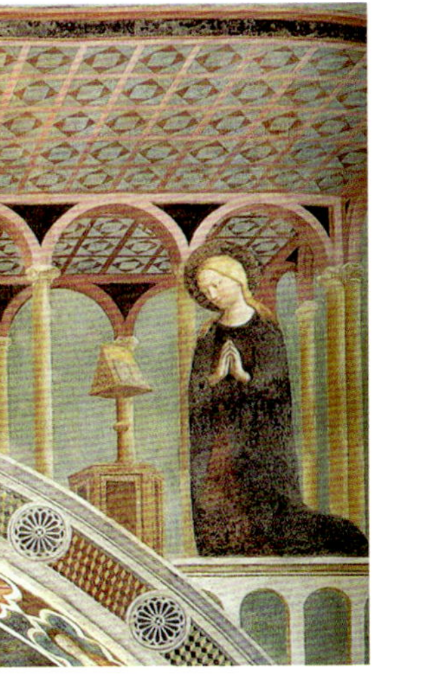

Fig. 38. Masolino, Annunciation, c. 1428/30, Rome, San Clemente

1434. The decoration of the convent of San Marco, financed by the Medici, had left a deep impression on Eugene IV, who slept there the night before its inauguration, on 6 January 1443. It is no surprise that the pope called Fra Angelico to Rome in early 1445, a few months after his return to the city, to have him contribute to the *renovatio urbis* he ambitioned. For Eugene and his successor Nicholas V, Angelico painted no fewer than three chapels in the Vatican complex; he may also have frescoed the cloister of the Dominican convent of Santa Maria sopra Minerva, where he was staying—and in the sacristy of which Fouquet's *Portrait of Eugene IV* hung.[34] Many interesting comparisons have been drawn between Fouquet's works and the only chapel by Fra Angelico to have survived, the Nicoline Chapel in the Vatican palace; as it was made under the auspices of Nicholas V, too direct connections should be avoided—Fouquet may never have seen these frescoes. Nevertheless, the affinity between the art of both artists in light, space, composition, and knowledge of antiquity cannot be exaggerated. These qualities are also the ones of a pupil of Fra Angelico's, Benozzo Gozzoli, who was extremely interested in antique motifs (cf. cat. 10), executed exquisite miniatures with portraits of popes (fig. 39), and later surrounded a *Madonna and Child* (fig. 14) with blue and red cherubs—a resemblance to the panel from the *Melun Diptych* now in Antwerp that should be seen as a cultural affinity, not as a direct influence.[35] Even if Piero della Francesca and Andrea del Castagno were not active in Rome yet, the artistic

panorama in that city between 1443 and 1447 was rich enough to have provided Fouquet with a deep knowledge of Italian Renaissance art.[36]

A hotly debated question remains: how did Fouquet obtain the honor of portraying Pope Eugene IV? Did he arrive in Italy known to have been a sovereign's portraitist, bringing along a likeness of Charles VII (fig. 3)?[37] The latter was precisely one of the persons represented in a chapel in the Vatican painted during the Quattrocento, a

Fig. 39. Benozzo Gozzoli, Portrait of Eugene IV, Joachim da Fiore, Vaticina Pontificum, c. 1440/45, London, British Library, Harley Ms 1340, fol. 11v

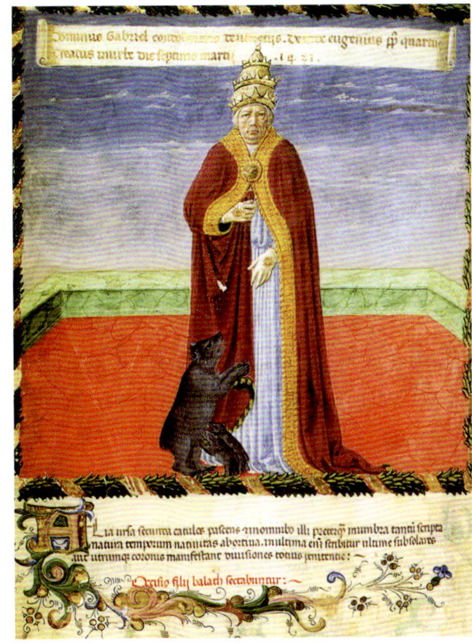

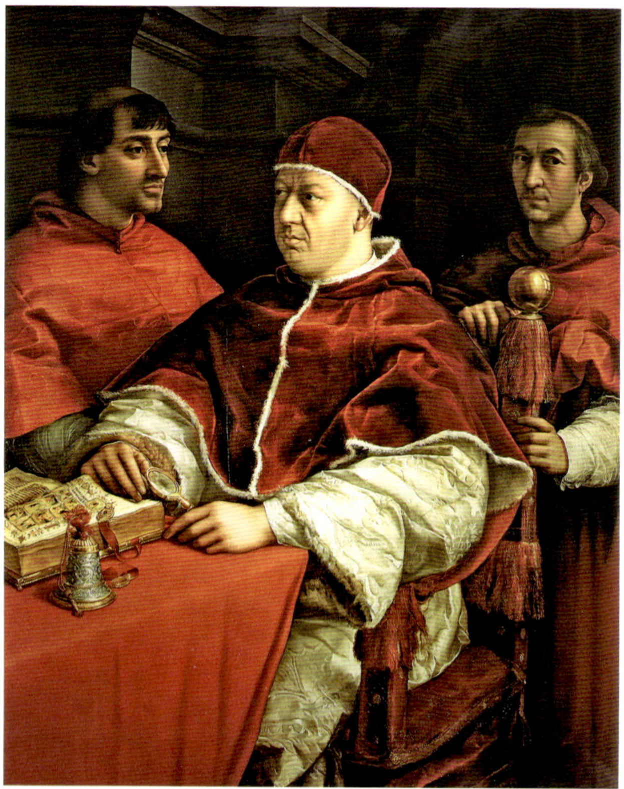

Fig. 40. Raphael, Portrait of Pope Leo X between Two of his Nephews, 1518/20, Florence, Galleria degli Uffizi

chapel that might have been decorated by Fra Angelico and his workshop, even if Giorgio Vasari attributed it, quite implausibly, to the late 15th century Milanese painter Bramantino.[38] But Vasari may have been right in saying that, when the chapel was destroyed to make room for the famous *Stanze*, Raphael asked his assistants to copy these portraits "so beautiful and well done that they needed only a word to come alive".[39] A description that is certainly a *topos*, but that strangely echoes the words in which Fouquet's *Portrait of Eugene IV with two of his relatives* was described.[40] Could Raphael have been receptive to the new realism in portraiture introduced by Fouquet, a realism that allowed him to portray the pope not in profile, as was the tradition in Italy, but in three-quarter view; and not to limit the representation to the face, as was often the case in Flanders, but include the arms in the composition (fig. 30)? The *Portrait of Pope Leo X between two of his nephews* (fig. 40) may reflect this influence; but in the absence of Fouquet's original work, and with so little information at hand, perhaps the best attitude is, alas, to remain cautious.[41]

My thanks to Julien Chapuis, Gerardo de Simone, Sophie Egly, Stephan Kemperdick, Douglas Kline, and Christine Seidel.

1   Laclotte, 1967, p. 40.
2   On the rediscovery of Fouquet and of early French painting, see Martin 2004 *specim.* pp. 51-52.
3   See Avril in Cat, Paris 2003, pp.96-98; Sricchia Santoro 2003, pp. 50-53, who suggests that the "relatives" were members of the Franciscans and Augustinians, but also possibly from the pope's family.
4   Laclotte 1967, p. 38.
5   New York, Pierpont Morgan Library, ms. M. 834; Cat. Paris 2003, no. 28.
6   Laclotte 1967, p. 38. At that time, Michel Laclotte considered the miniature of St Luke a copy from a lost illustration by Fouquet from the *Hours of Etienne Chevalier*; the author later accepted fully Fouquet's authorship (Laclotte 1995, p. 99), a position that is now consensual among scholars.
7   Laclotte 1967, p. 35.
8   See note 21 below.
9   Causa 1954, pp. 17-18.
10   Lombardi 1983, pp. 70-83 sums up the propositions that have been made about this sojourn.
11   Sricchia Santoro 2003. The earlier reference is Sricchia Santoro 1979, p. 102.
12   Sricchia Santoro 2003, pp. 55-56. The juxtaposition had already been made by Sricchia Santoro 1979, pp. 132- 133 but with the traditional attributions. In 2003, Fiorella Sricchia Santoro also attributed to Fouquet the SS John the Baptist, Augustine, and Thomas Aquinas from the *Crucifixion*.
13   Sricchia Santoro 2003, p. 59.
14   The already cited article of Sricchia Santoro 1979 is a good example of this tendency. The journey of Jan van Eyck in Italy was postulated by Sterling, 1976, p. 29, in a famous article, where the representation of snowy mountains in the oeuvre of van Eyck was interpreted as evidence of a direct knowledge of the Alps. Interestingly Sterling 1971, p. 9 had used earlier the same argumentation for Fouquet.
15   A chapter has been published in Longhi 1995, pp. 15-30.
16   Longhi 1914; cf. Rowley 2014, pp. 10.
17   Longhi 1927, ed. 1963, p. 72.
18   On the probable activity of Piero della Francesca in Rome during the mid-1450s, before his documented stay in 1458/59, see Pinelli 2002. Piero della Francesca is documented in Florence in 1439, when he was working with Domenico Veneziano; his presence in the workshop of Fra Filippo Lippi in 1442 has also been suggested by Di Lorenzo 2004, pp. 291-292.
19   Longhi 1952a. See also Longhi 1952b, ed. 1979, p. 25; Longhi 1952c, ed. 1975, p. 84; and Longhi 1955, ed. 1979, p. 30. Among the scholars who published their studies in the periodical directed by Longhi, *Paragone*, one can cite: Toesca 1952; Causa, 1954, pp. 17-18; Castelfranchi Vegas 1966, p. 44.
20   Fiorella Sricchia Santoro graduated under Roberto Longhi in the University of Florence, while Michel Laclotte has never hidden his debt towards one of his "*quatre maîtres*" (Laclotte 2003, pp. 310-325). The presence of Fouquet in Florence has been especially endorsed by Luciano Bellosi, a former student of Longhi who would coin the term "*pittura di luce*" ("painting of light") to describe the artistic scene of Florence in the 1440s: see Bellosi 1992, pp. 49.
21   The Neapolitan attributions did not seduce every art historian, Sterling 1971, note 2; Cat. Madrid 2001, no. 52 (Gennaro Toscano); Thiébaut 2006, p. 50. For an opposite view, see Cianfarini 2000, pp. 386-387.
22   Sricchia Santoro 2003, p. 56. The documentation of the Orvieto chapel names many collaborators of Fra Angelico, but the name of Fouquet never appears.
23   The attribution is due to Pächt 1974, who used his proposition to reaffirm the links between Fouquet and Jacopo Bellini he had already postulated in Pächt 1940/41. The supposed influence of the drawings of Jacopo Bellini on Fouquet was also an argument for Sterling 1971, pp. 12-13 to think of a possible trip to Venice. On the *Portrait of Gonella*, see Avril 2003, pp. 94-96, where this attribution is even doubted.
24   Schwager 1970, p. 209. Reynaud 1981, p. 78 note 4 observes only a superficial analogy between the two buildings; while Avril in Cat. Paris 2003, pp. 272, cat. 32 attributes the manuscript to a close collaborator of Fouquet, which would evidently weaken the argumentation. The same chronological problem is also present for the *Assumption of the Virgin* by Andrea del Castagno painted in 1449/1450 for the Florentine church of San Miniato tra le Torri and now in the Gemäldegalerie, Berlin, that Sterling 1971, p. 11 proposed as a model for the scene of the same subject in the *Hours of Etienne Chevalier*.
25   Evans 1985.
26   Evans 1985, p. 48 was also puzzled by the fact that this alleged reference was inserted in a book whose recipient had never come to Florence and could not understand the allusion; c.f. also Evans 1989.
27   Sterling 1971, p. 17 has also insisted on Fouquet's supposed interest in the Tuscan landscape.
28   See the argumentations of Sricchia Santoro 2003, pp. 50-53. Filarete fled Rome in 1447 because he was accused of theft of relics.
29   The unrealistic supposition by Schaefer 1967, p. 196 that Fouquet participated in the casting of the doors has not been followed. On the relationship between Fouquet and Filarete, see also: Cianfarini 1997.
30   On the arrival of the work in Rome, see Esch 1978, p. 211.
31   On the use of *putti* by Fouquet in relationship with Donatello, see Caglioti 2015, pp. 27-29.
32   Sterling 1988, pp. 22-23 first linked to Fouquet the fresco, the composition of which was initially more monumental than it is now. It has been attributed to Cimabue and Giotto, but is by the hand of a local painter influenced by Giotto (Bellosi 1998, p. 15). For possible (in my opinion questionable) influences on Fouquet of 14th-century Italian painting, see Richards 2007. On the lost portrait by Gentile da Fabriano, see Christiansen 1982, p. 136.
33   On this *Annunciation*, interestingly dismissed by art historical literature, see the lecture I proposed at the Fondazione Zeri in Bologna on 19 September 2016 ("Alla ricerca dell'Annunciazione di Masaccio vista da Giorgio Vasari a San Niccolò Oltrarno") available online and soon to be published.
34   On the Roman period of Fra Angelico, see De Simone 2009 and the forthcoming De Simone 2017.
35   On the Detroit *Madonna*, see Cole Ahl 1996, pp. 214-215, who makes no mention of Fouquet. I thank Stephan Kemperdick for suggesting this comparison.
36   On the presence of Piero in Rome, see note 18 above. Andrea del Castagno is documented in Rome in 1454, for decorations he made in the Vatican palace; for his supposed relationship with Fouquet, see note 24; and Sterling 1988, pp. 24-26.
37   Sterling 1987 suggested this was not the Louvre portrait, but an earlier version, now lost, but known through copies.
38   Reynaud 1981, p. 80, n. 44.
39   Vasari, 1568, III, p. 259.
40   Cf. Thiébaut 2003, pp. 29-32.
41   For this comparison, see Focillon 1936, p. 29; Schwager 1970.

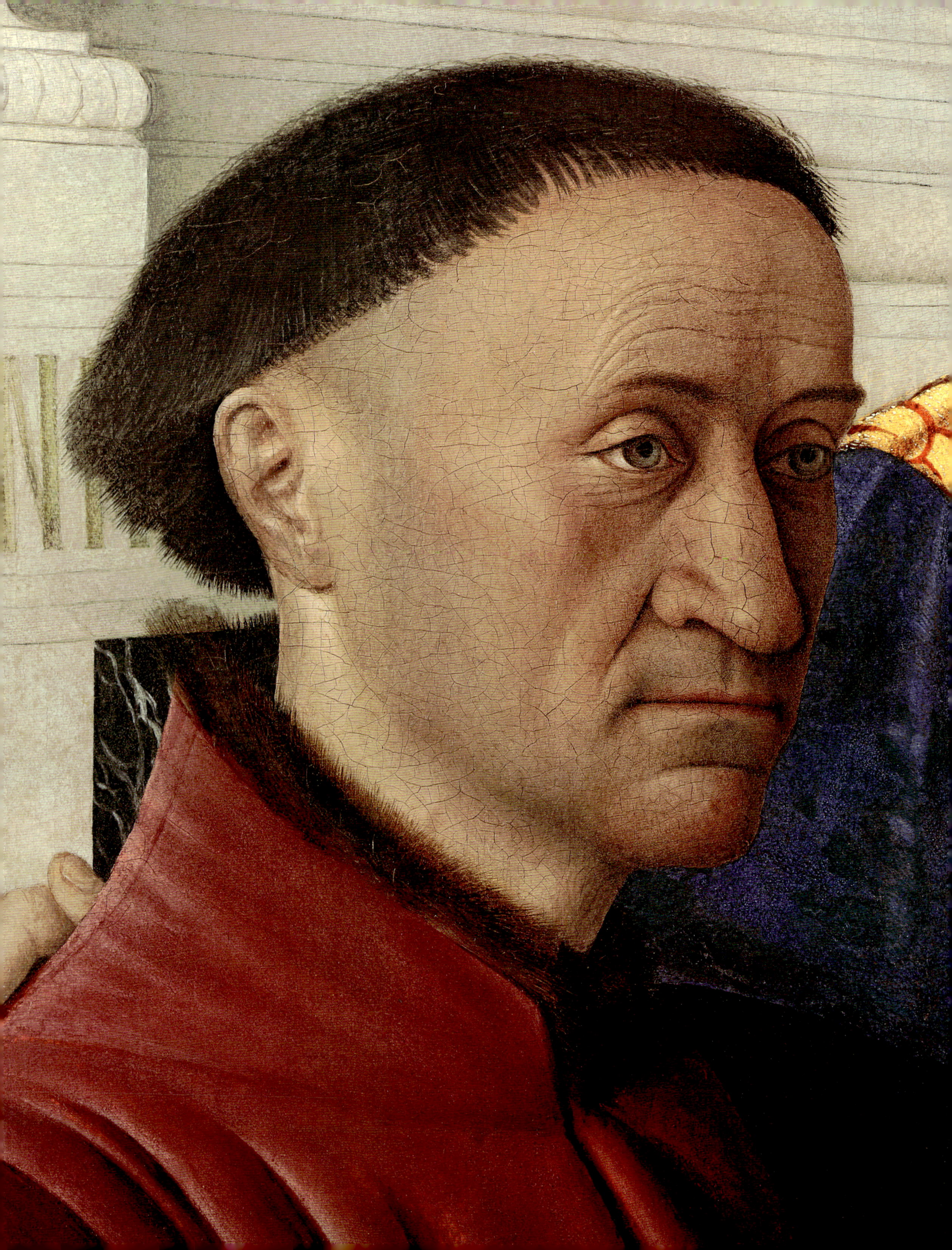

Eberhard König

ÉTIENNE CHEVALIER AS A CLIENT
OF JEAN FOUQUET

Instead of simply referring to customers or clients, art historians love to use terms like "patron" or "donor," all too often forgetting that it is impossible to donate something to oneself. Clients who ordered small devotional images or even prayer books for their own use and had themselves depicted in them may have been ever so pious;[1] but the images, which they alone could contemplate (at least during their own lifetimes), were not donations, and could only have served other purposes to which art historians have given little thought.[2]

Praying with Prayer Books and Diptychs

Jean de Tavernier depicted Philip the Good (fig. 42), probably in 1454, kneeling at a *prie-dieu* with prayer book and diptych before him.[3] The panels of the diptych, scarcely larger than the pages of the prayer book, once again show the duke of Burgundy against a gold background, kneeling in prayer to the Madonna.[4] Jean Fouquet probably never painted a genre-like image of this kind with both a prayer book and a devotional image; but he did portray one and the same gentleman praying in both a diptych (fig. 41, cat. 1) and a double page in a prayer book (fig. 43), which in turn is often described as a diptych.[5] In both images, the arch-martyr Stephen presents his namesake, the royal treasurer Étienne Chevalier, to the Madonna.[6]

The oldest documentary source for the two panel paintings, which are now in Berlin and Antwerp, dates to around 1660 and describes the panels as a diptych on the wall above the double tomb of the patron and his wife Catherine Budé in the collegiate church of Notre-Dame in Melun.[7] Since Catherine, who died on August 24, 1452, is not depicted, the diptych may have been intended for Étienne Chevalier's home in Paris.[8] The house, which gave the Rue de la Verrerie its name and—as Guillebert de Mets reported in 1434—allegedly had more windows than the year had days, was not built by Étienne; rather, it had already belonged to Miles Baillet (1348/50–1424), the treasurer of Charles VI, and was known for mass being said there every day.[9] However, the diptych could also have been intended for the altar in Chevalier's chapel in the collegiate church of Melun.

When Étienne Chevalier opened his prayer book to the Hours of the Virgin (fig. 43), he knelt beneath an image that showed both him and St. Stephen in life size. In both Paris and Melun, the rectangular window reflected in the knobs of the Madonna's throne could have been interpreted as an allusion to Chevalier's splendid house, even if it did not even remotely correspond to the imaginary architecture painted by Fouquet. As a work of art in its own right—one that also reinforced the now-lost epitaph inscription in the collegiate church—the juxtaposition of the Antwerp Madonna and the Berlin panel brought a double incongruity into the space where Étienne Chevalier may have used these images: for the background of the Antwerp *Virgin and Child* with its red and blue angels contrasts starkly with the Renaissance architecture of the Berlin wing.

In the book of hours, the arch-martyr Stephen likewise presents Étienne Chevalier to the Mother of God, but here she suckles the Christ Child at her breast. The angels, who form a heavenly orchestra with instruments at the left and sing in a choir on the right, appear not as putti-like seraphim and cherubim, but rather as youthful figures of varying ages grouped by the color of their robes, with only the youngest singers at the right clothed entirely in white. The location appears to be the forecourt of a Renaissance palace;[10] the portal at the end of the courtyard, however—a tall Gothic embrasure framing a classical shell niche—is a closed gate, a *porta clausa* symbolic of Mary's virginity. Thus the setting represents the goal of every pious worshipper, for under the open sky, Étienne Chevalier kneels in the realm of the Queen of Angels. He numbers among the *gens de robe longue* of the French royal court;[11] ironically, one might even mistake him for one of the lawyer saints of the poor, Yvo of Tréguier or Homobonus of Cremona,[12] especially since his jurist's robe is the only fabric in the miniature not accentuated with gold.[13] Compared to Jean de Tavernier's frontispiece for Philip the Good, this image clearly manifests the tremendous ambition inherent in Fouquet's transposition of the royal treasurer, of all people, into the heavenly realm; the latter's name and office, moreover, are inscribed into a frieze beneath putti who appear against a sky-blue background, exhibiting the golden monogram "e&e" on purple and green shields. The impression arises—just as in the marshal Boucicaut's book of hours a generation before[14]—that it is not Étienne Chevalier, but rather the Virgin Mary who is a guest in this place. Thus a profound contrast appears between this patron and Philip the Good—the "Great Duke of the Occident," as the Burgundian called himself—a difference that is difficult to reconcile with the respective historical roles of the two gentlemen.

A Jurist from Melun in the Service of Two Kings

Étienne Chevalier was born in Melun, where an "ostel Jehan Chevalier" is mentioned in 1402 in the prosperous parish of St. Aspais and where Étienne's father was lay

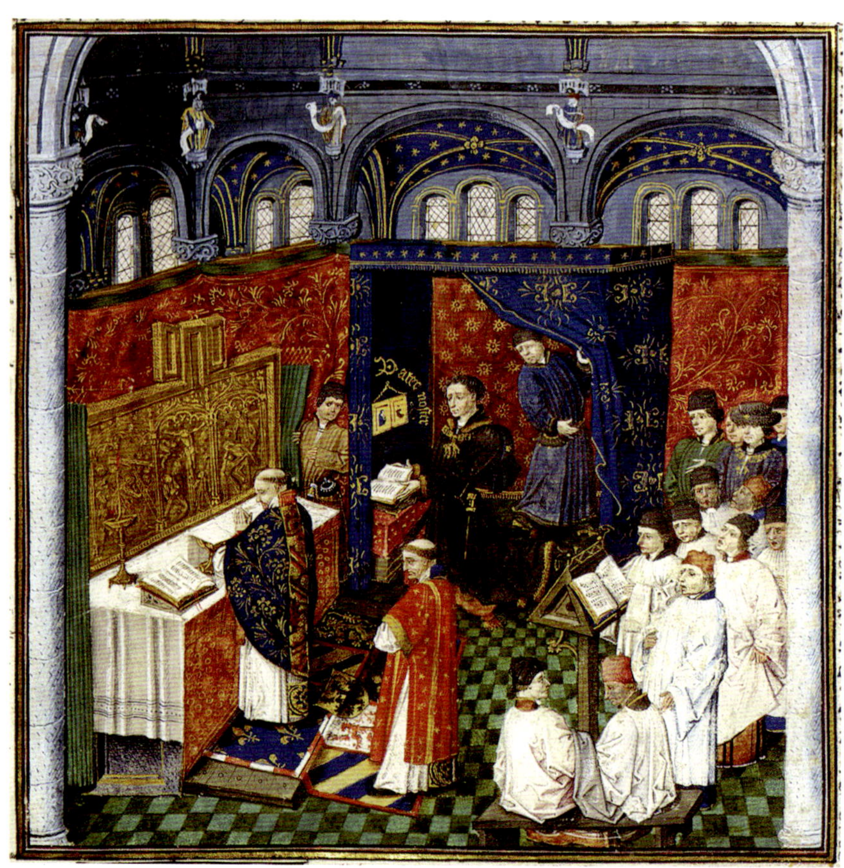

Fig. 42. Jean de Tavernier, Philip the Good Praying, *Traité de l'oraison dominicale*, after 1454, Brussels, Bibliothèque Royale, ms. 9092, fol. 9

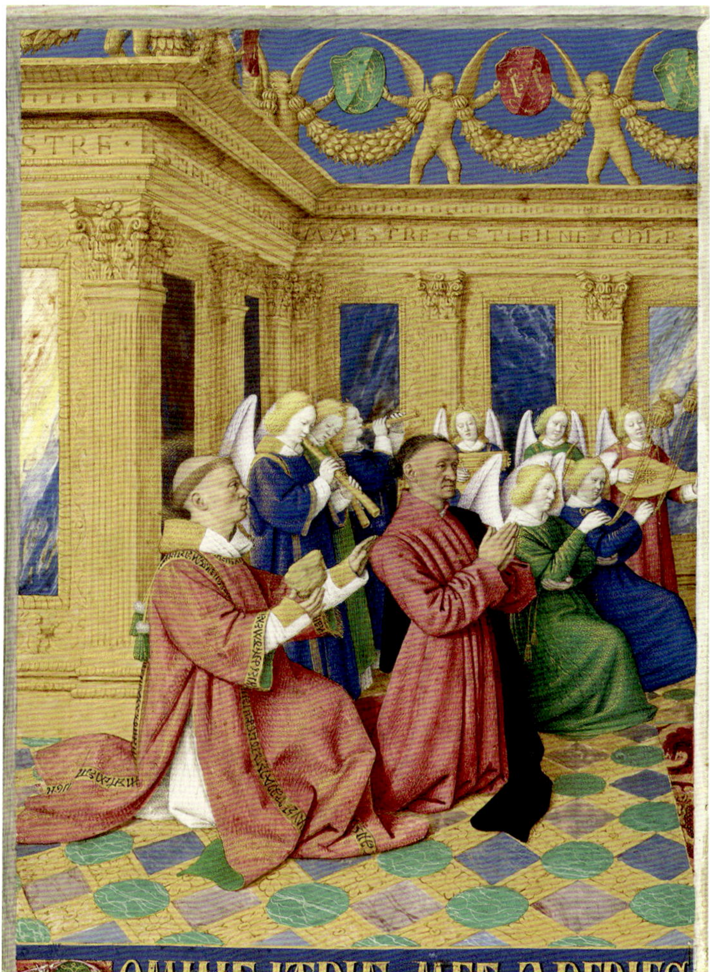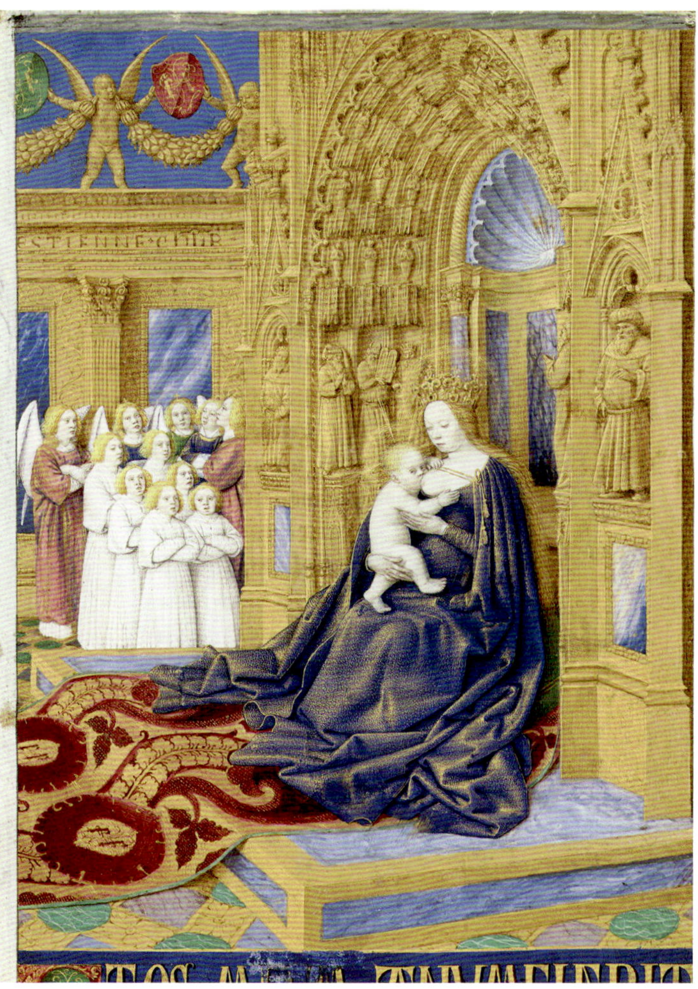

Fig. 43. Jean Fouquet, *Étienne Chevalier before the Virgin*, formerly a double page from the *Hours of Étienne Chevalier*, Chantilly, Musée Condé

procurator of the abbey of Saint-Père.[15] In 1444 Étienne married Catherine, a daughter of the Parisian jurist Dreux Budé, from whom he had assumed the office of *Contrôleur général des aides en Languedoc* the year before. Widowed early on, he seems never to have married again. He died in September 1474; the couple's shared bronze tomb slab, which also depicts four children—a boy and three girls— is recorded in Gaignière's albums (fig. 52).[16]

Beginning in 1426, Étienne Chevalier[17] served as secretary and *maître de la chambre aux deniers* (thus responsible for finances) to the constable Arthur de Richemont. The Chevaliers, both father and son, declared their loyalty to the Dauphin Charles, who laid claim to the crown in Bourges and whom Jean Chevalier served as secretary beginning in 1423. Around 1441, Étienne left the service of Arthur de Richemont, from whom the English had taken

the appanage of Richmond, and entered the service of the royal family, at first probably for the Dauphin Louis, the later King Louis XI, for whom he was still working as *maître de la chambre aux deniers* in April 1443.[18]

As early as June 24, 1442, Étienne Chevalier lent the king himself 1100 *livres tournois*; in 1443 he was appointed royal secretary. He soon became the tax auditor of Languedoc, then also of Languedoil and Outre-Seine. He traveled to England, Brittany, and Burgundy for Charles VII; in 1449, he was appointed to the crown council as *maître de la Chambre des comptes* and was later made *contrôleur de la recette générale des finances*. Finally, on March 20, 1452, he was named *trésorier de France*, the highest financial office in the kingdom.[19]

Together with Jacques Cœur and the doctor Robert Poitevin, Étienne Chevalier served as executor of the estate[20] of Agnès Sorel, the king's mistress. Later he would do the same for Charles VII himself, though here in 1461 he ran afoul of Jean de Montespedon, called Houast, who imprisoned him and his father-in-law Dreux Budé in Montargis before the dead king's successor secured their release. Already by late November 1461, Étienne Chevalier, who for a short time had served in the *Chambre des comptes* under Jean Bureau,[21] was again signing royal doc-uments. In early 1462, he accompanied Louis XI to the south and then to Tours. In 1463, together with the admiral of France Jean de Montauban[22] and the royal secretary Jean Bourré, Étienne Chevalier—now royal treasurer once again—conveyed the massive sum of 200,000 *écus d'or* to Philip the Good of Burgundy, in order to buy back the cities on the Somme for France. In the civil war of the *Ligue du Bien public* in 1465, Étienne Chevalier remained

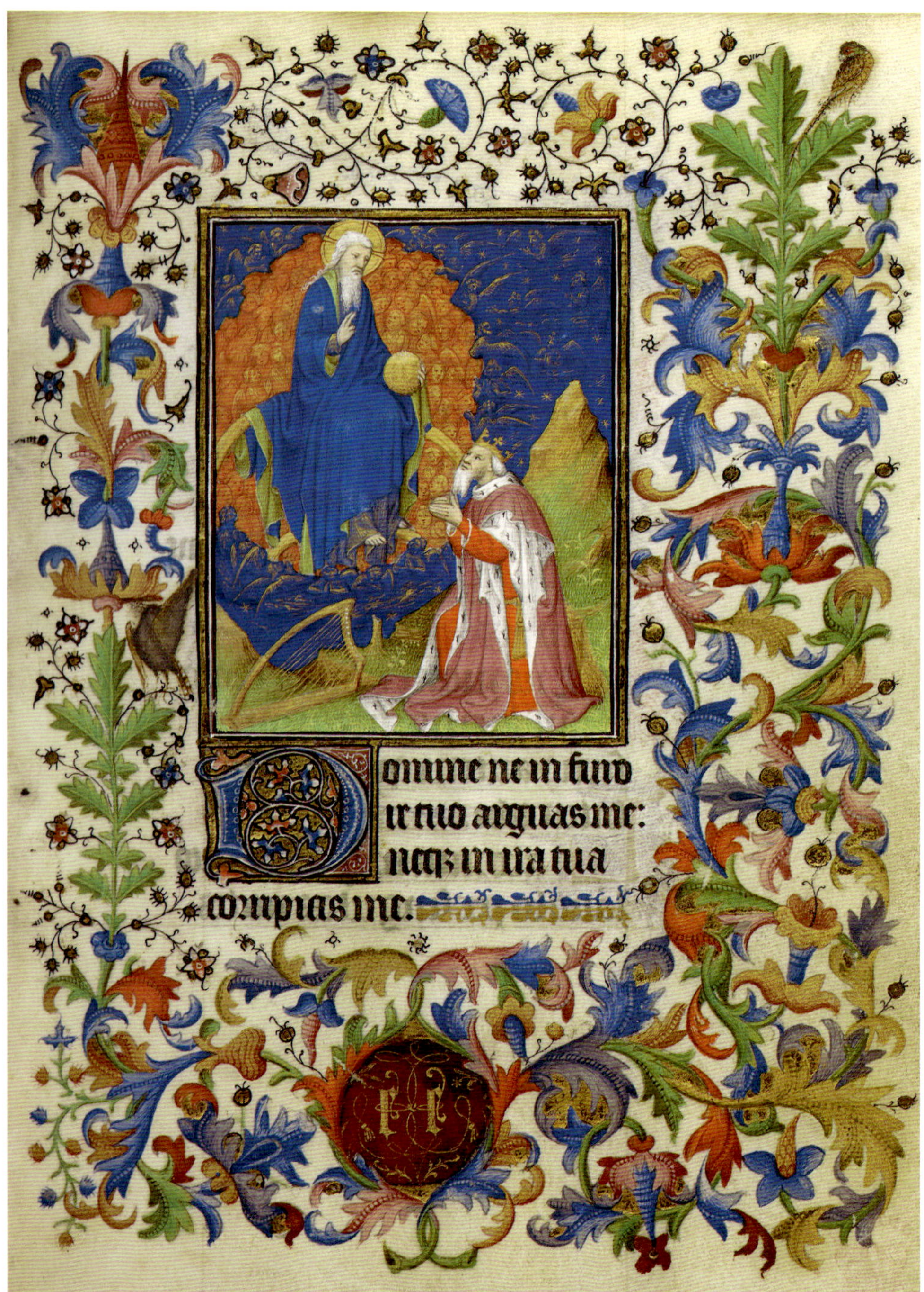

Fig. 44. Boucicaut Master, King David Praying, *Book of Hours*, ca. 1415/20, owned by Étienne Chevalier, London, British Library, Add. Ms. 16997, fol. 90

loyal to the king, whom he even entertained in his house in Paris. He relinquished his offices only shortly before his death on September 3 or September 14, 1474, and Philibert Boutillat began service as the new treasurer on November 10, 1473.[23]

The Double "e" with Love Knot

The name Étienne Chevalier, or "Stephen Knight," already gives rise to confusion.[24] The "aristocratic" association is only a surname; for unlike his wife's parents, apparently the treasurer was not entitled to bear a coat of arms.[25] In all the works Jean Fouquet created for him, he is identified as MAISTRE ESTIENNE CHEVALIER in antique epigraphy and even more frequently with the golden letters "e&e" in Gothic miniscule connected by a love knot. His position as *maître de la Chambre des comptes* from 1449 on is emphasized by inscriptions in both the Berlin panel (cat. 1) and the book of hours (on the double page for the Hours of the Virgin, on the house of Zacharias in the Visitation, and on the temple front behind the Marriage of the Virgin). His title and name frame the golden scenes from the legend of St. Martin. In the initial for Hilarius of Poitiers, they appear on a curved shield; elsewhere, shields of the same kind, preferably on a purple ground but also on green, are labeled with the golden letters "e&e." The double "e" as a pair of letters decorates numerous miniatures in inexhaustible variety, and Jean Fouquet used a shield of this same kind to paint over an older coat of arms beneath the David image by the Boucicaut Master in the latter's London book of hours (fig. 44).[26]

The late Gothic script that suppresses the middle bar of the "e" may tempt us to read "e&c" and interpret it either as the monogram of Étienne and Catherine Budé or, despite the love knot, simply as the initial letters of the first name Étienne and the last name Chevalier. Yet the initial for the Marian prayer *Stabat mater*,[27] following five pairs of "e&e" written in miniscule, suddenly shows a clearly legible "E&E."[28] A simple solution would be to interpret the monogram as the first and last letters of the name "Étienne"—as in the *Livre du Cuer d'amours espris*, where René d'Anjou associates the initials "V" und "E" used by Jean de Berry with the girl's name VRSINE, a reference to an early liaison of the Duke.[29]

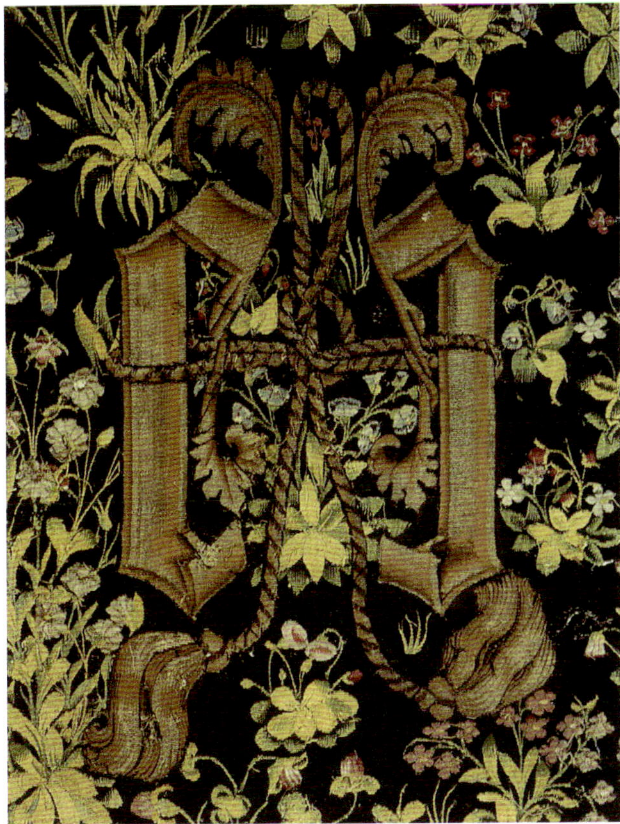

Fig. 45. Millefleur tapestry of Philip the Good of Burgundy, Brussels 1466, Bern, Historisches Museum, detail

With Michel Zink one could observe that "E est une lettre de malheur,"[30] since the letter "E" makes a wailing sound and the lower-case "e" looks puny;[31] there, however, we would be nearly on a par with Alexandre Dumas, who honored the E from his true first name Edmond in *The Count of Monte Christo*. In any case, the letter E was associated with "Eva," whose name becomes redemptive only when it is reversed into "Ave."[32] Seen in this light, the double "e" might express the pain of the widower Étienne Chevalier, who evidently commissioned both his book of hours and the Berlin-Antwerp diptych only after the death of Catherine Budé.

Yet the "e&e" connected by a love knot was not an isolated phenomenon, particularly in the 1450s. At the same time Fouquet was working for Étienne Chevalier, the abovementioned duke of Burgundy devised a similar sign for himself, without having been widowed.[33] From 1453 on, all major works executed for Philip the Good of Burgundy[34] were marked with "e&e," though here the right-hand letter was reversed. In the famous millefleur tapestry in Bern, bands of gilded metal, transformed into the letter "e" by chains or cords (thus sometimes causing them to be interpreted as the letter "c" [35]) appear in splendor around Philip's coat of arms along with the fire-steel and flint of the Golden Fleece (fig. 45).[36] An entire *chambre* of such hangings was created by Jehan de Haze of Brussels in 1466 for this sole documented commission for a series of tapestries by Philip the Good. The mirrored letters even appear on Philip's tomb slab of 1468 in the Church of Our Lady in Bruges.[37] This line of tradition, in which the letters become increasingly illegible, also includes the black-and-white monograms in the *Voustre Demeure Hours*, where the monogram "C&M" in Antiqua letters refers to Charles the Bold and his third wife Margaret of York, whom he married in 1468.[38]

At first Philip used the monogram PHE, which combined PH and E, the first and last letters of his name. Anna Rapp-Buri und Monica Stucky-Schürer suggest that he then replaced this formula with the first and last vowels of his name, incorrectly written as Ph*e*lipp*e*. Another explanation for Philip the Good's use of the two "e"s was advanced by Florens Deuchler on the basis of the point in time when the Burgundian duke adopted the mirrored letters as his personal insignia: it occurred in 1453, apparently immediately after the conquest of Constantinople by the Turks and shortly before Philip took the *Vœu du faisan*, the solemn oath to undertake a crusade, on February 17, 1454 in Lille. From that point on, Deuchler maintains, Philip conceived of himself as *eques ecclesiae*, knight of the Church.[39] Unfortunately it is difficult to attribute the same intentions to Étienne Chevalier: while *eques* is indeed the Latin equivalent of "chevalier", the French name "Étienne" hardly fits with the Latin surname "eques," though on the whole the affectation MAISTRE ESTIENNE CHEVALIER veritably trumpets the aspiration to knighthood.

Here at the latest it becomes necessary to place the "e&e" within a broader context than that of mere private individuals. Around 1400, the letter "e" appears over and over again in the margins of the *Wenceslas Bible* in Vienna. A plausible explanation has long eluded scholars; Diethelm Gresch, however, has been able to assign a very concrete meaning to the "e," not only in the manuscript borders, but also in architecture, specifically a contemporaneous "e"

chiseled into the stone above the council chamber in the Old Town Hall in Prague.[40] In Wenceslas' German-language manuscript, the letter "e" consistently appears alongside biblical passages relating to the divine Law—for in fact "E" was a word in its own right, a noun that referred to the law not of man, but of God. Echoes of this meaning resonate in German words such as *Ehe* and *Ehre* as well as the adjective *ewig*, derived from "E." In the adjective *ehern*, it constitutes the opposite of metallic, expressed in the distinction between the Bronze Age and the Age of Iron (*Ehernem Zeitalter*); the French language likewise reflects this distinction with the aurally related *airain*.[41]

Of course word formations associated with the *eherne Gesetz Gottes* were far removed from the French of Philip the Good of Burgundy, and even further from the linguistic usage of Étienne Chevalier. Yet it was precisely in the realm of heraldry that connections between the kingdom of France and the Roman Empire of the Kaiser were kept alive. Our point of reference for the "e" is even closer: under King Wenceslas, Prague was allied to France, and Fouquet himself produced striking miniatures depicting the visit to Paris of Wenceslas and his father, the emperor Charles IV, in January 1378.[42]

The Ambitions of a New Class of Patrons

In Paris, Étienne Chevalier could simply have walked around the corner from his splendid townhouse in order to commission both his diptych and his book of hours from the atelier that had dominated painting in the capital city for half a century: the workshop of the family of Haincelin de Haguenau, now identified as the Bedford Master,[43] on the Rue Quincampoix, a street that today still runs northward from the Rue de la Verrerie. Étienne's familiarity with this address before he approached Fouquet is evidenced by his copy of Boccaccio's *Decameron* from the 1440s:[44] the eleven column-width illuminations in the manuscript were painted by the Dunois Master (fig. 46), an artist named after a sumptuous book of hours made for the same Jean de Dunois who for decades worked closely with Étienne Chevalier in the crown council of Charles VII and Louis XI.[45] The Dunois Master is considered the younger Haincelin, if one wants to distinguish generations within the workshop.[46] The manuscript was

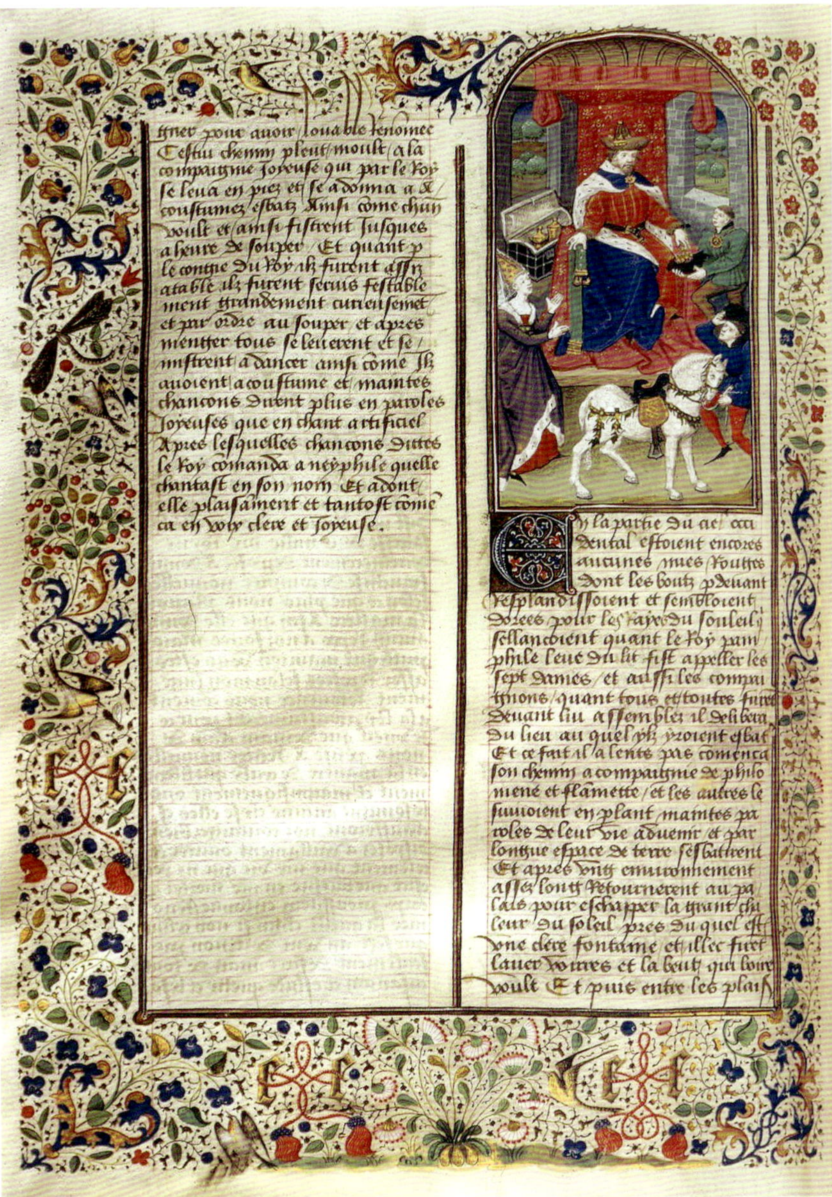

Fig. 46. Dunois Master, Griselda, *Boccaccio of Étienne Chevalier*, 1440s, Cambridge/Mass., Houghton Library, MS Richardson 31, fol. 233v

created in the 1440s, and the fact that the borders of all eleven illuminated pages are designed for the golden "e&e" also proves that the monogram should not be interpreted as a response to the death of Étienne's wife.

Yet for the magnificent works that would earn him a place in art history on the eve of the Renaissance, the royal treasurer decided against a Parisian workshop that had not only been highly esteemed since the days of Jean de Berry, but at that time was developing an impressive new visual language in the work of recently-arrived artists like the Master of Jean Rolin.[47] He also passed over another Parisian artist, a pioneering painter from the North now called

after Dreux Budé; the Master of Dreux Budé—perhaps one of the Vulcop brothers—had painted a crucifixion triptych (now in multiple locations around the world) for Étienne Chevalier's wife's parents, and had also created the epoch-making *Parlement of Paris Altarpiece* around 1450.[48] One could surmise that the royal treasurer rejected the bourgeois art of the metropolis in favor of the new star ascending at the royal court of Tours, that of Jean Fouquet. But who, aside from the artist himself, was responsible for the rise of this new art? While Fouquet did make a portrait of Charles VII and later also painted a miniature of Louis XI with the Order of St. Michael,[49] his breakthrough came with the works for Étienne Chevalier; they mark the beginning of his striking new art. Moreover, it was Étienne Chevalier who inspired his own son-in-law Laurent Girard to have the Munich Boccaccio illuminated in Fouquet's workshop.[50]

Certainly Christine Seidel has succeeded in revising the overly negative image of Charles VII's patronage;[51] as a patron, however, Étienne Chevalier outstripped not only the king, but even the latter's son Louis XI. Apparently the new, unusual, daring art of Jean Fouquet at first held little appeal for the high nobility, who preferred to rely instead upon tried and tested formulas for dynastic legitimation. The above-mentioned marshal Boucicaut and Étienne Chevalier shared two decisive features: both of them promoted major examples of an especially bold, progressive art at the French royal court, and both proved at the same time that artistic expertise was better suited to their own social class, inscribing themselves into art history with innovative works and surpassing in heraldic ambition anything the old nobility dared to do.

The generosity of Étienne Chevalier fits this picture: Anne D. Hedeman explains the unusual image at the end of Étienne's *Decameron* as the knightly virtue of munificence. The image shows Griselda, not driven to misery by her spouse, but lavished with benefits in the end (fig. 46)—for Hedeman "a complement to Étienne Chevalier himself who may have seen himself mirrored in the scene of munificence."[52]

In light of this social assessment, the comparison with Philip the Good of Burgundy seems inadmissible only from the strict perspective of a nobility fixated on origin: after all, the duke belonged to the House of Valois. But the *Grand Duc d'Occident* was not a king, and in his striving for a royal crown, his son Charles the Bold showed how vehemently Burgundy regretted this gap.[53] For this reason, the way in which the two dukes of Burgundy employed progressive art to advance their agenda differs decisively from the attitude of their tradition-bound relatives at the French court.

Since it can hardly be coincidental that both Étienne Chevalier and Philip the Good adopted the "e&e" in the 1450s, forming their monograms with only the first and last letters of *Étienne* or the first and last vowel of Ph*elipp*e, let us return once more to the tempting association with the "e" in the *Wenceslas Bible*. The invocation of a rare

and noble word of highest ethical value—one that came, moreover, from a foreign culture ennobled by the imperial court—may represent the culmination of the tendency manifested in the double page of the Hours of the Virgin in the *Hours of Étienne Chevalier*: the treasurer of France, who lacks only the gold on his robe in order to belong to the highest sphere, seeks to leave behind the social limitations that he deems already to have practically overcome in his service to the king.

Though in a different way than the *nouveau-riche* Chevalier—who came from the class of jurists, financial officials, and councilmen without aristocratic legitimation—Philip the Good pursued a similar goal. With his "e," he too endorsed the highest ethical principles. Étienne Chevalier, however, insisted that his art monumentalize him in an even more overwhelming way than the duke of Burgundy. For this reason, we should observe him as he prays in front of the Berlin-Antwerp diptych, holding his book of hours in his hand.

1   Many thanks to Élisabeth Antoine, Tony Deimling, and Christine Seidel for advice and assistance.

2   See the volume by Dominic Olariu from 2004, with contributions by Albert Châtelet and myself, as well as König 1987.

3   *Traité de l'oraison dominicale*, after 1454; Brussels, KBR, ms. 9092, fol. 9. For Châtelet 2009, fig. 8, p. 164, images of suppliants are surrogates for their presence, as if the portrait could pray on behalf of the person represented. For the manuscript, see Cat. Los Angeles/ London 2003, no. 34, pp. 220-221.

4   Precedents include the miniatures in Berry's *Belles Heures* (New York, Cloisters), where a servant draws back a curtain to reveal a praying woman (fol. 91v) as well as a praying man (fol. 91); König 2004, p. 83, figs. pp. 85, 43.

5   Jean de Berry's *Brussels Hours* shows the duke with patron saints in grisaille on the verso and the Madonna on the recto; Brussels, KBR, Ms. 11060-61, pp. 10-11; Meiss 1967 speaks of "The Initial Diptych" (pp. 202-208). Cat. Paris 2004, no. 45, pp. 109-111 and fig. 25. The tradition leads to the *Hours of Louis de Laval*; Paris, BnF, latin 920, fol. 50v-51; Avril in Cat. 2003, no. 52; most recently Seidel 2017, pp. 26-28 and 53-58.

6   Chantilly, Musée Condé, Ms. 70; most recently Reynaud 2006, no. 4-5, pp. 39-45.

7   Godefroy 1661, pp. 885-886; additional material in the Godefroy manuscript Ms. 241, fol. 385, in the Bibl. de l'Institut, Paris; Schaefer 1975, pp. 98-99.

8   According to Châtelet 2009, pp. 160-161.

9   After speaking in summary fashion of the houses of noble lords, Guillebert des Mets (Le Roux de Lincy 1855) explains at the end of Ch. xxv: "Entre lesquelx estoit l'ostel de sire Mille Baillet en la Voirrie, qui estoit tresorier du roy; ou quel hostel estoit une chappelle où l'en célébroit chascun jour l'office divin… si y avoit des voirières autant qu'il a des jours en l'an" (p. 69, and in the commentary by Le Roux de Lincy, pp. XLI¯XLII). Schaefer 2000, p. 294, makes reference to Champion 1931, p. 146.

10 Fouquet surpasses the *sacra conversazione* by Fra Angelico (Museo di San Marco, Florence) as well as Domenico Veneziano's *Santa Lucia de'*

Magnoli Altarpiece of 1446 (Uffizi). Most closely related is Andrea del Castagno's *Last Supper* in the refectory of Sant'Apollonia in Florence.

11 Members of the royal council wore long robes if they did not belong to the nobility, in contrast to the *gens de robe courte* such as the duke of Burgundy.

12 Homobonus appears in the Basilika of the Bode Museum in a *Sacra Conversazione* painted by Bartolomeo Montagna in 1500 (or 1515) from the collection of the Gemäldegalerie in Berlin.

13 As noted in Reynaud 2006, p. 42 n. 4.

14 Paris, Musée Jacquemart-André, Ms. 2; Meiss 1968, fig. 1-42; it is especially noticeable in the tent where the Virgin is crowned by Christ (fol. 95v; ibid., Fig. 36) as well as in the tapestries surrounding the theophany for the Hours of the Trinity (fol. 118v; Fig. 39). The heraldry of the marshal Boucicaut, however, is disfigured, since Aymar de Poitiers had the marshal's coat of arms largely overpainted with his own crude colors at the end of the 15th century. See also Châtelet 2000, pp. 216-319.

15 Étienne Chevalier has never been studied in detail, and the literature has contented itself with minimal evidence; see Förstel 2008. The anonymous French article in Wikipedia is unusually well-researched.

16 Paris, BnF, Dép. des Estampes, Rés Pe-11a, fol. 47; individual images without decorative context; Paris, BnF, Dép. des Estampes, Oa 15, fol. 16-17; Schaefer 1975, Fig. 3.

17 Since in 1426 Chevalier is referred to as MAISTRE, i.e. Master, his birth year would have to fall shortly after 1400, as noted in Schaefer 1975, p. 7.

18 Favier 2001, p. 112.

19 During that period his signature is more frequent than virtually any other member of the council, as Gaussin 1982 explains and Contamine 2017, p. 403, summarizes.

20 Courcelles 1824, pp. 2-3; most recently Contamine 2017, p. 281.

21 *Ordonnances des rois de France de la troisième race*, Vol. XV, p. 11.

22 Jean de Montauban owned books of hours that contrast in the most glaring way with those of Fouquet, such as the extraordinarily splendid lat. 18026 in the BnF in Paris, most recently Cat. Paris 1993, no. 93; in 2001, the library of Rennes was able to acquire a second, hitherto unknown example (Ms. 1834).

23 Vaesen, Charavay 1895, pp. 183-184, n. 1.

24 The Abbé Bertin, who visited Melun in 1717, did not even consider Chevalier a surname, and identified the person buried there and represented in the Berlin picture only as Étienne (*Extraits du carnet de voyage de l'Abbé Bertin*, Paris, BnF, fr. 8224, p. 556; Schaefer 1975, p. 13).

25 The identification of Dreux Budé and his wife as the patrons of a crucifixion triptych is based on this coat of arms (d'argent au chevron de gueules, accompagné de trois grappes de raisins); Sterling 1990, pp. 54-75; the panels are divided between the J. Paul Getty Museum in Los Angeles, the Louvre, and the Musée Fabre in Montpellier. A grisaille in a French private collection shows a variation of the woman from the right wing; Sterling 1990, pp. 50-53.

26 London, BL, Add. Ms. 16997, fol. 90; Cat. Paris 2003, no. 25, pp. 218-219.

27 Reynaud 2006, no. 28, pp. 136-141, with fig. p. 137.

28 As indicated by Reynaud 2006, p. 18; the second case she mentions is not so clear, since taken by itself the rather unsuccessful "E&e" in the small initial for the *Visitation* (there no. 6, pp. 46-49, fig. p. 47) could also be read as "E&c."

29 Meiss 1967, pp. 95ff. discusses this legend, quoting the twelve verses from the *Cuer d'amours espris* after Smital, Winkler 1926, II, pp. 101ff.

30 Zink 2004, p. 35; it should be noted, however, that Zink's book does not present itself as a philological study, but rather numbers among the author's remarkable poetic attempts to make medieval ideas comprehensible and accessible to a broader public.

31 Huon le Roi describes the small "e" as follows: "N'a de lonc gaires ne de lé/ Petit et corbé le veés." ("it is neither very long nor very wide, you see it as small and curved"); Zink 2004, p. 35.

32 "Mainte dolors commence en E./ Vous entendés bien que sans E/ Ne pourroit nus nommer Evain; En cest mont somes par E vain" ("Much sorrow begins with E; You understand that no one could be called Eve

without E; in this world the E makes us mortal"—here, for the sake of the rhyme, the hybrid male name Evain is used, perhaps even in analogy to Yvain from the Round Table of King Arthur); Zink 2004, p. 36.

33 Philip's third wife, Isabella of Portugal (1397-1471), survived the duke by four years.

34 Rapp-Buri, Stucky-Schürer, pp. 129-132 with illustrations on p. 130 of the ivory *Throne-of- Grace Trinity* and the court goblet from the Weltliche Schatzkammer in Vienna.

35 Rapp-Buri, Stucky-Schürer 2001, pp. 118, 440, n. 420.

36 Rapp-Buri, Stucky-Schürer 2001, pp. 115-143, esp. pp. 129-132.

37 Drawing in Rapp-Buri, Stucky-Schürer 2001, fig. 124, p. 132.

38 For this book of hours, which is divided between the national library in Madrid (Ms. Vit. 25-5), the Kupferstichkabinett in Berlin (78 B 13), and the Philadelphia Museum of Art (No. 343), see Cat. Los Angeles/ London 2003, no. 20, as well as my essay König 2013.

39 Florens Deuchler in Cat. Bern 1963, passim; echoed by Francis Salet in a review in the *Bulletin monumental* CXXII, 1964, p. 122.

40 Vienna, ÖNB, cod. 2759-2764; Gresch 2003; for the Bible, see Jenni, Theisen text volume pp. 158–212 (no. 5), illustration and index volume fig. 144-192.

41 The association is clearest in the work of Auguste Rodin, whose statue of a youth became famous under the title *L'Age d'airain*. In the context of Bismarck's reputation as the "Iron Chancellor," however, the work also alludes to the *Age de bronze*, considered the nobler of the Ages of Man.

42 *Grandes Chroniques*, Paris, BnF, fr. 6465, fol. 441-444v; most recently Cat. Paris 2003, no. 26, fig. pp. 244-246.

43 New approaches, as well as the most important sources, are presented in Villela-Petit 2003; in this regard, see my older perspective in König 2007, pp. 31-38. Objections to the notion of two painters named Haincelin, however, are still current, as in Rouse and Rouse 2000, II, pp. 73ff.; see König 2017.

44 Cambridge/Mass., Houghton Library, MS Richardson 31; most recently Cat. Boston 2016, no. 187. Christine Seidel was kind enough to remind me of this manuscript.

45 London, British Library, Ms. H.Y. Thompson 3; most recently Châtelet 2008.

46 In Cat. Paris 1993, p. 36, Nicole Reynaud first made the suggestion, now generally accepted, that the artist whom Eleanor Spencer had referred to as the "Bedford chief associate" be designated as the Dunois Master.

47 This painter's work appears, for example, in the Brussels copy of the *Horloge de Sapience*; Spencer 1963; see Cat. Paris 1993, pp. 38-45, as well as König 2017, nos. 22-23.

48 Paris, Louvre; Sterling 1990, pp. 36-49, although there the piece is attributed to an artist from Tournai working in Paris, whom Sterling would like to identify with Louis le Duc; Lorentz 2004; for the date, see also McKendrick 2007.

49 Paris, BnF, fr. 19819; Cat. Paris 2003, no. 29.

50 Munich, BSB, cod. gall. 6; Cat. Paris 2003, no. 32. The obvious contrast between the image of the *Lit de justice de Vendôme*—prefaced to the manuscript and independent of the text— and the rest of the illuminations inspired Avril in this catalogue to attribute only the full-page miniature to Jean Fouquet and to identify another artist besides him, the "Master of the Munich Boccaccio," a close associate and probably his son. He then attributed the Fouquet- esque miniatures in the *Antiquités Judaïques* to this same painter, although these are the only works documented for Jean Fouquet himself in a note from the 15th century. Consequently, the enamel with the self-portrait from the frame of the *Melun Diptych* assumes a decisive role in the identification of the painter's hand (see the essay by Élisabeth Antoine in this volume).

51 Seidel 2017, above all pp. 126-208.

52 Cat. Boston 2016, p. 223.

53 On these efforts, see most recently the multiple editions, in different languages, of Cat. Bern/Bruges/Vienna 2008/09, Ch. 4, on the duke's meeting with Emperor Frederick III.

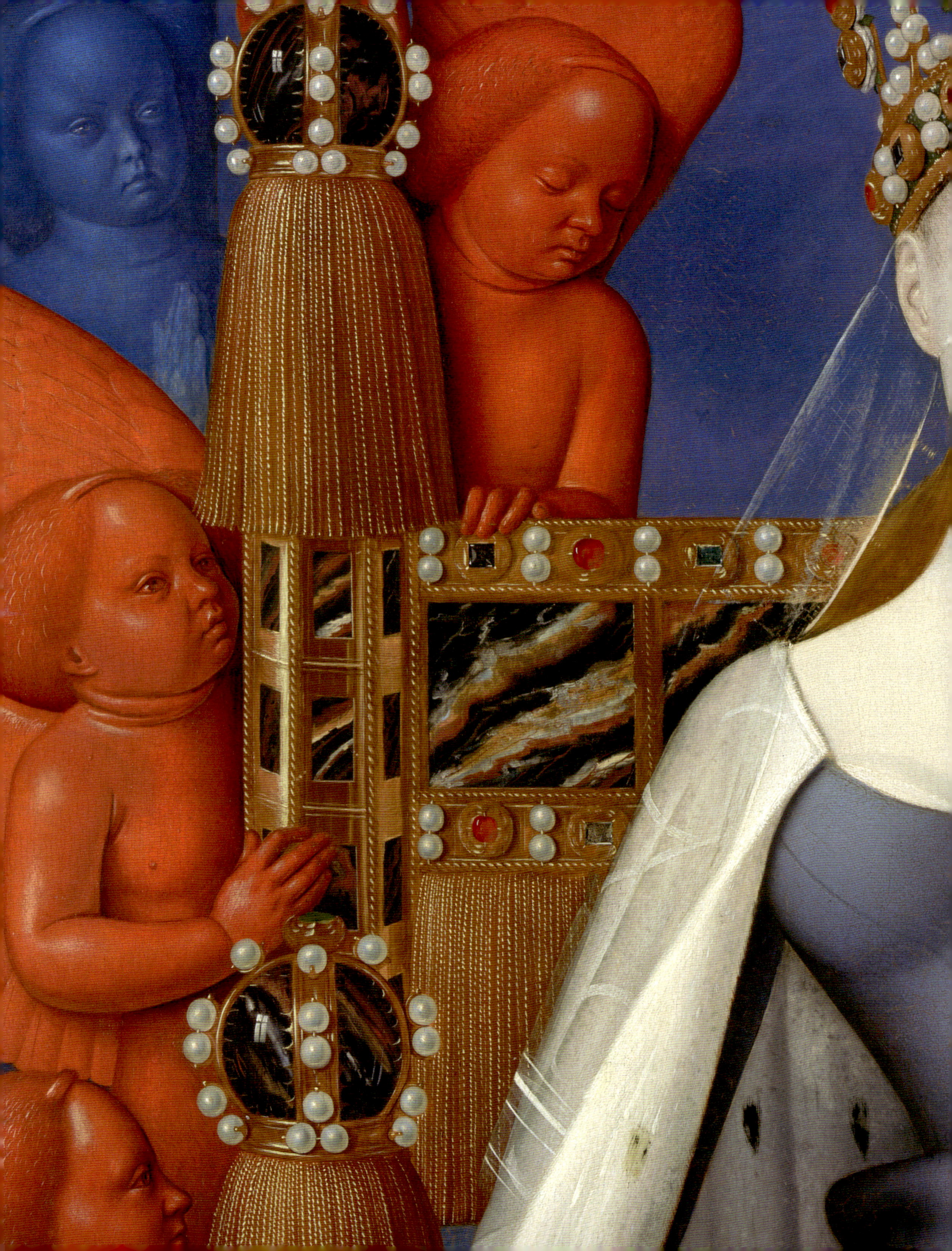

Brigitte Kurmann-Schwarz

REGINA ANGELORUM ET MISERICORDIAE – ICONOGRAPHY AND ICONOGRAPHIC MODELS OF THE MADONNA IN FOUQUET'S *MELUN DIPTYCH*

To this day, few sacred images are as disconcerting to the modern viewer as the Madonna of the *Melun Diptych*. With her tightly corseted wasp-waist, her high, domed, fashionably shaved forehead, and her white skin, the Virgin appears as a delicate half-figure turning slightly toward the right, as if the viewer, like Étienne Chevalier's patron saint in the donor panel, were looking at her frontal figure from the left at a slight angle. While the heavy drapery makes it difficult to tell whether the Virgin is seated or standing, the Child's seated position in the folds of her white mantle indicates that his Mother must have lowered herself into the partially visible throne. Wearing a delicate, transparent veil and a heavy crown, she inclines her head to gaze at the Christ Child. The laces of her bodice are loosened and her left breast is exposed, as if she were preparing to nurse. The Child, however, gazes attentively toward the left wing of the diptych, pointing to the donor panel with the outstretched index finger of his left hand. His gaze and gesture set in motion a dialogue between the painted figures in both panels, across the barrier of the frame that once separated them.

The sacred pair are surrounded by child-like angels in red and blue, whose colors identify them as the highest hierarchies of the nine choirs of angels. The red seraphim bear the throne, while the blue cherubim raise their hands adoringly to the Mother of God and the Child. The inward curve of the throne to the Virgin's right indicates that her seat is a *sella curulis*—a folding chair with X-shaped legs. Polished onyx, pearls, gems set in gold, and golden tassels adorn the backrest of the throne. The spheres crowning the vertical elements of the throne to the right of the Virgin show reflections of a window with crossbars. Reflected light also gleams on the rounded bodies of the angels, as if they were three-dimensional sculptures fashioned of a hard, polished material. The form of the Madonna with her domed forehead and spherical breasts, the plump body of the Christ Child, and the voluminous folds of the garments are all reminiscent of sculptural figures, with body parts approximating basic geometric forms.

The following discussion of the Antwerp *Virgin and Child* will take this sculptural quality as a point of departure and will explore the role of the precious ornamentation both of the Virgin and of her throne. In addition, questions related to the iconographic tradition of this extraordinary image of Mary will also be addressed, including the motif of the displaying of the breast and the Virgin's rank as the Queen of Angels. As we will see, the diptych was commissioned in connection with Étienne Chevalier's decision to be buried in the church of Notre-Dame of Melun; thus the patron's choice of pictorial motifs must be understood in the context of intercession for the salvation of his soul. As a high-ranking official, moreover, Chevalier was intimately acquainted with the prevailing artistic taste at court, a fact which helps explain his ambitions for the aesthetic form and iconography of the diptych. Finally, the artistic devices that characterize the Madonna as a sacred image in the medieval tradition will be investigated, along with the painting's reception since the early modern period.

Albert Châtelet and other authors were struck by the sculpture-like appearance of the Virgin, leading them to suggest that in this painting, Étienne Chevalier was depicted praying not in front of Mary herself, but in front of her image.[1] And in fact most mid-15th-century images of the Virgin and Child north of the Alps were indeed sculptures, painted and often covered in metal.[2] Although patron and artist chose a version of the Madonna unusual for their time, their intent was to remain within the tradition of sculptural representations of the Virgin and Child. In this respect, Jean Fouquet was not alone: as Jeffrey F. Hamburger has shown,[3] Netherlandish painters, too, legitimated their innovative paintings by invoking the tradition of Marian statues and reliquaries. The three-dimensional bodies of painted Madonnas seem like sculptures, while their garments, richly adorned with gold and precious stones, resemble the containers that held the relics of the saints.[4] These artists further enhanced the complexity of their images by combining naturalism with symbolic meaning.[5] Jean Fouquet, too, visualized the extraordinary sanctity of his pictorial subject by alluding to older media and their particular aesthetic, as well as by reproducing in paint the precious materiality of such objects.

In the case of the Antwerp *Virgin and Child*, Châtelet has identified the motif of the *Sedes sapientiae* as determinative for Fouquet's painting.[6] This image type, which was usually carved in wood (less often in stone) and painted, emerged toward the end of the first millennium[7] and was widely used for seated figures of the Madonna in the Middle Ages and beyond. In its early form, which continued on into the later Middle Ages in some regions, the image has a severe, static effect; yet despite its aloofness, it was so valued by the faithful that it has survived in great numbers to the present day.[8] More than any other motif, it represented the mystery of the Incarnation, the event that set in motion the divine plan of salvation, and showed the Blessed Mother—whom theologians identified with the Church—as the throne of the God-Man Christ. The sculptural group thus played the role of intermediary between contemporary viewers praying for help and the sacred personages in heaven who were embodied in the sculpture.[9]

From the beginning, the image of the *Sedes sapientiae* included variations showing the Child frontally enthroned on his Mother's lap or seated at an angle to her left,[10] as for example in the Imad-Madonna in Paderborn (ca. 1060)[11] or the Madonna from the Cluniac priory church of Saint-Martin-des-Champs in Paris (ca. 1135, now in Saint-Denis, fig. 48).[12] The version embodied in these two examples was also adopted by Jean Fouquet for the Antwerp *Virgin and Child*. The spheres decorating the backrest of the throne likewise connect Fouquet's painting to the oldest known seated figures in sacred sculpture, such as the figural reliquary of St. Foy in Conques (ca. 1000)[13] or the statue of Notre-Dame-sous-Terre in the cathedral of Chartres (ca. 1029), which was destroyed in 1793.[14]

In contrast to the cathedra-like throne of the earliest seated figures, Fouquet depicts the Virgin on a *faldistorium* with back- and armrests, the folding seat of ancient dignitaries. Although this form occurs only seldom north of the Alps,[15] it had constituted a status symbol of rulership ever since the early Middle Ages, as evidenced by

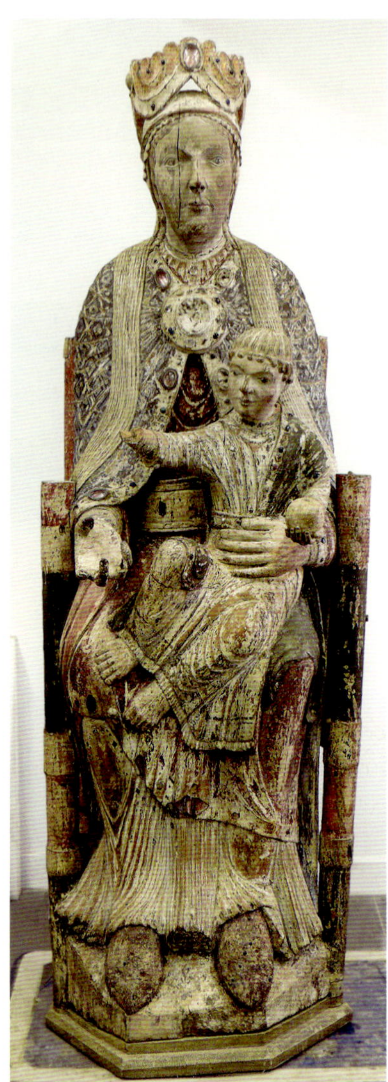

Fig. 48. Seated Virgin from the Cluniac priory church of Saint-Martin-des-Champs, Paris, ca. 1135, Saint-Denis, Basilique

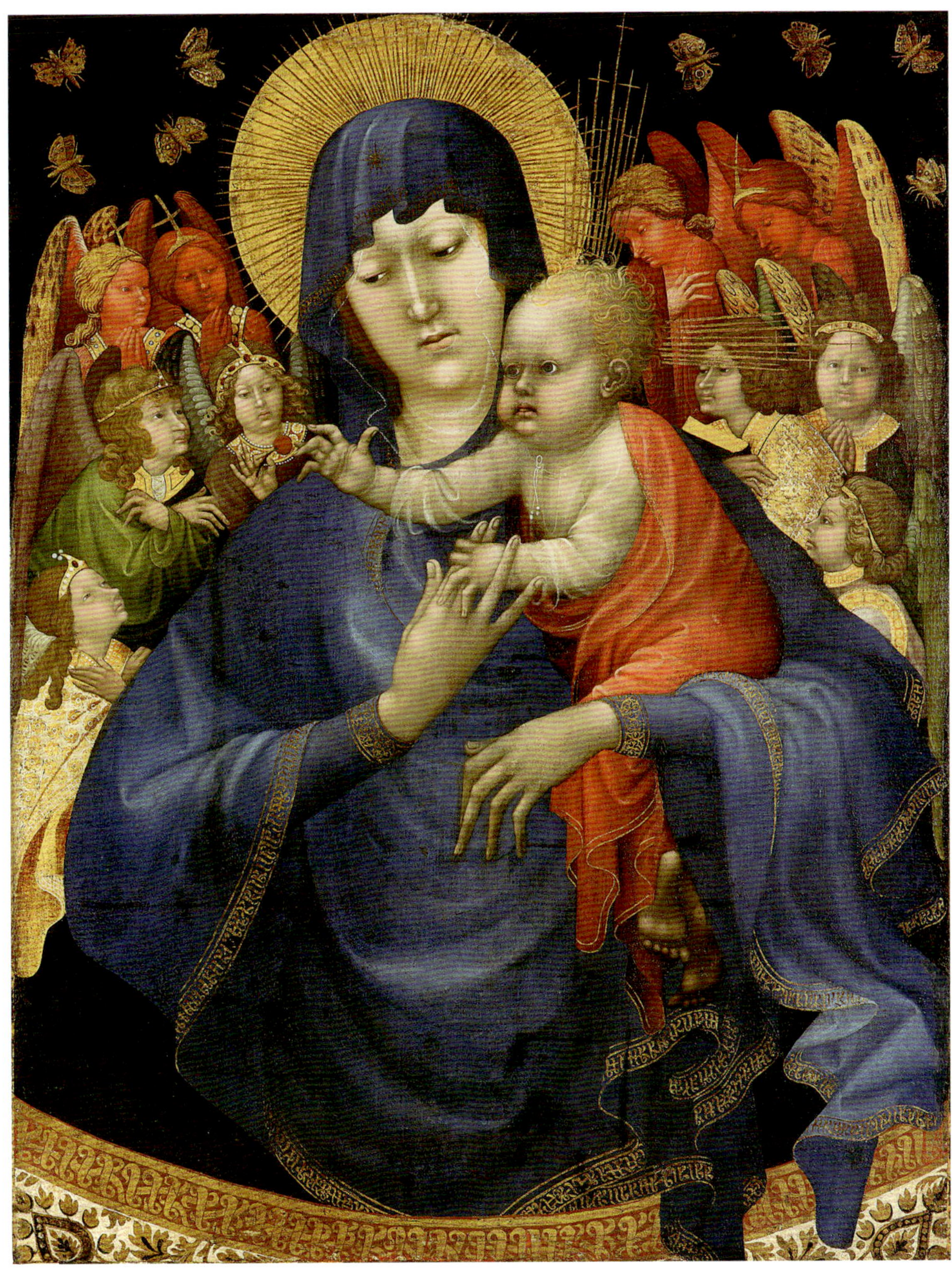

Fig. 49. Jean Malouel (?), *Virgin with Butterflies (Virgin and Child with Angels)*, ca. 1410-1415, Berlin, Gemäldegalerie

the so-called Throne of Dagobert. The latter, a precious object fashioned of gilt bronze, also includes spherical forms atop the back- and armrests of the throne, some of which are shaped like heads.[16] Closer to Fouquet's time, the archbishop's throne in the cathedral of York was also supplied with decorative fringes like those on the throne in the Antwerp *Virgin and Child*.[17] Visual representations of King Charles V frequently show him seated on this kind of throne.[18] Jean Fouquet himself depicted the royal *faldistorium* multiple times in the *Grandes Chroniques de France*.[19] Quite obviously, it was considered a sign of royal dignity in medieval France, and along with the crown, costly garments, and ermine-lined mantle, emphasized the Virgin's rank as the Queen of Heaven.[20]

In his painting, however, Fouquet not only invoked the tradition of the Mother of God as the Queen of Heaven in the form of the *Sedes sapientiae*, but also embraced a new pictorial type. Since 1400, half-figure panel paintings of the Madonna had become an established type north of the Alps; presumably, imported icons were the inspiration for this motif.[21] Until now, scholars have assumed that Fouquet knew the motif of the half-figure Virgin and Child with angels from Italy; Châtelet and others pointed to reliefs of the Madonna by Bernardo and Antonio Rossellino as well as the putti on Donatello's *Cantoria* in the cathedral of Florence.[22] The design of Italian marble reliefs was also used to explain the absence of illusionistic space, the unusually white skin of the figures, and the *sella curulis* in the Antwerp *Virgin and Child*.[23] At the same time, however, it has also been rightly emphasized

that in contrast to the Italian reliefs, Fouquet shows the Virgin positioned almost frontally. Thus the painter did not simply reproduce Italian models, but was also inspired by French images of the Virgin familiar to him. The same is generally also assumed for the red and blue angels, which are traced back to late Gothic manuscript and glass painting such as the stained glass created for Jacques Coeur in the cathedral of Bourges (1451),[24] where God the Father appears in a corona of fiery angels along with blue heavenly musicians.

Jean Fouquet was not the first artist at a French court to use the motif of a monumental half-figure Madonna. Nicole Reynaud has called attention to the *Butterfly Madonna (Virgin and Child with Angels)* in the Gemäldegalerie in Berlin (fig. 49),[25] which is attributed to the Burgundian court painter Jean Malouel and is one of the oldest surviving paintings on canvas.[26] Although the Berlin painting differs from the Antwerp *Virgin and Child* in its presentation of the Mother of God as a standing figure,[27] the two Madonnas are cropped in a similar manner, and Malouel's painting has approximately the same dimensions as Fouquet's panel. The two Madonnas also resemble one another in their frontal poses, as well as other aspects of the iconography: like Fouquet, the older painter shows Mary surrounded by angels, four of whom are identified as seraphim by their red color, while the rest are assigned to the other eight choirs by their varying diadems.[28] The superior quality of the Berlin *Butterfly Madonna* suggests a high-ranking patron, perhaps Duke John the Fearless of Burgundy.[29]

Another feature shared by the Madonnas in Berlin and Antwerp is the painterly rendering of goldsmiths' work. While in Malouel's painting the representation of precious metalwork is confined to the diadems of the angels, in Fouquet's panel both the throne and the Virgin herself are adorned with gold and jewels. The reflection of a real window in the Virgin's throne confirms the interpretation that the patron is praying before an image of the Madonna; as we will see, however, Fouquet's intentions go beyond the mere material representation of an image.

The precious stones and pearls that adorn the throne (fig. 47) have rarely been analyzed in depth. Yet as mentioned above, it is clear that Fouquet associated his painting with the aesthetics of goldwork, above all of reliquar-

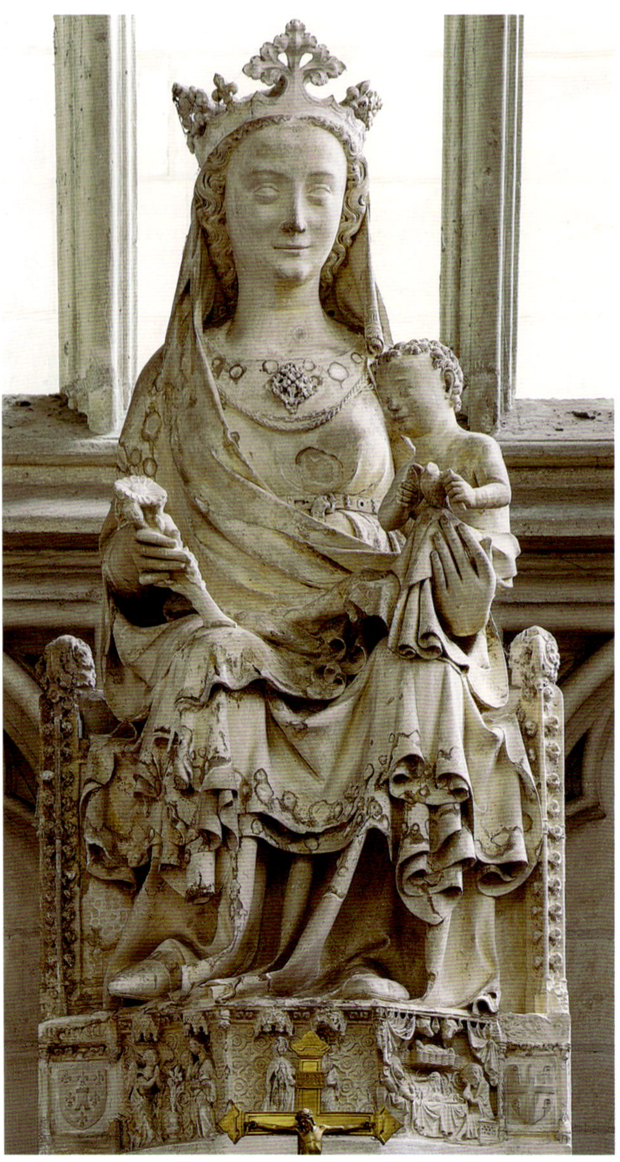

Fig. 50. Madonna of Manuel de Jaune, 1334, Sens Cathedral, Chapel of Notre Dame

ies.[30] This aspect does not necessarily represent an innovation on the part of 15th-century painters, for earlier *Sedes sapientiae* figures like the above-mentioned Virgin from Saint-Martin-des-Champs in Paris (fig. 48) had been richly decorated with gems. The ornamentation of this statue evokes precious silk fabrics, while glass paste decorated the borders of the Virgin's tunic as well as her mantle, which is fastened with an oversize fibula. The heavy crown of the Mother of God is likewise ornamented with glass paste. The rich decoration of many seated Madonna figures not only emphasized her rank as the Queen of Heaven, but also frequently reflected the function of such statues as reliquaries.[31] An important example of the continuation of the tradition of the *Sedes sapientiae* as reliquary into the late Middle Ages is the carved stone figure of the enthroned Virgin from the Chapel of Notre Dame in Sens Cathedral, dated to 1334 (fig. 50). It was once painted in color, gilded, and decorated with gem-like, figurally painted glass paste, and stood in a painted shrine. Changes in the 16th century and a radical restoration in the 19th century destroyed this splendor, so that now only the indentations for the glass paste are visible on the bare stone figure.[32] As the examples in Saint-Denis and Sens show, the conspicuous representation of precious and semiprecious stones, pearls, and goldwork in the Antwerp *Virgin and Child* not only emphasizes the painter's exceptional skill in the illusionistic rendering of precious materials, but at the same time connects the painting with objects that were highly venerated or contained the relics of the saints.

The unusually white skin of both Mary and the Child in the Antwerp panel points in the same direction. The white is reminiscent not only of marble sculpture, but also of the courtly gold and enamel sculptures known as *émail sur ronde-bosse d'or*.[33] No other medium combined plasticity and preciousness in such an ideal way as these enameled gold figures, which were pieced together into three-dimensional images called *joyaux*, or gems. Fouquet and Étienne Chevalier could have known such objects, for around 1450 they were probably still present in large numbers in church treasuries and aristocratic collections. Like the Antwerp *Virgin and Child*, the figures on the *Goldenes Rössl* in Altötting (1405),[34] the *Holy Thorn Reliquary* in the British Museum (ca. 1400),[35] or the *Chocques Triptych* in the Rijksmuseum (ca. 1390-1400)[36]—to men

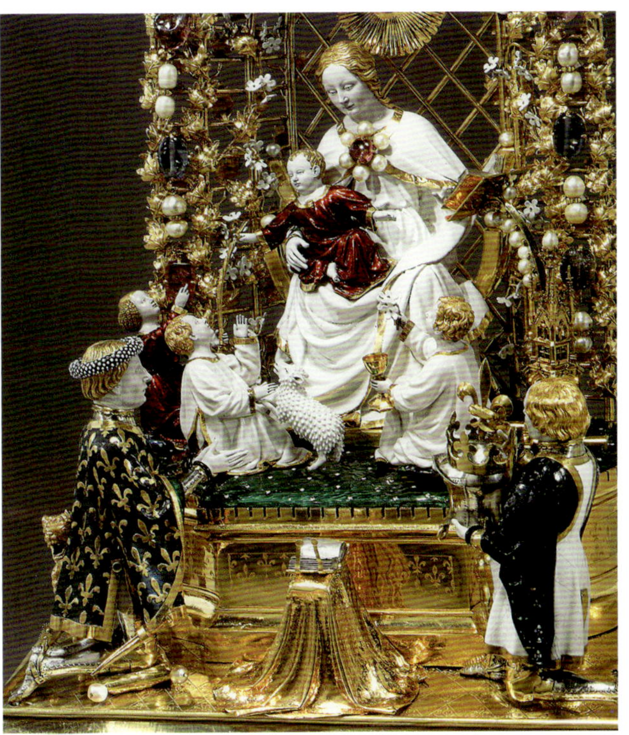

Fig. 51. Virgin and Child from the *Goldenes Rössl*, Paris, 1405, Altötting, Kapellstiftung, Treasury of the Heilige Kapelle

tion only especially spectacular examples—show the flesh tones in pure white. In addition, the *Goldenes Rössl* and the *Holy Thorn Reliquary* are richly adorned with pearls and gemstones. Despite the chronological and stylistic differences, the parallels between the Madonna of the *Goldenes Rössl* (fig. 51) and the Antwerp *Virgin and Child* are striking, and pertain not only to the white skin tone, but also to the form of the throne, which in both cases is a *sella curulis*.[37] In its relation to these gold and enamel sculptures, the remarkable aesthetic of the panel painting once again establishes a connection to some of the most sacred objects associated with the saints and venerated by the faithful. Even if the Melun Virgin strongly resembled the secular ladies of the royal court by virtue of her figure type, her pale complexion, the form of her clothing, and her crown, it was precisely these same characteristics that pointed to a sacred context closely linked to the understanding of salvation.[38] This association likewise explains the motif of the displaying of the breast and the representation of Mary as the Queen of Angels.

The modern viewer is taken aback by the fashionable details of clothing and hairstyle as well as by the displaying of the breast, the *ostentatio uberum*. In ancient and medieval tradition, however, this gesture had nothing to do with fashionable demeanor, decadence, or even godlessness; rather, it was understood as a gesture of ardent pleading by women for the benefit of sons and husbands. Although scholars have known the significance of the display of the breast and its longstanding tradition, they have still had difficulty coming to terms with it. Some authors have resorted to embarrassed silence on the topic, while at the same time offering an extremely negative assessment of the picture as a whole, as is the case, for example, with Huizinga.[39] Others have viewed the Antwerp *Virgin and Child* as a portrait of King Charles VII's mistress Agnès Sorel,[40] whose lax standards of dress were decried above all by the chroniclers of the Burgundian court,

Fig. 52. Drawing of the Tomb slab of Étienne Chevalier and Catherine Budé in Notre-Dame of Melun, Paris, Bibliothèque nationale de France, Est. Pe II a, fol. 41

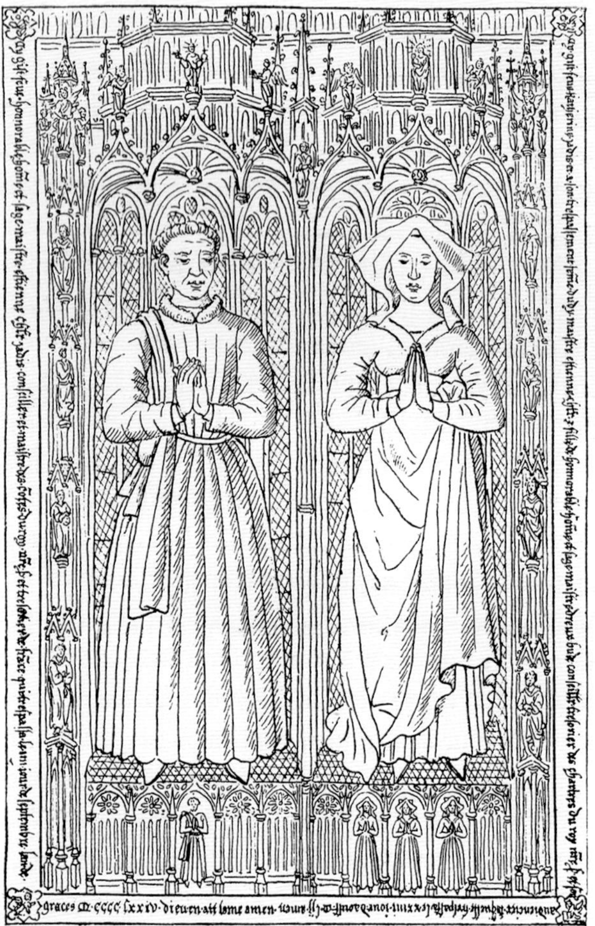

a source by no means sympathetic to the king.[41] Claude Schaefer is one of the few who has explored the connection between the *ostentatio uberum* and the provisions made by Étienne Chevalier for the salvation of his soul.[42] The chain of intercession represented on the diptych, which connects the patron's name saint Stephen with Mary and Christ,[43] as well as Chevalier's liturgical foundations, his brass epitaph, and the tomb panel with images of the treasurer and his wife Catherine Budé, who had died in 1452 (fig. 52)—all these demonstrate that the representation of the Virgin displaying her breast belongs in the context of liturgical intercession. Although Schaefer recognized this reference, in his opinion the *ostentatio uberum* motif in the *Melun Diptych* conveyed a different meaning than the motif of *Maria lactans* and images of intercession.[44] More recent studies of depictions of Mary displaying her breast, however, indicate that all three pictorial motifs are closely associated with ideas about salvation that would have been familiar to viewers at the time the diptych was created.[45]

In the Gospel of Luke (11:27), the mother of Christ is explicitly mentioned as the one who nursed the child Jesus at her breast. Thus based on the Evangelist's authority, the breasts of Mary were used beginning in early Christian times as an argument for the human as well as the divine nature of the Savior.[46] Since Christ needed his mother's milk, he must have had a truly human body. Throughout all periods of church history, the humanity of Christ, his human suffering and dying, has been central to the Christian understanding of salvation; written sources on this theme date as far back as the second and third centuries. It took longer, however, for this argumentation to gain widespread representation in visual images.[47] The nursing Mother of God first appeared above all in the art of the Eastern Church; not until the 12th and 13th centuries did it become common in the pictorial media of the West.[48] The earliest representations of the *ostentatio uberum* were made before the year 1300 in the context of the theme of judgment.

Among the many titles of the Mother of God, her identification as *Mater* and *Regina misericordiae*, Mother and Queen of Mercy, plays a central role in the present context.[49] As Maria Ecclesia, she bestows upon Christians the pure milk of mercy and intercedes for them at the judgment by reminding the stern judge of the breasts that

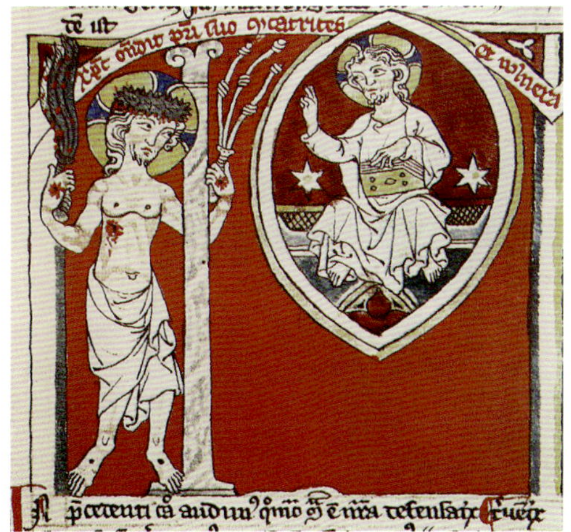
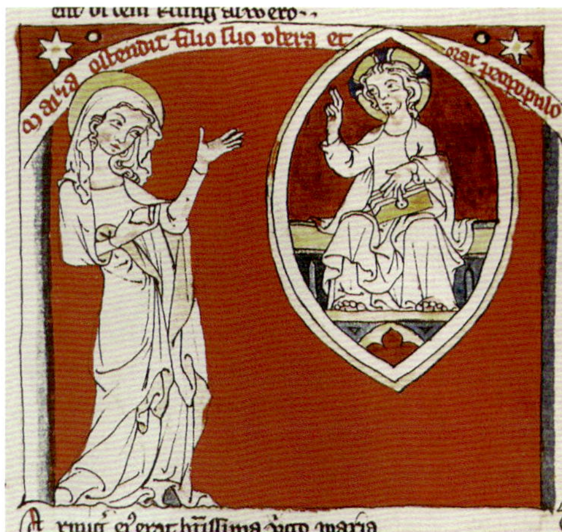

Fig. 53. The Intercession of the Virgin and Christ, from the *Speculum Humanae Salvationis*, ca. 1330, Kremsmünster, Benediktinerstift, Cod. Cremifanensis 243

nursed him. While the faithful of the Middle Ages may not have been familiar with the theological discussions, they still believed in an afterlife to which their souls would go after death. Whether they would go to heaven, purgatory, or hell until the final judgment was decided by Christ the judge.[50] All Christians, probably including Étienne Chevalier, awaited this event with great fear.[51] All their hopes were set on the Mother of Christ;[52] she displayed her breast in order to lend the greatest urgency to her plea for mercy.

The direct literary sources for the image originated in the 11th century. For Anselm of Canterbury, the Virgin is the refuge of sinners because she once nursed the judge at her breast.[53] A century later, Arnold of Chartres, abbot of Bonneval, first formulated the idea that Mary exposes her breast as she prays to her Son for humanity, and that the latter, in turn, reminds God the Father of his sacrifice by showing him his wounds.[54] Arnold's conception was translated into visual form in the *Speculum humanae salvationis*, an illustrated typological book composed in the early 14th century, and was widely disseminated among clergy and laity; the manuscript in Kremsmünster, for example, includes multiple depictions of the intercession of Christ and Mary (fig. 53). Already previously in his *Liber de laudibus Sanctae Mariae*, Richard of Saint-Laurent had come to the conclusion that no one can be against those for whom the Mother of God intercedes.[55] Sermons and vernacular poetry such as the *Advocacie Nostre Dame Sainte Marie* (ca. 1320) disseminated these ideas: in the *Advocacie*, Mary speaks the following words to the judge:

Ta mère suy, mère m'appeles
Beau fils, regarde les mameles
De quoi aleiter te souloie.[56]

The oldest images of the Virgin displaying her breast are found in English representations of the Last Judgment in the last quarter of the 13th century;[57] a little later, the motif appears in Italy[58] and the Upper Rhine.[59] A depiction of the intercession of Mary and Christ from the wing of an altarpiece by a painter from the workshop of Konrad Witz (fig. 54), created around the same time as the Antwerp *Virgin and Child* (ca. 1445-1450) and now in Basel, is particularly striking;[60] not only does Christ point to his wounds and Mary display her breast, but the Virgin also includes a female patron in the intercession, taking her by the hand.

In the first half of the 14th century, the motif of the interceding Virgin displaying her breast was already so familiar to French artists that the manuscript painter Jean Pucelle included it in a miniature of the *Miracle de Notre Dame* by Gauthier de Coincy around 1330, although the corresponding text does not mention it at all.[61] The story tells of the sudden death of a marauding knight: as his soul leaves his body, he is set upon by demons (fig. 55). But since the deceased man had been a fervent devotee of the Virgin his entire life, the Mother of God, together with the angels, prays to Christ for his soul. By displaying her breast, she lends such impetus to her request that her Son is moved to mercy. Hardly has the request been made when two angels intervene in the course of events and rescue the knight's soul from the hands of the demons.

The ardent intercession of Mary, manifested in the displaying of her breast, must also have been central to Étienne Chevalier's hope of salvation, and Fouquet intensifies the weight of the patron's request by showing it brought before the Queen of Angels. The latter title arose from the belief that angels had carried the Mother of God into heaven after her death.[62] Unlike the Ascension of Christ, the Assumption of the Virgin is not described in the biblical text and thus remained controversial until it was established as dogma in 1950. Basing their argument on St. Jerome and Dionysius the Areopagite, theologians as early as the Carolingian period (Paschasius Ratbertus, Paul the Deacon, and Ambrose Autpert) developed the foundations for the doctrine of the bodily assumption of Mary into heaven and her powerful position within the heavenly hierarchy.[63] Fouquet distilled the iconography of the coronation of the Virgin amid choirs of angels to its essence by reducing the heavenly hierarchy to two ranks of angels along with their Queen.[64] Although she is exalted, Mary's humble gaze toward her Child makes clear that she is subordinate to her Son and it is he who will judge the souls of the dead.[65]

Despite the reference to grand hierarchical compositions, the depiction of the Madonna and Child as half-figures—"zooming in" on them, as it were—and the child-like appearance of the angels emphasize the impression of intimacy. Sixten Ringbom has described this type of image as a "close up,"[66] bringing the viewer nearer to the holy per-

Fig. 54. Workshop of Konrad Witz, The Intercession of the Virgin and Christ, altarpiece wing, Basel, ca. 1445-1450, Basel, Kunstmuseum

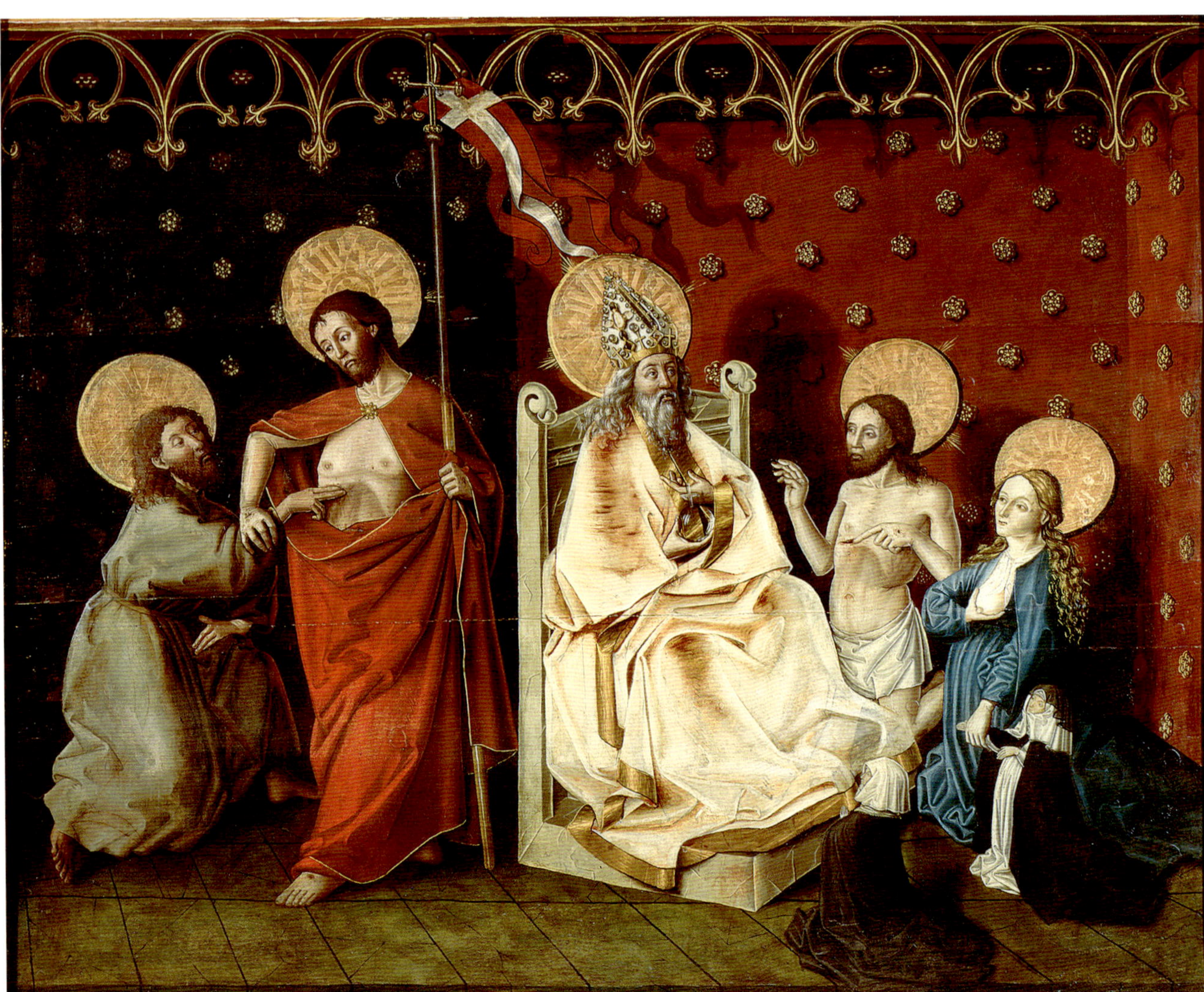

sonages. Although Ringbom was more concerned with narrative representations than with timeless images for veneration like the *Melun Diptych*, the latter was probably likewise intended to express the close proximity between viewer and saint.

If we return to high medieval examples of the *Sedes sapientiae*, we notice that in these sculpture groups, as in Jean Malouel's painting in Berlin, the Child is clothed. By the 14th century, however, he appears naked in most cases, or simply wrapped loosely in a cloth, as in the above-mentioned Madonna from the cathedral of Sens (fig. 50). The Child's nakedness, like the mother's milk which he as an infant needs, emphasizes Christ's human nature, which was given to the Savior by Mary.[67] The pointing gesture, on the other hand, identifies the child Jesus as God, who fulfills the promise of salvation to Étienne Chevalier. With his active motion, the Child transcends the mere imitation of a work of art and elevates the image of the Madonna and Child to the level of an apparition.

Fouquet's painting isolates the scene of Mary's effectual intercession before Christ, removing it from the context of general or individual judgment and transferring it to the realm of prayer for the salvation of a specific patron. The latter's name is chiseled onto a pillar of the room in which he appears with his patron saint, and the attention of the Christ Child is focused solely on him. Although Chevalier does not see the Savior—his gaze is directed forward at an angle, past the apparition on the right-hand panel—his inner eye perceives the scene observed by St. Stephen and the viewer of the diptych. Indeed, the diptych format offered the artist an ideal way to distinguish between the world of the suppliant and the sphere of the divine.[68] While the posture and gestures of the figures connect the two images, the internal structure of the two panels and the frame that once surrounded them separates the patron from the heavenly realm. Although the figures on the Antwerp panel seem almost tangible in their plasticity, both the frame and the figure of Mary create distance to the patron and viewer:[69] with an energetic gesture, the Virgin draws her white mantle protectively in front of her body, parallel to the picture plane, while the cape falling straight down from her right shoulder creates a barrier between her and the image of the patron.[70] The unnaturally bright skin of the Madonna and

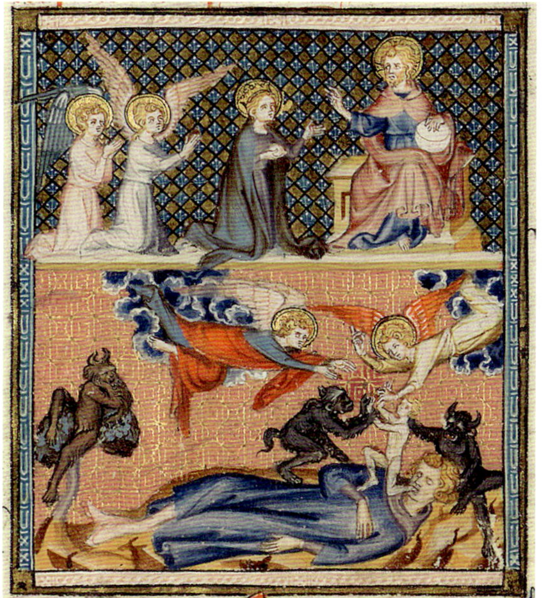

Fig. 55. Jean Pucelle, The Virgin interceding to save the soul of a suddenly deceased knight, from *The Miracles of Our Lady* by Gauthier de Coincy, ca. 1330, Paris, Bibliothèque nationale de France, ms. n. a. f. 24541, fol. 61v

Child likewise produces a feeling of distance from the viewer. Although Chevalier is in close proximity to the Mother of God, the form of the picture and the barriers built into the representation serve to divide him from the holy pair. These observations show that Fouquet based his image on medieval modes of representation, relying on the aesthetics of sculptures and reliquaries. His picture is intended to confront the viewer, not with a secular female ruler, but with the Queen of Angels and of Mercy in the heavenly realm—a truth that is higher and ultimately invisible.

Since the early 17th century, however, Fouquet's Madonna has been associated with an earthly person, with Agnès Sorel,[71] the mistress of King Charles VII. This opinion arose not only due to Fouquet's depiction of the Virgin in the clothing of a secular queen, but above all because of her exposed breast—the devotional significance of which has just been explained in detail. Fouquet's image of the Virgin was associated with the criticism leveled by the Burgundian chronicler Chastellain, who described the plunging necklines worn by the royal mistress.[72] Around the same time, the first criticisms were being directed at the motif of Mary displaying her breast and the religious understandings associated with it, and above all at the reliquaries of the Virgin's milk.[73] Finally, the Reformers of the first half of the 16th century not only condemned these objects, but also viewed the image of Mary with an exposed breast not as the promise of salvation, but as a scandal.[74] This example shows the degree to which even the motifs of sacred images can be products of their time.[75]

Initially, preachers and theologians of the post-Tridentine period defended the image of the Virgin interceding with exposed breast, since it was deeply anchored in the imagination of the people.[76] Yet even among Catholics, the naked female breast in the context of sacred images came to be viewed as an offence against religious decorum.[77] Thus since the 16th century, such images have conveyed a different message to their viewers than was previously the case. While in the Antwerp *Virgin and Child* the *ostentatio uberum* could still represent the Mother of God's ardent intercession for the salvation of humanity, in the age of confessionalism it increasingly became the object of suspicion—so much so that, unlike Jean Fouquet and his patron, who understood the image of Mary with exposed breast as the *Regina misericordiae*,[78] early modern viewers like Denis Godefroy could only conceive of the presumed portrait of the mistress of Charles VII as a reference to the Queen of Heaven.

1   Châtelet 1975, pp. 127-138. The differing approaches to the representation of space in the two panels led to the assumption that they had been created by different artists; Durrieu 1911, p. 731.

2   Belting 1990, pp. 331-345, 466.

3   Hamburger 2000, pp. 47-69.

4   Belting 1990, pp. 471-474.

5   Hamburger 2000, p. 52; Signori 2014, pp. 41-42.

6   Châtelet 1975, pp. 130.

7   Belting 1990, pp. 333-336.

8   Forsyth 1972, pp. 8-30. On the later development of the seated Madonna, cf. Le Pogam 2013, pp. 131-145.

9   Forsyth 1972, pp. 8-9, 22-30.

10   See the works listed in Forsyth 1972.

11   Endemann 2009 (2011), pp. 121-148.

12   Plagnieux 2013a, pp. 118-128; idem 2010, p. 208.

13   Fricke 2007, pp. 45-48, 52-56; Schramm 1954, pp. 353-354.

14   Delaporte, 1965, pp. 9-32. More recently, the image from Chartres has been assigned a later date, since it is first mentioned in documents from the late 14th century; Hediger, Kurmann-Schwarz 2014, pp. 141-142.

15   Gaborit 2013, p. 152.

16   Paris, Cabinet des Médailles; Schramm 1954, pp. 326-331, fig. 36. As Hoffmann 2004, p. 12, has most recently explained, the throne consists of an older *faldistorium* without a backrest, presumably made for Clovis I in 508, to which back- and armrests were added later.

17   Dervieu 1910, pp. 215-220; Milnes 1982, pp. 61-64.

18   Sterling 1987, pp. 187-192.

19   Paris, Bibliothèque nationale, ms. fr. 6465. See Avril, Gousset, Guenée 1987, pl. 21, 32, 41, 42.

20   On the tradition of the Virgin as the Queen of Heaven, see Russo 1996, pp. 203-208.

21   Reference is made to works such as the panel of Notre-Dame des Grâces in Cambrai, which the canon Fursy de Bruille brought back from Rome in 1440 and which was disseminated through copies in the 1450s; Belting 1990, pp. 490-492. Artists including Rogier van der Weyden made use of the half-figure Madonna; Cat. Washington/Antwerp 2006/07, pp. 246-263. The Madonna images by Rogier belonged to diptychs; Kemperdick 1999, pp. 105-111; De Vos 1999, pp. 111-116, 298-301, 305-307, 323-327.

22   If Fouquet had already returned to Tours in 1448, he could not have known the works mentioned in the literature—neither the tondo of the Madonna from the tomb of Leonardo Bruni in Santa Croce by Bernardo Rossellino, 1448-1450 (Poeschke 1990, p. 136, fig. 188), nor the relief of the Madonna by Antonio Rossellino, ca. 1465, New York (Langhanke 2013, pp. 220-231, fig. 72). In contrast to Fouquet's painting, the Christ Child in the Italian works is clothed; only the relief in San Clemente da Rignano from the late 1450s, attributed to Antonio Rossellino, likewise shows a naked Child; Langhanke 2013, pp. 199-208, fig. 66. On the *Cantoria*, 1433-1438, see Poeschke 1990, pp. 105-106.

23   Châtelet 1975, pp. 129-130. Châtelet makes reference above all to a relief in New York attributed to Antonio Rosselino; in terms of motif, however, Fouquet's painting is closer to the relief in San Clemente a Rignano (see n. 22).

24   Châtelet 1975, p. 128. Reynaud 1981, p. 21, makes reference to the book of hours from 1415/20 that was owned by Chevalier; London, British Library, Add. 16997, fol. 90 shows God the Father surrounded by red and blue angels (see fig. 44). Avril refers to manuscript illumination and stained glass in Cat. Paris 2003, p. 125, and explicitly to the stained glass in Bourges; Kurmann-Schwarz 1988, pp. 17-19, 30-33. For addenda on dating, see Kurmann- Schwarz 1999, pp. 143-149.

25   Reynaud 1981, p. 22.

26   Winkler 1959, p. 189; Meiss, Eisler 1960, pp. 239-240; Lorentz 2004, pp. 96-98; Roelofs 2005, pp. 48-51; Schmidt 2008, pp. 20-29, who also refutes the reconstruction of the piece as the right wing of a diptych; Cat. Rotterdam 2012, pp. 128-129 (Katrin Dyballa).

27   Like the older Virgins in Bohemia, e.g. the Raudnitz Madonna, ca. 1390, or the Westphalian Fröndenberg Virgin, ca. 1410 (Museum Dortmund); Belting 1990, pp. 484-490.

28   Schmidt 2008, p. 22, with reference to Bruderer Eichberg 1998, pp. 62-67, 83-85.

29   The duke traveled frequently, which may explain the use of lightweight canvas for the painting; Schmidt 2008, pp. 26-27.

30   Hamburger 2000, pp. 50-53.

31   Forsyth 1972, pp. 31-38.

32   Kurmann-Schwarz 2017, pp. 313-317.

33   Eikelmann 1995a, pp. 112-130.

34   Eikelmann 1995b, pp. 52-57.

35   Eikelmann 1995a, p. 118.

36   Taburet-Delahaye 2004, pp. 170-171.

37   See also Kahsnitz 1995, pp. 68-69.

38   Hamburger 2000, pp. 47-52.

39   In his 1919 book *The Waning of the Middle Ages*, Johan Huizinga articulated his unease over the Antwerp panel as follows: "... the Madonna is, in fact, represented here according to the canons of contemporary fashion: there is the bulging shaven forehead, the rounded breasts, placed high and wide apart, the high and slender waist. The bizarre inscrutable expression of the Madonna's face, the red and blue cherubim surrounding her, all contribute to give this painting an air of decadent impiety (...)." He ends with the comment: "There is a flavor of blasphemous boldness about the whole, unsurpassed by any artist of the Renais-

sance." Huizinga 1999, pp. 142-143. Schreiner 2011, p. 227, likewise wonders whether the picture was based on the sexual fantasies of monks, but comes to the conclusion that not every religious feeling has to be interpreted erotically. Miles 2008, pp. 47-48, on the other hand, emphasizes this aspect and refers to depictions of the Virgin with naked breasts as "men's images"; accordingly, she stresses the erotic content of the Antwerp *Virgin* (ibid., p. 83).

40 Most recently Cat. Paris 2003, pp. 128-129.

41 Henzler 2012, p. 57, quoting Georges Chastellain. The author makes a convincing case that the king's mistress, who came from the lower nobility, violated the courtly dress code with her wardrobe. One must also take into account that reports about the French court from the pen of a Burgundian historiographer would have been less than objective.

42 Schaefer 1994, pp. 148-149, and idem 2000, p. 295. Regarding the spatial context, see Förstel 2008, pp. 96-107.

43 Schaefer 2000, p. 296, however, associates the chain of intercession with the Marian prayer *Obsecro te*.

44 The difficulty of distinguishing between the motifs becomes apparent in diptychs by Rogier van der Weyden, which likewise oscillate between *ostentatio uberum* and *Maria lactans*; see the diptychs of Jean Gros (Tournai and Chicago, ca. 1455-1460) and Laurent Froimont (Caen and Brussels, ca. 1463-1464). The ambiguity is especially striking in the latter work, which more closely resembles an *ostentatio uberum*, since Mary not only exposes her breast, but also places her hands together in prayer.

45 Seidel 1977, pp. 70-79; Kretzenbacher 1981, pp. 42-66; Marti, Mondini 1994, pp. 79-90; Schreiner 2011, pp. 216-237.

46 "Blessed is the womb that bore You, and the breasts which nursed You." See Marti, Mondini 1994, p. 80. Theologians also associated the *ubera matris* with the Song of Solomon; Seidel 1977, pp. 49-50; Schreiner 1011, pp. 212-216.

47 Marti, Mondini 1994, p. 80, trace the motif back to Coptic art of the 6th century; Schreiner 2011, p. 215. However, isolated earlier representations also exist, such as the wall painting in the Catacomb of Priscilla in Rome (probably 2nd century), Russo 1996, pp. 176-180.

48 Marti, Mondini, p. 81; one of the earliest examples is the Madonna of Dom Rupert in Liège, ca. 1150; Fulton 2002, pp. 344-350.

49 Seidel 1977, pp. 70-77; Schreiner 2011, pp. 223-225, points to Mechthild of Magdeburg.

50 Jezler 1994, pp. 13-26.

51 Kretzenbacher 1982, p. 9.

52 The role of Mary as intercessor was established very early; Russo 1996, pp. 180-181, 210- 215.

53 Seidel 1977, p. 73.

54 Seidel 1977, pp. 73-74; Kretzenbacher 1981, pp. 67-70; Marti, Mondini 1994, p. 80.

55 Seidel 1977, p. 74.

56 "I am your mother, mother you call me beautiful son, look at the breasts with which I nursed you" (translation by the author); Seidel 1977, p. 74; for the manuscripts, see https://www.arlima.net/ad/advocacie_nostre_dame.html.

57 Marti, Mondini 1994, p. 81, fig. 47, p. 79, London, British Library, Add. 38116, fol. 13, *Last Judgment*, after 1280.

58 See especially Seidel 1977, pp. 70-77.

59 Marti, Mondini 1994, p. 81, fig. 49 (Freiburg, Minster, nave XXIII, tracery, ca. 1330/40; Becksmann 2010, vol. 1, pp. 304-305; vol. 2, fig. 141-143).

60 Basel, Kunstmuseum, Cat. Basel 2011, pp. 169-181 (Stephan Kemperdick).

61 Marti, Mondini 1994, p. 82, fig. 51; for the manuscript, see Focillon 1950, p. 38, fig. XVI.

62 Bruderer Eichberg 2008, pp. 171-180.

63 Ibid., pp. 174-176.

64 Italian painters had already reduced the number of figures in order to create a more intimate representation of Mary's position at the head of the angel hierarchy; Bruderer Eichberg 2008, pp. 171-174.

65 On Mary's rank with respect to Christ, see Russo 1996, pp. 185-188, 209-217.

66 Ringbom 1984, pp. 39-52.

67 Kurmann-Schwarz 2017, pp. 328-329.

68 Signori 2014, pp. 41-45; Wolfthal 2011, pp. 105-109; Schmidt 2006, pp. 16-19.

69 Hamburger 2000, p. 49. On the Virgin's long mantle as a barrier to her approachability, see Russo 1996, pp. 184-185.

70 The white rather than blue mantle of the Virgin goes back to the *Revelations* of St. Bridget of Sweden; Schiller 1966, pp. 88-90.

71 For Agnès Sorel, see most recently Henzler 2012, pp. 21-23, 30-31, 37-41, 133-143.

72 Ibid., pp. 56-58.

73 Schreiner 2011, pp. 207-212.

74 Marti, Mondini 1994, pp. 84-85.

75 Schreiner 2011, pp. 234-237.

76 As late as 1570, Molanus still advocated this iconography of intercession; Marti, Mondini 1994, p. 85.

77 On the confessional critique of the religious image, see Göttler 1990, pp. 263-297.

78 Schaefer 1994, p. 356.

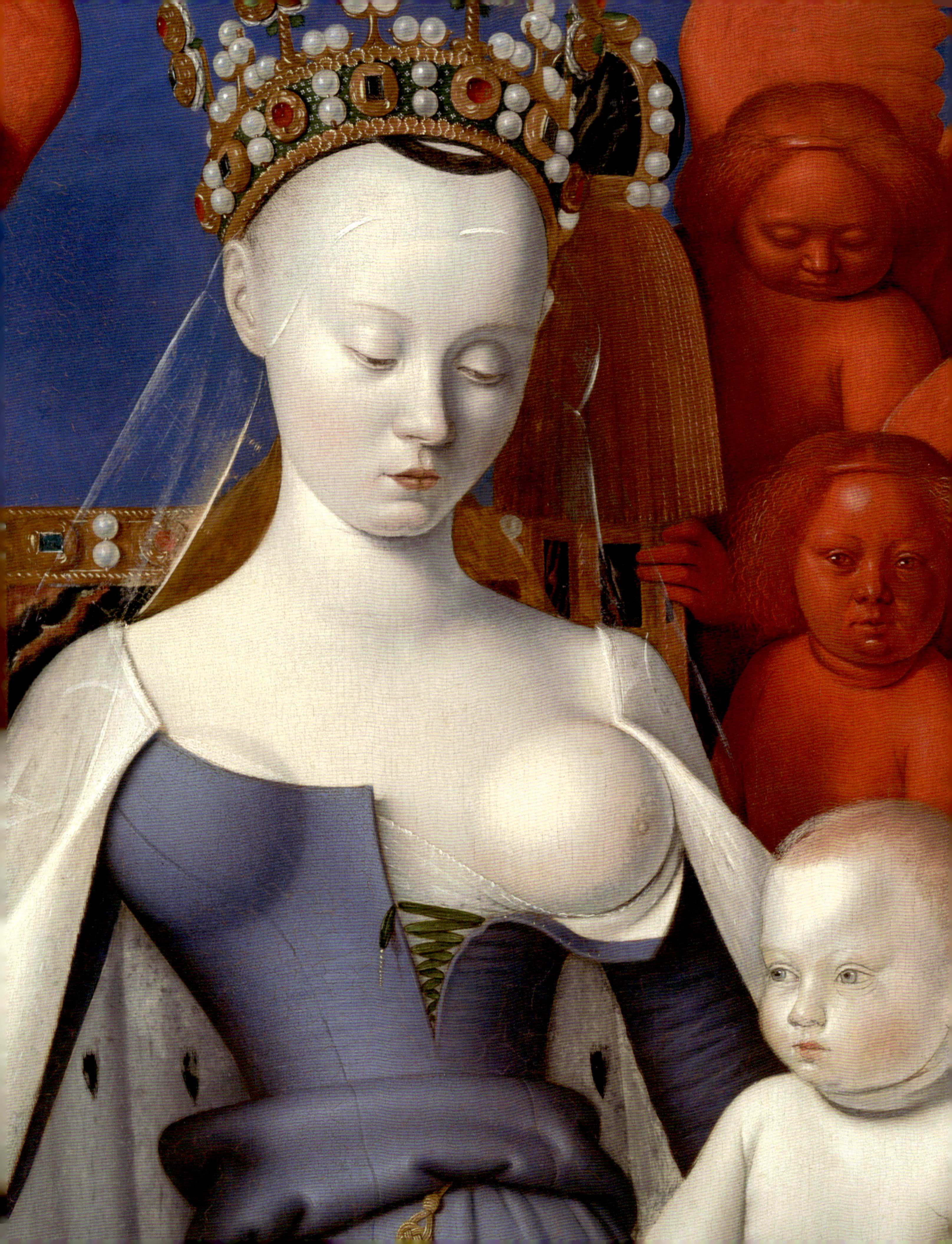

Thomas Kren

THE MELUN VIRGIN,
AGNÈS SOREL, AND THE COURT OF CHARLES VII[1]

The Melun Virgin Mary is Agnès Sorel, Charles VII's deeply mourned mistress, who died suddenly on February 9, 1450, while carrying the king's child. Remarkably, she has continued to live in memory long after her death. A tradition, dating back to the earliest written record of this painting in 1608, associates the Virgin's distinctive features, painted ca. 1452-55, with her fabled beauty: on a visit to Melun the young Louis XIII was told that the king's mistress was depicted as the Virgin in the diptych.[2] A late sixteenth-century portrait, known in several versions, transforms the image of the Virgin into a lay woman, who displays the same disconcertingly exposed breast (fig. 57).[3] Clearly based on the *Melun Virgin*, the later painting bears an inscription identifying its subject as Agnès Sorel.[4] She has remained the subject of books and novels down to the present day.[5]

Today most scholars accept this traditional identification. While no images actually made in Agnès' lifetime survive, a number of reliable portraits have come down to us. A lost life drawing by Jean Fouquet, painter of the *Melun Diptych*, is preserved in two careful copies from the sixteenth century (cat. 5).[6] Still more striking is the resemblance of her tomb effigy at Loches, which Charles commissioned from an unknown sculptor shortly after her death (fig. 58).[7] It represents the same small but pronounced—and slightly dimpled—chin, elegantly curved eye brows, long, straight nose that is fleshier at the bottom, noble forehead, and hair pulled tightly back at the sides to emphasize the splendid planes of her face.

The *Melun Diptych* and its representation of the Virgin belong to a turning point in French art, when the demand for painted portraiture was expanding rapidly across Europe and in particular at the French court. In-deed, Fouquet contributed profoundly to its success; even prior to his receiving the commission for the *Melun Diptych*, he was praised for making his subjects "genuinely appear properly alive."[8] In several respects the *Melun Virgin* is unprecedented: a portrait of a royal mistress, represented as the Virgin, and specifically the nursing Virgin, with a heightened naturalism that imparts an erotic charge. The subject of the nursing Virgin was widespread across Europe, but still fraught because the female breast was also a source of sexual arousal.[9] While the *Melun Virgin* pushed the boundaries of its pictorial category so aggressively that it lacks immediate successors, it also announced a triumphal new category of

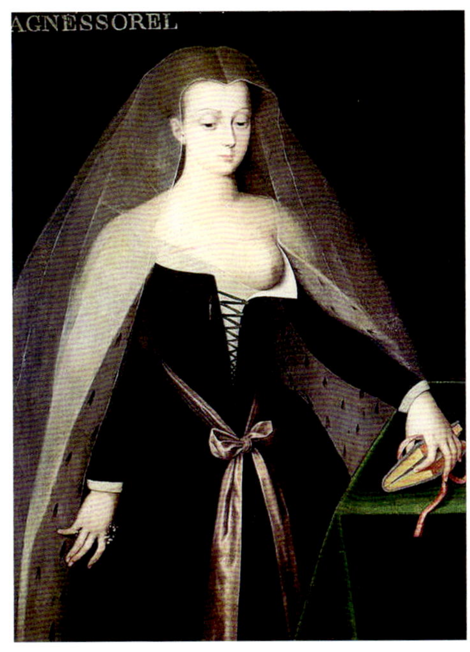

Fig. 57. Anonymos, Posthumous Portrait of Agnès Sorel, after the *Melun Virgin*, canvas, ca. 1560/1600, whereabouts unknown

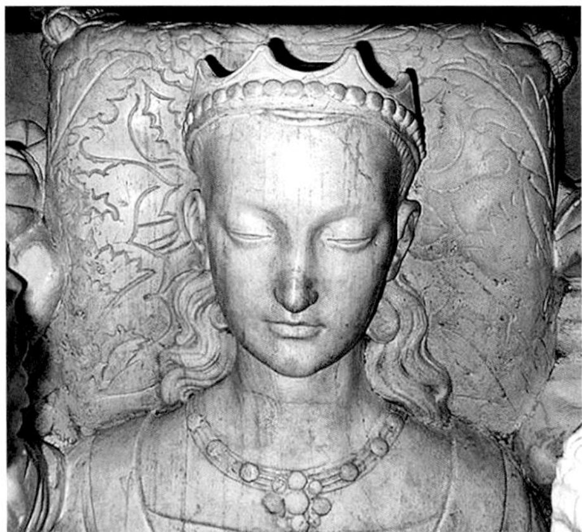

Fig. 58. Tomb Figure of Agnès Sorel (Detail), alabaster, probably 1450s, collegiate church St. Ours, Loches

French painting, the nude mistress portrait. This essay considers the cultural conditions that shaped this masterpiece: Agnès' life at court, the place of eroticism in French religious imagery at court, and the relationships between court artists and their patrons.

The *Melun Virgin* shows the Virgin Mary seated with the Christ child on her lap surrounded by a heavenly host of cherubim and seraphim. While her delicate features betray her youth, the Virgin sits regally and tall, her neck long, her eyes downcast. The child sits equally erect on her lap, his glance directed to the patron on the opposite panel. She supports her son with her proper left hand, but does not embrace him. While her left breast is fully exposed, Mother and Child do not otherwise interact. The Virgin wears an ermine cloak and a jeweled crown of pearls, rubies, and other precious stones which identifies her as Queen of Heaven. She is seated in a similarly bejeweled and tasseled throne of marble and gold, set against the rich blue vault of heaven itself. It is an image at once monumental and highly theatrical. Despite the Virgin's appropriately inward and modest expression, the artist has conveyed powerfully the model's physical beauty and charisma.

The panel was the right wing of a diptych, the other showing St. Stephen presenting Étienne Chevalier (d. 1474) within its own monumental setting, a decidedly Italianate classical hall of cream, yellow, and parti-colored marble (cat. 1, fig. 93). The son of a royal courtier, Chevalier entered the service of Charles VII in 1442 and quickly became a member of his inner circle. He was named Trea-

surer of France in 1452, around the time the diptych was painted (and the same year his wife, Catherine Budé died). But the genesis of the composition with the Virgin and Child was initially distinct from the companion donor panel, as shall be demonstrated below, such that Chevalier's relationship to the right panel may be secondary to that of another patron.

The Antwerp panel offers a radical approach to a popular devotional subject, the *Virgo lactans,* the Virgin suckling the Christ child. It appeared previously in a diptych format in the imposing miniatures added in the 1380s to the Duke of Berry's *Très Belles Heures* (fig. 19). The scene with the Virgin and child contains many of the same elements as the *Melun Virgin,* a monumental throne, a host of angels (albeit on a smaller scale) behind the throne, and the inward, contemplative expression of Mary. She also wears an elegant, if plainer, gown and mantel, with stylish ties. A striking difference in Berry's illuminated diptych, however, is that the Christ child is actually nursing, his lips at her nipple and one hand on the partially exposed breast. Moreover, He is comfortably nestled in the Virgin's lap, his body framed by hers. With one leg raised on her proper right knee and the other dangling between her knees, the effect is one of great intimacy. The subject is incontrovertibly the *Virgo lactans.* By contrast in Fouquet's version the nursing has not commenced and seems uncertain. The Virgin's breast is exposed, indeed fully and more dramatically than in Berry's diptych, but the Christ child ignores it and the Virgin makes no gesture of invitation.

The *Virgo lactans* by the highly original Rohan Master, ca. 1430, more closely anticipates the character of the *Melun Virgin* (fig. 59). As in the Berry miniature the Child is held tight to the breast and he also looks out at the viewer. The relationship of mother and child is once again an intimate one. At the same time, this Virgin is a comparable type to Agnès, youthful, pretty, and voluptuous. Her gown has a tight-fitting bodice, snug at the waist, partially laced up the center but undone at the softly lit breast, all features of the gown in the painting that contribute to Agnès's sensuality. Here, however, the illuminator decorously covers the shoulders and breastbone with material from the headdress, following a convention of the fifteenth century in northern Europe acknowledging that some modesty was required.

In her study of the *Virgo lactans* in fifteenth-century Florence, Megan Holmes remarked that "the range of meanings associated with the bare-breasted woman was extensive and highly charged."[10] Besides other Christian themes such as Charity, bare-breasted classical heroines included Cleopatra and Lucretia but also everyday adulterers and prostitutes; erotic content was usually central to these narratives. Moreover, the rise of naturalism contributed significantly to the sensuality of naked flesh, whether the subject was Christian, which it was largely initially, or secular. This was the case with both Tuscan and French court art, where the theme of the *Virgo lactans* enjoyed favor.

In fact, Fouquet himself had returned from Tuscany and Rome a year or two before he began to work on the image of Agnès Sorel as the nursing Virgin. He would have seen comparable large-scale examples such as that by Masolino in Munich (fig. 60) where the Virgin's upper body, including the area above her breast, is discreetly covered. Likely due to the unease over this type of ambiguous yet vivid nudity, the *Virgo lactans* began to fade in popularity in Tuscany during the 1440s, largely disappearing for several decades.[11]

A few years after he completed the *Melun Diptych* Fouquet again depicted the nursing Virgin in the book of hours he created for Étienne Chevalier (fig. 43), but more canonically. He depicts the Virgin's upper body more decorously, with a narrower opening across the breasts and golden cords across the breastbone to hold the mantel in place.[12] As art began to imitate nature more methodically, the tensions between the role of the Virgin's breast as a source of maternal and spiritual nourishment and its sensual appeal grew. In the *Melun Diptych* Fouquet heightens the latter by disengaging Mary from the activity of nursing while isolating her exposed breast. She declines to offer it or raise the Christ child up to it while he ignores it completely, his gaze and gesture focused on the patron opposite. The intimate contact essential to the iconography of a *Virgo lactans* is wanting here. Moreover, the geometric purity of the bare breast, painted with heightened attention to texture and detail, makes it, arguably, a *subject* of the painting.

The anomalous character of the relationship Fouquet depicts is underscored by the fact that several works that copied or imitated features of the Antwerp panel invari-

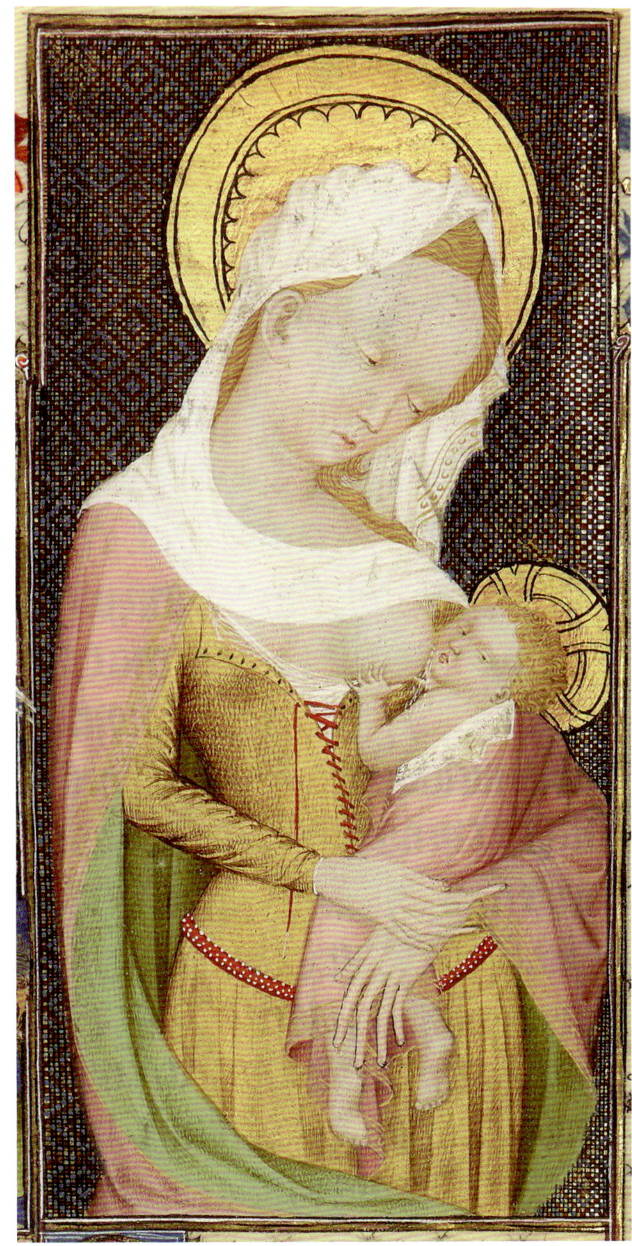

Fig. 59. Rohan Master, Virgo lactans, Rohan Book of Hours, ca. 1430, Paris, Bibliothèque nationale de France, ms. Lat.9471, fol. 33v.

ably did so only partially, always returning the iconography overtly to the narrative of the *Virgo lactans*.[13] None of these examples repeats the central inaction of the Christ child, ignoring the Virgin's nominally proffered breast. A French silver stained glass roundel from the end of the century repeats the unusual motif of the fully exposed breast, while reorienting the child toward it (fig. 61). The glass designer "corrects" Fouquet's transgressive iconography. Likewise, in a miniature of the Child in the arms of a Virgin with her breast exposed, her gaze and embrace link the Child's body more intimately to hers (Lille, fig. 62).[14] Fouquet was doubtless aware of the acceptable norms of the *virgo lactans* tradition and conveniently overlooked these parameters with the *Melun Virgin*.

One of the most distinctive departures of Fouquet's Virgin from the conventional iconography of the *Virgo lactans* resides in her attire. In comparison even with the form-fitting costume of the Virgin in the Rohan Hours and Masolino's painting (figs. 59, 60), her gown is finely-tailored, aristocratic, and modish. Indeed, the late 1440s and 1450s were a decade of economic pros-

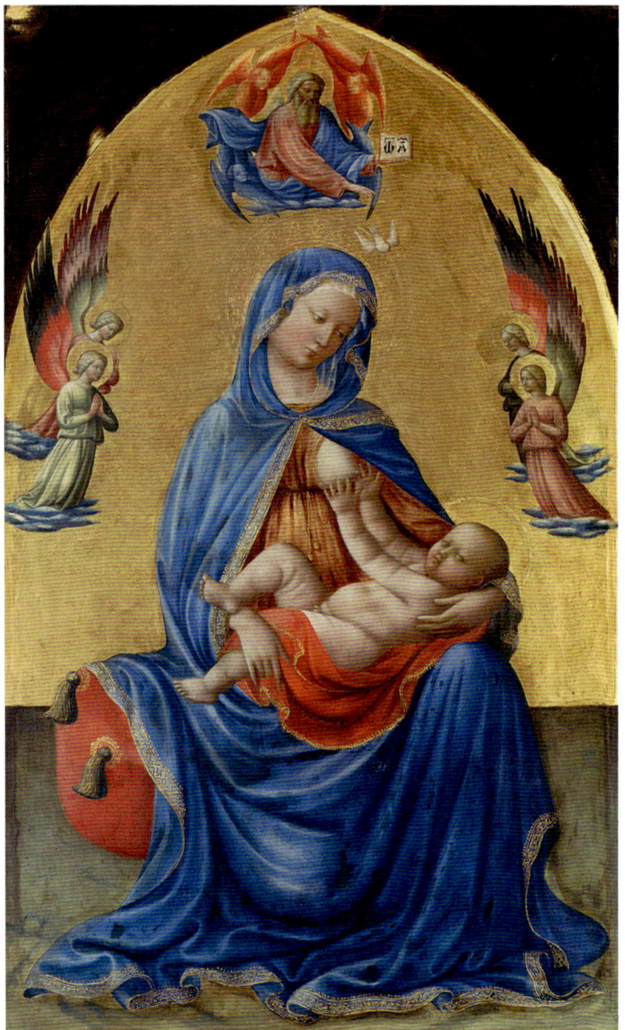

Fig. 60. Masolino da Panicale, Virgo lactans, ca. 1425, Munich, Alte Pinakothek

perity in France and correspondingly high fashion at court.[15] The *Melun Virgin* wears the snug-fitting *cote hardie*, which tightly cinches her waist, and over her shoulders a royal, ermine-lined cloak. This attire, superfluously opulent for the Queen of Heaven, underscores the reality that the king's mistress had supplanted the queen, Marie d'Anjou, in his life. At the time of Agnès' death, five years into their relationship, the child she was carrying would have been her and Charles' fourth together. Besides being more beautifully dressed, Agnès was by many accounts also more visible at court than the queen.

The potentially scandalous appearance of Fouquet's Virgin is suggested by the commentary of Jean Juvenal des Ursins, the influential archbishop of Rheims. In 1445, when his brother Guillaume became the royal Chancellor, the prelate lamented the conditions at court: "… in his own household… the king should prohibit openings in front through which you can see the women's nipples and breasts, and the great furred trains, girdles, and other things, because they are so displeasing to God and the world."[16] While Juvenal was hardly the first cleric to lament lascivious court dress,[17] and did not single out Agnès by name, others were less guarded. George Chastellain, a Burgundian courtier who spent several months at the French court on visits in 1446 and 1447, was close to the royal councilor Pierre Brézé, who like Agnès had formerly attended the Angevin court. Nevertheless, Chastellain complained about the way Agnès Sorel displayed her neck, shoulders, and bosom.[18] Implying that she even exposed her nipples, he claimed "100,000 murmurs" rose against her.[19] Such a controversial way of dressing was scarcely appropriate in a religious image. In short, Fouquet's Virgin would have been viewed as partially nude; the disarray of her gown[20] only heightens the eroticism of what is revealed.[21]

Agnès Sorel at the Court of Charles VII

Agnès Sorel was born around 1422, the daughter of Jean Soreau, Lord of Coudun. She first appears in 1443 as a modestly remunerated member of the household of Isabella of Lorraine, duchess of Anjou and sister-in-law of queen Marie. When Charles VII met her, he was smitten,

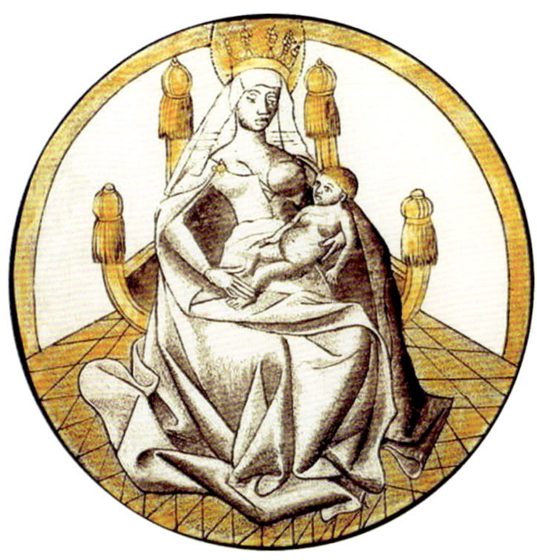

Fig. 61. French, Virgo lactans, Stained Glass, second half of the 15ᵗʰ century, Rodez, Musée Fenaille

and by the end of 1444 she had left the retinue of the duchess for the household of the queen. But her sensational beauty caused a stir at court and was often remarked upon.[22] The knight Olivier de la Marche, accompanying Isabel of Portugal, duchess of Burgundy, on a state visit to the French court, remarked "She was the most beautiful woman I have ever seen",[23] while Jean Chartier, the official chronicler of Charles' reign, thought her one of the most beautiful women in the world.[24] She came to be called "La belle Agnès" as many accounts from the time attest.[25] Charles awarded Agnès the title of Dame de Beauté-sur-Marne, the first of a number of royal properties and pensions she received, which guaranteed a substantial income. She appears to have belonged to the circle of the king's closest advisers including Chevalier, Brézé, and Jacques Coeur, the king's *argentier* and principle financier. Chevalier and Coeur served as executors of her will.

As noted, Agnès enjoyed a highly visible life at court; according to Chastellain she was treated better than the queen.[26] Charles is described as "besotted" with her, and she remained his devoted mistress until her untimely death in Normandy in February, 1450.[27] She had gone there to join the king on a military campaign when she became ill, dying suddenly and somewhat mysteriously. In contrast, while Marie d'Anjou bore Charles fourteen children, the last in 1446, the king and queen appear to have lived quite separate lives, and

she did not rush to his side when he was on his death bed in July, 1461.[28]

Agnès' fashionable and extravagant dress was also criticized as above her station.[29] At a time when sumptuary laws carefully dictated the clothes appropriate to different classes, she raised eyebrows for dressing like a duchess. Chartier wrote that she had the finest "fur-trimmed gowns, gold necklaces, and precious stones."[30] Chastellain said she not only had the most beautiful clothes, reflecting the status of a grand dame,[31] but also the most beautiful jewelry and rings, linen and vessels, tapestries and bed clothes.

Agnès was evidently highly conscious of the power of her physical charms not only to please Charles, but also to influence wider opinion, even if this shocked some and provoked criticism. Undoubtedly many, including her lover, admired the generous cleavage she displayed, an admiration that could have informed the choice of the *Virgo lactans* as a subject for the *Melun Diptych*; elements of the Queen of Heaven's uncommonly *chic* royal costume may also have evoked memories of Agnès' self-presentation. Nevertheless, despite the comments of her critics, the latter did not necessarily include a completely unveiled breast. At the same time, the *Melun Virgin's* fully bared breast has no equivalent in representations up to that time.

Two Melun Virgins?

The approximate date given to the *Melun Virgin* of ca. 1452-1455, several years after Agnès' death, indicates that the image was commemorative.[32] But the story of its genesis is more complicated than that circumstance might suggest. The very close relationship of both Agnès and Chevalier with the king raises the larger question whether the original audience for this image was actually intended to be the monarch himself. In fact, Fouquet also painted an earlier version of the composition that showed the Virgin with an exposed breast; oddly, it was left unfinished and ultimately abandoned. That image was partially scraped away to facilitate over-painting with a likeness of King Charles, ca. 1450 (fig. 11, 13).[33] Moreover, a pouncing from the lost work served as the starting point for the composition now in Antwerp.

Whatever the reason for abandoning this initial version, Fouquet rightly judged his invention significant enough to carefully record. A number of possibilities occur. Did the king, or perhaps a courtier from his inner circle, commission the initial work for Charles' pleasure? Does the subject of the overpainting, the king himself, indicate that it was commissioned by the same individual? Was Agnès then still alive? Might the Queen, who had tolerated for more than five years the mistress who bore Charles three children, finally put her foot down, demanding the destruction of a blasphemous glorification of her victorious rival? And/or was the king's new mistress, a niece of Agnès according to Chastellain, troubled by the reminder of her relative and predecessor's tragic and mysterious death?[34] It seems plausible that discomfort both with the devotional painting's real subject and its eroticism caused the abandonment of the first effort. Whatever the circumstances, the Antwerp painting became a memorial to Agnès.

Artist as Courtier

The principal agent of the originality and boldness of the *Melun Diptych* was surely the artist himself, whose exceptional inventiveness and genius was already admired in his lifetime. He marshaled his artistic gifts in the service of a powerful patron and an extraordinary circumstance, the lionizing at court of the king's mistress. Already in France by the end of the fourteenth century, especially in aristocratic circles, artistic invention and variety were increasingly prized alongside the traditional delight in precious materials. As Hans Belting initially observed with regard to the early fifteenth century in France, "A private taste addicted to innovation became the target for a production that profited from a competition between collectors."[35] Moreover, the prospect for artists to become part of a noble household, even as *valet de chambre*, offered opportunities for a more personal relationship with their aristocratic patrons.[36]

At the start of the fifteenth century, the skill and ingenuity of the Limbourg Brothers famously transformed a block of wood into a *trompe l'oeil* luxury manuscript as an *étrenne* for their devoted patron, the bibliophile John, duke of Berry.[37] The *étrennes,* the court tradition of gifts exchanged at New Year's, comprised an arena where members of the household, including artists, courtiers, family members, and other princes could strengthen their relationships with their powerful noble patrons and lords. The duke's own rewards to Pol de Limbourg included a house in Bourges and various jewelry, as well as arranging the artist's marriage to a pre-adolescent girl despite the protestations of her mother; the duke endeavored to facilitate the nuptials with the girl's kidnapping.[38] In return, the brothers supplied the duke not only with extravagant *étrennes,* but also with his most refined and inventive illuminated devotional manuscripts, fashioned to appeal to his taste for the sensual and provocative in ways that complemented his own transgressive erotic inclinations. The duke who sought, much to the dismay of his peers, to take an underage girl as his second wife and reputedly had a weakness for liaisons with working class men, may have found the Limbourgs kindred spirits.[39] The *Belles Heures* and the *Très Riches Heures* boldly marry pious devotional content to eroticism. They contain uncommon Christian subjects, depicting sensual female and male nudes (fig. 63), beautiful youths, scenes of flagellation and self-flagellation, graphic depictions of seduction, a cross-dressing monk, and an array of phallic motifs throughout the miniatures (fig. 64), all intended to entertain the viewer and very likely to complement private erotic inclinations.[40]

The January miniature of the *Très Riches Heures* places the duke in his own richly appointed milieu surrounded by a wealth of the treasures he had collected, commissioned, and loved (fig. 64). The scene may represent the occasion of the annual gift-exchange. Prominent in the foreground of his teeming entourage are handsome and extravagantly outfitted male servants.[41] The young cup-bearer at the left has one of the mechanical tools of his vocation dangling suggestively from his groin. The duke, a collector of antiquities including coins, cameos, and medals, would have noted with appropriate amusement the allusion to Ganymede, cupbearer to Jupiter by day and the god's lover by night.[42] As Robert Mills points out, "Ganymede functions playfully…to render the duke godlike: waited on by a series of beautiful young men [the duke] effectively becomes a second Jupiter."

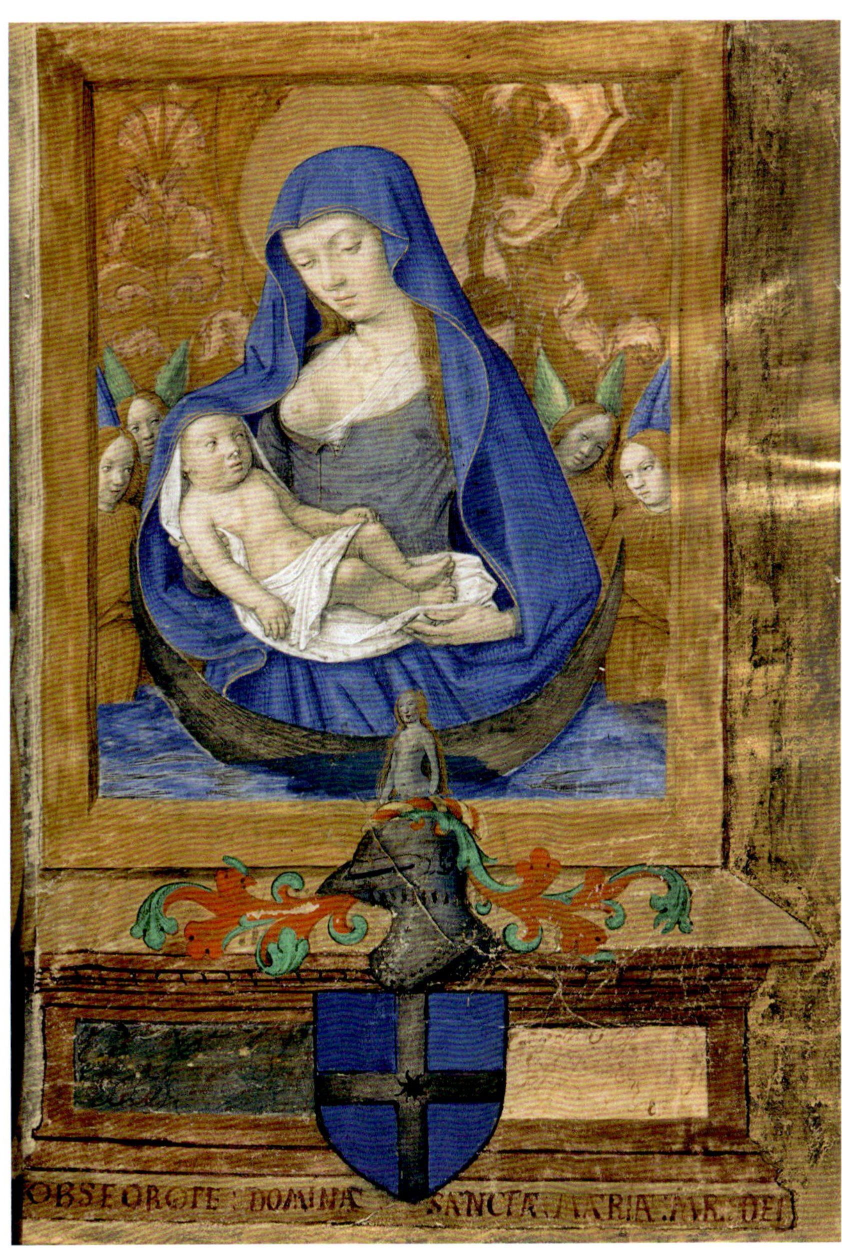

Fig. 62. French, Virgo lactans, detached Miniature from a Book of Hours, ca. 1485/90, Lille, Palais des Beaux-Arts

Thus, the Limbourgs were sophisticated portraitists; they understood that the portrait was about both likeness and the subject's aspirations and self-image.[43] In sheer ambition the January miniature is unlike any other portrait up to that time, an innovation that allowed the artists to flatter an enormous ego in ways both obvious and subtle. Within the framework of this highly personal artist/patron relationship, the Limbourgs became the first artists in France to explore the sensual nude as an artistic theme, drawing in part on the models of ancient art from the duke's collection. Ultimately the sensuality and eroticism which pervades the *Belles Heures* and the *Très riches Heures* provides a new departure, one where the tastes of their patron benefited from a complimentary sensibility in his artists.

At the same time, where the focus on sensuality and naked flesh in the *Belles Heures* disrupts the tradition of overwhelmingly pious iconography in devotional books, the Limbourgs may have taken their visual impetus not only from the duke but from popular imagery that is now lost to us. In 1402, only four years after the first arrival of the Nijmegen-born brothers in Paris, the same

year they entered the service of the Burgundian Duke
Philip the Bold, the eminent Parisian theologian Jean
Gerson warned in a sermon about, "the filthy corruption
of boys and adolescents by shameful and nude pictures
offered for sale in the very temples and sacred places...
Christian boys—oh, horror—are here initiated (…) into
the world of obscene songs, gestures, and habits (…)."[44]
Significantly, in 1402 the three brothers themselves likely
ranged in age from 14 to 17.[45] While we do not know
the character of Gerson's "nude and shameful pictures",
their availability in "the very temples and sacred places",
suggest that they may have been religious images, scenes
from the lives of the saints and the Passion of Christ.
Might those artists fashioning images for public sale
likewise have selected narratives of sexual temptation
and the torture of female saints in order to depict fully
or partially unclothed naked figures or other scenes of
eroticism? It bears noting that Gerson's objections to
nudity—in that time the term "nudity" would have encompassed partial nudity such as the *Melun Virgin's*—

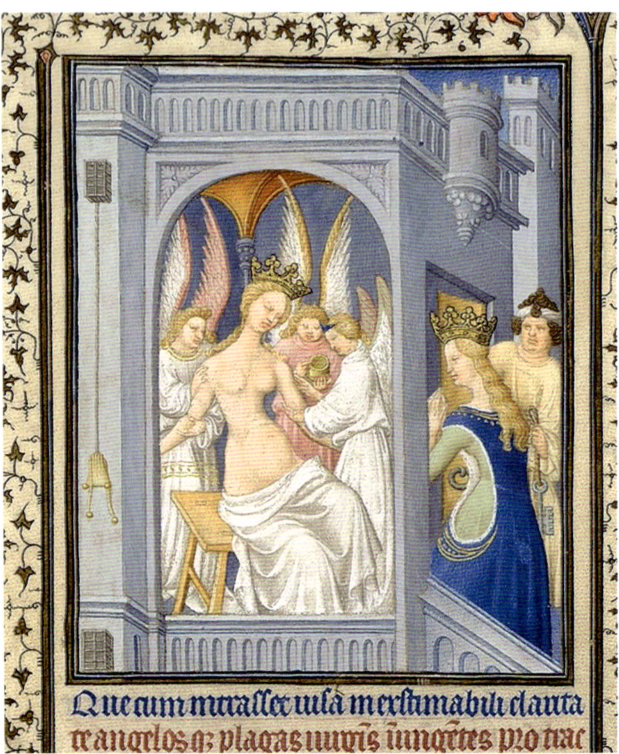

Fig. 63. Limbourg Brothers, Saint Catherine nursed by Angels and visited
by the Empress, Belles Heures of Jean, Duke of Berry, New York, The Cloisters
Collection, 54.1.1, fol. 17v

belong to a larger desire to steer youth away from illicit
sexuality to which music, images, and social behavior
might all contribute. In that sense, then, the complaints
of clerics and other observers about women's bared
breasts at the court of Charles VII, including Agnès
Sorel's, are not only about decorum, but also about the
larger court culture; implicit is a view of these women as
courtesans who had a debilitating impact on the men
serving the crown. Even lacking contemporary responses
to either of Fouquet's versions of the *Melun Virgin*, other
than the seemingly precipitous destruction of the first
version, it is reasonable to imagine objections to a work
that enshrines feminine behavior viewed as abhorrent
by clerics and by many lay observers.

To return to the case of the Duke of Berry, he was
almost certainly complicit in the Limbourgs' choices for
ever more sensual and explicit imagery in the *Belles
Heures* and the *Très Riches Heures*. The duke ordered a
second campaign of miniatures for the *Belles Heures*
which increased the concentration of both storytelling
scenes and sensuality. The second campaign adopted an
unconventional format that substituted for the strictly
devotional content of the book a narrative content, i.e.,
in place of the traditional prayers and meditations, short
captions that maximized the number of miniatures and
specified the provocative narratives to be depicted. The
success of this encouraged the duke to award the brothers
an even more ambitious commission in the *Très Riches
Heures.* In short, the duke knew what he was getting.
For similar reasons, it seems likely that the patron of the
original version of the *Melun Diptych*, whether it was
the king himself or a loyal courtier, understood that
Fouquet could immortalize Agnès' beauty in an extraordinary manner. In the atmosphere of Charles' court,
where Agnès seems to have cast such a powerful spell,
certain rules of decorum had already been bent, not
least by Agnès herself. Those involved undoubtedly understood that prominent court observers such as Archbishop Juvenal des Ursins would be displeased, but they
did not care. Technically, access to luxury devotional art
made for elites in France was relatively easily controlled
by the work's owner. Like books of hours, diptychs could
easily be closed. The *Melun Virgin* may have been intended originally only for the pleasure of the king and
his closest advisors.

In this respect, it is important to keep in mind Reynaud's comment that Fouquet's portrait of Charles VII represents something new in Western art. It is the first half-length, nearly frontal, independent portrait that is also life-size.[46] And despite the king's unprepossessing presence in the painting, its direct, lifelike quality certainly had no equal up to that time and must have had a tremendous impact. Moreover, the first version of the *Melun Virgin*, the lost original portrait drawing of Agnès Sorel, and the portrait of Charles are likely among the first works Fouquet created upon his return from Italy. They bespeak an artist capitalizing on his success in Italy and confidently ingratiating himself with new clients. At Rome, he had acquired celebrity with his now lost portrait of Pope Eugenius IV. It was for this work that he received accolades for making his sitters "genuinely appear properly alive."

Given this pivotal moment in the history of portraiture, envisioning a comparably life-size image of the king's mistress, even disguised as a devotional subject, was itself radical on the part of both patron and artist, notwithstanding the nudity. Yet, there was also a historic precedent for depicting the mistress of a ruler in the nude; both Fouquet and some members of the court of Charles were likely aware of it. Pliny's *Natural History* was a text well known in France during the Middle Ages. It had enjoyed a revival of interest since the time of Petrarch and Boccaccio, both writers greatly admired in France. The Duke of Berry, for example, had owned a large, richly illuminated copy.[47] In the *Natural History* Pliny related a story of the esteemed classical painter Apelles, who was called upon by his patron, Alexander the Great, to portray his beloved mistress, the beautiful Campaspe. Apelles painted her in the nude and during the course of their sittings fell in love with her. Alexander recognized this and, in a magnanimous gesture, offered Campaspe to the painter.[48]

For Fouquet, his triumphant Italian experience may have served to enhance his own sense of the relevance of the story of Campaspe, returning to the royal court when Agnès Sorel's position was secure. Moreover, Fouquet's time in Florence not only exposed him to a supercharged artistic environment, but also placed him within a burgeoning humanist milieu. Sricchia Santoro makes a compelling argument that the artist met Fra Angelico there

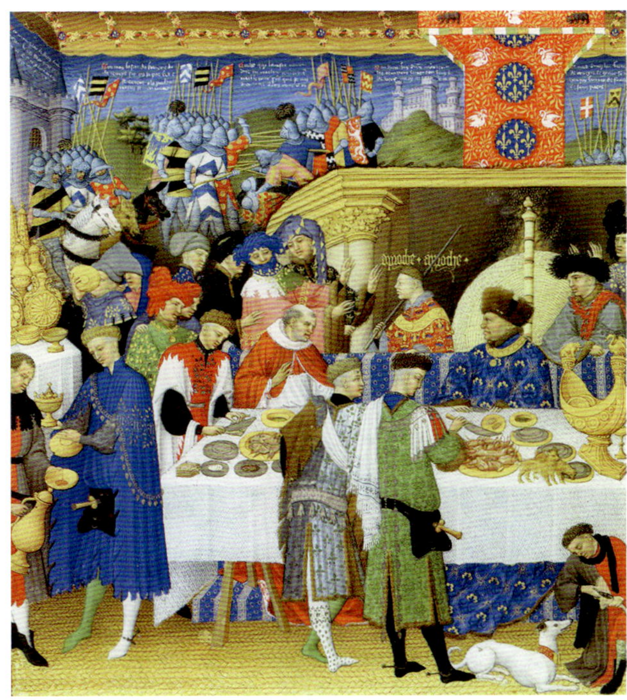

Fig. 64. Limbourg Brothers, January, Très Riches Heures of Jean, Duke of Berry, Chantilly, Musée Condé, ms. 65, fol. 1v

and went on together to Rome, and possibly Orvieto, where they likely collaborated.[49] In addition to myriad individual works of art by the great artists then active that Fouquet encountered in Florence and Rome,[50] his own work upon his return to France betrays an awareness of the new Albertian ideas of image-making being explored during the 1440s.[51] Moreover, inspired by Pliny, Leon Battista Alberti in his treatise *On Painting* relates stories about ancient painters including Apelles. Written in Latin around 1435, it was translated into Italian shortly thereafter, and quickly widely discussed. Another Florentine deeply indebted to the *Natural History*, Lorenzo Ghiberti began his *Commentaries* in 1447, and recounted in it the story of Apelles and Campaspe.[52] So the likelihood of Fouquet's awareness of the classical precedent in strong. Moreover, his ability to cast the King of France as Alexander the Great, however obliquely, to his Apelles, and the King's beloved Agnès Sorel as the legendary Campaspe, in a memorable work of art offered an extraordinary path to ingratiating himself with the court.

To our pairings of Valois prince/artist-courtier, I add a less-defined relationship that is so provocative, it deserves to be considered, if judiciously. It concerns Charles VIII, grandson of Charles VII, and a lost memory book, likely a manuscript that was compiled while he was on his Italian campaigns. It was discovered in his tent following the retreat of the French forces at the battle of Fornovo on July 6, 1495, and judged of sufficient interest to be the beneficiary of several eyewitness descriptions.[53] The book consists of depictions "*al naturale*" of many women of different attire and ages "*per loro violate in molte citate*". One account describes the women as prostitutes. In fact, Charles' troops in Italy got a notorious reputation among the populace for the rampant violation of women and girls. The loss of the book prevents us from knowing the precise character of the images. Ulrich Pfisterer raised the question whether they might even constitute a chronicle of "erotic positions" in the ancient tradition, also anticipating Giulio Romano's *I modi*.[54] The implication is that the book was created by an artist (or artists?)—the phrase *al naturale* would seem to imply some skill involved—imbedded with the troops and—somehow—documenting the features (*ritratte)* of the king's (and/or his men's?) "conquests" and/or rape victims.

The promiscuity of princes was, of course, the rule rather than the exception and to a large degree accepted. Charles' Valois rival, Philip the Good, Duke of Burgundy, was much more successful at fathering children by his mistresses than by his wives[55] and by one account Charles VII, after Agnès, had a mistress who was also involved in procuring teenage girls for him.[56] While we might want to distinguish a seemingly deep love such as Charles for Agnès from random sexual encounters, the question arises whether a ruler's impulse to commemorate his loves in an image is a new one? Is Charles VIII's memory book, or "Book of Beloveds", thinkable without the existence of the *Melun Virgin*? Had the possibilities of fifteenth-century art *al naturale*, the more lifelike and potentially sensual style of representation embodied by Fouquet, opened up avenues to fulfill some rulers needs' for witness to their own sexual potency via images of their lovers?[57] Certainly in the relationship between patron and artist-courtier, the artistic demands of the "Book of Beloveds" would seem to raise the bar in complexity. As Pfisterer emphasizes, the historic issues around erotic cultures and behaviors are complex ones to disentangle.

The Female Nude in Christian Art: A Coda

The decision to paint the king's mistress partially nude as the Virgin Mary within an altarpiece intended for private prayer and meditation, especially a work that may have been inspired or explained by an ancient precedent, seems strange, even disconcerting today. In France during the fifteenth-century Christian subject matter and especially devotional art, consisting of private altarpieces and lavish prayer books, were pre-eminent. Often this was where artistic innovation was found, as the *Melun Diptych* so splendidly makes clear. Illuminated devotional books, in particular, were the focus of a lively market with strong competition among collectors for the most beautiful examples carried out by outstanding artists. Moreover, for the history of the nude in France the next step continues to play out within Christian art, almost entirely within the expensively decorated pages of book of hours. As a consequence, the immediate successors to Fouquet's showing Agnès Sorel as the Virgin embody, not surprisingly, similar contradictions. Although his influential original is lost today, Fouquet himself appears to have been the creator of a new iconography for the subject of *Bathing Bathsheba*, in which she is shown completely nude, nearly full-length, and partially submerged in the garden fountain where King David first set eyes upon her.[58] The image is designed to illustrate the Seven Penitential Psalms, a canonical text of books of hours, then thought to have been authored by King David himself. While a miniature in a private prayer book is necessarily much smaller than the relatively large Antwerp panel—a few inches versus several feet—this iconography is also more explicit and unprecedented. In Fouquet's concept Bathsheba is fully nude, even her genitals are uncovered. The most faithful surviving version to Fouquet's lost original is likely the modest miniature in a book of hours from the 1460s, when Fouquet was still very active (fig. 65). Although here the copyist awkwardly provides a transparent veil to cover Bathsheba's groin, the figure otherwise probably closely reflects Fouquet's idea. She looks modestly downward, turning away from the gaze of King David in the entryway to the palace. Her body also gently and gracefully turns to the side, while still displaying her resplendent beauty to the book's reader.

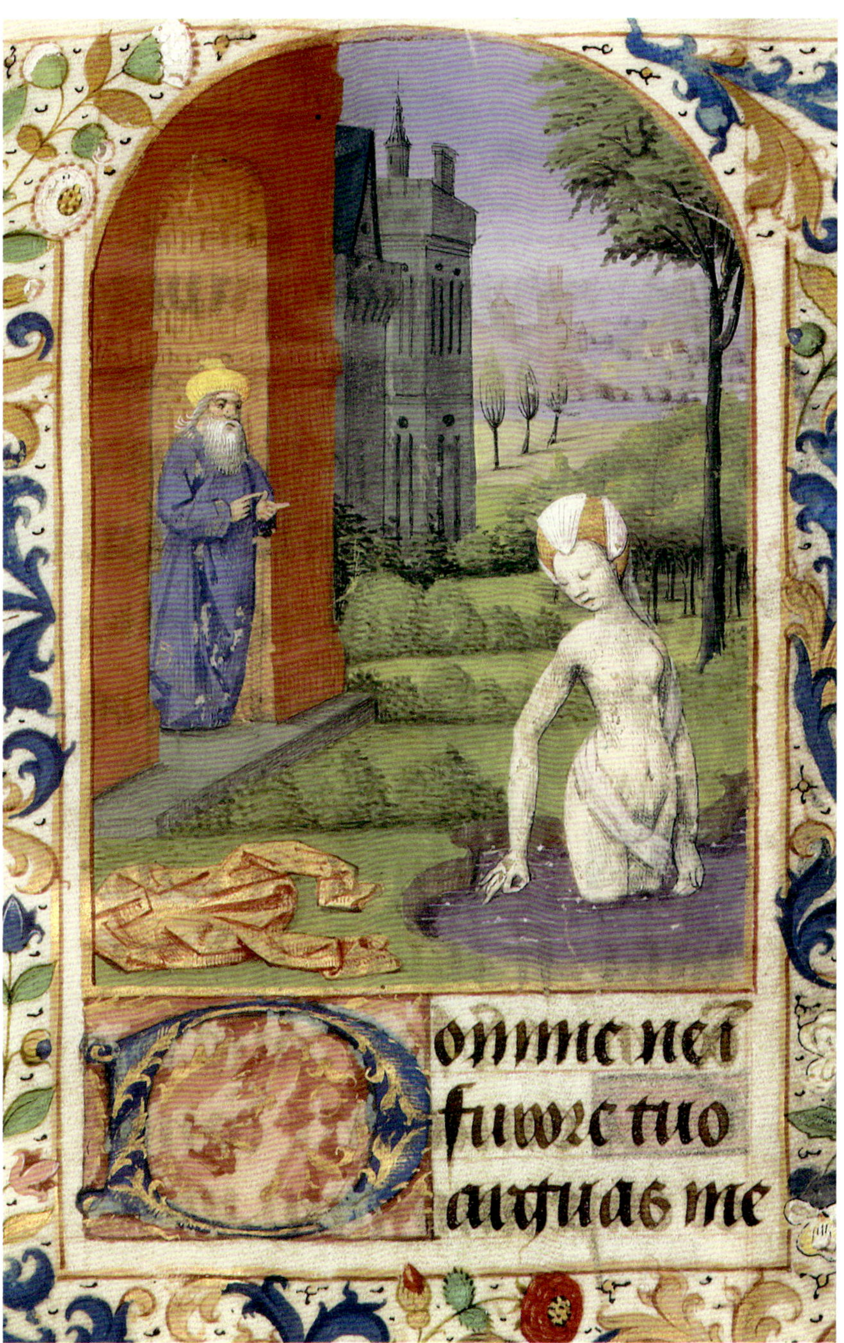

Fig. 65. French (copy after Fouquet), Bathing Bathsheba, Book of Hours, 1460s, St. Petersburg, Russian Academy of Sciences, Ms. O.104, fol. 118r

The heroine's inward expression is reminiscent of the *Melun Virgin*, while the downward gaze and twist of the torso may reflect Fouquet's study of classical marbles in Italy. The turban was a motif that Fouquet favored in his depictions of certain female figures and is found as early as the 1450s.

In contrast to the *Melun Virgin*, Fouquet's invention had an immediate and enduring impact. The new *Bathing Bathsheba* supplanted the standard iconography of the Penitential Psalms, which had been the Penitent King David, shown kneeling in his royal robes beseeching God for forgiveness for his capital sins of adultery (with Bathsheba) and murder (of her husband). For the next three generations, well into the sixteenth century, a sensual nude Bathsheba appears regularly in books of hours made for men and women.

In Christian teachings, however, the subject of Bathsheba was a deeply moralizing one. She was much written about and discussed, held up in the fourteenth and fifteenth century as a seductress, a married woman, who aroused the desires of the unsuspecting King, an exemplar of behavior to avoid for young women.[59] Women often received the present of a book of hours at a young age, during adolescence and/or at the time of marrying and so the image of Bathsheba might well carry a specific meaning for them. Significantly, however, many of the most sophisticated and beautiful of the French *Bathing Bathsheba*s, including the most explicitly erotic, were those made for men's prayer books. An example for King Louis XII seems particularly appropriate in the present context (fig. 66). It is typical of many depictions of the nude Bathsheba in her flirtatious gaze at the viewer while a leering water spout in the form of a *chatte*, also a slang term for prostitute, provides coarse humor.[60] Just as Charles VII and his courtiers would have seen in the *Melun Virgin* first and foremost a commemoration of his beloved as well as an awe-inspiring beauty of the court, the images of *Bathing Bathsheba* offered sensual pleasures that were more generic but comparably extra-devotional. Thus, while pictorially the

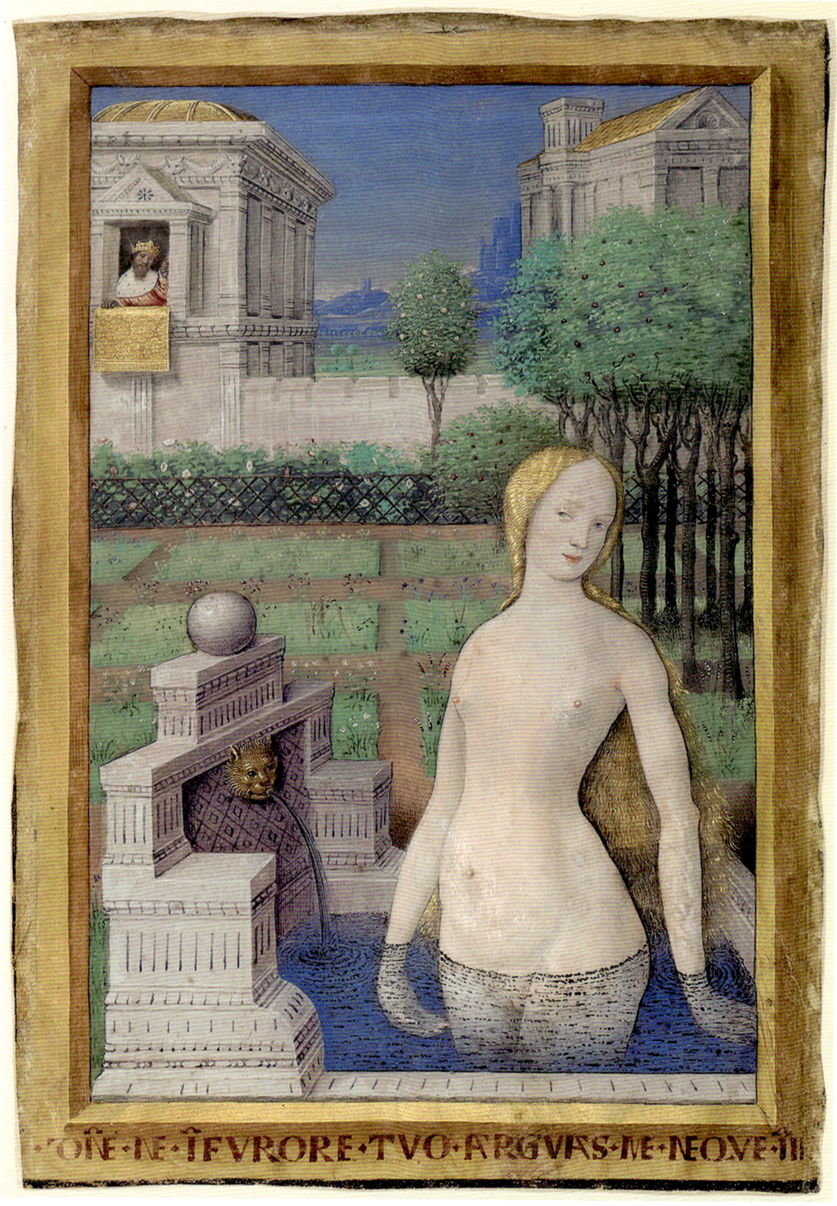

Fig. 66. Jean Bourdichon, Bathing Bathsheba, Book of Hours of Louis XII, 1498/99, Los Angeles, The J. Paul Getty Museum, Ms. 79

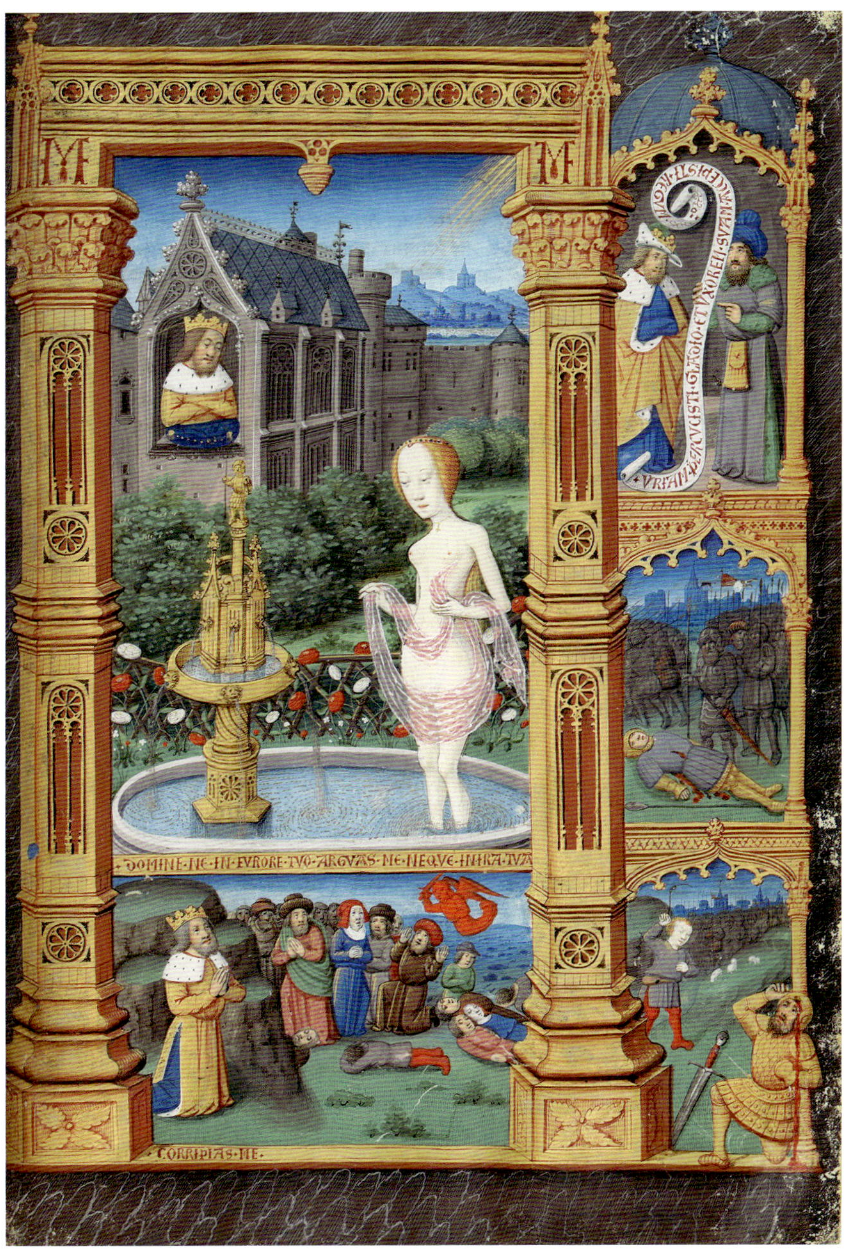

Fig. 67. Master of Catherine de Coëtivy, Bathing Bathsheba, Book of Hours of Marguerite de Coëtivy, Chantilly, Musée Condé, Ms. 74, fol. 61r

Melun Virgin lacked for several generations a succession, for example, in a line of painted French mistress portraits, it marks a turning point in the establishment of the sensual female nude as a popular motif within French art.

It is fitting then to conclude by noting that one of the countless French devotional miniatures of the *Bathing Bathsheba* was specifically conceived to preserve the memory of *la belle Agnès*. As noted, Charles and Agnès had three children, all of whom lived to adulthood and who, through the efforts of Charles and then his son, Louis

XI, made good marriages to prominent men. The eldest, Marie, married Olivier de Coëtivy, who had aided the king in the re-conquest of Normandy. Their daughter, Marguerite de Coëtivy, commissioned a splendid large book of hours, likely after the death of her spouse François de Pons, Count of Montfort, in 1504. It features a distinctive miniature of the *Bathing Bathsheba* (fig. 67), not least for the manner in which the bather discreetly covers her lower quarters with a veil while her inward expression recalls the modesty of Fouquet's *Bathsheba*. She also wears a diadem reminiscent of the one Marguerite's grandmother, Agnès Sorel, wears in her tomb effigy at Loches (fig. 58). Perhaps most striking is the depiction of King David. He wears the ermine collar worn by kings of France and his palace looks less like a palace than the royal *Sainte-Chapelle* in Paris. Thus, this singular miniature acknowledges Marguerite's descent from Charles VII while alluding to her grandmother's legendary beauty and implicitly, through the adultery of David and Bathsheba, to the illicit nature of that relationship.[61] Significantly, Agnès' three daughters were also considered beauties, undoubtedly a source of familial pride. The iconography also suggests that the beauty of Agnès Sorel encompassed more than just her face. Thus, in Marguerite's book of hours, without alluding to the *Melun Virgin*, the devotional art of a subsequent generation continues to do the work of keeping Agnès' memory—and legend—alive.

As the *Melun Virgin* makes clear, the origins of the nude in France are bound up with forces often at odds with one another: a powerful but dominant Christian spiritual culture deeply entwined with the crown, and a giddy court environment with a taste for luxury and innovation in a newly prosperous nation. The extraordinary invention that the *Melun Virgin* and the companion donor panel represent, realized from Jean Fouquet's melding of northern and southern Europe visual language and techniques, is inseparable from this environment. In a similar way, the myriad innovations of the Limbourg Brothers in the *Belles Heures* and the *Très Riches Heures* arose from the atmosphere and tone that the voracious, luxury-loving Duke of Berry created at his court. The result is an art that is modern not only in its verisimilitude, but also in its specificity, ultimately an art that, even in its strangeness, is intimate, personal, and individual. It is an art where nudity is often inseparable from the erotic. Created at the same moment when life-size portraiture is also emerging at the Valois court, the *Melun Virgin* seems to push the limits of a visual language so new it had only just been established. The tensions it embodies, between the spiritual and the sensual, the sacred and the profane, are still felt. This essay has argued that the eroticism of the *Melun Virgin* made it a radical work at the time of its creation. Having lost none of its power over the centuries, it still seems radical today.

1   I want to thank for close readings of drafts of this paper Mark L. Evans, Bruce Robertson, Margaret Scott, Linda Bauer, and George Bauer. Arguments contained in this paper were developed in presentations at the Art Institute of Chicago, St. Louis University, Rice University, and the Center for Advanced Study in the Visual Arts. I want to thank Martha Wolff, Susan L'Engle, Diane Wolfthal, and Elizabeth Cropper, respectively, for the invitations to institutions and Prof. Cropper for the appointment as the Edmund J. Safra Professor at CASVA in 2016.

2   Avril in Cat. Paris 2003, p. 130, under no. 8.

3   Museé de l'Histoire de France, Château de Versailles, and Château de Mouchy, Paris; Miles 2008, p. 83, pl. 3; Vale 1974, fig. 4.

4   Kervyn de Lettenhove in Chastellain 1864, p. 366, n. 1.

5   A couple of modern examples are a popular historical study: Champion 1931 and the novel by Bourin 1970.

6   Avril in Cat. Paris 2003, 128, 149-153, cat. nos. 7, 14, 15.

7   Avril in Cat. Paris 2003, 128, cat. no. 7; Lombardi 1978, pp. 5, 10, fig. 9.

8   Regarding the artist's now lost portrait of Pope Eugene IV and two companions: "...il quale fe[ce] a Rome papa Eugenio e du' altri de' suoi appresso di lui, che veramente parevano vivi proprio..." Antonio Averulino (called Filarete), Trattato d'architettura, between 1461 and 1464, quoted from Cat. Paris 2003, p. 98.

9   Holmes 1997, pp. 167-195.

10   Holmes 1997, p. 187.

11   Holmes 1997, p. 178.

12   Examples of other Virgo lactans with these features include Simon Marmion, Saint Bernard and the Madonna Lactans, a full-page miniature removed from a prayer book, (Los Angeles, J. Paul Getty Museum, ms. 32), and examples by Rogier van der Weyden or workshop in Caen, Musée des Beaux-Arts (Collection Mancel), Tournai, Musée des Beaux-Arts, and Art Institute of Chicago.

13   Avril in Cat. Paris 2003, 129-130.

14   Cat. Paris 2003, pp. 384-5, no. 50. For other examples see Cat. Paris 2003, p. 129, ill. 2, no. 49, pp. 382-3.

15   On this costume see the detailed analysis by Scott 1980, pp. 150-151.

16   "Que le roy, en son hostel mesmes, il mist remesde tant en ouvertures en par devant, par lesquelles on voit les tetins, tettes et seing des femmes, et les grans queues fourrées, chesnes, et aultres choses. Car celles sont trop desplaisans à Dieu et au monde." (Paris, Bibliothèque nationale de France, ms. fr. 2701, fol. 55v). English translation from Vale 1974, p. 94. Elizabeth Morrison and Zrinka Stahuljak kindly assisted with translations from Old French.

17   Vale 1974, p. 94.

18   "Descouvroit les espaules et le sein devant, jusques aux tettins; donnoit à toute baudeur loy et cours, fust à homme, fust à femme; n'estudioit qu'en vanité, jour et nuit, pour desvoyer gens et pour faire et donner exemple aux preudes femmes de perdition d'honneur, de vergogne et de bonnes moeurs; et tant et si avant en avoit-elle bonne main." Chastellain 1864, IV, p. 366.

19   "Dont toutevoies cent mille murmures sourdoient contre elle, et non moins contre le roy." Chastellain 1864, IV, p. 366.

20   Miles 2008, 83.

21   The dress historian Margaret Scott has characterized the Virgin's self-presentation as "blatant exhibitionism." (Scott 1980, p. 151).

22   See especially Champion 1931, pp. 31-34.

23   "Certes c'estoit une des plus belles femmes que je vy oncques", Olivier de la Marche 1884, p. 55; also quoted by Lettenhove in Chastellain 1864, p. 365, n. 1.

24   "...qu'entre les belles, c'estoit ... la plus belle du monde...", Chartier 1858, p. 183.

25   Champion 1931.

26   "avoir son quartier de maison en l'hostel du roy, ordonné et appointié mieux que elle; avoir compagnie de bruit de femmes et en plus grand nombres que le sien; avoit et vour toute l'affinité des seigneurs et des nobles et du roi mesme, se faire devers elle", Chastellain 1864, IV, p. 365.

27 Chastellain 1864, IV, pp. 366, 365.

28 Vale 1974, p. 190.

29 "Elle menait, on le voyait bien, aussi grand train qu'une comtesse ou une duchesse," remarked an anonymous Parisian diarist on the occasion of Agnes's visit to the city in 1448, Journal d'un bourgeois 1963, p. 179.

30 Chartier 1858, II, p. 181, on Sorel pp. 181-186.

31 "Portoit queues un tiers plus longue qu'oncques princess de ce royaume, plus haut atour qu'à demi, robes plus couteuses, et de tout ce qui à ribaudise et dissolution pouvoit traire en fait d'habillement, de cela fut-elle produiseresse et inventeresse." Chastellain 1864, IV, p. 366.

32 Avril in Cat. Paris 2003, 121- 130, no. 8.

33 Reynaud 1981, p. 14; Reynaud 1983.

34 Chastellain 1864, IV, pp. 366-368.

35 Belting 1994, p. 424.

36 Perkinson 2009.

37 Inventory of 1413, no. 994, Guiffrey 1896.

38 For an account of the gift exchanges and the bizarre affair of the abduction of Gillette la Mercière, see Niessen, Roelofs, van Veen-Liefrink 2005 pp. 20-22.

39 Camille 2001.

40 Camille 2001, pp. 7-32; Driver 2012, pp. 149-182; Lindquist 2017, pp. 173-207.

41 Camille 2001.

42 Camille 2001, p. 15; Mills 2015, p. 231.

43 Perkinson 2009, pp. 189-277, has shown how the arena of portraiture was an ideal one for flattering and patron.

44 Sermon G. 10; Glorieux 1973, p. 28; English translation in Brown 1989, p. 241.

45 Niessen, Roelofs, Van Veen-Liefrink 2005, p. 15

46 Reynaud 1981, p. 15.

47 Turin, Biblioteca Nazionale Universitaria, Mss I.I.24-I.I.25, damaged in the fire of 1904; see Armstrong 1983, pp. 29-35.

48 Pliny, Historia Naturalis, 35.85-87.

49 Sricchia Santoro 2003, pp. 50-63.

50 Inglis 2011, pp. 43-51.

51 Sricchia Santoro 2003, p. 62.

52 McHam 2013, pp. 49, 322.

53 "vi fu trovato un libro nel quale sotto diversi habiti & etate: al naturale erano depicte molte femine per loro violate in molte citate: e seco il potravano per memoria" Corio 1503. "In quella preda vidi io un libro, nel quale erano dipinte varie imagini di meretrici sotto diverso habiot, & età, ritratte al natural; secondo che la lascivia & amore l'haveva tratto in ciascuna città, queste portava egli seco dipinte per ricordarsene poi." Benedetti 1549, fol. 31r.

54 Pfisterer 2011, p. 480.

55 Vaughn 2002, p. 133.

56 Du Fresne de Beaucourt, 1891, p. 9.

57 Pfisterer 2016, pp. 181-184.

58 Kren 2010.

59 Kren 2005, pp. 50-51; Kren 2010, p. 169.

60 Kren 2005, pp. 57-58.

61 Kren 2010, pp. 175-178.

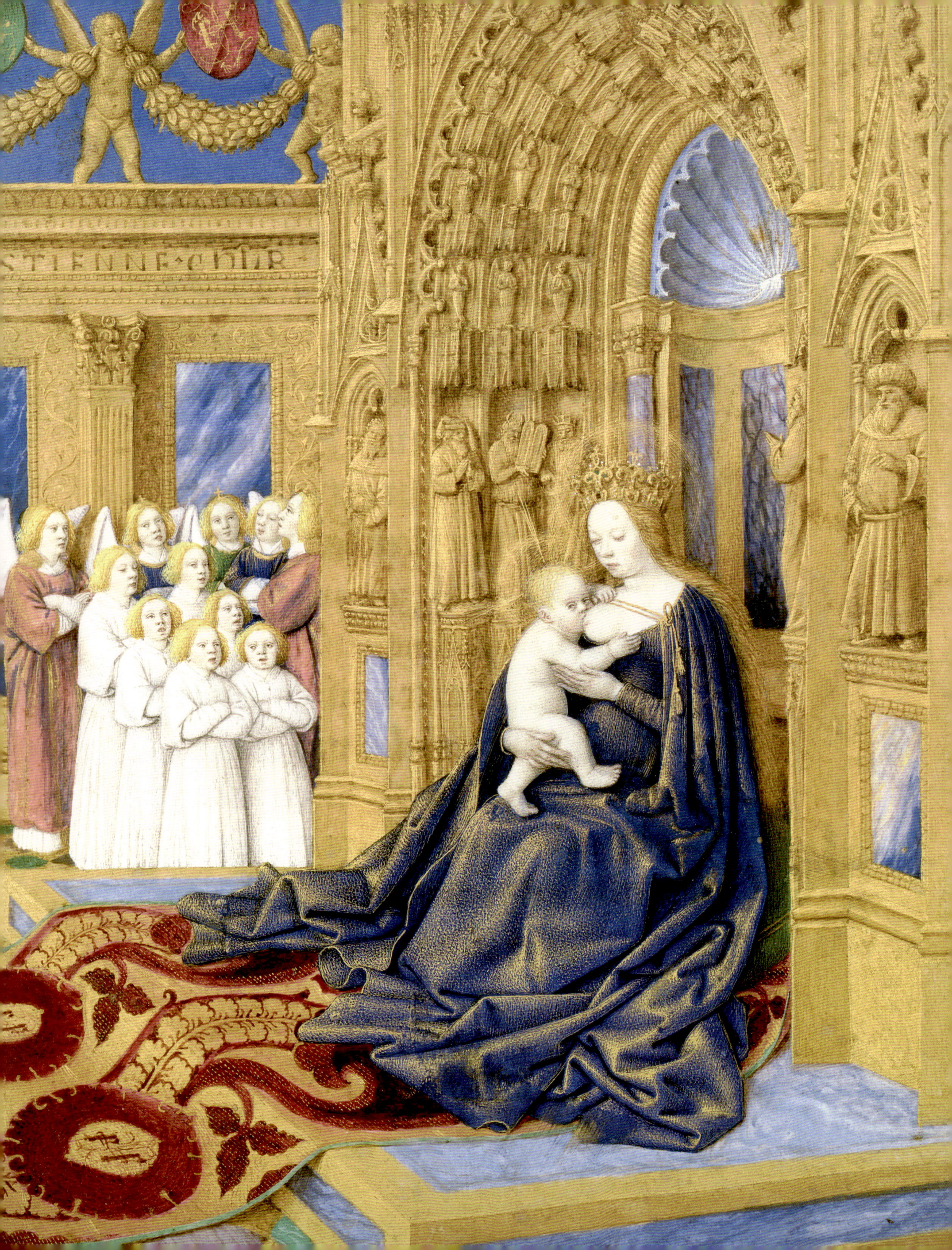
STIENNE·CHR

Peter Kurmann

RENAISSANCE IN THE FORECOURT OF HEAVEN – JEAN FOUQUET AS A PAINTER OF ARCHITECTURE

The *Melun Diptych* depicts a supernatural vision bestowed upon Étienne Chevalier. The viewer of the diptych observes what the patron can see only with his inner eye, since in the real, physical world it is invisible to him as he gazes past it: a vision of the Madonna surrounded by angels. Equally apparent to the viewer of the painting is Étienne Chevalier's name saint, who stands alongside him, laying his hand on his shoulder. A gold-heightened inscription on the base of the pilaster at the left edge of the Berlin panel records Étienne Chevalier's name,[1] as if to document and authenticate the vision. The apparition transports the patron from the earthly realm to the heavenly one, but the painter alludes to the earthly surroundings of both viewer and patron by depicting the reflection of a cross-barred window in the two onyx spheres on the backrest of the Madonna's throne. By incorporating an element from the patron's earthly reality into the heavenly scene, the painter indicates that the vision is taking place in Étienne Chevalier's familiar environment: one of the rooms of a magnificent stone townhouse, which in the 15th century would have been distinguished by its cross-barred windows. This reference to the earthly world, reflected in the heavenly Throne of Wisdom, reminds the viewer that a holy life in the here and now is the condition for entrance into the eternal Paradise. This reminder, in turn, conveys an encoded request to viewers of the image to pray for the salvation of the patron's soul, thereby earning for themselves merits in heaven.[2]

But what kind of a space is this, in which Étienne Chevalier and St. Stephen find themselves? If the onyx spheres are to be believed, it does not belong to the earthly realm, for otherwise the space would be reflected in them along with the windows. Certainly the banquet halls and dwelling chambers of the castles and palaces of the upper classes in 15th-century France looked nothing like this room, of which we see only a small portion, consisting of the lower part of a single wall and a small section of floor paved with costly marble tiles. The wall is paneled in white marble with a high dado supporting an order of pilasters. Panels of intensely glowing polychrome marble between the pilasters are paired with a decorative rhomboid pattern on the dado.[3] The picture is cropped in such a way that we see no more than the lower third of the elevation, but we can imagine a high, imposing hall of a considerable extent continuing beyond the right-hand border of the picture and receding further into depth. For the period shortly after the middle of the 15th century when this work was most likely painted, this kind of composition was highly unusual, even by Italian standards. In the 14th and 15th centuries, Italian artists preferred to depict entire rooms when representing figures and scenes in architectural interiors.[4] Giotto, however, had painted partial views of rooms in several frescoes in Assisi, allowing some parts of the space to be cut off by the edges of the picture and in some cases omitting the ceiling as well.[5] When the viewer stands before an image depicting a section of a room which at the same time is imagined to be larger, the distance between the viewer and the subject represented seems to diminish. The same holds true for the donor

Fig. 68. Jean Fouquet, *Maria lactans*, from the *Hours of Étienne Chevalier*, Chantilly, Musée Condé

panel from Melun. Since here the physically perceptible room is only suggested—an impression intensified by the positioning of the protagonists, who draw close to the front edge of the picture and fill almost the entire composition—the viewer is unavoidably pulled into the vision bestowed upon Étienne Chevalier. As for the latter, his gaze into infinity[6] and his highly focused facial expression clearly indicate that he quite literally has eyes for nothing else.

For a mid-15th-century French painting, however, what is even more unusual than the cropping of the image is the architectural language employed by the artist to depict the interior space. It is the architectural language of classical antiquity, presumably mediated by the early Italian Renaissance. Along with a number of illuminations from the *Hours of Étienne Chevalier*, painted by Fouquet around the same time,[7] the Berlin donor panel likely represents the earliest manifesto of the Renaissance of the Italian Quattrocento north of the Alps. It is evident that this kind of architectural image could emerge only as a result of Fouquet's journey to Italy;[8] the artist could have acquired his understanding of antique architecture only through direct contact with ancient monuments or those of the contemporary Renaissance in Italy. Thus the pilasters of the wall paneling are supported by Attic bases, whose profile corresponds to the classical pattern used, for example, by Alberti on the pedestals and columns of the corner pilasters and main portal of the façade of S. Maria Novella in Florence.[9] The cropping of the Melun donor panel obscures the pilaster capitals from view, but we can well imagine that if Fouquet had included them, he would have rendered them as classical Corinthian capitals. The latter had been introduced in Florence during the second third of the 15th century by Brunelleschi as well as by Alberti and his circle, for example in S. Pancrazio (Capella Rucellai and entrance front), the Pazzi Chapel at S. Croce, and again on the façade of S. Maria Novella.[10] Fouquet himself used this same capital type in a number of miniatures, along with capitals from other column orders.[11] The most striking are the classical Corinthian capitals on the second donor image he painted for Étienne Chevalier, the two-page illumination from the *Hours of Étienne Chevalier* (fig. 43, 68)[12]—likewise a double image that repeats the theme of the *Melun Diptych*, though in a somewhat different con-

figuration. In contrast to the panel painting in Berlin, in the manuscript illumination the space in which the scene takes place is visible not merely in part, but in its entirety. From a slightly elevated vantage point, the viewer sees the entire long side of a large hall as well as its narrow sides, opening up the entire space within which the event occurs.[13] Most of this space is filled with the actors in the scene, all of whom are represented in full figure. Once again, the kneeling Étienne Chevalier presents himself as donor and suppliant before the enthroned Madonna; once again, he is accompanied by St. Stephen, who now also kneels to the right of him. This time, the throne on which the Madonna is seated is completely concealed by the folds of her mantle; here, she not only shows the Child her breast, but also nurses him. This work thus depicts a closer relationship between Mother and Child than in the diptych; moreover, the Christ Child does not look at Étienne Chevalier, but rather turns his head and his gaze toward the viewer of the image (who, however, is virtually identifiable with Étienne Chevalier as the owner of the book of hours). The space between the main figures, who occupy the front of the middle ground, and the walls at the back is almost completely filled with a host of angels—singing on the Virgin's side, playing instruments on the donor's side. The singing angels represent the praising heavenly hosts, while the angels with instruments harmoniously accompany the human soul after death on its way to heaven through the spheres.[14] Thus this image, too, is closely associated with the patron's plea for salvation, which he directs to the Virgin.

Behind the Madonna's throne, the entire narrow side of the room is filled with an elaborate Gothic portal, to which we will return later. The other walls are decorated with the same classicizing[15] paneling we see on the donor painting from Melun; in the book of hours, however, the paneling is shown in its full height, with Corinthian capitals, entablature, and cornice. Above, a blue sky seems to open up, where our attention is drawn to putti holding garlands of grain. Is the viewer supposed to interpret the putti and the sky as a painted fiction, or as a living reality? What, in fact, constitutes reality in in this picture? Until now, scholars have almost always interpreted the donor's spatial environment in the double image—both in the *Melun Diptych* and in the book of hours—as an earthly reality. However, we would maintain that this room also belongs to heaven and constitutes part of the vision. Confirmation for this interpretation is provided above all by the antique architecture of the double image in the book of hours. In the first place, this architecture optically connects the donor with the Mother of God, so that there is no longer any separation between the supernatural realm and the earthly world; this connection is also reinforced by the presence of angels in both parts of the space. Furthermore, the unreal, golden preciousness of the architecture points to the spiritual realm—which incidentally also holds true for the wall paneling in the donor image from Melun: to the degree that it departs from almost archeological exactness in its rendering of antique models, it does so in order to call forth the impression of a special opulence, as in the delicate leaf pattern on the shafts of all the pilasters, chiseled in or painted on in fine lines.

It is no coincidence that Fouquet chose antique architecture as the "stage set" for the vision of Étienne Chevalier, for this architectural style conveyed a message essential to the interpretation of both donor images. In his vision, the patron has come to the very threshold of the Holy of Holies, but has not yet crossed into it, and still finds himself in the antechamber, as it were, of the eternal Paradise. In the book of hours, the Gothic portal that leads to this paradise is still closed, and indeed is occupied by a Renaissance niche: the Virgin Mary must still offer up her intercession. The golden forecourt of Paradise is radiant in the forms of classical antiquity; it is one of the many mansions in the Father's house (John 14:2). In mid-15th-century France, antique architecture was an absolute novelty: the stark clarity of its formal language verged on the miraculous. Thus at that time, no better setting could have been imagined for a vision which, in itself, was also something miraculous.

In both of Étienne Chevalier's donor images, the depiction of marble panels between the pilasters on the walls establishes an association with the ancient architectural technique of incrustation. This practice had enjoyed a long tradition in Italy since antiquity. It is safe to assume that most major buildings in Roman times were covered with marble facing; certainly Fouquet would have seen the remains of such incrustation in Rome, and in the 15th century there were probably more surviving examples

than today.[16] The Pantheon alone offered a variety of specimens.[17] Naturally, there had also been painted imitations of marble paneling in antiquity,[18] and this practice was widespread in the Middle Ages as well. Did Fouquet model his images on the painted versions, or was he more strongly influenced by monumental architecture? Fully preserved examples of incrustation were visible in Florence in buildings that we now consider representatives of a "proto-Renaissance" due to their use of antique forms;[19] the most outstanding of these are the Baptistery of Florence and S. Miniato al Monte.[20] However, even as late as the end of the 15th century, the exterior of a quintessential central-plan Renaissance building like S. Maria delle Carceri in Prato was covered in marble facing in an obvious reference to the architectural incrustation of the past.[21]

Despite the transcendent nature of the scene, the "heavenly forecourt" in the two donor pictures by Fouquet is presented as a realistically rendered architectural interior. Thus it makes sense to look for precedents in Italy, both in churches and in the interiors of monumental public buildings or private palaces. In this context it is important to note that Fouquet combines two different elements—flat marble panels covering the wall, and an elevation showing a Corinthian pilaster order in high relief—thus making this configuration something other than true "incrustation architecture".

The search for a series of pilasters alternating with wall panels in 15th-century Italian church architecture yields no results, unless one feels compelled to mention the decoration of the upper part of the wall compartments between the chapel entrances in the nave of the Tempio Malatestiano in Rimini.[22] There, however, the rows of flat pilasters serve only as ornamentation and show none of the structural understanding of antique architecture that informs Fouquet's painted elevations. Equally fruitless is the search for precedents in secular Italian architecture. The only example of pilasters in relief on the interior of a secular building that predates Fouquet's compositions, at least in terms of its conception, is the *salone* in the Palazzo di Parte Guelfa in Florence, although here care is advised in view of the extensive restorations undertaken on this building.[23] Of the pilaster orders represented in Italian painting, only the one from Piero della Francesca's 1451 fresco of Sigismondo Malatesta kneeling before his name saint (Tempio Malatestiano, Rimini) can be dated to around the same time as Fouquet's pictures; there, however, the architectural elements are arranged in an entirely different manner than in Fouquet's paintings of the "forecourt of heaven".[24] In Italy, painted orders of pilasters are rare during the second half of the Quattrocento, an observation that holds true both for the walls of real spaces—for example the Sala dei Gigli in the Palazzo Vecchio in Florence from the 1480s—and those that appear in paintings and frescoes.[25]

In contrast to painted orders of pilasters in interior spaces, painted marble occurs relatively frequently in the Italian art of the Trecento and Quattrocento. Although the tradition of painted marble certainly goes back to late antiquity, most artists of the later Middle Ages and the Renaissance would have looked to Giotto for the rendering of marble. Giotto had painted figures of the Virtues and Vices alternating with fictive marble panels on the dado of the Scrovegni Chapel in Padua,[26] and later he painted marble panels again in the Bardi and Peruzzi chapels in S. Croce in Florence.[27] One need only spend time in this church to observe how the motif spread among Giotto's successors: Maso di Banco painted square marble panels as wall facing[28] and Taddeo Gaddi included the motif on the stairway of the temple,[29] while the Master of the Rinuccini Chapel likewise adopted it in a somewhat different form.[30]

Scholars have rightly emphasized the importance of Fra Angelico for Jean Fouquet's artistic development. The two artists probably met in Rome,[31] and given this assumption, it is certainly no coincidence that incrusted polychrome marble panels of the type depicted by Fra Angelico in some of his paintings recur in Fouquet's images of the "forecourt of paradise". Particularly noteworthy in this respect are two panels painted by Fra Angelico with scenes from the legend of Saints Cosmas and Damian. The panels come from the predella of the high altar of S. Marco in Florence and are now in Munich. The scene in which the saints appear before the proconsul along with their brothers takes place in front of a background wall consisting of an order of columns, marble panels, and an entablature (fig. 69).[32] The analogy to the wall design of Fouquet's donor image in the book of hours is striking: one would only need to replace the Ionic order with a Corinthian one and change the colors

of the wall panels to arrive at a composition very similar to that used by Fouquet in the donor images of Étienne Chevalier. In the second painting by Fra Angelico, the proconsul, tormented by demons, is seated in front of a wall incrusted with marble panels, whose gleaming surfaces and lively veining recall certain wall panels in both versions of Fouquet's "heavenly forecourt" (fig. 70).[33] Such details bear witness to the way in which the younger of the two great masters adopted and varied the formal inventions of the elder, integrating them into different contexts.

Do these marble panels have special meaning? We would not ask this question if the trendy art historian and philosopher Georges Didi-Huberman had not raised it. In a wide-ranging study of a number of major works by Fra Angelico, Didi-Huberman discusses in depth the possible meaning of the four fictive marble panels painted by the artist beneath the *Sacra conversazione* (known as the *Madonna of the Shadows*) in the east corridor of the cloister of S. Marco in Florence.[34] Here the painter was supposedly concerned with the fundamental question of whether the divine can be represented in images. According to St. Augustine, the mystery of the Incarnation is conveyed through signs, whose indexical character can include dissemblance; in this sense, the stone is a dissimilar figure for the divine. The marble panels can signify many things: the cornerstone, the rock, but also the tomb of Christ and therewith also Mary, who likewise contained the Savior within her body. Didi-Huberman supports his theses with numerous passages from theological and philosophical treatises of late antiquity and the Middle Ages; but whether Fra Angelico had read all these sources is anything but certain, and thus it remains questionable whether the painter was the great intellectual which, according to Didi-Huberman, he would have to have been.[35] And in fact this multilayered interpretation has already yielded to a simpler reading, one that understands the polychrome marble fundamentally as a "figure of Christ".[36] This conception would also explain why the great representations of the Last Supper by Andrea del Castagno (Cenacolo di S. Apollonia, Florence)[37] und Domenico Ghirlandaio (refectory, S. Marco, Florence)[38] show gigantic wall panels of varicolored marble extending the entire length of the picture area. On the other hand, however, in his wall paintings from the Villa Carducci-

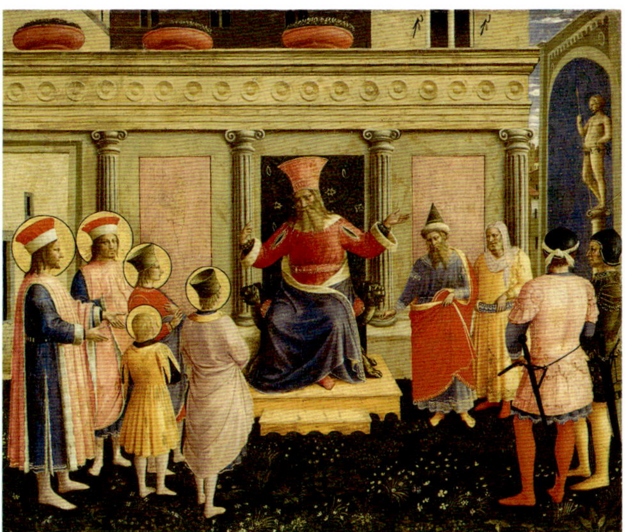

Fig. 69. Fra Angelico, *Saints Cosmas and Damian with their Brothers before the Proconsul Lysias*, Munich, Alte Pinakothek

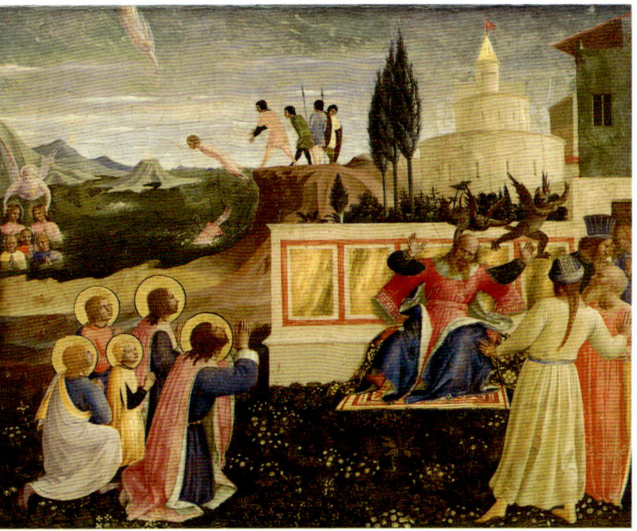

Fig. 70. Fra Angelico, *Proconsul Lysias Possessed by Demons; Saints Cosmas and Damian are Thrown into the Sea*, Munich, Alte Pinakothek

Pandolfini in Legnaia, this same Andrea del Castagno also used painted panels of colored marble as the background for his very secular *Uomini illustri*, who appear in the company of a number of female figures from antiquity.[39] In this pictorial context, do the panels symbolize the physical strength of the heroes, or the strength of their moral resolve? And in the case of the two scenes by Fra Angelico from the legend of Saints Cosmas and Damian, might the motif even point to something negative, namely to the wealth and arrogance of the tyrants who imposed martyrdom on the two saints? If so, it would be no coincidence that the marble panels in both paintings are located near the villain. If this interpretation were tenable, the spectrum of possible meanings for this decorative architectural element could extend from the forecourt of heaven all the way to the demons of hell.

In the case of the two donor images of Étienne Chevalier, the marble panels, derived from tradition by way of Fra Angelico, unequivocally serve to signify heavenly splendor. Fouquet's inspiration for combining a three-dimensional pilaster elevation with incrusted marble panels probably came directly from Fra Angelico. The Frenchman's close relationship with the great Dominican and his knowledge of the latter's work down to the smallest details is evidenced by such elements as the previously mentioned leaf pattern on the pilaster shafts in the donor panel in Berlin. The same motif is found in a similar, if somewhat more

abstracted form in Fra Angelico's fresco of St. Lawrence before the emperor Decius from the Capella Niccolina in the Vatican (fig. 71).[40] There the leaf pattern decorates the pilasters framing the niche where the emperor sits in judgment.[41] Since the exact dates of Fouquet's journey to Italy are uncertain, we must assume that even if he did not see the actual frescoes in the Vatican, which were executed in the late 1440s, at least he was privy to Fra Angelico's working drawings. It is likely that the French artist produced a certain number of sketches and drawings on the basis of these and many other prototypes,[42] study material that would have remained with him throughout his life. It is significant to note, however, that with only one exception, Fouquet never rendered any kind of large building in its entirety in the antique style. Instead of depicting complete buildings, he contented himself with the repro-

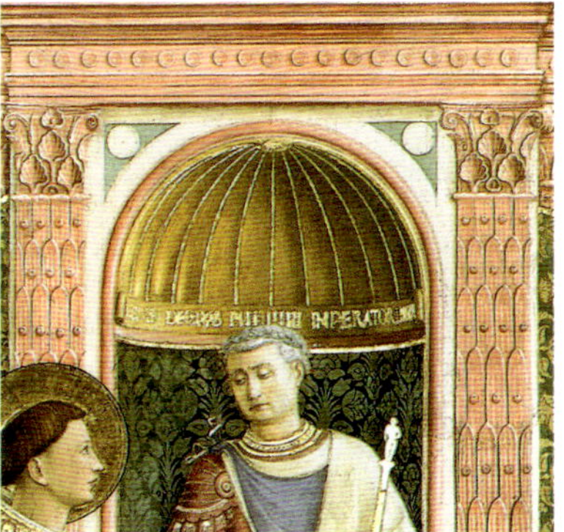

Fig. 71. Fra Angelico, *St. Lawrence before Decius*, ca. 1450, Vatican, Capella Niccolina, detail

103

duction of parts[43]—whether porticos,[44] paneling on walls and stage-like daises,[45] triumphal arches,[46] columns,[47] or putti holding shields.[48] It is also striking how few examples of antique architecture are found within the scope of Fouquet's oeuvre as a whole.[49] All the more significant, therefore, is the illumination in the *Grandes Chroniques de France* (BnF, fr. 6465, fol. 89 v) showing the coronation of Charlemagne in the interior of Old St. Peter's.[50] Here the artist not only depicts a late antique building in its entirety, but shows it exactly as it appeared during his time. The archaeologically correct rendering of Old St. Peter's strongly suggests that the artist relied upon his Roman sketchbook, which presupposes a certain historical consciousness: the historically authenticated event is placed within a pictorial setting rendered with equal historical accuracy.

It seems plausible that the distinctive character of the antique architecture of Italy would have deepened the aspiring master's awareness of the special qualities of the Gothic style native to the regions north of the Alps. Although we know nothing about his training or the beginning of his artistic activity, Fouquet's preference for Gothic buildings, along with many other indicators, suggests that he learned his profession in the milieu of so-called Early Netherlandish painting. This supposition is supported not only by the accuracy of his imaginary buildings and cityscapes, but above all also by his ability to realistically render parts of existing buildings (and in rare instances even overall views). The exact observation of architecture was not an absolute novelty at the time the young Fouquet would have received his training. The earliest exact architectural portraits in the entire history of art are found in the *Très Riches Heures* of the Duc de Berry,[51] where exterior views of fortifications and castles appear in the calendar pages and in the miniature of the *Temptation of Christ*. These "portraits" evince an astonishing degree of accuracy. The motivation for this precision probably had little to do with the desire to depict earthly buildings as representations or prefigurations of the Heavenly Jerusalem;[52] rather, the intention was to present the architectural perfection of the castles and their well-ordered surroundings as the sign of a *buon governo*, as had been the case already in the corresponding portions of the famous fresco by Ambrogio Lorenzetti in Siena.[53] The castles are presented as surrogates for the "good rulers", and topographical accuracy in their representation was the highest imperative in order to unequivocally identify the castles with their particular rulers. The extremely precise portraits of fortresses, cities, and villages in the domain of the Duke of Auvergne, Bourbonnais, and Forez that appear in the *Armorial* of Guillaume Revel from the 1450s can be understood in the same sense.[54] Here, too, exactness of rendering is by no means an artistic concern, but rather a political or administrative one.

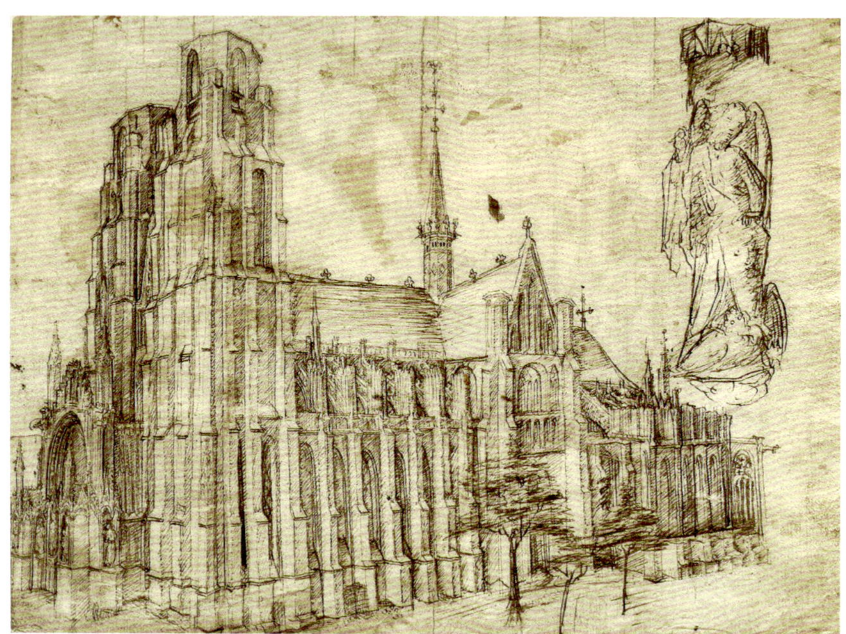

Fig. 72. Master of Girart de Roussillon(?), *Large Church*, ca. 1450, pen and ink on paper, 21.3 x 28 cm, Erlangen, Universitätsbibliothek, Graphische Sammlung

Quite different in nature are those representations of architecture from the first half of the 15th century that can be described as "realistic architectural fantasies". Such images could reflect a purely artistic intention, as with a drawing in Erlangen, or could be imbued with iconographic significance, as in the so-called *Madonna in the Church* by Jan van Eyck, now in the Gemäldegalerie in Berlin. Always, however, such images were derived from examples of real architecture that were defamiliarized or recombined in new ways. An anonymous pen drawing from around 1450, now in Erlangen (fig. 72), is a kind of capriccio that arbitrarily combines elements from various Gothic cathedrals in Normandy: the façade of Bayeux, the nave of Notre-Dame in Rouen, and the transepts of Lisieux and Coutances.[55] This *mixtum compositum* was probably a study by means of which an aspiring artist could prove his familiarity with buildings in a particular local area. Much more important from an art historical standpoint is the so-called *Virgin in the Church* by Jan van Eyck (fig. 73).[56] As a number of copies suggest, this painting was the left panel of a diptych whose right-hand portion showed a kneeling donor.[57] The analogy of the subject matter to that of the donor images of Étienne Chevalier is striking: in both cases, the patron of the image beholds the Madonna in a vision, and in both, the apparition takes place in the heavenly realm. Van Eyck envisions heaven as a Gothic cathedral, thus invoking the ancient *topos* of the church building as symbolic of the various ontological modes of the church: as the community of believers consisting of "living stones" and as a symbol of eternal blessedness in the form of the Heavenly Jerusalem. Fouquet, on the other hand, clothes his vision of heaven in the Renaissance garb he had only just discovered in Italy. Nevertheless, he does not depart from the old understanding of church architecture as an image of heaven, and for him as a French artist—just as for van Eyck as a Netherlandish one—the highest form of church architecture could only be the Gothic cathedral, a creation of France. This sensibility may testify to an awakening national consciousness,[58] but bears even stronger witness to an understanding of liturgical hierarchies: in Gothic France, the *mater ecclesia* of a diocese was normally the grandest building far and wide. It is probably for this reason that Fouquet conjures up an entire Gothic portal from the

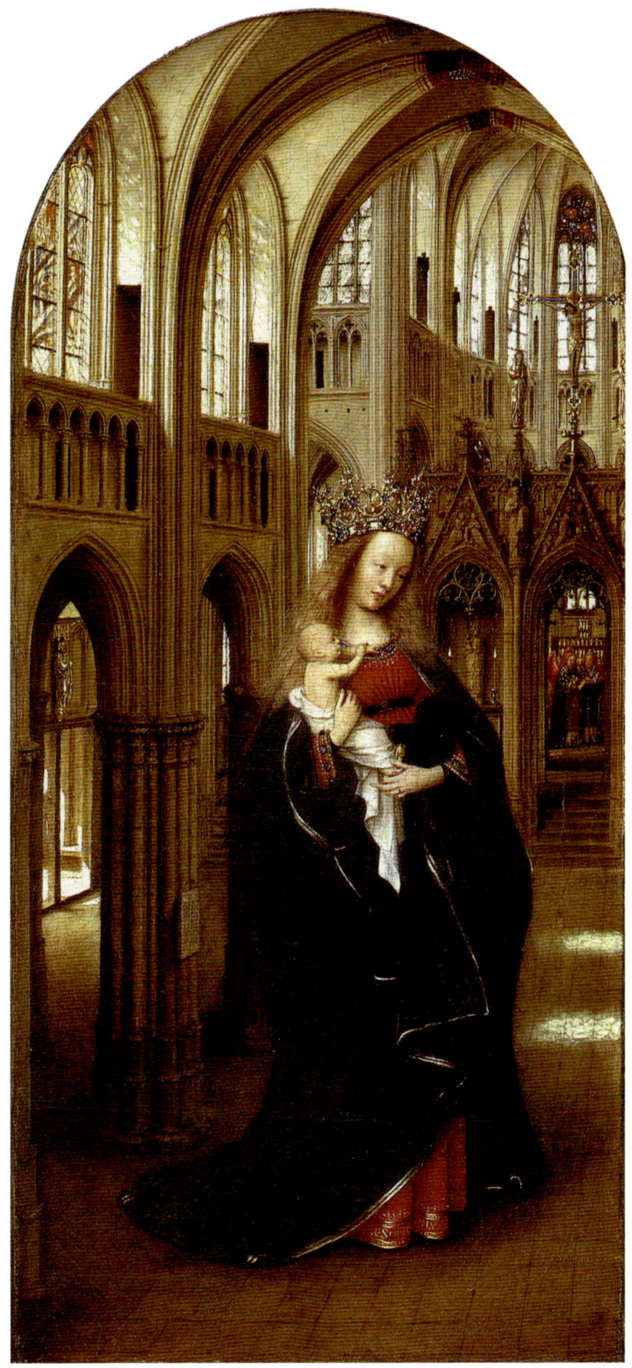

Fig. 73. Jan van Eyck, *Madonna in the Church*, ca. 1440, Berlin, Gemäldegalerie SMB

realm of the cathedrals for the *Hours of Étienne Chevalier*, inserting it into an *aula caelestis* that is otherwise dominated by antique forms; here, too, the Mother of God becomes a kind of "Virgin in the Church" (fig. 68).[59] Fouquet's substitution of a Renaissance niche for the

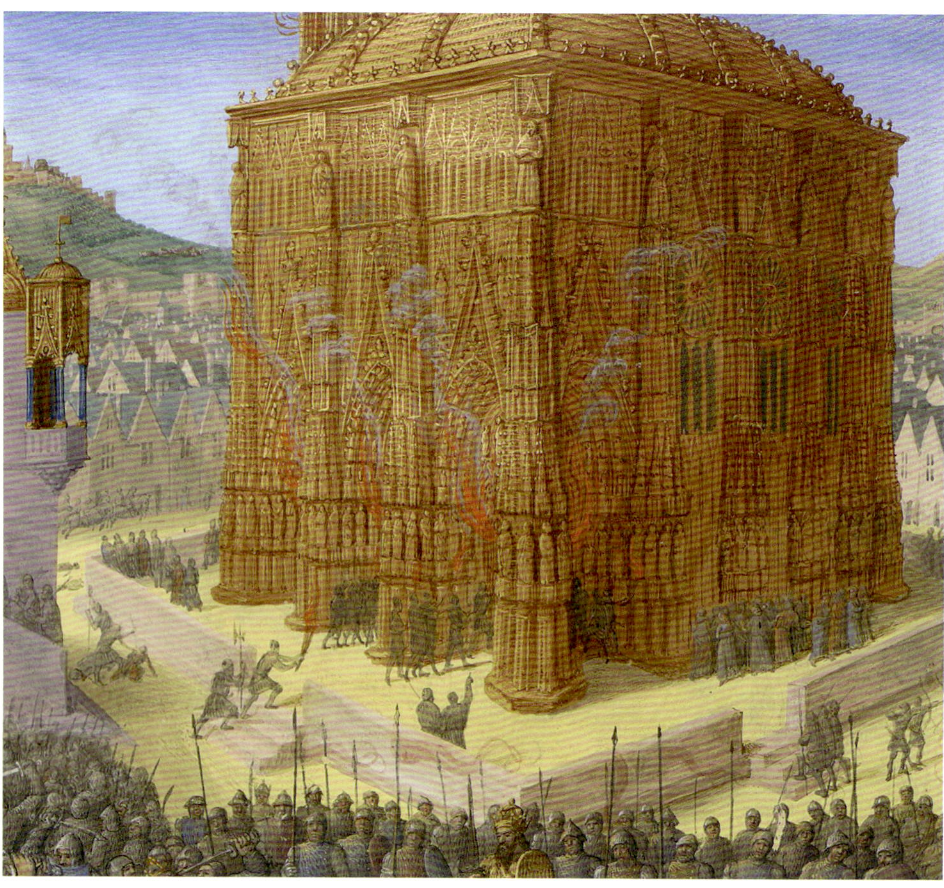

Fig. 74. Jean Fouquet or the Master of the Munich Boccaccio, *Antiquités judaïques*, Book X, *The Burning of the Temple*, detail, Paris, BN, fr. 247, fol. 213v

tympanum and doors of this church portal, however, is especially subtle, for in so doing he associates the traditional image of the church with the new "marvel" of antique architecture.[60] And since the Mother of God sits in front of a Renaissance niche, the distance between her and the donor, who is likewise surrounded by antique forms, seems to diminish.

The meticulously rendered Gothic forms of the church portal alone demonstrate the exceptional development of Fouquet's understanding of architecture. In this respect he stands in the tradition of Jan van Eyck, who could certainly be described as an architect in disguise. The painting of the *Madonna in the Church* shows that if he had been commissioned to do so, van Eyck would have been fully capable of producing the design for a great cathedral with all the details of ground plan and elevation; in other words, the church depicted on the Berlin panel could be built in reality. For this reason, some have claimed that van Eyck illustrated an existing building that has since disappeared, such as the old

cathedral of St. Lambert in Liège. But Jan's church interior is, and remains, his own unique invention. While he did employ components from existing monumental sacred buildings in Flanders and Brabant, he combined them so skillfully into a new overall composition that the imaginary building takes on the character of a believable, though in fact only illusory reality: the piers of the nave are derived from the Church of Our Lady at Bruges, the triforium and upper gallery from the Basilica of Our Lady at Tongeren, and the triforium as well as the clerestory in the choir from the church of St. John (now St. Bavo) at Ghent. There is no doubt that Jan van Eyck would have been capable of painting an accurate, realistic rendering of a specific building, but apparently he was either not interested in doing so or was not given the opportunity.[61]

Like Jan van Eyck, Jean Fouquet knew how to take individual elements from real, existing Gothic buildings and expertly combine them into a new composition. Proof of his ability to do so is offered by two nearly identical rep-

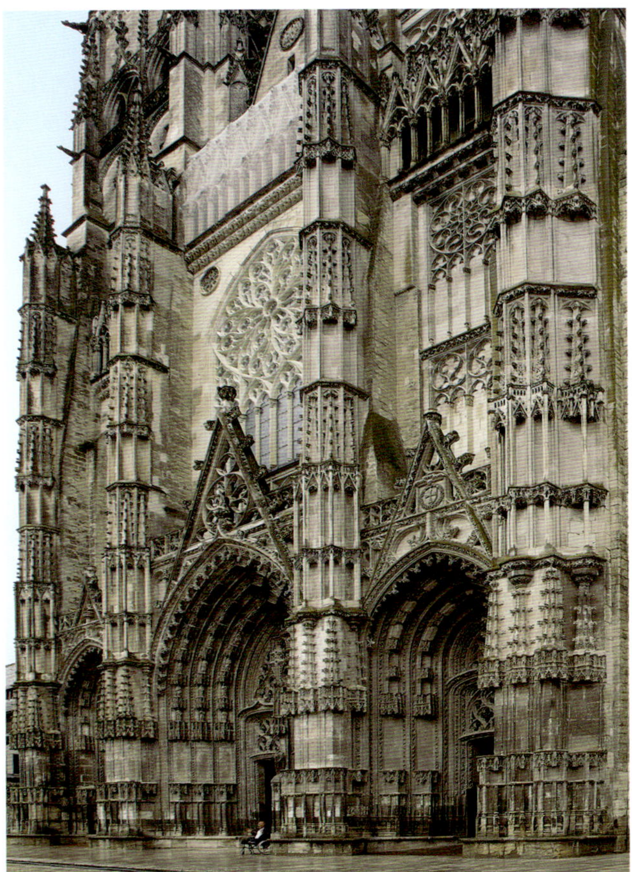

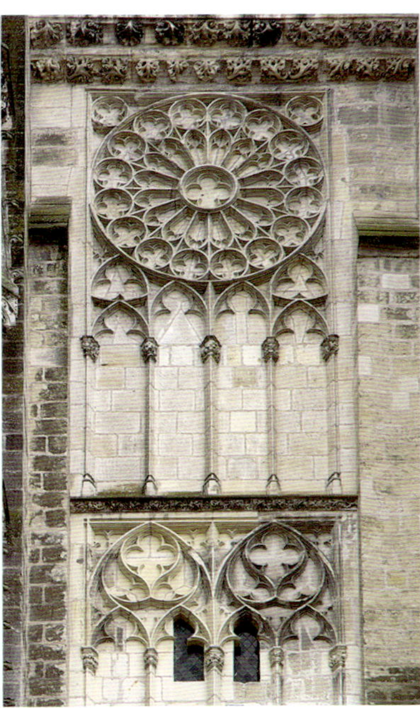

Fig. 76. Tours, cathedral, west façade, blind rose window below north tower

Fig. 75. Tours, cathedral, west façade from the southwest

resentations of the Jewish Temple from the *Antiquités judaïques*, both of which paraphrase the west front of the cathedral of Tours up to the height of the open galleries of the towers. The images in question depict the construction (Paris, BN, fr. 247, fol. 163) and the burning of the Temple (ibid., fol. 213 v).[62] In the image of the construction of the Temple, the right side of the building is cropped, while the burning of the Temple shows the entire structure; for this reason, the latter miniature will serve for comparison with the façade from Tours (fig. 74). On the cathedral of Tours, the late Romanesque façade of the 12th century was covered over with late Gothic forms in the *style flamboyant* (fig. 75), placing the architectural ornamentation only a little earlier than Fouquet's illuminations.[63] The façade consists of three deep portal bays, separated by strongly projecting buttresses and articulated by blind ornamentation with a giant tracery window in the center. Fouquet altered the prototype by transposing the design of the west façade of Tours onto an imaginary rectangular central-plan building.

Since he doubled the height of the portals in comparison to the real building, he omitted the zone of the (blind) windows beneath the gallery at the base of the open stories of the towers. The painter took the narrow Romanesque side of the façade, still visible on the original building, and multiplied it into five bays on the main side of his Temple, reformulating it in the *style flamboyant* and including three giant tracery windows, each framed by a portal bay.[64] Fouquet's understanding of the specific character of the west façade of Tours is evidenced by his consistent repetition of the main motif of the buttresses—their corners rounded by multiple niches for figural sculpture stacked one above the other—on the corners of his painted central-plan building, thereby suggesting freestanding piers behind which an entry hall might be located. There is no such entry hall, however; as the miniature of the construction of the temple on fol. 163 makes clear, the buttresses form an architectural unity with the jambs and archivolts on all the portals. On each of the corners of Fouquet's imaginary building, two portals

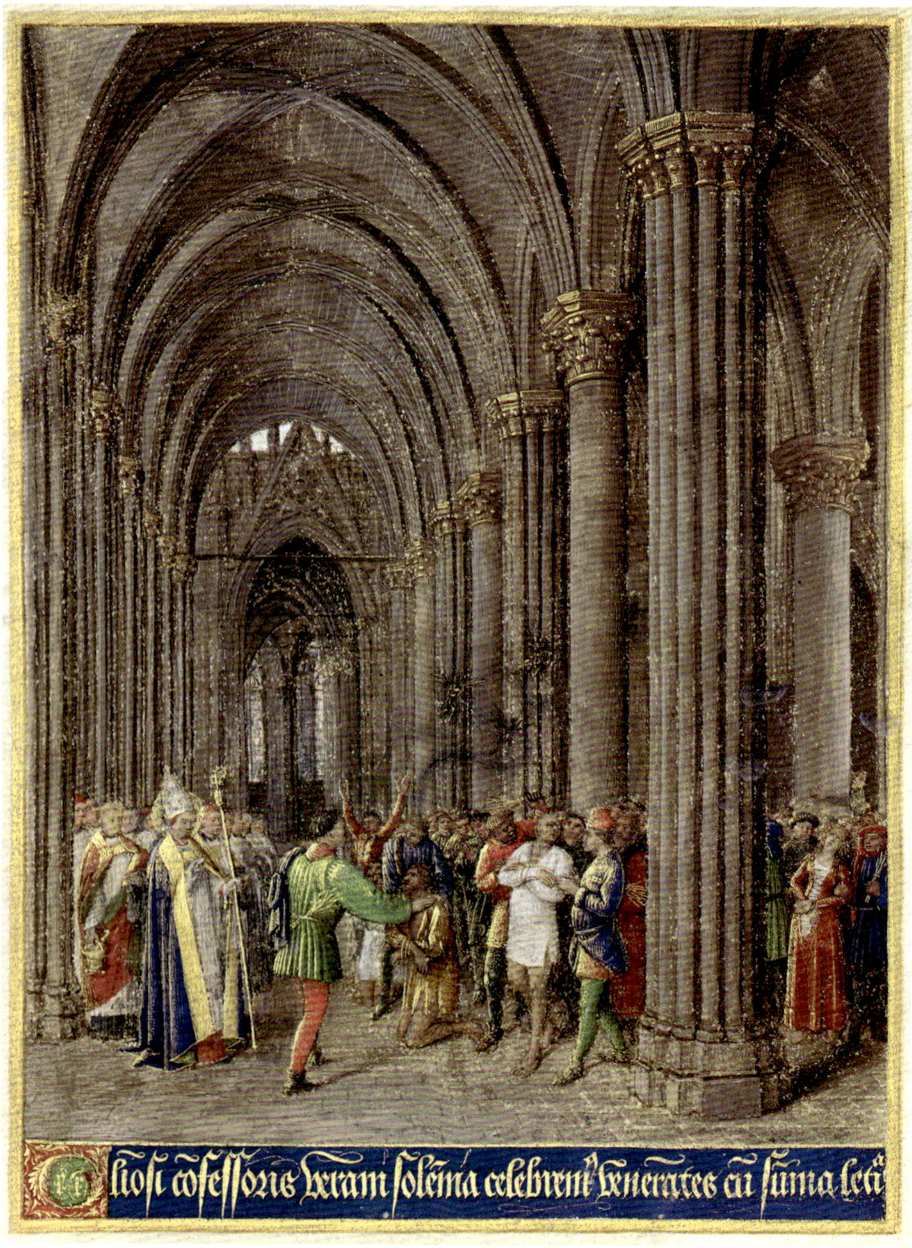

Fig. 77. Jean Fouquet, *St. Veranus Heals the Demon-Possessed*, from the *Hours of Étienne Chevalier*, Paris, Musée Marmottan, donation Daniel Wildenstein, ms. 153

meet at a right angle. The cathedral of Nantes, with its two-tower façade erected in the second third of the 15ᵗʰ century, offers a concrete example of this motif: statue niches superimposed on the buttresses serve to optically connect the portal jambs at either edge of the façade to adjacent portals standing at a right angle to the west. While this disposition is very similar to Fouquet's Jewish Temple,[65] the formal language of the painted building in the *Antiquités judaïques* is exclusively that of the masons' workshop from the cathedral in Tours. Fouquet adopts it

down to the smallest detail; even the anachronistic rayonnant rose window in each of the three tracery windows on the long side of the Temple is found on the actual building in the zone of blind tracery beneath the north tower (fig. 76). The question of the historical relationship between the specific example of the west façade of Nantes and Fouquet's conception of the Jewish temple remains open. Be that as it may, it is evident that Fouquet used existing features from the major work of large-scale architecture in his home city, built during his lifetime, to

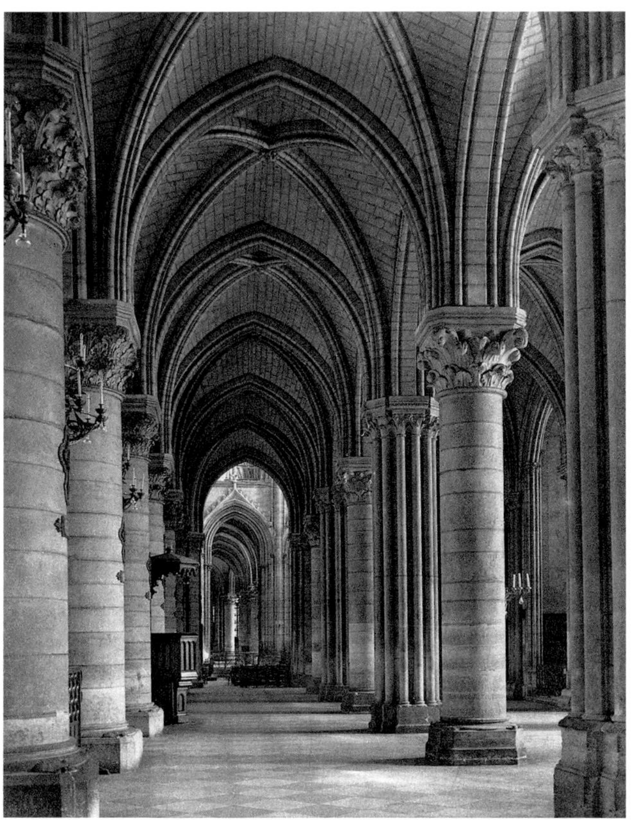

Fig. 78. Paris, Notre-Dame, nave, south side aisle from the west

create a fictive manifesto of precious craftsmanship that would have made any goldsmith proud, not only due to its golden coloration, but also because of its refinement. The fact that the Jewish Temple appears here in the form of a Christian church underlines the continuity between the Old and New Testaments.

There is no doubt that Fouquet's Jewish Temple represents a high point for the pictorial type of the realistic architectural fantasy. Since the painter drew the formal material for his composition exclusively from a single existing building,[66] the effect of a believable, illusionistic reality created by the artist—already observable in van Eyck's *Madonna in the Church*—is increased exponentially. Due to its coherence of structure and ornamentation, the fictive building takes on the quality of an architectural portrait—and it is only a small step from a work like this to an accurate, realistic rendering and thus a true architectural portrait. Jean Fouquet is in fact the creator of the earliest portrait of an existing interior space in the entire history of art: while Pieter Jansz.

Saenredam is rightly considered "the first portrait painter of the Dutch church interior",[67] about 200 years earlier Fouquet had rendered the interior of a large cathedral with perfect, realistic accuracy (fig. 77).[68] The image in question comes from the *Hours of Étienne Chevalier* and depicts the two northern side aisles of the nave of Notre-Dame in Paris as the setting for a scene in which St. Veranus, bishop of Cavaillon, heals the demon-possessed (fig. 78).[69] The representation of the architecture seems to have been so important to the manuscript painter that he departed from the layout used for bishop saints in order to gain space for a full-page illumination. The only connection between St. Veranus and the cathedral of the French capital derives from the fact that the southern French bishop was especially venerated in the parish church of Saint-Vrain near Plessis-le-Comte—a possession of Étienne Chevalier—which belonged to the diocese of Paris.[70] We are left with the impression that the artist welcomed any excuse to paint part of the interior space of the Paris cathedral, for one can hardly imagine that this largely unknown saint enjoyed particular veneration in Paris.

This illumination in the *Hours of Étienne Chevalier* is Fouquet's most brilliant "architecture piece". The topography of the church is described so accurately that as viewers we can recognize our own vantage point: we stand in the westernmost bay of the outer side aisle[71] on the north side of the cathedral and look eastward toward the transept, down the magnificent row of alternating compound piers and round columns. All the details, such as the base of the compound pier in the right foreground, agree perfectly with reality.[72] The only simplification undertaken by the manuscript illuminator was to systematically replace the leaf capitals with bud forms. In accord with High Gothic ideals, Fouquet makes the supports more slender than they actually are, but that is artistic license rather than "inaccuracy". The same can be said of the arch at the entrance to the side aisle of the choir on the east wall of the transept, which appears in the left background of the picture. Like its prototype in the cathedral, it carries a gable, but Fouquet's gable is steeper than the real one and is connected to the tracery posts of a large window or glazed triforium overhead, which is not present in the real church since this is where the gallery is located. It is obvious that here, Fouquet intentionally "overinterpreted"[73] the alterations undertaken on the early Gothic transept in the second half of the 13th century, representing them with great expertise and sensitivity to the qualities of the High Gothic style of around 1300.[74] But it is not these "archaeological" observations that constitute the tremendous artistic value of this manuscript illumination, but rather its outstanding qualities of composition and lighting. The building, which stands in monumental serenity as if created for eternity, radiating the salvific power of the church, contrasts with the swirling mass of people that accompany the wildly gesticulating victims of demon-possession. Next to them, the clerics stand as motionless as the piers, a point of stability echoing the architecture. The space is suffused with an even half-light, appropriate to the dignity of the scene, yet strong enough to model the contours of the architectural members. The cathedral itself has become the subject of the picture.[75] It seems, then, that no further evidence or analysis[76] is needed to secure a place for Jean Fouquet among the greatest painters of architecture in the history of art.

1   [CHEVAL]IER ESTIEN[NE]

2   Bialostocki 1970, pp. 168-169, suggests a different reading of this motif, interpreting it as a symbol of Mary's virginity. The fact that the message of the onyx spheres—whatever it was intended to be—would no longer have been recognizable after the installation of the diptych in Notre-Dame in Melun due to the distance between the painting and the viewer does not exclude an iconological interpretation; for this it would suffice that the element was important to the painter and his patron.

3   Since the donor and his patron saint obscure two-thirds of the dado, only one iteration of the pattern is visible on the wall bay in the background; other decorative forms alternating with the rhombus would also be conceivable.

4   Kwastek 2001, p. 15.

5   Kwastek 2001, p. 33.

6   "Étienne Chevalier regarde vers l'Enfant, mais dans le vide" (Schaefer 2000, p. 299 n. 12).

7   Ca. 1452-1460; see Avril 2003, p. 193.

8   See the essay by Neville Rowley in this volume.

9   Syndikus 1996, pp. 145-146, fig. 199.

10   Syndikus 1996, pp. 54-60, fig. 38, 39, 42-44. Cf. the antique capital in S. Miniato al Monte (ibid., fig. 34).

11   The composite capital appears, for example, in the Visitation (Schaefer 1994, p. 53) and the Marriage of the Virgin (ibid., p. 91) in the Hours of Étienne Chevalier.

12   Ca. 1452-1460, see Avril 2003, p. 193.

13   On the concept of the Schauöffnung, see Kemp 1996, pp. 29 ff., 55 ff.

14   Clouzot 2007, pp. 276-293.

15   Since the distinction between the monuments of "real" classical antiquity and those of the Renaissance is not our primary concern here, we will subsume both of them under the generic terms "classical" and "antique".

16   For discussion of remains or traces of incrustation in areas belonging to the city of Rome, see Bitterer 2013.

17   Waddel 2008, Ch. 14, pp. 139-146.

18   An example would be the painted rectangular marble fields, both vertical and horizontal, beneath the figural bands of the Capella graeca in the Catacomb of Priscilla; see Aurea Roma 2000, p. 313.

19   For the concept and the most important examples, see Brucher 1987, pp. 160-170.

20   Both examples also show the rhomboid pattern used by Fouquet in the Melun donor panel.

21   Niebaum 2016, vol. 1, pp. 184-205, here pp. 204-205.

22   Paolucci 2010, vol. 1, pp. 49-121, here p. 75, vol. 2, pl. 44-47, 89, 264, 323, 325.

23   The pilasters may have been planned by Brunelleschi as early as the 1430s, but they were not executed by Maso di Bartolomeo until the 1450s; see Zervas 1987, pp. 221- 223.

24   Frommel 2016, pp. 80-81.

25   This observation is easily verified by the numerous representations of Italian interior spaces illustrated in Kwastek 2000 and Roettgen 1996, as well as in Roettgen 1997. In the realm of manuscript illumination, there are even fewer examples. In miniatures of the 14th and 15th centuries, the walls of interior spaces are depicted either as bare masonry or are covered with wall hangings or wooden paneling. See the numerous illustrations in Oledzka 2016; only one example stands out as an exception, showing a wall and window-frame faced with pilasters and entablature: the Explication des actes des apôtres, Paris, ca. 1510, Brit. Library, Harley MS 4393, fol. 2 r, fig. p. 48.

26   Flores D'Arcais 1995, fig. pp. 134-135, 141.

27   Flores D'Arcais 1995, fig. pp. 251, 257.

28   Baldini 1985, fig. pp. 113, 114.

29   Baldini 1985, fig. pp. 134, 137; here the panels of the side platform are even decorated with a rhomboid mosaic.

30   Baldini 1985, fig. p. 180.

31   See the essay by Neville Rowley in this volume.

32   Spike 1997, cat. 71 c, pp. 226-227.

33   Spike 1997, cat. 71 d, pp. 226-227.

34   Didi-Huberman 1995.

35   Ortheil 1995.

36   Gerbron 2012 a); Gerbron 2012 b).

37   Dunlop 2015, pp. 21-28, 36, fig. 1-5, 76.

38   Marchand 2003.

39   Dunlop 2015, pp. 69-89, fig. 29-42.

40   Spike 1997, cat. 105 c, pp. 248-249.

41   In the fresco by Fra Angelico, the leaves are strongly stylized with a brick-shaped outline. In the portrait of Jouvenel des Ursins, this shape suggests the leaves of the bear's breech plant, probably an allusion to the portrait subject's name (cf. Schaefer 1994, p. 203). The pilasters on the donor panel of Étienne Chevalier in Berlin, on the other hand, show stylized acanthus leaves.

42   On this point, see Inglis 2011, pp. 35 ff.

43   For the sake of brevity, the following notes will cite only a selection of relevant examples, using the illustration numbers in Schaefer 1994 rather than names and titles.

44   Fig. 29, 114, 133, 140.

45   Fig. 36, 42, 46, 47, 61, 65.

46   Fig. 51, 126.

47   Fig. 143, 144.

48   Fig. 24, 62, 65.

49   Isolated examples of open chapel-like spaces can hardly be interpreted as representative instances of the depiction of complete antique buildings, as Inglis seems to assume (see Schaefer 1994, fig. 133 and Inglis 2011, p. 143, fig. 139).

50   Schaefer 1994, p. 174, fig. p. 175.

51   Longnon/Cazelles 1969.

52   Müller 2000.

53   Schmidt 2003.

54   Fournier 1973.

55   Kurmann 2004; Buck 2009, pp. 64-67, attributes the drawing to the Brussels Master of Girart de Roussillon and dates it to the mid-15th century, but does not mention our suggested identification of the individual building parts.

56   Kurmann 2010.

57   Ganz 2010.

58   Inglis 2011.

59   Schaefer 1994, p. 51; Reynaud 2006, pp. 41, 44-45.

60   Fouquet adopts the same pictorial strategy in his representation of the Fountain of the Apostles in the *Hours of Étienne Chevalier*, where he places a Gothic fountain in front of antique architecture (Schaefer 1994, p. 84 and fig. 48; Reynaud 2006, pp. 92-94.)

61   The depiction of the tower from the cathedral of Utrecht in both the *Ghent Altarpiece* and the cityscape of the *Madonna of the Chancellor Rolin* does represent an exception, but this isolated representation of a specific building in van Eyck's oeuvre is not enough to qualify the artist as a master of architectural portraiture. Dhanens' hypothesis that the choir ambulatory behind the *Virgin and Child with Canon van der Paele* was modeled on that of the Basilica of Our Lady in Maastricht is hardly convincing; in terms of scale alone, the two examples are divergent (Dhanens 1980, p. 223).

62   Schaefer 1994, p. 215, fig. 137, p. 219, fig. 139; Avril 2003, pp. 310 ff., fig. pp. 319 and 321. Here we are intentionally avoiding the controversial question of the different artists' hands at work in the miniatures from this codex, since in fact the design of the temple architecture discussed here can only be attributed to Fouquet.

63   See the somewhat vague information on the dating of the Tours façade in Andrault- Schmitt 2010, pp. 240-247; for the dating of the manuscript and illuminations of the *Antiquités judaïques*, see Avril 2003, p. 311; the miniatures relevant for the current context are dated "around 1465" or "around 1470-75".

64   The structure of the rightmost bay on the side of the Temple with five bays is obscured by the strongly projecting buttress to its left; for rea-

sons of symmetry, however, we may assume that Fouquet intended both corner bays to have a portal. The three middle bays with rose windows, however, were not intended to have portals, but instead show walls decorated with blind arcades, as we can clearly see in the miniature of the burning of the Temple. This observation holds true even though the buttresses of these three bays, like those of the portal bays, are decorated with statues.

65   Guillouët 2013, pp. 50-52.

66   Negligible differences between the rendering of individual architecture features in Fouquet's miniatures and the façade itself are due to later restorations on the church, visible above all in the area of the portal gables.

67   Jantzen 1910, p. 86.

68   The cathedral depicted by Rogier van der Weyden in his Antwerp painting of the Seven Sacraments cannot be considered a portrait of a specific building, since he combines features from the cathedral of Tournai with those from Gothic buildings in Brabant, especially St. Gudula in Brussels (see Sauerländer 1994).

69   Schaefer 1994, p. 126 and fig. 70; Reynaud 2006, pp. 196-199, fig. p. 197.

70   Reynaud 2006, p. 196.

71   In other words, the one directly behind the façade.

72   Because of superior lighting conditions in the southern side aisles, we have chosen a photograph of the latter as a parallel to the miniature. This, however, does not compromise the comparison, since the side aisles of the Paris nave are symmetrical in every respect.

73   Fouquet's version of the wall articulation of the transept is seen, for example, in the choir of the cathedral of Séez (ca. 1270-1300); see Grant 2005, p. 204.

74   Jalabert 1963, p. 38.

75   Reynaud 2006, p. 199.

76   Another image as precise and realistic as the interior of the Paris cathedral is Fouquet's portrait of the cathedral's west façade in the miniature "The Hand of God Drives out the Demons" from the *Hours of Étienne Chevalier*, a work already much-discussed by scholars (see the greatly enlarged detail reproduction in Reynaud 2006, p. 12).

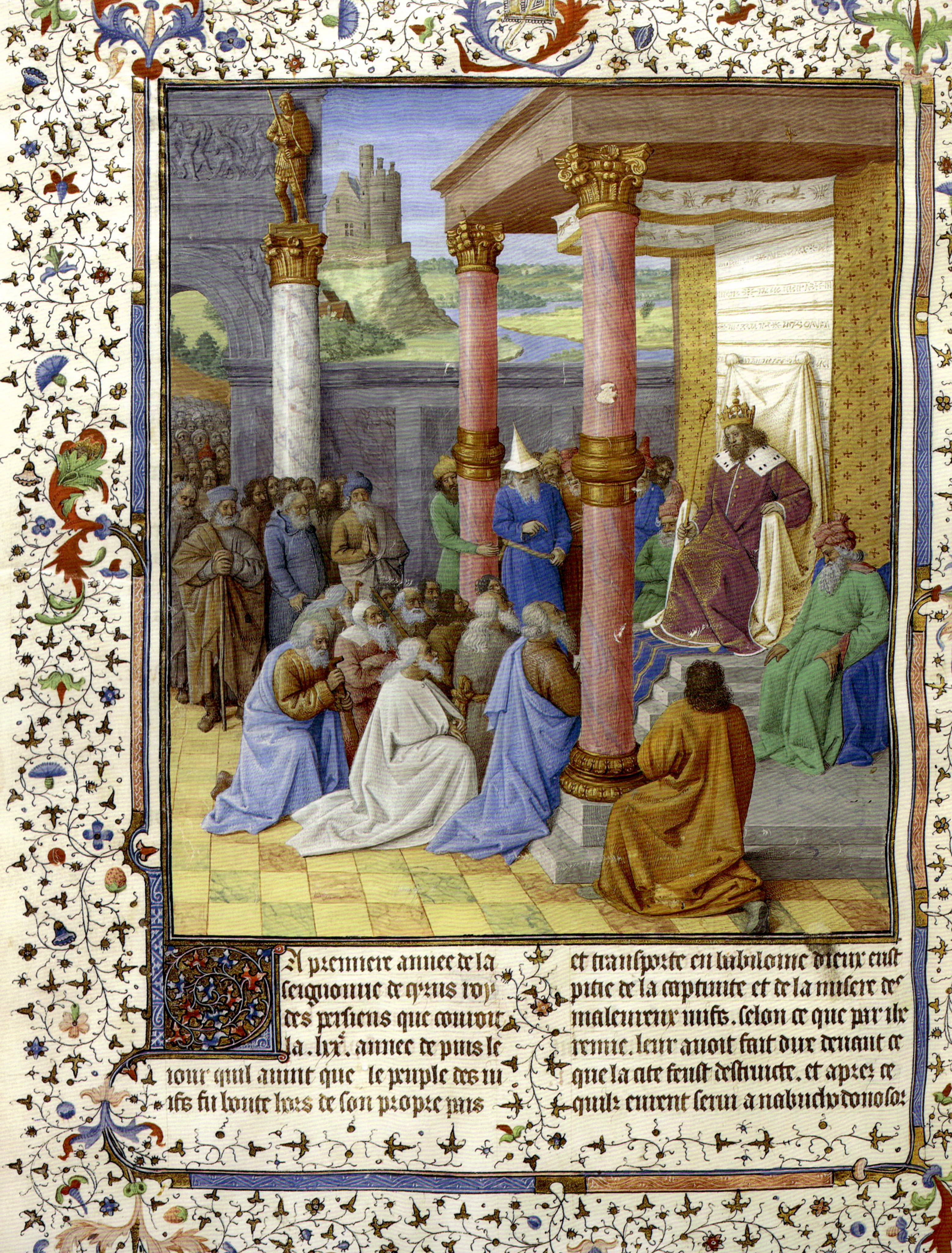

A premiere annee de la
seignourie de cyrus roy
des persiens que couroit
la .lxx. annee de puis le
iour quil auint que le peuple des iu
ifs fu boute hors de son propre pais
et transporte en babiloine dieux eust
pitie de la captiuite et de la misere des
maleureux iuifs. selon ce que par ihe
remie. leur auoit fait dure deuant ce
que la cite feust destruicte. et apres ce
quilz eurent seruj a nabuchodonoso:

Juliane von Fircks

„*EN GRANDS, RICHES ET DIVERS HABILLEMENS.*"[1]
VESTIMENTARY SPLENDOR AT THE COURT OF CHARLES VII
AND THE ENVISIONING OF LUXURY TEXTILES
IN THE WORK OF JEAN FOUQUET

Compared to the English duke of Bedford, who had resided in Paris as *regent de France* until 1435, and especially compared to the duke of Burgundy, the king of France was not a rich man. The poverty of the king and his retinue was lamented, for example, in a session of parliament held in Paris in 1437,[2] and the subsequent effort to improve the king's finances ("par n'importe quel moyen rehausser ses finances") involved levying immense taxes on the inhabitants of the capital city.[3]

The precarious financial situation of the monarchy contrasted starkly with the splendor and magnificence of the *joyeuse entrée*, the ceremonial entrance of the king into the capital city only shortly before.[4] For the inhabitants of Paris, this symbolic act made the change of power and the occupation by the French king a visible reality for the first time. The sequence and dramaturgy of this and similar events are recorded in detail in the *Chroniques du roi Charles VII* by Gilles le Bouvier (d. ca. 1455).[5] The triumphal character of the entrance and the overwhelming effect of the event were communicated to the spectators (as to the readers of the chronicle) in large measure by the splendid costumes of the knights. As we learn in regard to the entrance into the city of Rouen in 1449: "The king was accompanied by high lords, all clad in grand, rich, and diverse garments; some were draped entirely in gold fabric together with their horses,

while others wore velvet, embroidery, golden appliqués, damask, and satin fabrics according to various tastes and kinds".[6] Every participant in the parade was dressed according to his social standing, "chacun selon son degree".[7] Since the apparel served to represent an intact social order with the king at the pinnacle of the hierarchy, it had to manifest a corresponding degree of luxury, despite the shortness of funds. This display of weapons and textiles, as splendid and grand as possible—"avec la plus grande magnificence et avec un luxe royal"[8]—not only served to symbolically put the duke of Burgundy and the English monarch in their place; the intent was also to give visible form to an ideal image of the French monarchy, one that appeared well-ordered and unassailable.

A close connection exists between the ceremonial entrances of the king and the representation of fabrics and garments in the work of Jean Fouquet. The miniature on fol. 223 of the *Grandes Chroniques de France* (Fig. 80) represents the entry of King Philippe Auguste (r. 1180–1223) into the city of Tours, which had been conquered by the English.[9] Fouquet shows him in precisely the same way that Charles VII—who likewise drove the English out of French territories—would present himself on such occasions: in full armor, high on horseback, with an azure velvet caparison emblazoned with the *fleur-de-lis*.[10] At the *entrées* of Charles VII, pages bearing a blue velvet tunic with lilies and a gilded helmet crowned with a diadem and *fleur-de-lis* would go before the king in the procession.

Fig. 79. Jean Fouquet(?), The Magnanimity of Cyrus, *Les Antiquités judaïques*, ca. 1470, Paris, BNF, fr. 247, fol. 230v

Fouquet incorporated allusions to the victorious monarchy of Charles VII into the traditional scene of the *Adoration of the Magi* in the book of hours created for Étienne Chevalier (Fig. 81), presumably at the patron's request. It has long been recognized that the eldest of the Magi, who kneels before the Virgin and Child, bears the features of Charles VII. Furthermore, Claude Schaefer has interpreted the second-youngest magus, clothed in a long, fur-lined robe of white damask, as a role portrait of the Dauphin Louis, and the youngest in red as a portrait of Charles's second son, Charles de France.[11] The transposition of the biblical event into the contemporary world of Charles VII's France is achieved above all through the clothing and textile accessories: while Mary and Joseph are draped in timeless robes, the garments of the other figures show astonishing parallels to those worn at *entrées royales* and other official events. Over his golden hauberk Charles VII wears a fashionable, fur-lined *robe courte* of green velvet (one of his favorite articles of clothing in reality as well),[12] along with red hosiery and tall black boots with golden spurs. Schaefer has also observed that his fashionable white hat, adorned with a golden circlet and tassel, resembles the headdress Charles is described as wearing at the entrance into Rouen.[13]

A key element of Fouquet's composition is the arch-shaped row of lance-bearing soldiers standing shoulder to shoulder, shielding the Adoration scene from the battle in the background. This splendid guard seems to make reference to the reorganization of the army ordered by the king in 1444, in which lance-bearers (along with archers) recruited from the entire kingdom played a prominent role. Thomas Basin, bishop of Lisieux, reported that Charles VII was very proud of this administrative achievement.[14] Fouquet paints the soldiers wearing reflective armor and helmets crowned with tufts of green, white, and red ostrich feathers. Their tunics, likewise striped in the king's colors of red, white, and green, have short black sleeves and are embroidered all over with pearls. It is reported that at the entry into Rouen in 1449, the pages of Charles VII actually wore steel bracers and gilded helmets with ostrich feathers in various colors;[15] furthermore, "at the head rode the archers of the King of France, all clad in red, white, and green doublets studded with golden appliqués."[16] The parallel is astonishing, even if Fouquet's miniature replaces the archers with lance-bearers and includes pearl decoration instead of appliqués. In the background we see the troops of the French king seizing a castle; for contemporaries, the reference to the rapid advance of Charles VII and his recapture of English-occupied cities and fortifications would have been obvious.[17]

The particular effectiveness of the fabrics and garments in both the *Hours of Étienne Chevalier* and the *Melun Diptych* arises from the painter's perceptible interest in the consistency and appearance of textile materials, a fascination that is combined with a finely-honed gift of observation and the outstanding technical ability to translate observed forms into the language of painting. Fouquet uses realistic details, deliberately placed, to produce surprise and recognition in the viewer; in this way, some textiles take on the quality of signs or signals within the picture. This effect is seen, for example, in the double-page miniature depicting Étienne Chevalier venerating the enthroned Madonna (Fig. 43), where the train of fabric spread out beneath the Madonna is of particular interest for our purposes (Fig. 82a). With its corner extending over into the left-hand miniature, it contributes, like the painted architecture, to the illusion of a continuous space. Netherlandish painters usually depicted an oriental carpet in this position, while a cloth of honor made of velvet or patterned silk would be

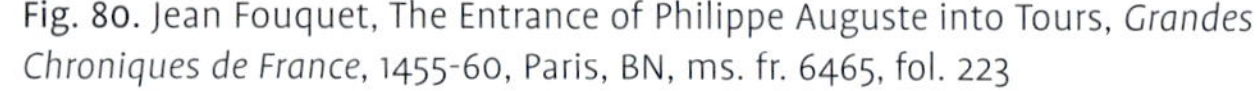

Fig. 80. Jean Fouquet, The Entrance of Philippe Auguste into Tours, *Grandes Chroniques de France*, 1455-60, Paris, BN, ms. fr. 6465, fol. 223

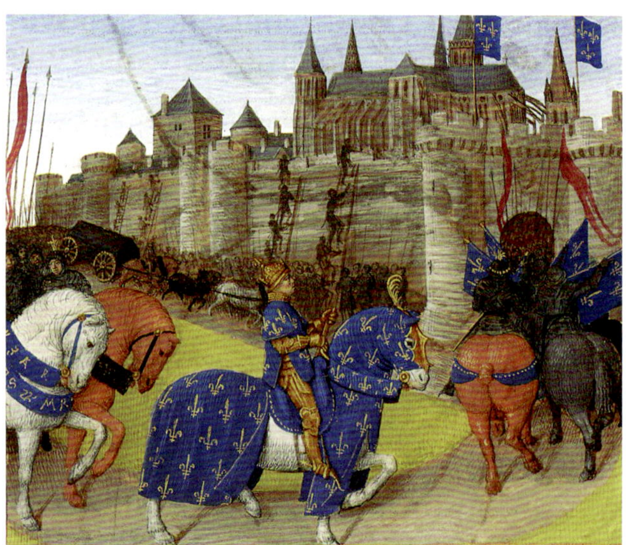

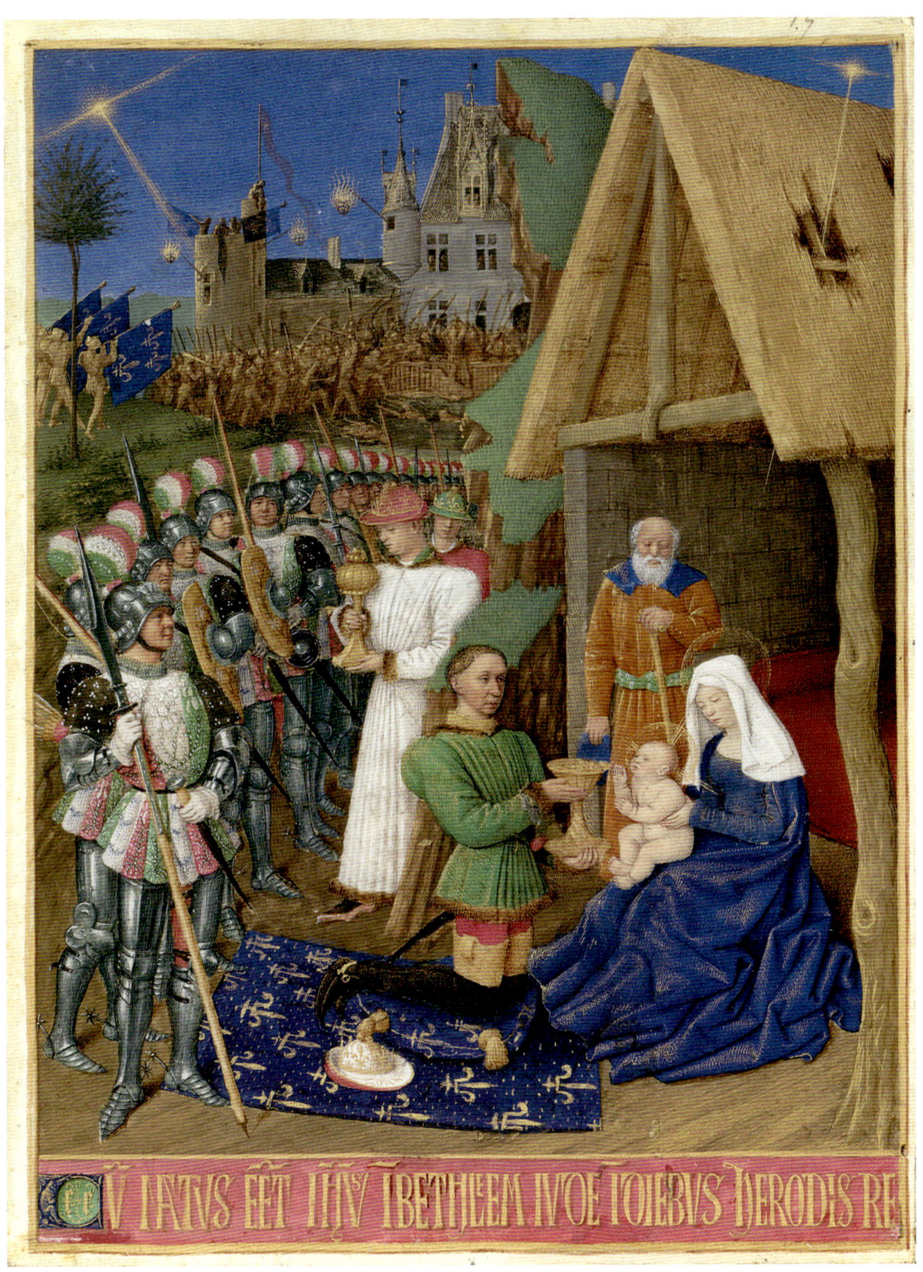

Fig. 81. Jean Fouquet, The Adoration of the Magi, *Hours of Étienne Chevalier*, ca. 1455, 16.5 x 12.2 cm, Chantilly, Musée Condé

hung behind the Madonna. Fouquet dispenses with both the throne and the cloth of honor and instead paints a golden portal in their place;[18] meanwhile, the cloth of honor is transposed to the floor beneath the Madonna's feet in place of the carpet. It is certainly no coincidence that the dark purple of the textile constitutes the deepest red tone in the entire miniature. The painted fabric underscores the magnificence of the Mother of God as effectively as the golden niche in which she is enthroned.

Fouquet renders the cloth as a splendid, deep-red velvet, presumably of Florentine origin, from around 1450, its pattern unfurling on a golden ground.[19] It is remarkable how meticulously the painter seeks to evoke the appearance of this material, which at that time was far more expensive than an oriental carpet. At the same time, however, it is clear that this is no actually existing fabric, but rather a composite of various velvets the artist had seen and which he now combined to produce a true paragon of textile art. Velvets were usually woven in panels that

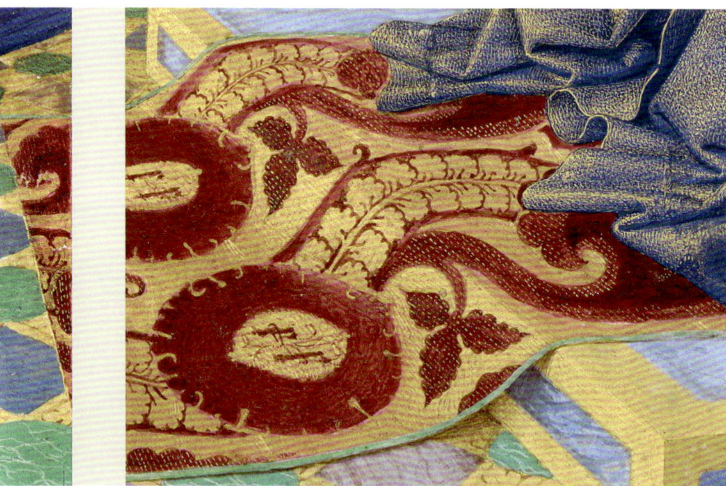

Fig. 82a. Jean Fouquet, Maria Lactans, *Hours of Étienne Chevalier*, Chantilly, Musée Condé, detail of brocade fabric b. Selvage of a red tiered silk velvet, Venice, second half of the 15th century, London, Victoria & Albert Museum, Inv. No. 55-1884

were narrow—often only 60 cm wide or less—but several meters long.[20] Real velvets from the 15th century had repeating patterns of enormous proportions: the width of the panel would accommodate only one, or at the most two, repetitions of the pattern. The woven panels were intended to be sewn together along the sides in order to enlarge the usable area, as we see in a cope of Italian silk velvet from the mid-15th century at Brasov in Transylvania (Fig. 83).[21]

The pattern of the velvet in Brasov is comparable to the painted fabric: palmettes and small branches producing leaves grow from a broad stem of velvet pile. And as in Fouquet's miniature, the width of the real fabric panel accommodates only two repetitions of the pattern.[22] The painted velvet, however, also includes a golden vine motif with a stem thickly set with leaves. In order to enhance the legibility of the image, Fouquet simplified the palmette with its inscribed pointed oval and the three leaves branching off the main stem; however, these generalized forms are not freely invented, but are copied from tiered velvets without gold (Fig. 82 b).

The abundance of gold, the varying levels of pile represented by different shades of purple, and finally the small golden dots indicating slipknots woven into the fabric—all these characteristics mark the fabric as an extraordinarily precious velvet. This assessment is also confirmed by the two narrow, bright green strips bordering the painted fabric panel on either side, a motif that con-

stitutes a relatively realistic depiction of the selvages marking the expensive purple velvet from Venice and Florence that was preferred in the courts of Europe (Fig. 82b).[23]

Finally, in an actual fabric, the signet "e&e" of the patron woven into the pointed oval of the palmette would have been a mark of the highest exclusivity. In reality only popes, kings, and high-ranking princes could afford a fabric decorated with their own coat of arms, personal device, or signet.[24] Such a product would have required a complete reconfiguration of the loom and would have meant customizing an extremely time- and cost-intensive serial procedure for a single patron. For Étienne Chevalier, a royal official who did not belong to the nobility, it is appropriate that in this image, the imaginary luxury fabric with his personal signet is reserved for the Madonna, since in reality such an article would have been well beyond his means. The mimetic quality of the painted textile elevates it far beyond the function of a decorative ornament; rather, it serves to imbue the image with courtly splendor and create an extremely contemporary impression. In effect, it appears as if the patron had presented an entire panel of velvet (in other words, a small fortune) to the Virgin Mary as a gift so that she might condescend to appear to him.

Fouquet's depiction of a panel of woven velvet, which includes even such details as the selvages, which would have disappeared when the fabric was worked, or the

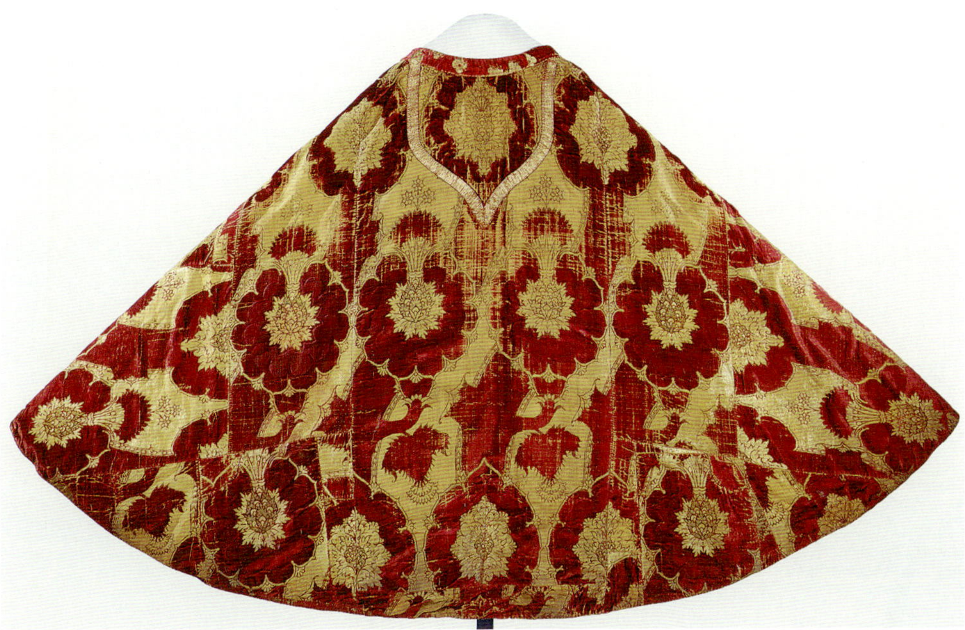

Fig. 83. Cope of Italian silk velvet, ca. 1450, Brasov (Transylvania), Black Church Inv. No. 341

straight cut of the front edge (Fig. 82a), presupposes direct visual experience. The patron may have desired the representation of this contemporary fabric, but he himself would hardly have owned an entire panel of it. It is more likely that the painter gained his astonishingly precise information from visits to the *argenterie,* the royal storehouse, where luxury textiles were stockpiled in large numbers. This scenario is all the more probable in light of the fact that in 1447, the *argenterie* had been transferred to Tours at the behest of Charles VII.[25]

Charles VII's preference for Tours (Fouquet's home town) may seem surprising, but among contemporaries his lack of interest in Paris was well known. The anonymous *Journal d'un bourgeois de Paris* includes the following entry for the year 1439: "A cette époque, ni le roi ni l'évêque ne s'occupait réellement du sort de la cité parisienne. Le roi était toujours en Berry et se moquait bien de l'Île de France, de la guerre ou de son peuple, comme s il avait été emprisonné chez les Sarrasins".[26]

The transfer of the royal storehouse to Tours occurred under the direction of the merchant Jacques Coeur, who held the office of *argentier.* The vestimentary splendor on display at the court of Charles VII was due in large measure to the indefatigable trading activities of this man, who supplied not only the king himself, but also his entire entourage with luxury goods from all over Europe and the Orient.[27] When the holdings of

the *argenterie* were audited after Jacques Coeur's arrest on July 31, 1451, they included around ten different types of silk fabrics, twenty kinds of cloth, fine and coarse linen, and precious, semi-precious and luxury furs, as well as armor, weapons, shields, garments, and headdresses.[28] The silk fabrics, including the velvets imported from Italy, consisted of a total of 554 recorded pieces and thus constituted the largest portion of the assortment of luxury goods. The position of trust Jacques Coeur enjoyed with Agnès Sorel—as manifested, for example, in her choice of him and Étienne Chevalier as the executors of her will in 1445—may have had to do with his function as the supplier of luxury goods for the court.[29]

Charles VII had first met Agnès in Toulouse in 1443, when she was a court lady to Isabella of Lorraine, wife of Duke René d'Anjou. The king reportedly elevated her to the status of official mistress during an *entrée royale* in 1444.[30] Olivier de la Marche, chronicler and member of the Burgundian court, saw her for the first time in Châlons-sur-Marne in 1445. He summarized her remarkable rise to prominence and her unusual role at court in a single sentence: "Le roi avait nouvellement élevé une pauvre demoiselle, gentilfemme nommée Agnès du Soret, à un tel triomphe et tel pouvoir que son état était à comparer aux grandes princesses du royaume".[31]

This newly acquired status as official mistress to Charles VII and the increase of power and wealth that accompanied it could be represented most clearly by means of clothing and jewelry. The position of mistress, for which there had been no precedent up to that point, was by no means unassailable and therefore had to be established externally all the more clearly. In this context, Agnès Sorel's luxurious clothing and extravagant lifestyle, much criticized by contemporaries, appear not only as an expression of personal vanity and indulgence, but above all as a sign of social self-assertion at court.

Unlike the king's previous lovers, Agnès had been elevated to the realm of social visibility by Charles VII himself, for example when he made a present to her of a castle, the "Chateau de Beauté." The jewelry Charles bestowed upon her during her seven years at his side was bought back after her death for a total of 20,600 *écus* (the yearly contribution to the queen was around 10,000 *écus*).[32] The fact that Agnès, with the approval and indeed at the wish of Charles VII, posed as the great lady with a visible presence at court necessarily put her in a position of dangerous competition with the French queen. Contemporaries like Georges Chastellain observed with suspicion how Agnès increasingly played the role of the actual female ruler at the king's side, a position to which she was in no way entitled. Significantly, the scandalous quality of this situation was associated above all with the material possessions of the mistress, which were viewed as inappropriate: "She had all the tokens of honor and services properly due to the queen; more beautiful bedclothes, better linens and blankets, better dishes, more beautiful rings and jewelry, finer cuisine, better everything."[33] Of course, as an advisor to the duke of Burgundy, Chastellain was an outsider as well as a potentially critically-minded observer. The acceptance of Agnès's queen-like status among the narrower circle of Charles VII's retainers, however, is clear from her representation as the Queen of Heaven in the *Melun Diptych* (Fig. 94).

Not only do the external features of the *Maria Lactans*, with her golden-blonde hair and snow-white skin, correspond to the chroniclers' descriptions of Agnès Sorel, but the identification of the figure with the royal mistress dates back to the early 17th century. Thus there can be no doubt that the painting is in fact a role portrait of

Agnès Sorel.[34] The representation of the Madonna with the features of the king's mistress is based on a complex calculation. The sensually provocative quality of her appearance consists not only in the exposure of the naked left breast, represented as a perfect sphere, but also in the presentation of the entire body with the help of fashion. The cut of her *cotte hardie*, open at the front, plays an essential role in defining the figure, which is further emphasized by such tailoring details as the seam running from the covered right breast down to the waist. The skirt gathered above the belt calls attention to the wasp-waist as a key attribute of feminine beauty;[35] the bunched fabric forms an opulent waistband from which the upper body emerges as a slender goblet. The shaved forehead and hair tied back at the neck to reveal a view of the throat and delicate ears reflects courtly fashion. While thus far the representation of the figure has more in common with a Venus than a Madonna, the connection to the traditional iconography of the Mother of God is established by means of abstract elements and fictive combinations: the *cotte hardie* is actually an undergarment, and in reality would not have been worn with only a mantle over it. The painter also omits any further characterization of the texture of the blue-gray fabric of the dress. The ermine-lined mantle, whose outside seems to consist of white damask with a large-scale pattern and which would have been quite heavy in weight, is attached to the neckline of the *cotte hardie* as a broad cape and has no fastener of its own. Its timeless cut resembles the classic mantles of the High Middle Ages, worn by Madonna statues and the figures of female saints in the 13th century.

In the left panel of the diptych, Étienne Chevalier did not have himself represented as a private individual. Rather, he is clothed in a fur-lined *robe longue*, the garment worn by members of the parliament in Paris and by royal officials.[36] In 1449, the chancellor Guillaume Jouvenal des Ursins had appeared in a *habit royal* at the *entrée royale* into the city of Rouen,[37] and he wears the same garment in his portrait by Fouquet, now in the Louvre (Fig. 123). The red robes worn by Chevalier and Jouvenal des Ursins, however, differ considerably in their cut. While the chancellor's garment with its broad shoulders strongly resembles the doublet of Charles VII in the portrait by Fouquet (Fig. 11), Étienne Chevalier's robe seems surprisingly antiquated. The stitched folds on the breast correspond to the fashions of the time around 1450, but the same cannot be said of the balloon-shaped cut of the sleeves or the standing collar. These elements reflect French-Burgundian court fashion from the period around 1415-1430 and actually belong to a *houppelande*, as comparison with fol. 7 from Pierre Salmon's "Dialogus" (Geneva, BGE, ms. Fr. 165) reveals, where three similarly clothed courtiers are gathered at the bed of King Charles VI.[38] Balloon sleeves of this kind also appear on the figure of the patron Jodocus Vijd on the exterior panels of Jan van Eyck's *Ghent Altarpiece* of 1432, as well as on the Burgundian chancellor's robe in van Eyck's *Madonna of the Chancellor Rolin* from around 1435, now in the Louvre. We may assume that the retrospective character of Chevalier's garment was intentional; the outdated official garb may have been intended to remind the viewer that Chevalier's position at court was a family tradition, since his own father had served as a royal notary.

Chevalier was of bourgeois origin. His social status derived exclusively from his position as *trésorier du roi*, one of the highest officials in the king's service. Charles VII, however, was notorious for a certain lack of loyalty with respect to his retainers;[39] in view of Jacques Coeur's dramatic fall from favor in 1451, Chevalier's diptych may also have been intended to express his profound obeisance to his lord. In this work, he caused himself to be represented as a royal official, prayerfully rapt in the vision of a Madonna whose heavenly beauty merged with the earthly beauty of the deceased royal mistress into a perfect ideal of feminine beauty in and of itself. When he also adorned the diptych with a frame of azure velvet decorated with gold embroidery and gold enamels (Fig. 16)—a reference to the Capetian colors—he did so not only for himself, but also for the king.

Chevalier probably ordered the diptych for the altar of his burial chapel in the collegiate church of Notre-Dame in Melun.[40] The church had been founded by the Capetian king Robert II (r. 996–1031), and for centuries was occasionally used by various rulers of France for special ceremonial occasions, such as the marriage of Isabella, the daughter of St. Louis, to Theobald of Navarre. By installing the diptych in the church at Melun, Chevalier paid his respects to both his own personal history

Fig. 84. Lampas with striped decoration, Mongolian Iran, 14th century, from a chasuble from Århus, Copenhagen, National Museum, Inv. No. CXXXVII

(Melun was his birthplace) and the customs of the royal family. The cut of St. Stephen's deep-blue dalmatic may likewise have been intended by the painter as a reference to the venerable age of the church: while the edging of the garment, rendered in genuine gold leaf, appears to be inspired by a contemporary Italian gold fabric with a large repeating pattern, in form and placement it echoes the *clavi* of an antique tunic. Fouquet's painterly approach to textiles was highly intentional and he knew how to use precious fabrics not only to evoke the splendor of the court of Charles VII, but also to envision the historical past. In 1465, the duke of Armagnac came to Tours and on this occasion commissioned Fouquet's workshop to illuminate a French translation of the *Antiquités judaïques* of Flavius Josephus, a work composed in the first century after Christ.[41] The miniature on fol. 230v (Fig. 79) shows the Persian king Cyrus granting permission to representatives of the twelve tribes of Israel to return to their homeland and reconstruct the temple. The ruler is clothed like a European king in a voluminous, ermine-lined purple robe and wears a golden hoop crown. His throne, equipped with a baldachin, is covered in snow-white fabric with a pattern of golden stripes, some of which are decorated with foreign letters. The top edge of the canopy shows a frieze with fleeing hares pursued by dogs. The decoration, consisting of bands of inscription and pairs of running animals, is so obviously derived from the Islamic culture of the Near East and is so characteristic of a certain type of historical silk textile that the painter could not possibly have invented it himself.[42] Rather, he had a very clear conception of the appearance of textiles of this kind imported from the Orient, as comparison with a woven silk in the National Museum in Copenhagen demonstrates (Fig. 84). The courtly interiors of his time, however, would no longer have included these fabrics, for their use was confined to the 13th and 14th centuries.

An inventory prepared after the death of Charles V of France (1380) bears witness to the fact that in that era, striped textiles had been an established part of the royal regalia.[43] It is fascinating to read that fabrics with striped patterns appear exclusively under the rubric "Couvertures de Sièges pour le Roy" (covers for the royal throne).[44] Paragraphs 1136 and 1137 of the inventory each refer to a striped silk used for a throne canopy. The textile listed under Number 1136 originated "oultre-mer" ("from beyond the sea"); it was striped in yellow and supplied with "lettres d'oultre-mer et bestellettes" ("oriental letters and little beasts"). Paragraph 1137 likewise mentions "une couverture pour le siège du Roy" made of a fabric from "oultre-mer," which also had lengthwise stripes. This throne covering was framed with azure velvet showing ten French coats of arms.[45] The later addition of embroidered edging with the *fleur-de-lis* signals the active appropriation of a foreign material by the court tailor: the embroidered symbols integrated it into a sign system with validity and relevance for the French court.

Against this background, the use of an antiquated striped brocade from the Near East to embellish the throne of the Persian king Cyrus in the miniature from the *Antiquités judaïques* seems perfectly consistent, and at the same time reveals a highly subtle approach to vestimentary tradition at the French royal court. For this reason, it is entirely probable that this invention was the achievement of Fouquet himself and not his workshop associates. Once again, the royal storerooms and treasuries must have been the place where the artist studied the old textiles that were no longer in use.

Thus even in a painterly detail such as the throne canopy of King Cyrus, Jean Fouquet proves himself a great artist and an intelligent mind, capable of using his works to reflect the burgeoning interest in ancient history within the milieu of Charles VII and the court of his ally René d'Anjou.[46] Fouquet's instrument was the brush rather than the pen, but as a contemporary witness of an epoch in which the French monarchy was reinventing itself, he is in no wise inferior to the great 15th-century chroniclers such as Chastellain, de la Marche, and Le Bouvier.

1   "In grand, rich, and diverse garments," as Gilles Le Bouvier describes the king's retinue at his entrance into Rouen in 1449; Le Bouvier 1979, p. 323.

2   A report of this session is included in the *Journal d'un Bourgeois de Paris* (1405–1449); cf. *Journal d'un Bourgeois* 2009, vol. II, p. 151, no. 702.

3   Ibid., pp. 151, no. 702 and 160-163, no. 725.

4   For the *entrée royale*, cf. Bryant 1986.

5   Le Bouvier 1979.

6   Ibid., p. 323.

7   Ibid., p. 324.

8   To quote Thomas Basin's description of the marriage of the sister of King Charles VII to the English King Henry V in 1420; Basin 1933, vol. I, p. 69.

9   Paris, Bibliothèque Nationale, ms. Fr. 6465; cf. Cat. Paris 2003, pp. 219-224, cat. no. 26 and p. 236, fig. at top.

10   Le Bouvier 1979, p. 323: "Le roy de France estoit armé de toutes pieces, monté sur ung cursier couvert jusques aux piez de veloux asur semé de fleurs de lis d'or…"

11   Schaefer 1994, p. 44.

12   Basin 1933, p. 281: "vétu [en robe] courte, comme il le faisait souvent – il usait d'étoffes de couleur verte…"

13   Schaefer 1994, p. 44. Le Bouvier 1979, p. 324: "en sa teste un chappel de veloux vermeil ouquel avoit au bout une houppe de fil d'or."

14   Ch. II, "Comment le Roit Charles … organisa sa cavallerie et forma 1500 lances ordinaires," Basin 1933, pp. 17-21.

15   Le Bouvier 1979, p. 324.

16   Ibid., p. 325.

17   Patricia Stirnemann identifies this scene as the battle of Castillon (1453); Stirnemann 2005, p. 10.

18   See the essay by Kurmann in this volume.

19   Michael Peter, Riggisberg, provided valuable assistance in the identification of the velvet.

20   Examples are found in Monnas 2012, pp. 64-65, cat. no. 6 (w. 44 cm); pp. 98-99, cat. no. 24 (l. 300 cm, w. 60 cm).

21   Patterned warp-pile velvet with two pile levels, stitched with gold threads, Italy, ca. 1450, Brasov (Transylvania), parament treasury of the Black Church, Inv. No. 341; cf. Wetter 2015, pp. 191-203, cat. no. 2.

22   Discernable in the central piece of the rear section of the cope, set off by seams.

23   Frequently, however, individual golden threads were also worked into the selvages; cf. Monnas 2012, pp. 25-26.

24   Ibid., p. 27; see Michael Peter's soon to be published introduction in Peter (forthcoming).

25   Mollat 1991, p. 31.

26   "At that time neither the king nor the bishop were truly concerned for the fate of the city of Paris. The king was always in Berry and cared nothing for the Île-de-France, the war, or his people, as if he had been imprisoned by the Saracens." *Journal d'un Bourgeois* 2009, vol. II, pp. 173-174, no. 761.

27   See the comprehensive studies by de Man 1950 and Mollat 1991.

28 Mollat 1991, pp. 35-38.
29 Wellman 2013, pp. 42-43.
30 Ibid., p. 37.
31 "The king had recently elevated a poor girl, a noblewoman named Agnès of Sorel, to such triumph and power that her status was comparable to that of the great princesses of the kingdom." Olivier de la Marche 1884, vol. II, p. 55.
32 Philippe 1983, p. 117.
33 "Elle avait tous états et services royaux devers elle comme si même eût la reine, plus beaux parement de lit, meilleurs linge et couverture, meilleure vaisselle, meilleurs bagues et joyaux, meilleure cuisine, meilleur tout..."; Chastellain 1864, Bd. IV, pp. 366.
34 Cf. the essays by Kemperdick and Kren in this volume.
35 Fouquet loved this motif, which was derived from everyday fashion, and used it in other works as well, e.g. in the glass roundel of ca. 1460 for Laurens Girard, now in the Musée national du Moyen Âge in Paris, Inv. Nr. Cl. 1037a; Cat. Paris 2003, pp. 164-165, cat. no. 18.
36 Bryant 1986, p. 85.
37 Le Bouvier 1979, p. 325: "...messire Guillaume Juvenal des Ursins, seigneur de Trainel et chancellier de France, vestu en habit royal de robe et chapperon forrez a ung mantel d'escarlate...".
38 Cat. New York 2011, pp. 130-131, fig. 32.
39 Mollat 1991, pp. 211-216.
40 See the essay by Kemperdick in this volume.
41 Paris, Bibliothèque Nationale, ms. fr. 247 (vol. I) and ms. Fr. 21013 (vol. II); Schaefer 1994, p. 204; Cat. Paris 2003, pp. 310-337, there attributed by François Avril to the Master of the Munich Boccaccio and Jean Bourdichon.
42 Cf. von Fircks 2016.
43 Labarte 1879.
44 Ibid., p. 149.
45 Ibid.
46 Without referencing Jean Fouquet, Nagel/Wood 2010 offer interesting perspectives on this subject.

Nanny Schrijvers

NO LOVE AT FIRST SIGHT –
FOUQUET'S *VIRGIN AND CHILD*
AND THE ROYAL MUSEUM OF FINE ARTS
IN ANTWERP

When Manfred Sellink recently interviewed Stephan Kemperdick in connection with the plan to reunite the Fouquet diptych,[1] his first question was: "In our museum, 'the Fouquet' is one of the most important pieces. Is it the same for you?" Clearly the *Virgin and Child with Seraphim and Cherubim* ranks as an undisputed masterpiece, a trophy of the museum. Since 2009, moreover, the panel has been included in the Flemish government's list of especially valuable pieces and as such enjoys special protection.

But it was by no means love at first sight. The Van Ertborn bequest,[2] to which the painting belonged, was duly welcomed by the museum's curators, but apparently in the mid-19th century the *Virgin and Child* was appreciated only to a limited extent, and the work was rarely described or commented upon. For a long time, the Antwerp museum behaved as a rather cool lover, and not until the 20th century did the painting gradually begin to receive more attention and come to be viewed as significant, perhaps as a result of the Paris Exposition of 1904.[3]

"We are children of our time, whether we like it or not"

In 1904, curator Pol De Mont[4] composed a survey[5] of the museum's collection of Old Masters: "In its strikingly decorative conception, the *Madonna with Child surrounded by Angels*, No. 132, shares the powerful form, but by no means the warm coloration of the panel with Étienne

Chevalier and his patron St. Stephen in Berlin, with which it was united in the church in Melun until 1775. The spirit and the style of both pictures are more Italian than Netherlandish […]."

The "powerful form" was also noted by Jacques Wappers,[6] who added that the starkness of the figures may have been derived from contemporaneous sculpture. Incidentally, the inclusion of the painting in Wappers' 1923 booklet on the collection represented a genuine elevation of its status, since only about fifty works of art were selected for the publication.[7]

Thus by the 1920s, the *Virgin and Child with Seraphim und Cherubim* had made it to the Top 50, and in their assessment of the painting the curators continually invoked its potential affinity to modern art. Form and color were essential elements in this connection: the previously noted monumentality and starkness were now associated with Cubism and the experiments of the avant-garde.

In 1939, Arthur Henry Cornette[8] explored the unusual appearance and style of the panel in more depth and compared it with the Berlin piece: "[…] Despite its subtle suggestiveness, this panel is more archaic than the one with the donor, which has a more lifelike effect [...]".[9] The archaism of the work, its return to "origins", likewise seemed modern. Cornette continued: "The form of the Virgin is striking in the firmness of its drawing and its spiritual character—one thinks of many Egyptian heads—and the painting's ever-increasing popularity can be explained by its undeniable relation to particular qualities of modern art". Two years later, Cornette went even further when he observed: "The comparison goes in both directions, toward Egypt and to Modigliani; across the centuries, the artists extend a hand to each other [...]".[10]

The painting has always been an "uncomfortable" work. The above-mentioned museum directors and early curators generally wrote with a tone of reserve. There was always a "but"; the work was doubted and compared, considerations were presented and opinions advanced, but no one dared to unequivocally call the work "beautiful" or "magnificent"—until chief curator Walther Vanbeselaere.[11] In 1959 he wrote: "Nothing is more changeable than the prevailing taste: as of now, the Madonna by Fouquet is considered the most superb painting in the Antwerp museum. It suits the taste of our time as its ideal embodiment".[12] Vanbeselaere also attempted to enlighten a broader audience in publications such as *Openbaar Kunstbezit* (*Public Art Collections*): "We are children of our time, whether we like it or not! Whatever one may think of abstract art, it still plays an important role in our conception of beauty. If many people nowadays view Fouquet's Madonna as the outstanding masterpiece in the Antwerp museum—a notion that would have been unthinkable 50 years ago!—then it is because of certain qualities that we now find brilliant and describe as admirable merits, but which were previously considered archaisms and imperfections and tolerated only with reservation".[13]

"The ungraceful child"

In his working copy of the inventory catalogue of 1948, Vanbeselaere made notes and corrections for a forthcoming revised edition. There he crossed out the words "het onbevallige kind" (the ungraceful child)—or, in the French edition, "un enfant peu gracieux"—a description already present in the catalogue entry of 1905 and that had been repeated in every edition since.

A survey of 19th-century inventory catalogues shows how little was known about the work at that time. The first catalogue in which it was recorded following the bequest of 1841 lists it under No. 106 as "école inconnue".[14] On the one hand, this designation may reflect the lack of appreciation for the work on the part of connoisseurs and museum officials; but on the other hand, Florent van Ert-

born's papers contain virtually no information on the panel, not even the details of its acquisition.[15] The work was not included in the catalogue begun by Van Ertborn,[16] which remained unfinished when he discontinued it in 1828.

The following example serves to illustrate this mixture of limited knowledge and lack of interest. In Cornette's 1938 monograph on the patronage of Chevalier van Ertborn, he recounts what he refers to as a "strange episode" involving Fouquet's *Virgin and Child*: "On January 22, 1848, a certain G. P. Green wrote the following to the archivist Verachter,[17] presumably in response to the inventory catalogue of 1845: 'I would like to know whether in your opinion, the picture is an original or a copy. To which epoch, and, if possible, to which master should the work be attributed? Where did the previous owner acquire the picture, and how did it come into his possession?' The archivist replied: 'The painting in question is a copy and has nothing to do with Agnès Sorel'".[18]

Three years later, in 1851, Theodoor van Lerius[19] added a number of *Rectifications et Additions* to his *Notice sur le catalogue du Musée d'Anvers*, including a note regarding Count de Laborde's[20] attribution of the *Virgin and Child* to Fouquet, which had been recorded in the (fairly brief) inventory catalogue of 1845: "Incidentally, he [de Laborde] identifies Jean Fouquet as the painter of picture No. 106, which according to Monsieur De Laet[21] depicts the Virgin with the Christ Child surrounded by red and blue angels and which is listed without an artist's name. He adds that this painting, which was acquired by the deceased Monsieur Florent van Ertborn in Paris, is certainly also a portrait of the famous Agnès Sorel. Here we have no intention of investigating whether as a painting, this work of art is in fact as remarkable as Monsieur de Laborde claims, but we must confess that his complaint about the current location of the work seems somewhat exaggerated to us."

Apparently Theodoor van Lerius was not very impressed with Count de Laborde's expertise; nevertheless, the entry was revised in the subsequent edition of the inventory catalogue and the phrase "école inconnue" disappeared. Count de Laborde's displeasure over the hanging of the painting was dismissed as exaggerated, and it seems that in this regard, no change would be forthcoming any time soon.

"High up"

The work was rarely mentioned in tourist travel guides; it appeared only occasionally in editions of *Baedeker* beginning in the 1880s, and then only very briefly with title and artist's name.[22] The French edition of 1888 includes the unusual statement that it was located "dans le haut," or "high up". Apparently the painting was hung high up on the wall—perhaps too high to be noticeable or clearly visible? A clue here is found in the preparatory documents for a catalogue of the Van Ertborn bequest, for which evaluations were solicited from eminent connoisseurs. Gustave Wappers, at that time director of the academy and the museum, wrote to more or less the same specialists who had previously advised Van Ertborn on his collecting activity. Sulpiz Boisserée[23] answered at great length on February 7, 1844, and wrote the following in regard to what was then designated as No. 82, the "Portrait of Agnès Sorel, from the German School":

"This painting is by no means a portrait of Agnès Sorel; it simply represents the Virgin Mary with the Child, accompanied by cherubim and seraphim. It would be preferable to dispense with this incorrect designation—not only because it is incorrect, but even more so because the name Agnès Sorel unfortunately attracts attention to that hideous painting, which should be banished to the darkest corner, if not done away with altogether. As far as the attribution to the German School is concerned, I know of no work from that school that would have even the slightest relation to this dreadful panel."[24]

Heinrich Gustav Hotho[25] had also written to Wappers that the painting did not belong to the German School, though he provided no further commentary. As mentioned earlier, at that time the work was designated as "École inconnue". Boisserée, on the other hand, had more to say. Incidentally, his description of the panel as "cette hideuse peinture"—that hideous painting—prefigures what would later be said of "modern art", and apparently his advice to hang the picture in the darkest corner was followed as well.

Sulpiz Boisserée's merciless rejection of the picture in 1844 contrasts starkly with the judgment rendered by Paul Vandenbroeck, present curator of 15th-century art, in 2014: "The interaction of physical and material beauty, an austere and extremely restrained design, a 'subliminal' erotic dimension, an unmistakable aloofness and an unreal, dream-like atmosphere make Fouquet's panel unique and an absolute masterpiece of 15th-century European art. The astute and open-minded Florent van Ertborn purchased this highly unusual work—which towers over all 15th-century French painting known to us—in the art market of post-revolutionary Paris. Today, Jean Fouquet's creation presents itself to us as an inextricable mixture of piety and eroticism, archaic dignity and a modern-seeming boldness."[26]

1   In the Antwerp museum journal *Zaal Z*; De Rynck 2017.

2   Chevalier Florent van Ertborn (Antwerp 1784–Den Haag 1840) was mayor of Antwerp from 1817 to 1828 and later governor of Utrecht. In addition to the many projects he realized for the harbor and city of Antwerp, he is remembered above all as a collector. The Van Ertborn bequest comprised 106 works of art, including a number of multipart works from the 14th, 15th, and 16th centuries. His preference for this epoch was unusual at the time; his art-loving family followed the more customary practice of collecting works from the 17th century. In assembling his unusual collection, he regularly received help and advice from other collectors and experts including the brothers Melchior and Sulpiz Boisserée and Gustav Friedrich Waagen, also lovers of 15th-century art.

3   1904, Paris du Louvre, Pavillon de Marsan, Exposition des Primitifs Français, no. 40.

4   Pol de Mont (Wambeek 1857–Berlin 1930), writer, curator from 1904 to 1919.

5   De Mont 1914, pp. 22ff.

6   Jacques Wappers, interim curator from 1919 to 1921, assistant curator until 1924.

7   Wappers 1923 pp. 16-17: "Une certaine raideur dans les figures de la Mère, de l'Enfant divin et des séraphins rouges et bleus qui entourent le trône, donnent à penser qu'on se trouve en présence de la reproduction d'une Vierge qui ornait l'oratoire d'Etienne Chevalier à l'èglise de Loches à laquelle ce tableau était destiné."

8   Arthur Henry Cornette (Antwerp 1880–Sint-Michiels-Bruges 1945) was a lawyer, university lecturer in art history, assistant curator beginning in 1924, and chief curator from 1929 to 1945.

9   Cornette 1939, pp. 57ff.

10   Cornette 1941, p. 26.

11   Walther Vanbeselaere (Zevekote 1908–Antwerp 1988) was chief curator of the Royal Museum of Fine Arts in Antwerp from 1948 to 1973.

12   Vanbeselaere 1959, no. 7 (reprint 1969, no. 51).

13   Vanbeselaere 1966, pp. 28-28b.

14   Cat. Antwerp 1845, no. 106: "H. 091., L. 0.81. École inconnue (Musée Van Ertborn), Vierge avec l'Enfant-Jésus entourée d'anges bleus et rouges."

15   For the practical implementation of the bequest, the paintings located in The Hague were listed first (November 19, 1840), followed by those in Antwerp (November 27, 1840); from this it emerges that the *Virgin and Child* was kept in The Hague. There is no further mention of the work.

16   Archive of the KMSK Antwerp; see Janssens 2002, pp. 85-112.

17   Frederik Verachter (1797–1870), the municipal librarian and archivist of Antwerp, was entrusted with the compilation of the inventory catalogue.

18   Cornette 1938, p. 31.

19   Theodoor Frans van Lerius (Antwerp 1819–Antwerp 1880) was a lawyer and author who regularly published on the history and painting of Antwerp.

20 Count Louis-Joseph-Alexandre de Laborde (Paris 1773–Paris 1842) was an antiquarian, historian, author, and member of the Académie des Sciences morales et politiques. In his work *La renaissance des arts à la cour de France* he mentions the *Virgin and Child* as a work by Fouquet.

21 Jan Alfred De Laet, literary scholar and teacher at the University of Ghent, was to write the inventory catalogue.

22 Baedeker 1888, p. 104.

23 Sulpiz Boisserée (Cologne 1783–Bonn 1854) was a historian and art collector together with his brother Melchior (Cologne 1786–Bonn 1851).

24 Archive of the KMSK Antwerp; the original is in French.

25 Heinrich Gustav Hotho (Berlin 1802–Berlin 1873) was a philosopher and art historian. Beginning in 1833 he was employed by Gustav Friedrich Waagen as assistant curator in the painting department of the Berlin Museum.

26 Vandenbroek 2014, pp. 131-133.

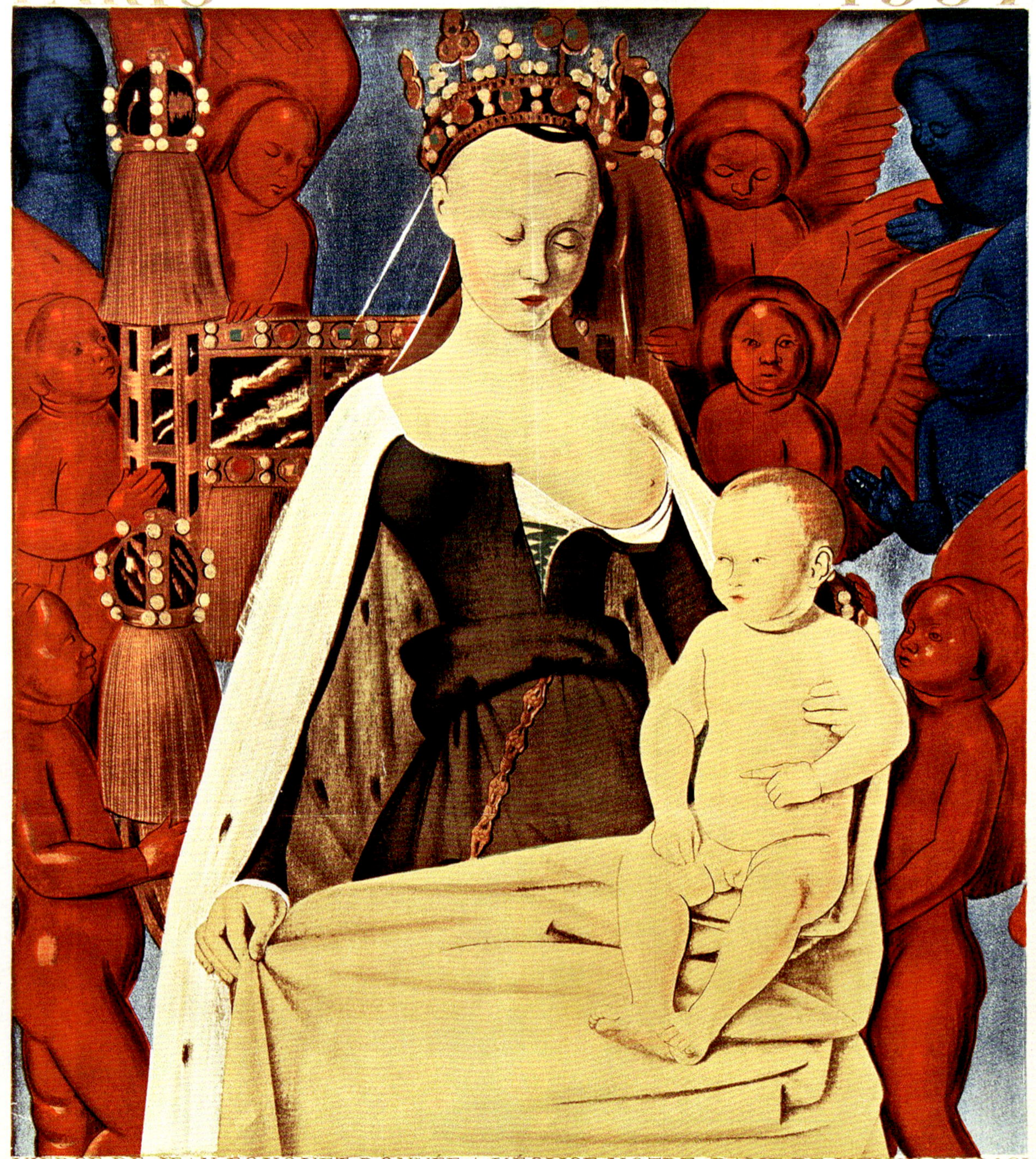

CHEFS D'ŒUVRE DE L'ART FRANÇAIS

AU PALAIS NATIONAL DES ARTS

AVENUE DU PRÉS! WILSON ET AVENUE DE TOKIO

JUIN - OCTOBRE 1937

Katrin Dyballa

PARIS 1937:
FOUQUET BETWEEN ALBERT SPEER AND GUERNICA

Exactly 80 years have passed since the two panels of Jean Fouquet's *Melun Diptych* were last seen together. The occasion was the *Exposition Internationale des Arts et Techniques dans la Vie Moderne*—the World's Fair—in Paris from May 25 to November 25, 1937 (fig. 86). Here, two years before the outbreak of World War II, the nations converged once more under the banner of peace and transformed the city of Paris. Not only did the numerous temporary buildings of the exposition give the city an entirely different character by day, but by night, as well, the illuminated pavilions turned it into a "cité lumière"(fig. 87).[1] Three hundred pavilions designed by around 300 architects under the direction of Jacques Gréber were erected over an area of about 100 hectares on the right and left banks of the Seine from the Eiffel Tower to the Trocadéro.[2] A total of 44 participating nations presented their cultural and technological achievements to an audience that ultimately numbered 31 million.[3] France, however, claimed the largest portion of the exhibition space, which was devoted to art and technology as two facets of human culture. Like all the previous World's Fairs, the event was intended to promote international peace and understanding;[4] yet perhaps more than any of its predecessors, this exposition was shaped by the nationalism of individual countries and constituted a focal point for political upheavals and conflicts in Europe.

Among the many attractions, the German and Soviet pavilions by Albert Speer and Boris Mihailovich Iofan (fig. 88) were especially impressive and caused a sensation, like the Eiffel Tower in 1889 or the Japanese Pavilion in 1900.[5] Placed across from each other on the north bank of the Seine, the massive, towering structures reflected the political rivalry and opposing ideologies of their respective states.[6] In contrast to the dramatic pathos of Vera Mukhina's monumental, 25-meter-high sculpture of a young couple striding forward, hammer and sickle held high in their uplifted hands, the German building—even taller than its counterpart, with a bronze eagle by Kurt Schmid-Ehmen—stood as a self-contained solitaire. In fact this effect was intended by Albert Speer: later in his memoirs, he recalled that he had deliberately conceived the design of the German Pavilion as a counterpart to the Soviet building, since he had known that that two pavilions would stand across from each other and had "just happened" to see the Soviet design, enabling him to respond to it.[7] Yet despite the rivalry between these two monumental, even oversize buildings, Max Horkheimer and Theodor W. Adorno viewed them as fundamentally similar: "The German and Russian Pavilions of the Paris World's Fair seemed to be of the same essence, and the decorative administrative and exhibition venues of industry hardly differ in authoritarian and other countries".[8]

The dominant, competing self-representation of the two states was quite apparent to observers—particularly on the German side. The Soviet Pavilion was not discussed in the German press, and visual illustrations were subjected to careful scenic direction. If the Russian building's inclusion in a photograph was absolutely unavoidable, then the caption had to make mention of it: In his *Streifzug durch die Pariser Weltausstellung*, for example, Guido Har-

Fig. 85. Poster for the exhibition *Chefs-d'œuvre de l'Art français*

bers commented that the Russian Pavilion stood "of all things" across from the German one.[9] Heinrich Hoffmann's illustrated volume simply observes: "Two buildings, two worldviews!"[10] In his travelogue *Das geistige Paris 1937*,[11] Gustav René Hocke, journalist for the Cologne newspaper *Kölnische Zeitung*, offered a more subtle characterization of public opinion in Paris. According to him, the French perception of the two pavilions and of the associated self-representation of the two states was very nuanced—to be sure, in favor of Germany: "Negative judgments of the German exhibition are very seldom heard. In contrast, the Russian banners and photographs are met with skepticism in most circles. While the objectivity of the German pavilion, including the architecture, finds approval, the propagandistic excess and violent pathos of the Russians is considered distasteful".[12] Although Hocke lays claim to "critical objectivity," his assessment is surprising and certainly reflects only one side of public opinion. A very different view was espoused by Christian Zervos, publisher of *Cahiers d'Art*, the artistic and literary journal closely associated with Pablo Picasso. Zervos criticized German ideological artistic production in the harshest terms and saw therein the demise of all aesthetics.[13] In his analysis of fascism, Walter Benjamin summarized this dilemma—the political exploitation of art, so palpable in Paris in 1937—in the following words: "Its [mankind's] self-alienation has reached such a degree that it can experience its own destruction as an aesthetic

pleasure of the first order. This is the situation of politics which Fascism is rendering aesthetic. Communism responds by politicizing art".[14]

At the 1936 Olympic Games in Berlin, the totalitarian National Socialist regime had made a point of presenting itself as peace-loving and cosmopolitan; now, at the Paris Exposition, it did the same. This idea was clearly formulated, for example, in the publication accompanying the German pavilion, which encouraged visitors—now that they had had the opportunity to become acquainted with German work and the "will to form," both of which were the "best guarantors of peace"—to visit Germany itself.[15] So that no one would feel excluded, the booklet was published in four languages: German, English, French, and Italian.

Yet Germany's actions had long contradicted this sentiment. Its support for Francisco Franco, for example, was caustically referenced in a review of the German Pavilion in the *Pariser Tageszeitung*, a German-language newspaper for exiles: "Germany wants to export—why doesn't it show its primary export to Spain: firebombs for the Basque country?".[16] Without a doubt, the collision of differing ideologies—National Socialism, Fascism, Stalinism, democracy—at close range at the Trocadéro in the summer of 1937 culminated in Pablo Picasso's large-scale painting *Guernica* (fig. 89). Exhibited at the Spanish Pavilion in the immediate vicinity of the German building, this work remains among the most enduring

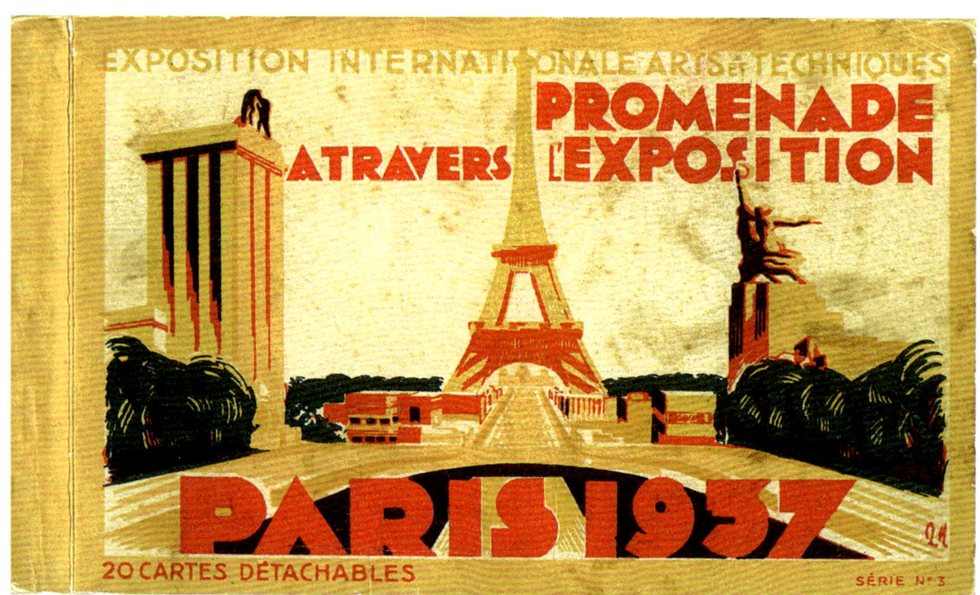

Fig. 86. Postcard booklet, Paris World's Fair, 1937

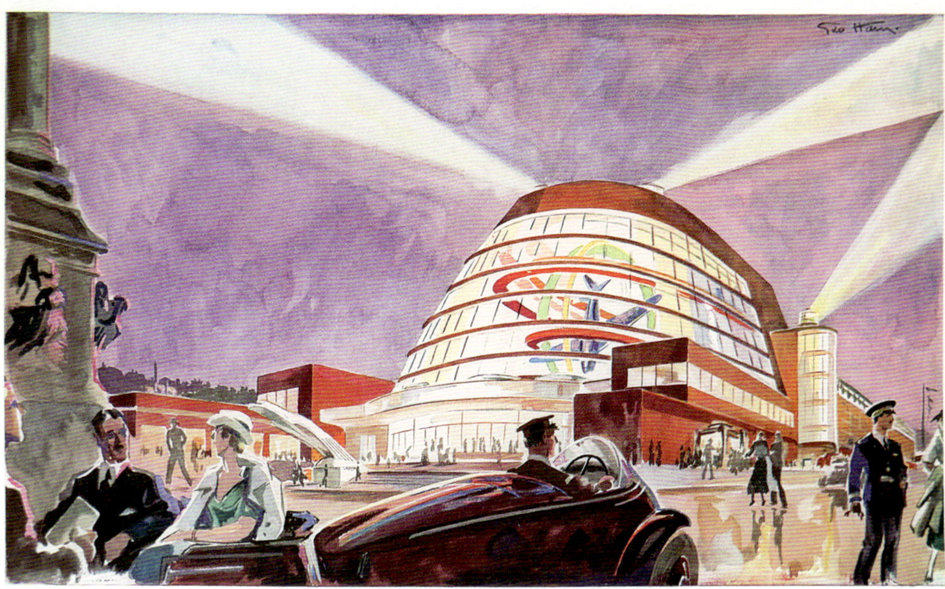

Fig. 87. Geo Ham, impression of the Aeronautic Pavilion, watercolor in *L'Illustration*, special edition, August 1937

legacies of the Paris World Exposition. The painting was Picasso's response to the Spanish Civil War and the destruction of the city of Guernica by the German Condor Legion in April 1937; as the artist himself stated: "It is my wish at this time to remind you that I always believed, and still believe, that artists who live and work with spiritual values cannot and should not remain indifferent to a conflict in which the highest values of humanity and civilization are at stake".[17] The particular significance of this work lay in its visualization of human suffering in the Spanish Civil War, placing it in diametric opposition to the maxim of the World's Fair—"to bring nations together under the banner of peace"—and imbuing Spain with profound significance as the defender of democracy and the republic.[18] The struggle for an uncertain future was not swept under the carpet, but was

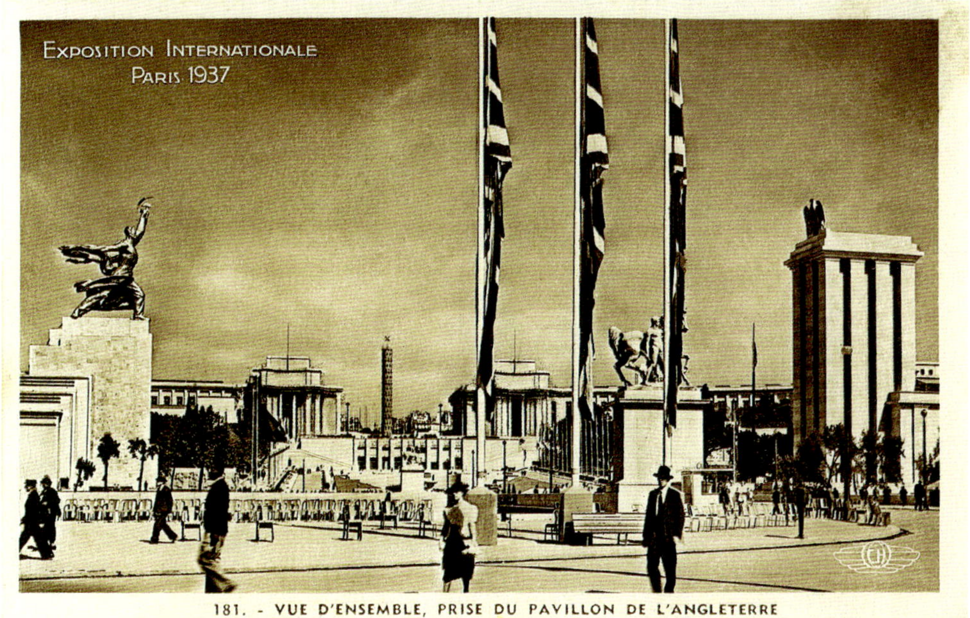

Fig. 88. Postcard of the Paris World's Fair with the German Pavilion and the Soviet Pavilion

openly acknowledged. Edmond Labbé, Commissar General of the Paris Exposition, even addressed this theme in his introduction to the *Livre d'Or officiel de l'exposition*, the organizers' official publication for the World's Fair: "Dans un monde sur lequel pèse lourdement la menace trouble des lendemains, il semblait, depuis quelque temps, que la civilisation eût commencé de douter d'elle-même, de ses valeurs, de ses vigueurs et de ses devoirs. Une sorte de découragement et de lassitude traversait les âmes, en y ébranlant presque jusqu'aux assises de l'espoir. Et voici que l'Exposition a surgi, tout d'un coup, dans un élan de volonté suprême et qu'elle est montée dans l'air comme un grand cri de confiance et d'ardeur de l'humanité tout entière".[19]

In addition to the above-mentioned attractions, the new Palais de Tokyo (fig. 90), a French building designed by Jean Claude Dondel and André Aubert on the avenue of the same name, also garnered significant attention—although less for its architecture than for its purpose. The building was intended to serve as the launching point for the exhibition of modern French art. Initially this may

Fig. 89. Entrance hall of the Spanish Pavilion with Pablo Picasso's *Guernica* and Alexander Calder's *Mercury Fountain*, page from *Cahiers d'Art* 12, 1937, p. 289

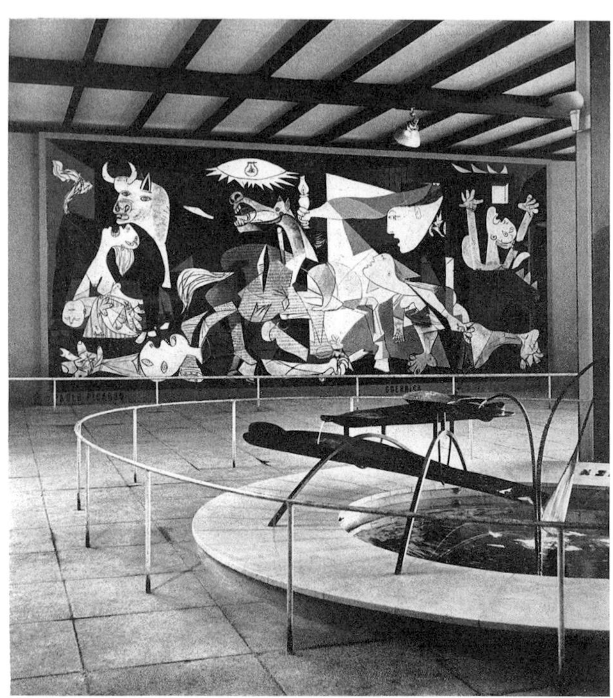

not seem remarkable, but here, for the first time, state and city were to become advocates for the new art: even after the closing of the World's Fair, the Palais de Tokyo would serve as the first museum for modern art in France. French painter Amédée Ozenfant waxed enthusiastic: "On pourra voir de la peinture française [contemporaine] en France! Ce sera rudement nouveau".[20] Gustav Hocke, too, recognized the achievements of modernism and observed that now visitors to museums of modern art would be able to see all those artists who had still been scorned or ridiculed in 1900.[21] Various buildings and institutions were involved in the realization of this ambitious exhibition project, for French art was to be exhibited at the World's Fair in multiple venues. In the initial stages of planning, it still seemed sufficient to limit the scope of the exhibition to contemporary art in relation to modern technology rather than trying to mount a retrospective. But Georges Huisman, Director General of Fine Arts, quickly realized that the new artistic currents should not be considered in isolation but should be understood in light of their origins: "Et il fut vite décidé qu'une vaste rétrospective, organisée à côté de l'Exposition Internationale, embrassant l'art français de ses origines jusqu'à l'époque contemporaine, constituerait, pour le plus grand profit de l'esthétique et des techniques d'aujourd'hui, la plus admirable des leçons et la plus pure joie des yeux et de l'esprit".[22] The same idea was formulated even more explicitly by Prime Minister Léon Blum in his foreword to the general catalogue of the exhibition: "Pour comprendre, pour goûter pleinement les réalisations contemporaines, il ne suffit pas de les replacer dans le milieu qui les a vu naître. Il faut encore les rattacher aux productions antérieures. Il faut les considérer comme la résultante d'une longue série d'efforts accomplis, dans la suite des siècles, par des hommes qui ont lutté pour discipliner la matière, pour parvenir à l'expression plastique de la vie, à la beauté des lignes, à l'harmonieuse éloquence des couleurs".[23]

Of course Huisman's concern for the pedagogical enlightenment of the public was not the only reason for including older art in the exhibition; probably more important was the opportunity to enhance the social acceptability of modern works and underscore the greatness of France's national artistic production. Shown next to and even in the same tradition as respected older works, modern art

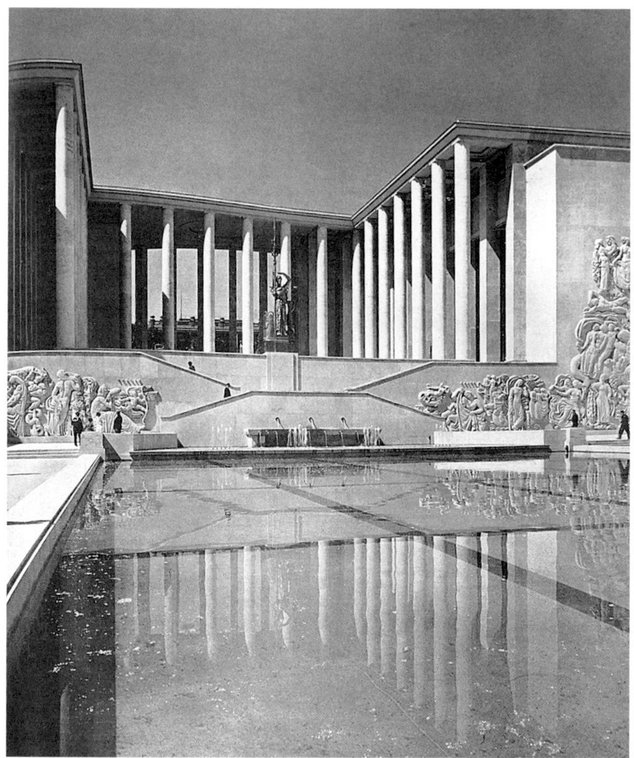

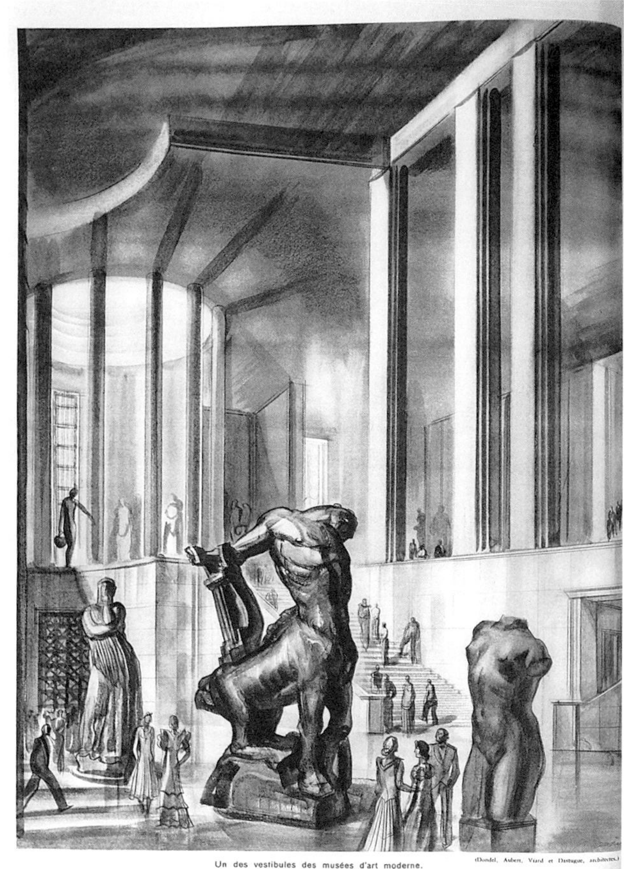

Fig. 90. View of the Musée de l'Art Moderne, venue for *Chefs-d'œuvre de l'Art français* and the Van Gogh exhibition

Fig. 91. Decaris, vestibule of the Musée de l'Art Moderne, charcoal drawing in *L'Illustration*, special edition, August 1937

would be ennobled and rendered more palatable to audiences of conservative taste.

And so in late 1936 the decision was made to show *Chefs-d'œuvre de l'art français*—an exhibition of French art from its beginnings to 1900—at the Palais de Tokyo.[24] In record time, no fewer than 1341 works from nearly every epoch and genre were brought together for this spectacular exhibition (fig. 91). The range of the medieval section was quite similar to the Paris exhibition of French primitives in 1904, which had shown 579 works.[25] The 1937 show, however, also included works as recent as Odilon Redon's *La Quadrige*. In all likelihood the design of the exhibition spaces was intentionally left unrecorded: only one photograph, taken during a visit by President Lebrun, shows the sober, modernist style of presentation in austere rooms illuminated by glass ceilings, too low for large-scale works (fig. 92).

The poster advertising the exhibition (fig. 85) employed a motif that still attracts attention, oscillating as it does between medieval piety and eroticism: Jean Fouquet's *Virgin and Child* from Antwerp, the pendant to the *Étienne Chevalier* in Berlin (cat. 1). Yet this motif was probably chosen not merely for its provocative strangeness, with the Mother of God (thought to be a disguised portrait of Agnès Sorel, mistress of King Charles VII) ostentatiously displaying her breast. Rather, Jean Fouquet was viewed as the founder of realistic painting in France, followed by Clouet and Corneille de Lyon.[26] Although the question of the origins of a genuinely French art was controversial, the concern now was to present a more unified picture; as education minister Jean Zay remarked, "Depuis les merveilles de notre moyen âge jusqu'à l'époque de Cézanne et de Seurat, on pouvait admirer la continuité prestigieuse de la tradition française".[27] There were two reasons for this: first of all, explicit allegiance was now being given to the idea that a nation's art contributed to its self-understanding and to identification with one's country; concretely, the retrospective was

131

viewed as a portrait of France.[28] Secondly, as mentioned, the exhibition was intended to position modern art within a broader context; this, however, only seemed possible if it were placed within the tradition of French art.

From a present-day perspective, the exhibition *Chefs-d'œuvre de l'art français* was organized in an astonishingly short time, bringing together works from the United States, the Soviet Union, the Netherlands, Belgium, Germany, and Great Britain. On February 19, 1937, a letter was issued from the French foreign minister to the German embassy in Paris, briefly presenting the exhibition project and announcing that René Huyghe, curator at the Louvre, would soon be departing for Germany to approach individual museums about loans.[29] A note verbale from the French delegation further emphasized the significance of this unique exhibition and urged accommodation of the request for loans; in return, every effort would be made to organize an exhibition of contemporary French art in Berlin in the following year.[30] And in fact just such a show was mounted the same year under the sponsorship of Hermann Goering: beginning on June 1, a total of 350 works by artists including Georges Braques, Jean Souverbie, Henri Matisse, Maurice Denis, and Charles Dufresne—but not Pablo Picasso—were shown at the Berlin Academy of the Arts.[31] It is all the more surprising to recall that the infamous exhibition *Entartete Kunst* ("degenerated art"), with its defamation of modern art, opened in Munich at almost exactly the same time, on

Fig. 92. The President of the Republic, Albert Lebrun, visits the exhibition *Chefs-d'œuvre de l'art français*, Hall of the 19ᵗʰ Century

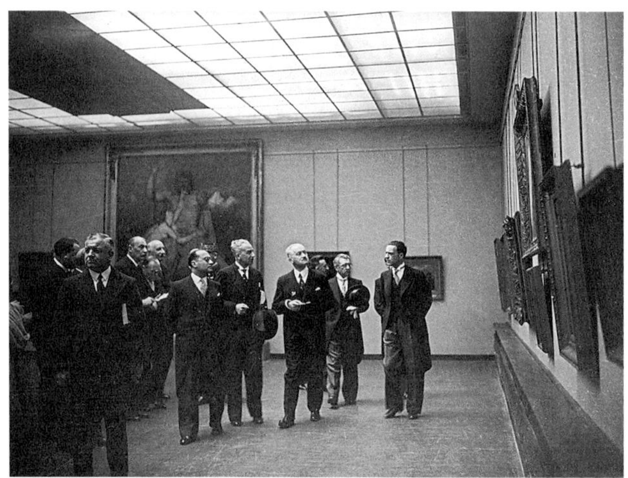

July 18. In Paris, too, this contradiction was palpable: on July 12, immediately adjacent to the German building, the Spanish Pavilion opened with the presentation of Picasso's *Guernica* (fig. 89).

As early as April 6, the German Ministry for Science, Education, and National Culture under Reichsminister Bernhard Rust approved the loan of the works requested in the March 3 note verbale, including eleven pieces from the Deutsches Museum and the Kaiser-Friedrich Museum in Berlin.[32] In the end, almost all of the requested works were lent: the *Diptych with Crucifixion and Man of Sorrows before the Virgin*, at that time still considered a French work (inv. 1620, today identified as Northern German), the *Coronation of the Virgin*, made in Paris around 1400 (inv. 1648), Jean Fouquet's *Étienne Chevalier*, Georges de La Tour's *St. Sebastian* (inv. 2046), Nicolas Poussin's *Landscape in the Roman Campagna with St. Matthew and the Angel* (inv. 478A), Pierre Mignard's *Portrait of Marie Mancini* (inv. 465[33]), Antoine Pesne's *Self-Portrait with Daughters Henriette Joyard and Marie de Rège before an Easel* (inv. 496B), and Antoine Watteau's *The French Comedy* (inv. 468). Further, the Berlin Kupferstichkabinett contributed Fouquet's portrait drawing of Guillaume Jouvenel (cf. cat. 3).[34] Equally first-class works came from the holdings of the former Berlin Royal Palace: Antoine Watteau's paintings *The Shop Sign of Gersaint* and *Peaceful Love* as well as *The Shepherds*, Nicolas Lancret's *Charmille* and *Dance in a Pavilion*, and finally Jean Siméon Chardin's *Lady Sealing a Letter*. Hocke described this generosity as "an excellent example of unreserved international cultural cooperation",[35] and the magazine *Weltkunst* emphasized that of the German lenders, the Berlin museums in particular had provided first-class works for the exhibition in Paris.[36] The Antwerp Museum of Fine Arts was equally generous and lent Fouquet's *Virgin and Child*.

But did the reunification of the two panels of the *Melun Diptych* attract attention? Robert Burnard, Secretary General of Fine Arts and co-organizer of the exhibition, referenced it in his commentary on the retrospective and mentioned the diptych as the first of the exhibited works: "Comment pourtant ne pas signaliser le diptyque de Jean Fouquet, qui réunit enfin, de nouveau, le portrait d'Étienne Chevalier, du musée de Berlin, et la Vierge d'Anvers?"[37] In the *Livre d'Or officiel de l'exposition*, as well, Burnard called attention to the Antwerp *Virgin and Child* in both text and illustration; here only a few works were mentioned by name, all of them paintings.[38] Amédée Ozenfant, on the other hand, said nothing about either the show or the exhibited works in his notes from his visit to the exhibition; what was important for him was that in the future, the new, specially constructed exhibition hall would become a museum for contemporary art.[39] The journal *Cahiers d'Art* briefly reviewed the exhibition of French masterworks and described it as "magnifique"; although no individual works were discussed, the review did include a quotation from Jean Zay invoking the unity of French art: "L'Exposition des chefs-d'œuvre proclame une fois de plus cette unité extraordinaire du style français […]".[40] More attention was paid to the exhibition of Van Gogh's work, also on view in the Palais de Tokyo, although the show's lighting, wall design, and picture framing received a devastating review.[41] In his travelogue *Das geistige Paris 1937*, Hocke discussed the art exhibitions in more detail, also considering their relation to the most recent World's Fair to have taken place in Paris, the exposition of 1900. Echoing Georges Huisman, he once again expounded the meaning and purpose of an exhibition of French art from the late Middle Ages to the end of the 19th century. By this means, the state could develop a program of artistic instruction that would play an essential role in the renaissance of French taste;[42] the exhibition would be imbued with the totality of the French spirit. Hocke, however, did not review any individual works, and the same holds true for reports on the Paris exposition in the daily press; the Jewish newspaper *Der Morgen*, for example, mentioned the "incomparable exhibition of French art from the early Middle Ages to the threshold of the present", but did not provide further details.[43] Paul Westheim's review of the *Chefs-d'œuvre de l'art français* in the *Pariser Tageszeitung* on July 27 emphasized the artistic achievement of portrait painters, citing Nicolas Froment's donor portraits of René d'Anjou and Jeanne de Laval as well as the portraits by Jean Fouquet.[44] Westheim described the exhibition as highly successful and as "an intellectual and sensual experience with an astounding, enthralling series of masterpieces, incontestable masterpieces".[45] A report in the *Revue de l'art*, as well, briefly alluded to Jean Fouquet's achievement in

portraiture and mentioned the *Étienne Chevalier* as the earliest example of a half-figure portrait, but then devoted fuller attention to 17th-century painting as the true beginning of French art.[46]

Reviews in the daily press were rare in comparison to the exhibition of 1904. The works of Jean Fouquet, however, were appreciated above all by the artists of French Post-Cubism.[47] Although they had certainly known Fouquet before 1937, the renewed presentation of his art at the Paris Exposition likely left a more profound impression.[48] Maurice Estève, Jean René Bazaine, and Roger Bissière paid homage to Fouquet's *Virgin and Child* by referencing it in their works, while Jean Hélion, whose abstract painting was anchored in the rectilinear forms of Piet Mondrian and Theo van Doesburg, was inspired by Fouquet with an impulse to add diagonal lines and curves to his art: "S'enrichissant ainsi, le signe minimum allait au-devant de cette image de la Vierge que je gardais comme une icône dans mon atelier. Il me semblait que tout ce qui manquait à l'abstraction était là: un jeu subtil de courbes et de nuances, une combinaison d'à-plats et de volumes, un luxe sobre de détails, enfin, toute la vie".[49]

In 1936, French art historian and medievalist Henri Focillon had already described the cubistic force of Jean Fouquet, which for him lived on in modern art: "[…] et qui se perpétue comme un héritage permanent dans les formes les plus élevées de l'art moderne".[50]

Two years later, Symbolist painter Maurice Denis explicitly articulated the importance of the repeated viewing of works by great masters. In his book on religious art, he especially emphasized the exemplary nature and expressive power of Fouquet's *Virgin and Child*—both its coloration and its contours, which he viewed as typically French—and even gave it a full-page color illustration in his book: "Sa couleur, à base de rouge, de bleu et de gris clair infiniment variés, est caractéristique du goût français, et il a enfin le sens des valeurs comme Corot, à la fois subtil et robuste".[51] Denis' observations were likely inspired not only by Fouquet, but also by French art historian Germain Bazin. The latter had already paid particular attention to Fouquet in his essay on medieval art in the publication accompanying the exhibition *Chefs-d'œuvre de l'art français* and had crowned him as an icon of French art: "Jean Fouquet donne de l'esthétique française une des définitions les plus authentiques".[52] In Fouquet, Bazin saw the convergence of everything that would later distinguish Camille Corot: "vision locale, non universaliste comme celle des flamands bornée à ce que l'œil peut embrasser, c'est-à-dire à l'horizon humain, simplification des plans, justesse des valeurs, association de l'Homme à la Nature, c'est déjà tout Corot".[53] In his discussion, Bazin made explicit reference to the Antwerp *Virgin and Child*; for him, this work had approached the very brink of abstraction through its simplification of forms and could be described as one of the "chefs-d'œuvre de l'art français" par excellence.[54] He saw it as the very embodiment of the French soul and the absolute expression of the Gothic, and in its purity found it comparable to French glass painting of the 13th century: "[…] le sein de la Vierge est une sphère d'ivoire, l'enfant est de cristal. Cette peinture claire, limpide, dénuée de tout esprit charnel est aussi pure, aussi immatérielle que les images peintes sur les verrières du XIIIe siècle; la suprême élégance du trait est la manifestation ultime de l'élégance linéaire du gothique".[55]

In his review of the 1904 exhibition *Primitifs français*, Durrieu had been less enthusiastic about Fouquet's *Virgin and Child* and had described it as mediocre: "[…] une œuvre médiocre très inférieure en tout cas aux portraits d'hommes. Il faut tenir compte, il est vrai, des altérations du temps qui ont pu en dénaturer les mérites. Mais, malgré tout, cette Vierge a dû toujours avoir les aspects bien maussade".[56] Thirty years later, such negative judgments had disappeared and the *Virgin and Child*, no longer perceived as morose, was chosen to adorn a poster (fig. 85). At the Paris Exposition of 1937—an opportunity for France, in particular, to engage in comprehensive self-representation—Jean Fouquet could be celebrated as the father of French painting.

1   Gréber 1937, p. 1.
2   Cf. Barker 2003, p. 10.
3   The official *Livre d'Or* of the exposition (1937, p. 11) lists 44 participating nations; Edmond Labbé, Commissar General of the Paris Exposition, however, only mentions 42 (ibid., p. 19). The idea of peaceful cooperation was repeatedly emphasized, for example by Claus Schrempf in his remarks on Gustav R. Hocke's *Kultur und Leben*; cf. Schrempf 1938, p. 7.
4   Graf 1997, p. 104.
5   Hocke 1937, p. 8.
6   Cf. Bushart 1985, p. 106.

7   Speer 1969, pp. 94-95; Graf 1997, p. 106.
8   Quoted in Spies 2003, p. 65. This observation by the social philosophers occurs in the chapter "Aufklärung als Massenbetrug" in *Dialektik der Aufklärung* (M. Horkheimer, Gesammelte Schriften vol. 5, Frankfurt 1987, p. 145). The quotation here is taken from the first version of the text, which was published in a small edition in 1944 as a hectographic typescript of the Institut für Sozialforschung. The sentence "Der dt. und russ. Pavillon…" was later deleted by the authors. After extensive analysis, Ades 1996, p. 61, comes to a different conclusion, characterizing the buildings as fundamentally different.
9   Harbers 1937, p. 271; see also Graf 1997, p. 110.
10   Hoffmann 1937, p. 105. The report in the *Völkischer Beobachter* mentions the Soviet building only in passing; *Völkischer Beobachter*, May 26, 1937, no. 145, p. 2, and May 27, 1937, no. 147, p. 3.
11   Hocke 1937, first published as a series of four articles in the *Kölnische Zeitung* in 1937, cf. *Kölnische Zeitung* no. 331, July 4, 1937, p. 3; no. 332, July 5, p. 6; no. 335, July 6, 1937, p. 2; no. 339, July 8, 1937, p. 1. Reviewed in *Leipziger Nachrichten* by Claus Schrempf in 1938.
12   Hocke 1937, p. 8.
13   Zervos 1936, p. 209; cf. Ades 1996, pp. 61-62.
14   Benjamin 1968, p. 242; cf. Ades 1996, p. 62.
15   Hoffmann 1937, p. 115. The theme of peace was emphasized by all participating nations, including the Soviet Union: "C'est pays dirigé par le Parti de Lenine-Staline qui incarne les plus belles aspirations vers la Paix, le Progrès, la Civilisation et le plus noble idéal humain" ("It is the country run by the party of Lenin and Stalin that embodies the finest aspirations for Peace, Progress, Civilization, and the most noble human ideal"), in: *Livre d'Or* 1937, p. 514.
16   "Pariser Weltausstellung," in: *Pariser Tageszeitung*, May 24, 1937, vol. 2, no. 346, p. 4.
17   Quoted in Barr 1966, p. 264.
18   Ades 1996, p. 58.
19   Ades 1996, p. 58: "In a world heavily burdened by the dark threat of the future, it has seemed for some time as if civilization had begun to doubt itself, its values, its powers, and its duties. A kind of discouragement and lassitude has come over our souls, shaking them to the very ground of hope. And now the Exposition has suddenly appeared with a force of supreme will, ascending skyward like a great cry of confidence and fervor from the whole of humanity." Labbé 1937, pp. 24-25.
20   Ozenfant 1937, p. 246: "One will be able to see [contemporary] French painting in France! That will be something completely new." Beginning in 1961, the Palais de Tokyo housed the Musée d'Art moderne de la Ville de Paris and the Musée national d'Art moderne in its two wings; the latter moved to the Centre Pompidou in 1977. Today the building is home to the contemporary art center "Le Palais de Tokyo."
21   Cf. Graf 1997, p. 116; here Hocke refers to Georges Huismann, cf. n. 11, no. 331, p. 3.
22   Huisman in Cat. Paris 1937b, p. VI: "It was quickly decided that a vast retrospective, organized by the International Exposition and encompassing French art from its origins up to the present, would provide the most admirable lessons and the purest joy for the eyes and spirit and would be of the greatest benefit to the aesthetics and technology of today." Cf. also Robert Burnard, Secretary General of the Museums of Fine Arts, in the *Livre d'o r* 1937, p. 64, and Ozenfant 1937, p. 246.
23   Léon Blum in Cat. Paris 1937a, first page of the foreword: "In order to understand and fully appreciate the contemporary pieces, it is not enough to place them in the milieu in which they originated. They should be connected once again to earlier works. They should be viewed as the result of a long series of accomplishments, over the course of centuries, by men who have struggled to discipline the material in order to attain the vivid expression of life, the beauty of lines, the harmonious eloquence of colors." Multiple publications accompanied the exhibition, including a general catalogue with a volume of illustrations with black and white plates of 162 works (Cat. Paris 1937a). A two-volume catalogue was also published with a selection of 397 works; the

first volume was devoted entirely to painting, while the second dealt with other artistic genres (Cat. Paris 1937b).

24 An exhibition of Van Gogh was also on view in the same venue. Contemporary, living artists, on the other hand, were shown at the Petit Palais and the Jeu de Paume in two exhibitions: "Les Maîtres de l'Art Indépendant"—primarily with works by Picasso, Matisse, Braque, and Rouault—and "Origine et Développement de l'Art International Indépendant," with Fauvist, Cubist, Dadaist, Surrealist, Abstract, and Constructivist art. Cf. Contensou, in Cat. Paris 1987, p. 12 and Ades in Cat. London/Barcelona/Berlin 1996, p. 59.

25 Cat. Paris 1904.

26 Cf. Bouyer 1937, p. 166.

27 Zay 1937, p. 80: "From the marvels of the Middle Ages to the epoch of Cézanne and Seurat, one could admire the illustrious continuity of the French tradition."

28 Cf. Huyghe 1937, p. 3; Henri Focillon in Cat. Paris 1937a, p. 13; cf. Kangaslathi 2011, pp. 129, 138 n. 42.

29 SMB-ZA, GG 258, Akte F-370-37, p. 1; special thanks here go to Sven Haase (Zentralarchiv).

30 SMB-ZA, GG 258, Akte F-370-37, p. 21.

31 *Die Weltkunst*, vol. 11, no. 24/25, from June 20, 1937, p. 2; Rakint 1937, pp. 196-197.

32 SMB-ZA, GG 258, Akte F-370-37, pp. 22, 24; the list also included Hamburg, Bremen, Munich, Hannover, Dresden, Kassel, Essen, Frankfurt, and Potsdam.

33 Now identified as a portrait of Clelia Cesarini Colonna, attributed to Jacob Ferdinand Voet.

34 Cf. Cat. Paris 1937a, no. 438 p. 210.

35 Cf. n. 11, no. 331, p. 3.

36 *Die Weltkunst*, vol. 11, no. 32/33, from August 15, 1937, p. 6.

37 Burnard 1937a, seventh page of his text: "How could one fail to mention the diptych by Jean Fouquet, which once again reunites the portrait of Étienne Chevalier from the museum in Berlin with the Virgin from Antwerp?"

38 Burnard 1937b, pp. 65, 67.

39 Quoted in Willet in: Cat. London/Barcelona/Berlin 1996, p. 117.

40 Jean Zay in *Cahiers d'Art* 12, 1937, p. 162: "The exhibition of masterworks once again proclaims this extraordinary unity of the French style [...]."

41 *Cahiers d'Art* 12, 1937, pp. 98-99.

42 Cf. Graf 1997, pp. 114-115; Hocke 1937, p. 10; Cat. Paris 1937b, p. VI.

43 H.B. in *Der Morgen* 13, no. 4, 1937, p. 141.

44 Westheim 1937, p. 4.

45 Paul Westheim reported on the *Chefs-d'œuvre* exhibition in the *Pariser Tageszeitung*, July 27, 1937, no. 2, 409, p. 4.

46 Bouyer 1937, pp. 165-166.

47 Reviews by: Lord 1937, p. 93, who does not mention Fouquet; Dimier 1938, pp. 171-174, who mentions some individual works, but not Fouquet. The most detailed review is the one by Bouyer in *Revue de l'Art* 1937.

48 Cf. François-René Martin, in: Cat. Paris 2008, p. 92.

49 Jean Hélion, "Notre-Dame de l'abstraction," in: *Le Nouvel Observateur*, December 21, 1984, pp. 70-71, here p. 70: "A small, enriching sign went out from this image of the Virgin that I kept like an icon in my atelier. It seemed to me that everything missing from abstraction was present here: a subtle play of curves and nuances, a combination of planes and volumes, a sober abundance of details, in short, all of life." Cf. Martin 2008, p. 92.

50 Focillon 1936, p. 32: "[...] and which perpetuates itself like an enduring legacy in the highest forms of modern art".

51 Denis 1939, p. 122; quoted in Martin 2008, p. 92: "His color, based on red, blue, and infinite variations of light gray, is characteristic of French taste, and ultimately his sense of values is like that of Corot, both subtle and robust".

52 Bazin 1937, p. 14: "Jean Fouquet gives the French aesthetic one of the most authentic definitions".

53 Bazin 1937, p. 14: "a local vision, not universalist like that of the Flemish, limited to what the eye can encompass, that is to the human horizon, simplification of planes, accuracy of values, association of Man and Nature, it is already entirely Corot".

54 Bazin 1937, p. 14.

55 Bazin 1937, p. 14: "[...] the breast of the Virgin is a sphere of ivory, the child is of crystal. This bright, crystalline painting, devoid of any carnal spirit, is as pure, as immaterial as 13th-century images painted on glass; the supreme elegance of line is the ultimate manifestation of the linear elegance of the Gothic".

56 Durrieu 1904, p. 81: "[...] a mediocre work, in any case much inferior to the male portraits. Of course one has to take into account the changes over time that may have diminished its merits. But despite all, this Virgin must have always seemed rather morose".

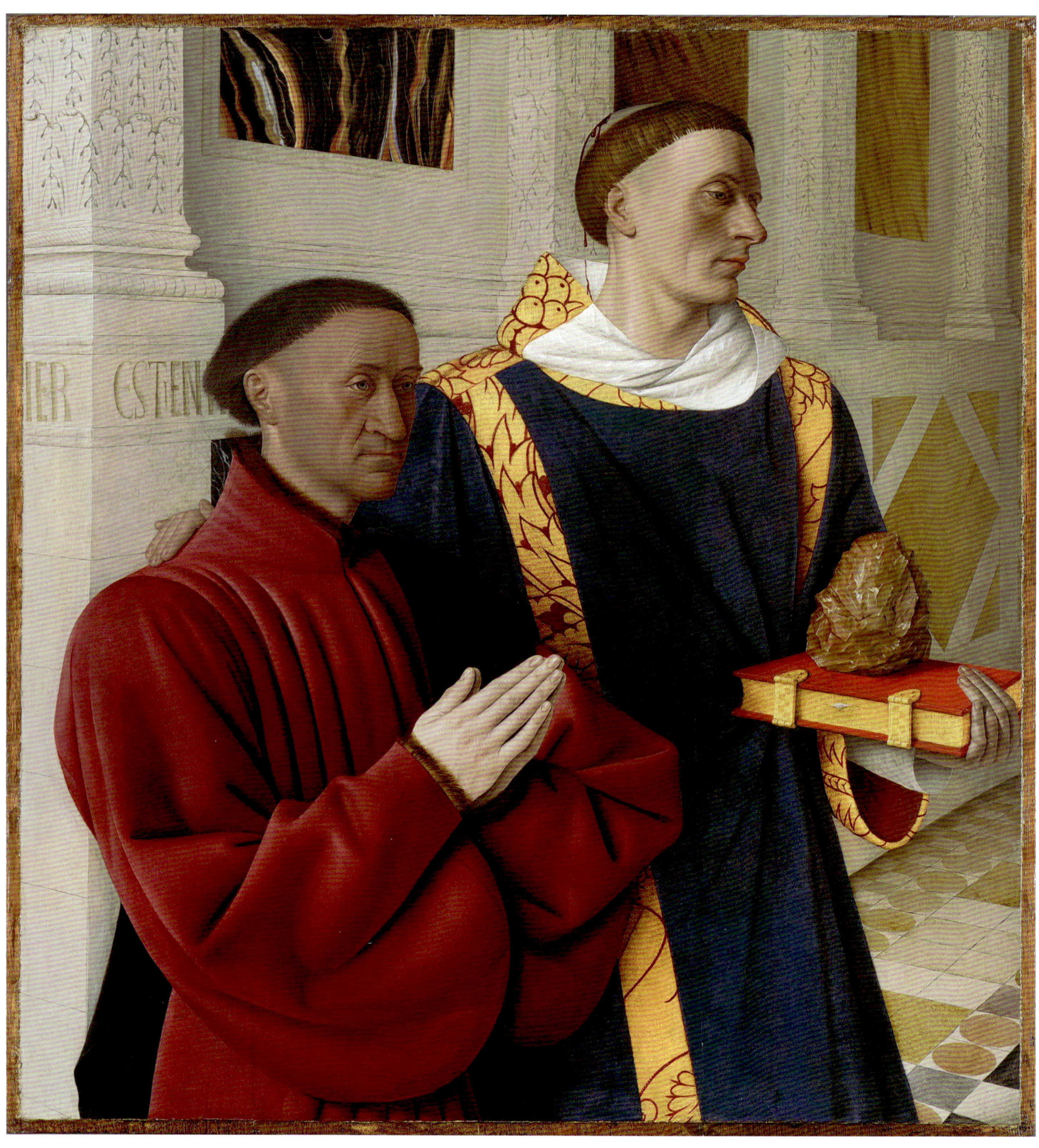

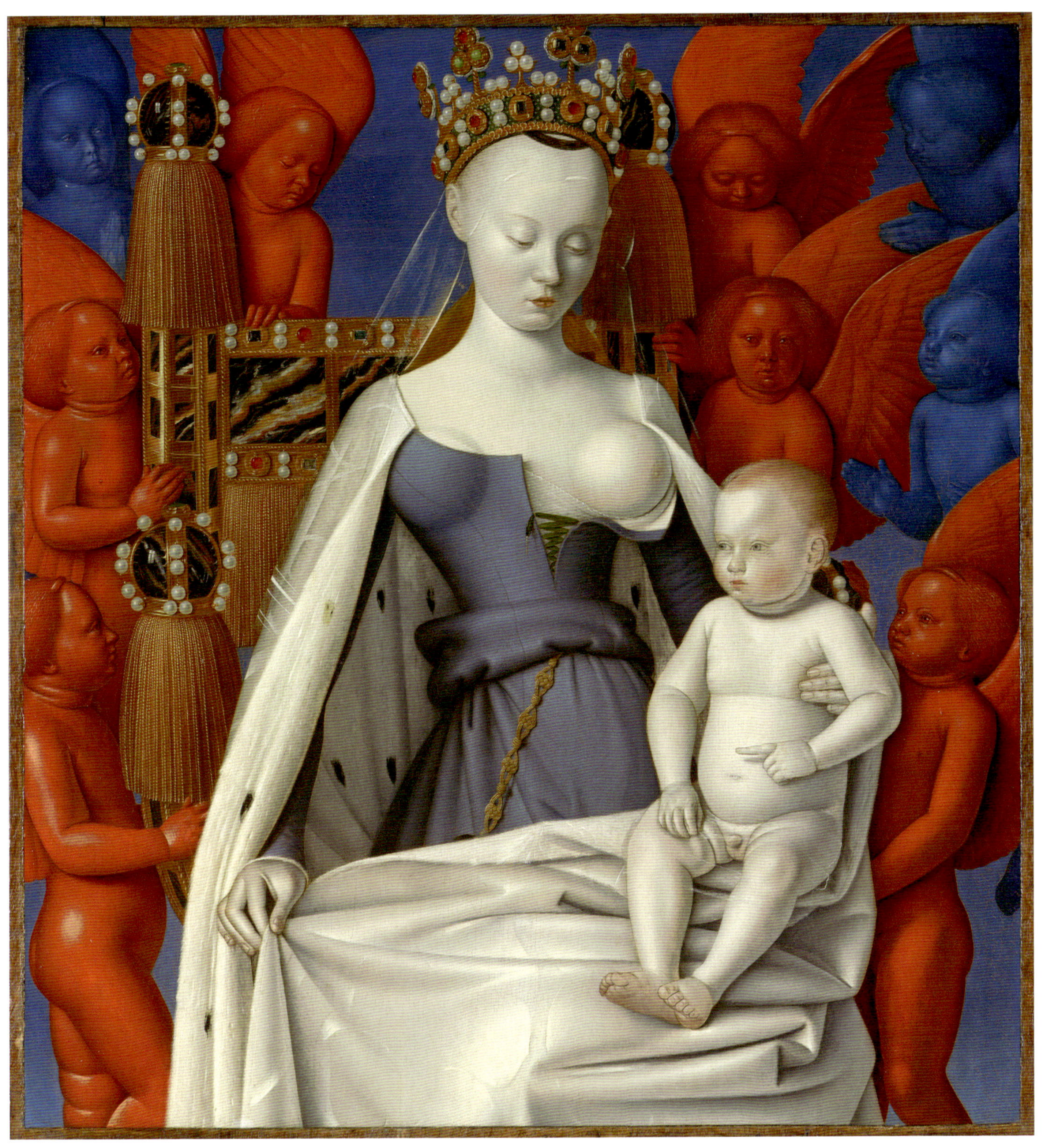

JEAN FOUQUET, THE MELUN DIPTYCH

ca. 1452/60

a) Left panel: *Étienne Chevalier and St. Stephen* (fig. 93)

Oak, 96.1-5 x 88.0 cm, thinned to 0.3-0.6 cm, cradled

Painted surface 94.0 x 85.4 cm

Inscription on architecture: (CHEVAL)IER ESTIENN(E); the same text apparently continued to the right, but is completely abraded there.

The panel was restored in 1986.

Gemäldegalerie, Staatliche Museen zu Berlin, Cat. No. 1617

b) Right panel: *Virgin and Child Surrounded by Angels* (fig. 94)

Oak, 94.2-3 x 85.3-5 cm, thickness 1.0-1.2 cm

Painted surface 91.6 x 83.0 cm

Inscription on the reverse, in black on the unpainted wooden surface: "La st vierge,/ sous les traits/ D'AGNÈS SOREL,/maitresse de Charles VII Roi de France/ morte en 1450/ce Tableau, qui êtoit/ dans le chœr de Nôtre Dame/ DE MEHUN,/ est un voeu de Mre ETIENNE/ Chevalier, un des Exécuteurs/ Testamentaires d'Agnès Sorel./ 1775/ Gaulthier/avocat" (fig. 95)

The panel was restored in 1995.

Antwerp, Koninklijk Museum voor Schone Kunsten, Inv. 132

Selected bibliography: Godefroy 1661, pp. 885 ff. – Waagen 1839, p. 372 – Grésy 1845 – de Laborde 1855, pp. 696-712 – Vallet de Viriville 1857 – Curmer 1864, pp. 87-90, 120 ff. – Friedländer 1896 – Bode 1896, pp. 6-9 – Cat. Paris 1904, pp. 17-19 (H. Bouchot) – Durrieu 1911, p. 731 – Wescher 1947, pp. 54-56 – Künstler 1975, pp. 13-18 – Châtelet 1975 – Schaefer 1975 – Lombardi 1978 – Sricchia Santoro 1978, p. 102 – Reynaud 1981, pp. 18-26, 90 – Reynaud 1983 – Sterling 1988, pp. 27-32 – Schaefer 1994, pp. 139-151, 290-292 – Vandenbroeck, Guislain-Wittermann 1996 – Cat. Paris 2003, No. 8 (F. Avril) – Van der Velden 2006, pp. 146 ff. – Förstel 2008, pp. 97-80 – Nash 2008, pp. 286-288 – Schaefer 2000 – Inglis 2011, pp. 10-13, 19 ff. – Vandenbroeck 2014, pp. 131-133

Provenance: The diptych was commissioned by Étienne Chevalier, presumably for his chapel at the east end of the collegiate church of Notre-Dame in Melun. In 1773/75, it was dismantled and the individual parts were sold. The *Virgin and Child* was acquired by Chevalier Florent van Ertborn (1784–1840, 1817–1828 mayor of Antwerp, later governor of Utrecht) in Paris at an unknown date and bequeathed to the Antwerp museum in 1841; at that time the painting was located in Utrecht. Its counterpart was discovered by the poet Clemens Brentano (1778–1842) in Munich at the beginning of the 19th century. He bought the panel and gave it to his brother, the banker Georg Brentano-Laroche (1775–1851) of Frankfurt am Main, since the latter already owned 40 illuminations that had been cut from the *Hours of Étienne Chevalier* and Clemens recognized the same artist's hand in the painting, as well as the same patron.[1] According to a diary entry by Sulpiz Boisserée, Georg had acquired the miniatures for 40 Louis d'or from the painter and dealer Peter Birmann in Basel shortly before September 18, 1816;[2] thus Clemens probably purchased the donor panel after this date. Following Georg Brentano's death, the panel and the miniatures passed to his son Ludwig, known as Louis (1811–1895), who kept them in his house near the Taunusanlage and made them available to interested viewers; Fouquet's two major works thus remained together in Frankfurt for about 75 years. In 1891, Henri d'Orléans, duc d'Aumale (1822–1897), bought the 40 miniatures from Louis Brentano for 250,000 francs and gave them to the Musée Condé in Chantilly, where they remain to this day. After Louis' death in 1895, the donor panel was purchased for the museum in Berlin for 80,000 marks from the heiress, Baroness Stuck-Brentano, with funds advanced by the Kaiser Friedrich Museums-Verein.[3]

The right panel, which was originally fixed, shows the Mother of God in extremely fashionable clothing, with an ermine mantle, laced bodice, and exposed left breast. The Christ Child sits in her left arm to the viewer's right. Six child-like angels in red, presumably seraphim, bear the Virgin's splendid golden throne, while three blue cherubim join them in front of a plain blue background. While the Virgin gazes at her divine Son, the latter looks to the left in the direction of the other panel and points toward the donor with his left index finger. In the left panel, Étienne Chevalier kneels in half-figure in the foreground, praying to the Virgin and Christ. He is clothed in a robe of costly dark-red velvet and has humbly removed his head gear, his *chaperon*, draping it over his left shoulder and onto his back. Behind him stands his patron saint, St. Stephen, who rests a hand protectively on his shoulder and likewise gazes across to the other wing. As a deacon, Stephen wears a blue, gold-trimmed dalmatic over his alb; around his neck is an amice, likewise ornamented in gold. On top of the book in his left hand lies his attribute and the instrument of his martyrdom, a sharp-edged stone. Blood from his stoning drips down the back of his head onto his collar. In the background, a Renaissance architecture recedes sharply into depth toward the right; its wall bears an inscription with the name and title of the patron. Both panels were originally supplied with splendid frames (fig. 16) and were connected with hinges. The left panel could be folded; its reverse was probably painted with a figural scene that was separated from the rest of the panel around 1775. It may have been a crucifixion, perhaps with a portrait of Chevalier's wife Catherine Budé, who had died in 1452.

The donor wing seems to have been attributed to Jean Fouquet for the first time in 1839 by Gustav Friedrich Waagen, who not only associated it with the miniatures that were likewise in Brentano's possession, but also succeeded in identifying the artist of both works by comparing them to illuminations from the *Antiquités judaïques*.[4] Waagen, however, doubted Fouquet's authorship of the Antwerp Madonna, while Léon de Laborde accepted it in 1855 and identified the two panels as the remains of the diptych in the collegiate church of Melun described by Denis Godefroy in 1661.[5] His attribution was accepted by virtually every scholar after him and was emphatically endorsed, for example, by Max J. Friedländer in 1896. Only Paul Durrieu still considered the *Virgin and Child* the work of an older master who had not yet been inspired by the Italian Renaissance.[6] Despite the existence of a description of the panels' original frame in Melun, the medallion with the artist's self-portrait, now in Paris (cat. 2), was not associated with the diptych until 1904, by Henri Bouchot;[7] in 1896, Max Friedländer still assumed that the enamels described by Godefroy would have measured about 15 cm in diameter.[8] An enamel of the same size[9] showing *The Choosing of the Seven Deacons*

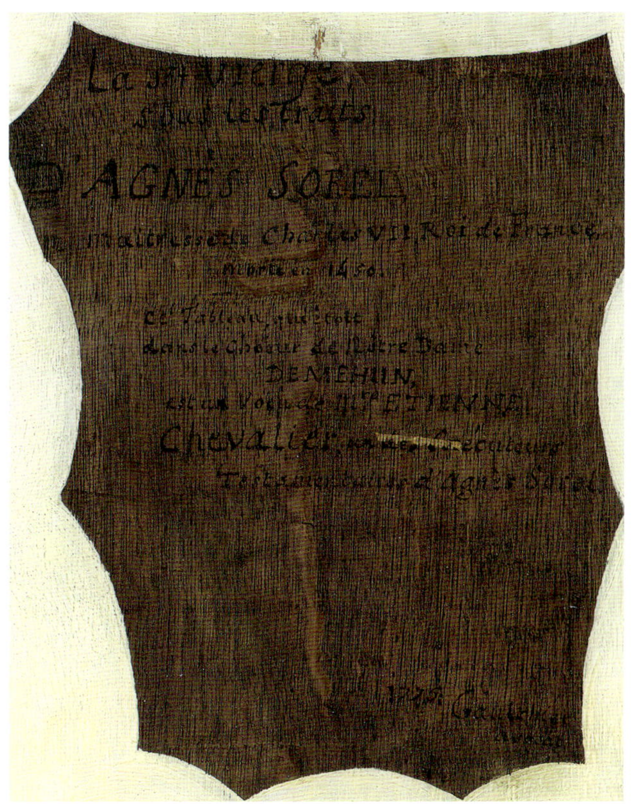

Fig. 95. Inscription of 1775 on the reverse of the Madonna panel

(fig. 15) was acquired by the Kunstgewerbemuseum in Berlin in 1891; not until 1904, however, was it recognized by Jean-Joseph Marquet de Vasselot as also belonging to the frame, and not until 1972 was the iconography identified by Marie-Madeleine Gauthier as a scene from the life of St. Stephen.[10]

In the extensive scholarly literature on the diptych, controversy has revolved above all around the question of whether the Virgin Mary bears the features of Agnès Sorel, as was rumored since the early 17th century at the latest and as the lawyer Gaulthier wrote on the back of the Madonna panel in 1775—no doubt in order to increase its sale value (fig. 95). De Laborde and Friedländer accepted this supposition, as did Claude Schaefer in 1975, Nicole Reynaud in 1981, and François Avril in 2003.[11] Albert Châtelet, on the other hand, argued strongly against it, and Schaefer later followed him, suggesting that the Virgin more likely bore the features of Chevalier's wife, Catherine Budé.[12]

Infrared reflectographies of the two panels taken in preparation for this exhibition reveal comparable underdraw-

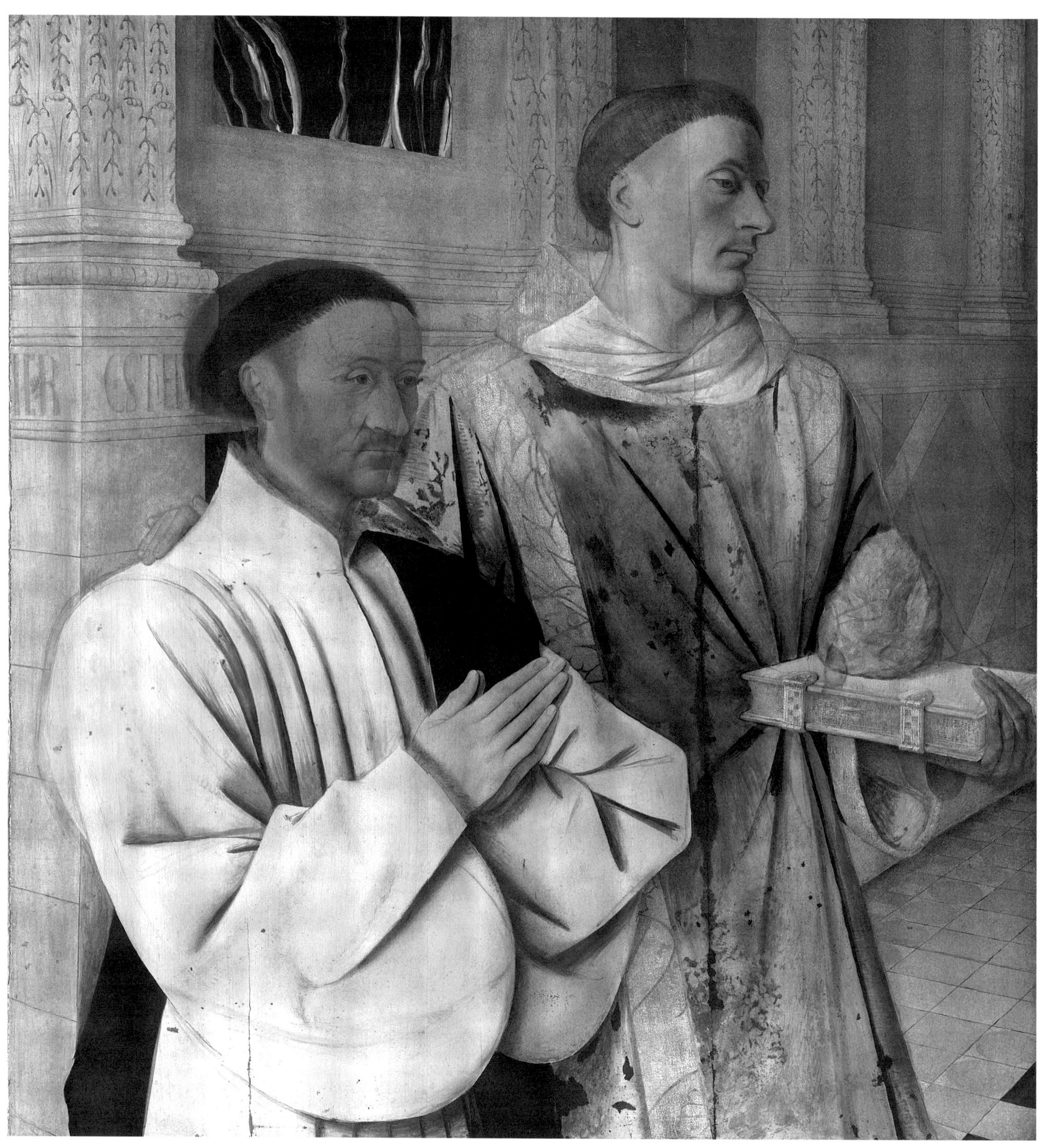

Fig. 96. Infrared reflectography of Donor panel, IRR by Christoph Schmidt, Berlin

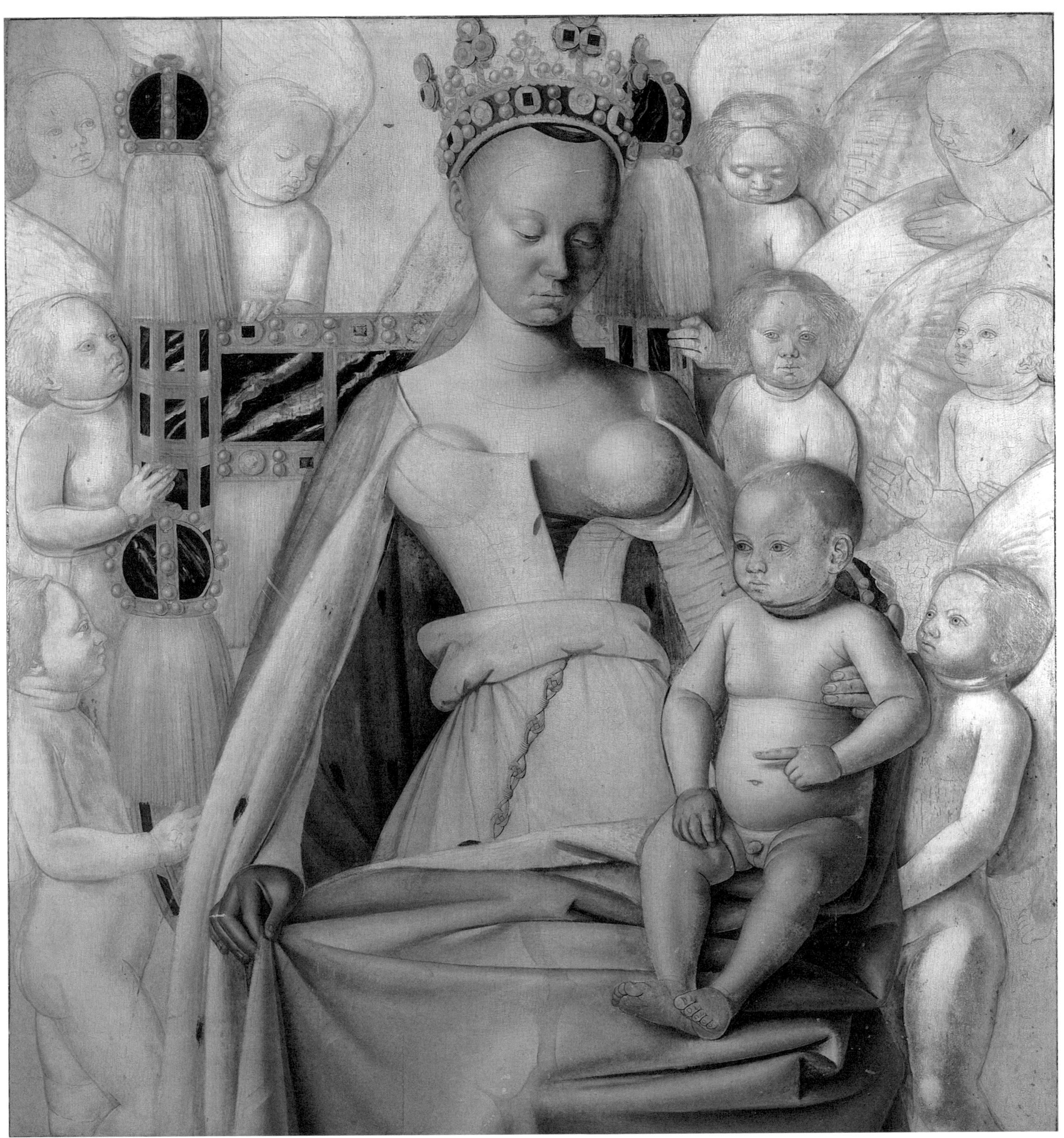

Fig. 97. Infrared reflectography of Virgin panel, IRR by Katrin Dyballa, Berlin

ings that are essentially linear and show only a few areas of hatching (fig. 96, 97). The donor panel, however, shows evidence of significantly more reworking than the Antwerp painting.[13] In the latter, changes were primarily made to the angels, and for the most part consisted only of minor alterations of contour, for example in the arm of the red angel on the left at the rear support of the throne. Somewhat more extensive changes are discernible in the lower right corner: a portion of the pelvic region of the front red angel was visible, revealing him as male, and the foot and toes of the blue angel at the right were drawn in detail further below. Traces of pounce marks like those on the donor panel appear on the faces of the red angel at the left next to the head of the Virgin and the red angel at the right front; thus it would seem that a cartoon was likewise used for the angels. Very few changes were made to the figures of the Virgin and Child—only a few pearls were omitted from the Madonna's crown—a fact that speaks for the exact repetition of the cartoon from the first version of the composition (fig. 97). In contrast to the angels, no pounce marks are visible here;[14] the question of whether this discrepancy, along with the slightly more significant changes to the angels, indicates that the latter were not depicted in the cartoon of the first version will not be addressed here. The figure of the Virgin does, however, show one remarkable alteration: the IRR reveals three non-concentric circle segments on her throat and decolleté (fig. 97). The two upper ones merely appear to indicate small, perfectly rounded wrinkles in her throat; the lower, larger one, however, suggests an object, like a higher neckline for the dress, although such would have accorded poorly with the exposed breast.[15] Was the figure originally depicted wearing a necklace? Such a motif would correspond to the jewelry represented on the tomb figure of Agnès Sorel (fig. 58), and if this conjecture is correct, it would provide further evidence for the identification of the mistress with the Madonna.

There are no contemporary documents for the work, and it is not mentioned until the year 1608.[16] A handwritten list of the properties and rents acquired by the church of Notre-Dame with the money donated by Éti-

enne Chevalier for his daily Mass contains no reference whatsoever to his chapel or his dispositions.[17] It is generally assumed that the diptych was painted after the death of Chevalier's wife Catherine Budé, which occurred in the summer of 1452; dendrochronological analysis confirms that the work was not created before the 1450s. The donor's portrait seems to be based on the same drawing as its counterpart in the double-page illumination in the book of hours (fig. 43). Chevalier's somewhat older appearance in the manuscript is probably mainly due to the painting's execution, for in his second portrait in the book of hours, in the *Entombment*, he seems younger than on the panel. Thus it seems impossible to determine the precise temporal relationship between the diptych and the book of hours; both can be dated to the period between 1452 and 1460.

Stephan Kemperdick

1 As communicated to the Comte de Laborde by Louis Brentano around 1850; see Curmer 1864, p. 88.

2 Boisserée 1978-1995, vol. 1, p. 360: Heidelberg, September 18, 1816.

3 Bode 1896, pp. 6-9; Stockhausen 1997, pp. 23ff.; the funds advanced by the Verein for the acquisition of the painting were repaid in 1897.

4 Waagen 1839, p. 372; the date of Robertet's entry, after 1488, was already known to him. For the manuscript, cf. Cat. Paris 2003, no. 34. Like Passavant 1833 before him, Waagen 1837, p. 415, recognized the affinity of the David miniature from Chevalier's book of hours, at that time in the Rogers collection in London, and that it had been intended for Étienne Chevalier.

5 De Laborde 1855, pp. 661-727; idem, in Curmer 1864, pp. 87-90.

6 Durrieu 1911, p. 731.

7 Cat. Paris 1904, pp. 17-19.

8 Friedländer 1896, pp. 212ff.

9 Its diameter, including the non-original frame with a branch motif, was 9 cm (Netzer 1999, no. 64); the photographic inventory card C III 16 from the Kunstgewerbemuseum in Köpenick specifies "diameter 7.5 cm" for the piece itself, apparently measured with the original edging, with a picture surface of ca. 6.9-7 cm. I am most grateful to Lothar Lambacher, Kunstgewerbemuseum Berlin, for this information.

10 Gauthier 1972, no. 252; likewise Reynaud 1981, pp. 23ff.

11 Reynaud 1981, pp. 20-22; Cat. Paris 2003, pp. 128ff.

12 Châtelet 1975; Schaefer 1994, pp. 146-148, quite differently from idem 1975, p. 100.

13 See the essay by Stelzig in this catalogue.

14 See the essay by Kemperdick in this volume.

15 The circle shape would not have been suitable for a veil over the bosom, like that of the Rohan Master (Fig. 59).

16 Héroard 1868, p. 323.

17 Melun, Archives départementales, doc. G 221; the majority of the manuscript must have been written after 1474, since a reference to "feu monseigneur maistre estienne chevalier" already occurs on one of the first pages.

Sandra Stelzig

RESULTS OF THE TECHNICAL ANALYSIS
OF JEAN FOUQUET'S PAINTING OF ÉTIENNE CHEVALIER
IN BERLIN

Fouquet's Berlin panel was subjected to a thorough analysis in preparation for the exhibition and as part of an ongoing cataloguing project in the Gemäldegalerie.[1] The results are based on microscopic examination, the evaluation of technical images from X-rays, infrared reflectography (IRR), and UV fluorescence,[2] and in certain areas micro X-ray fluorescence analysis (μ-XRF) for the identification of elements in pigments.[3] Since the painting formerly served as the left wing of a diptych, the right wing, the *Virgin and Child* now in Antwerp, should also be included in the investigation; as we will see, from a technical standpoint the two panels are closely related.[4]

The panel and the original frame

Like its counterpart, the Berlin painting was executed on an oak panel. The panel consists of four vertical boards which were butt jointed; each joint was secured with three long, thin, evenly-spaced dowels. In the middle joint, two heart sides are affixed to each other, while in the outer joints two sap sides meet, in accord with standard joinery practice.[5] The outer edges of the panel are not primed, indicating that it originally possessed a grooved frame that was primed and painted along with the panel. The same is true of the Antwerp painting. On the Berlin panel, the barbs show traces of gilding over a sand-colored layer containing numerous green particles. On the basis of their age, they could be interpreted as the remains of the polychromy of the original frame (fig. 98a). The width of the original frame between the two panels has been reconstructed by François Avril as 9-9.5 cm.[6]

The two panels of the diptych were separated from each other around 1775. When the former left painting was acquired by the Berlin museums in 1896, the panel had already undergone serious alteration: so much of the wood had been removed from the back that today the panel is only 3-5 mm thick and thus extremely fragile. In this process, the original dowel holes were cut in half, so that the dowels themselves, likewise halved, lie loose in their mortises. On both sides and in the upper right corner, a thin pinewood veneer was glued onto the back side in order to reinforce the partially overly-thinned panel; the transition between the veneer and the original panel was completely leveled. The contours of the veneered surface, however, are noticeably serrated, suggesting a saw cut. Apparently the panel was sawn apart, i.e., split lengthwise down through its thickness.[7] This in turn indicates that the original back side of the panel was elaborately painted, since otherwise it would probably not have been subjected to splitting, a procedure that was technically very complicated and could only be performed by specialists.[8] If there had been no painting on the back side, the panel would simply have been planed. Finally, the thinned panel was cradled. Since the cradle differs from the type commonly used in the Berlin museum, it is fairly certain that it was mounted before the panel was acquired in 1896.

Preparation of the surface with ground layer and imprimatura

The panel shows a light-colored ground whose consistent, weak X-ray absorption indicates that sizing was previously

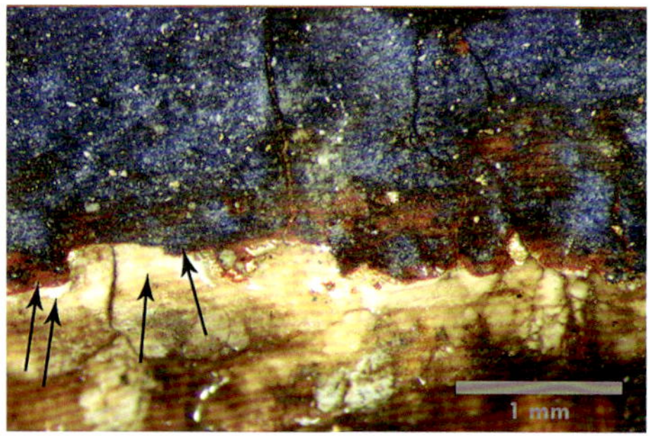

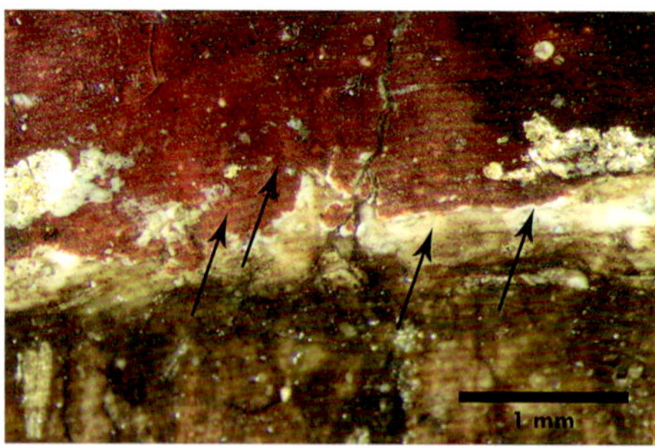

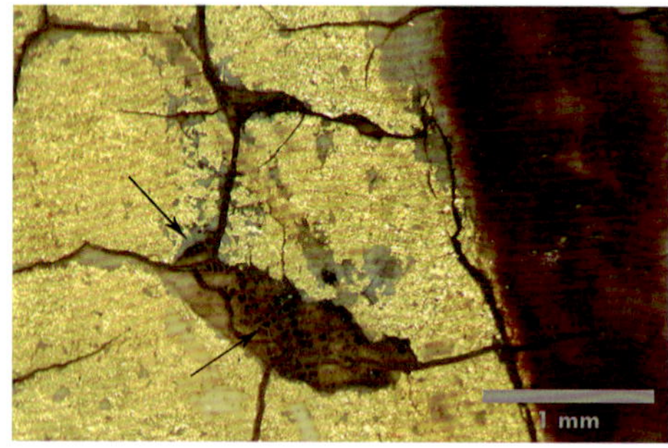

Fig. 98a. Lower edge of painting: light-colored ground, white imprimatura, reddish brown underpainting, and blue paint layer from the robe of St. Stephen; along the panel edge, remains of original gilding from the frame
b. Lower edge of painting: light-colored priming, white imprimatura, and two layers from Chevalier's red garment
c. Loss in the upper layers: underdrawing and white imprimatura visible beneath the gilding

Fig. 99. IRR: pounce marks

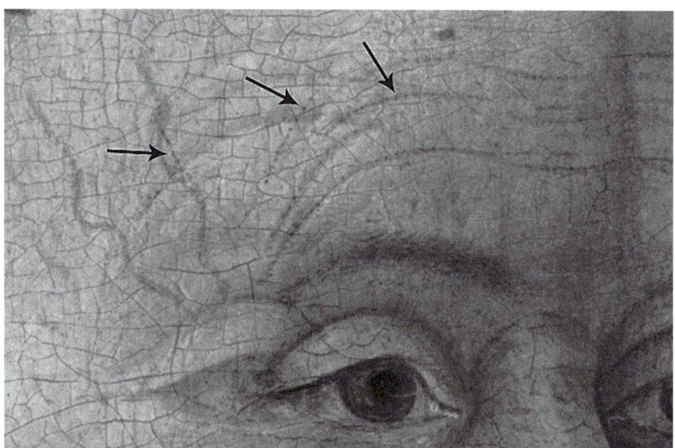

applied, filling the pores. The surface of the ground layer was carefully smoothed, leaving no traces of the work. Only a recessed groove along the inner frame edge remains, which either resulted from the sanding process itself or represents an engraved line intended to more clearly define the profile of the frame.

On top of the ground is a thin imprimatura in fine-particle pigment, probably containing lead white. It covered the first strokes of the underdrawing on the priming, permitting it to show through only faintly. The imprimatura was applied very evenly, so that the X-ray image reveals no brushstrokes. Microscopically, the imprimatura is perceptible in all areas of the work between the priming and the layers of paint (fig. 98b, c).

Underdrawing and pentimenti

The composition was carefully underdrawn using various media, and multiple times throughout the course of the work it was corrected, further developed, and reinforced. Traces of underdrawing are found on both the ground layer and the imprimatura.

In the earliest phase of the work for which we have evidence, a portrait drawing was transferred to the panel by means of pouncing, as indicated by a number of dotted lines revealed by the IRR in the head of Étienne Chevalier (fig. 99). The transfer of this drawing was probably preceded by an initial blocking out of the figures, into which the portrait was inserted. The IRR also shows the black strokes of underdrawing using a brush and a fluid medium with fine-particle pigment.[9]

A number of changes are visible in the paint layer, undertaken at various points in the working process. The stone in St. Stephen's hand was at first underdrawn significantly further to the left; the positions of hand and book in this initial design are not discernable. Individual strokes radiating from the stone can be interpreted as the folds of a robe over a bent arm.

At first, the bodies of both figures were broader in shape. To the right of St. Stephen, the original contour is still visible to the naked eye; the initial placement of his head further to the right is likewise apparent under UV fluorescence and in the IRR (fig. 100). The X-ray image shows that its position was changed before more paint was applied, that is, very early in the creation of the picture. The head of Étienne Chevalier, too, was initially planned for a different position and was later shifted to the right; here, however, the change was not made until the form had already been completely rendered in color (fig. 101). In order to revise it, the painter first covered the already finished head with light-colored paint, as indicated by the dense absorption in the X-ray that differs significantly from the other flesh-toned areas of the painting. The artist then incised the new contour line for the donor's head into the still-wet paint of the covering layer; this redrawing appears in the X-ray as dark lines. The shape of this second, revised head, however, exactly matches the first one, indicating that one and the same prototype was used both times. In the IRR, the interior lines of the portrait also appear twice, both versions showing dotted lines created by pouncing.

In this area, where the head was shifted during the working process, shrinkage cracks have developed in the uppermost layer, indicating that the artist executed the second version of the head on a layer of paint that was not yet completely dry (fig. 102). Cracks of the same kind are also observable in Jean Fouquet's *Portrait of Charles VII* in the Louvre, which was likewise executed on an intermediate covering layer. To all appearances, the artist used the same technical procedure in both paintings.[10]

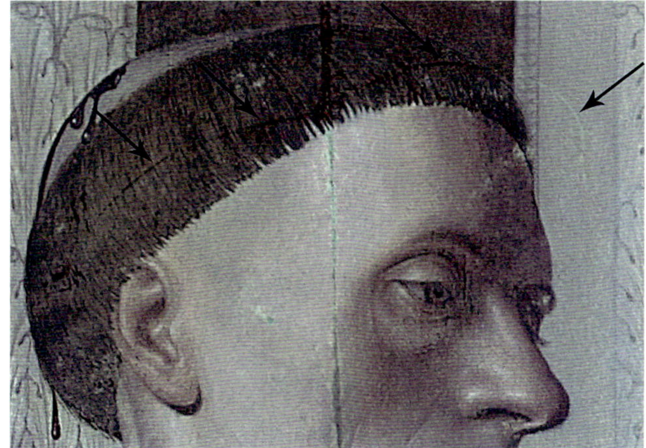

Fig. 100. UV fluorescence: contour of initial head position of St. Stephen

In 1983, Reynaud recognized the outlines of a Madonna exactly corresponding to the one in the *Melun Diptych* in the X-ray of the portrait of King Charles; Fouquet had completed an underpainting of the Virgin, but then painted over it in order to execute the royal portrait. Later, he recreated the same Madonna on another, somewhat larger panel, evidently using the existing older design. Here Reynaud had already surmised that pouncing was used, though without being able to prove the existence of pounce marks.

In the flesh tones of the donor, the results of the μ-XRF show iron oxide earth pigments containing only a little

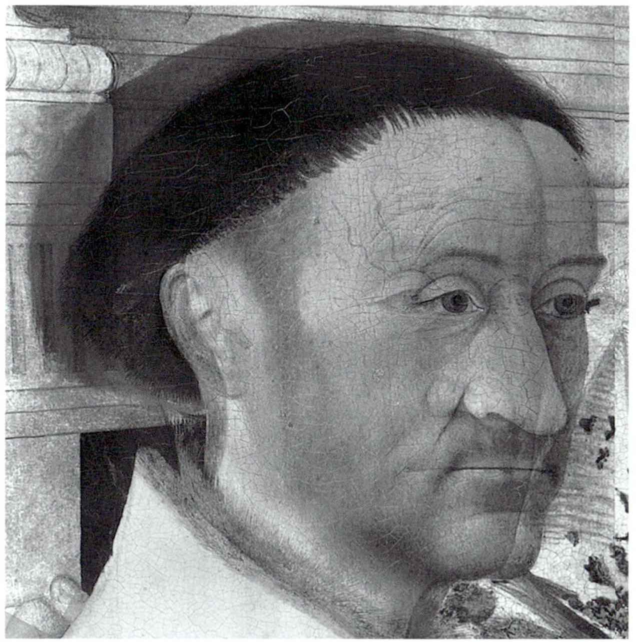

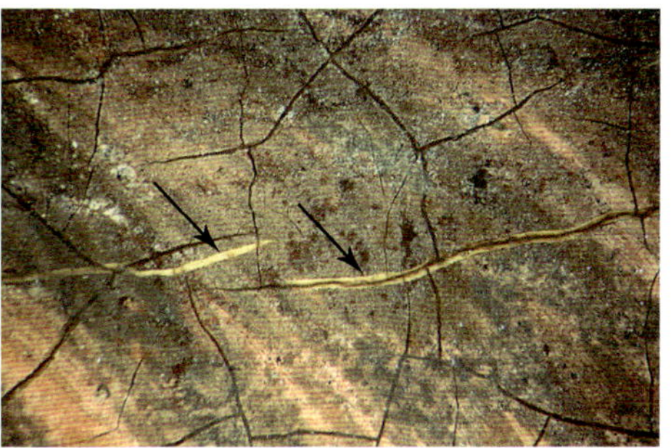

Fig. 101. IRR: head of Chevalier, shifted to the right, with visible doubling of contour lines and interior drawing

Fig. 102. Head of Chevalier, shrinkage cracks in paint layers over a light-colored, opaque intermediate layer

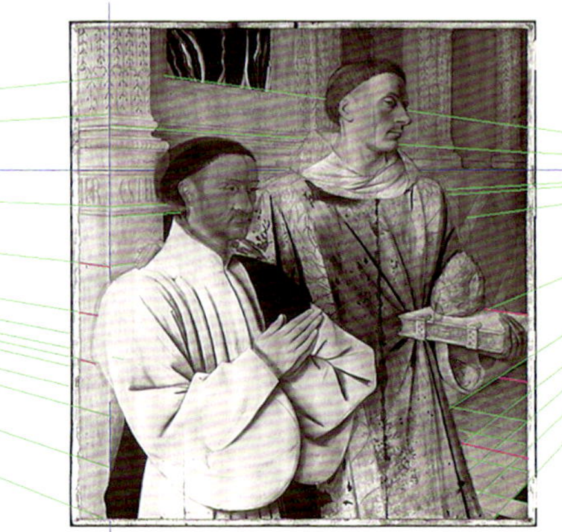

Fig. 103. Diagonal perspective with two vanishing points on a horizon line (blue)

vermillion. Measurements in his hands and in the head of the saint, on the other hand, indicate higher proportions of vermillion, fewer earth pigments, and in the hands even some lead-tin-yellow. The spectrums from both areas of light-colored flesh tone are very similar to each other.[11] It is possible that the artist intentionally rendered Étienne Chevalier's complexion somewhat darker, since his portrait in the book of hours painted by Jean Fouquet shows similarly dark tones.[12]

The perspective construction of pictorial space

The architecture of the background is precisely constructed in a diagonal perspective with two vanishing points located outside the painting; the left one is at a greater dis-

Fig. 104. Detail of fig. 103 with reconstructed orthogonals (green) and underdrawing (pink)

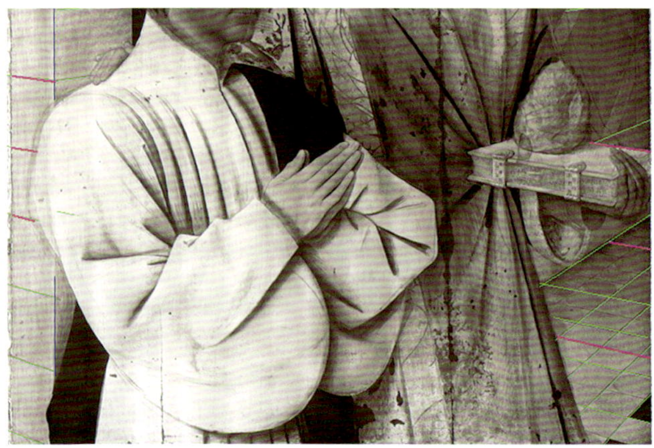

tance from the painting, while the right one is located at the chin of the Madonna in the corresponding panel in Antwerp (fig. 103).[13] Both points lie on the same horizon line, which runs along the upper edge of the inscribed frieze, slightly above Chevalier's eye level. The intersections of orthogonals from both vanishing points produce the geometrically correct foreshortening for the tile pattern; a construction of horizontals was not necessary here.

The IRR reveals several lines from the underdrawn perspective construction: at the left edge of the picture are short strokes that find their extension in the straight lines of the floor and the upper edge of the book on the right side of the painting (fig. 104). These strokes, however, do not correspond to anything represented in the image; they are purely for purposes of construction.

The straight lines of the perspective construction were established by thin strokes incised with a hard drawing tool into the imprimatura, which at this point was still wet, as evidenced by the dark lines in the X-ray image. The age-related craquelure of the paint layer follows these straight lines, so that they are discernable beneath the painting (fig. 105). These incised lines, however, do not pass through the figures, but carefully avoid them, indicating that the figures were first established, and then the background laid down.

In the head of St. Stephen, the incised lines stop at the contour visible in the painting, proving that the changes to the head must have occurred previously. With the head of Chevalier, on the other hand, the incised lines extend to the original position of the head, and thus lie beneath the flesh tone on the right-hand side. In the gilded areas, the incised lines of the architecture only extend as far as the contours; where the gilding was later painted over to reduce its area, no incised lines are observable.

Gilding

The areas of the panel to be gilded were established at approximately the same time as the background and were contoured by incised lines visible beneath the gold leaf in raking light (fig. 106). Apparently these contours were drawn before the application of the gold leaf, since the gold in the indentations is completely undamaged, and not afterwards to mark reductions in the gilded area.

The gilding was applied to a ground that was painted white in a fine-particle pigment, probably the imprimatura, and was fixed with an oil-size that is not visible to the microscope. The characteristically creased gold surface reveals an oily medium, apparently applied very thinly. In a number of places, the gilding was once again painted over to reduce its size, even before the addition of any of the painted red ornamentation or fabric texture. Surprisingly, overpainting was carried out even in rather large areas, without mechanically removing the gold leaf, which would have prevented adhesion problems. For example, the shoulder and the hood of St. Stephen were originally planned wider than they were ultimately executed. In this area, two nested, oval-shaped incised lines are visible with the microscope, probably representing a loop on the hood that was not executed in the painting. Gold leaf is found beneath part of the book cover and the stone; apparently the golden trim of the sleeve was at first supposed to extend further upward, rather than being covered by the book. The saint's fingers, too, which now clasp the book, are also partially painted on top of the gilding.

The large red ornamental pattern on the wide gold trim of St. Stephen's dalmatic was first underpainted in thin, transparent brown and then completed in red glazing. In addition, brown glazes were thinly applied for the shadows, in part using hatching strokes. After that, the fabric texture of the gold trim of the robe was added using small strokes in white and light yellow, which absorb the X-rays and appear bright, above all on the shoulder. The fore edge and clasps of the book also show brown glazes, which however are strongly abraded.

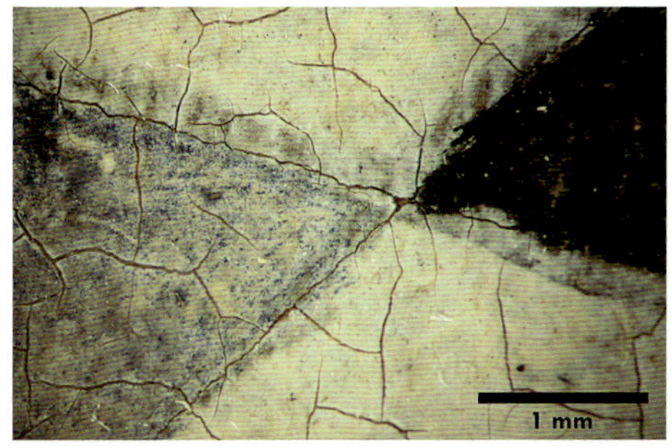

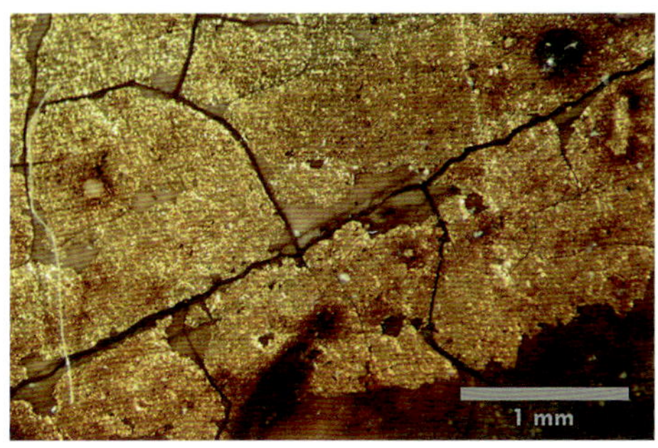

Fig. 105a. Floor tiles with craquelure following the incised construction lines
b. Incised underdrawing beneath gilding, visible as a faint gray abrasion in the paint crack in the middle of the picture

Localized underpainting and rendering in color

In the underpainting, the robes of the two figures, the stone, and St. Stephen's book were modeled in various nuances of red. According to the results of the μ-XRF, these layers contain varying proportions of vermillion and earth pigments; in Chevalier's garment and the book, characteristic pigment changes in the vermillion used for the underpainting later occurred. The stone was under-

Fig. 106. Incised lines along the contour of the gilding

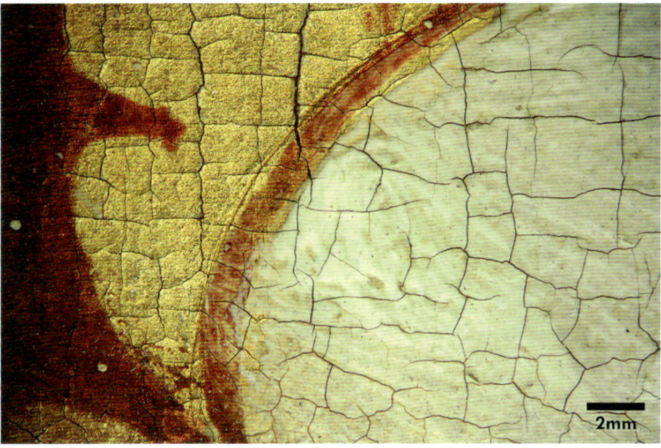

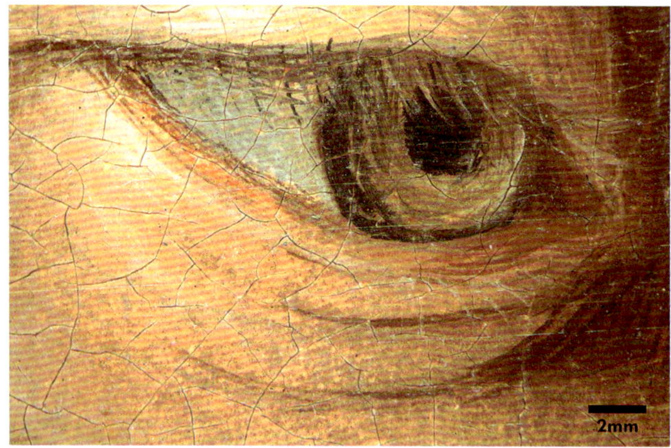

Fig. 107. Right eye of St. Stephen

painted in grayish-pink, the blue dalmatic in red-brown.[14] This kind of underpainting for blue areas is highly unusual, but also occurs in the Antwerp panel.[15] The blue robe was painted in an intense blue pigment over a large surface. Alterations in the color of the pigment in the direction of white suggest the use of expensive lapis lazuli, although the analysis was not able to definitively confirm this.[16] The red garment of the donor received its color from intense red glazes over an orange-red underpainting containing vermillion; its velvety surface was created by applying gossamer-fine veils of a fine-particle white pigment.

On the other hand, no preparatory layers are discernable beneath the flesh tones in the head and hands of St. Stephen. These areas were apparently modeled in thin layers on the light ground, which is confirmed by their

Fig. 108. Detail of fig. 107, eyelashes painted wet into wet

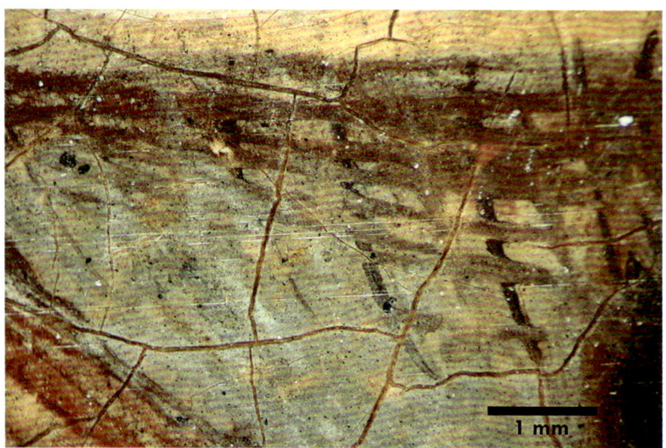

correspondingly weak X-ray absorption. The bluish veins on the forehead and temples were applied in blue pigment and were not covered with paint or intended to show through an additional layer. The cool light gray of the eyeball contains only black pigment, with no blue particles.

The background is developed in very thinly applied gray tones, which contain not only black pigment[17] but also red and red-brown particles; in certain areas, they were shaded with yellow glazes, creating finely nuanced gradations. The marbling of the stone incrustation to the left was developed in intense, opaque color, applied wet into wet.

Throughout the whole work, details were carefully executed and were frequently stippled with a fine brush. Effects of shading were achieved with thin glazes or hatching. On St. Stephen's eye, the iris was formed using fine concentric strokes; the lashes were applied with a thin brush and then leveled in a crosswise direction, wet into wet (fig. 107, 108). The parting of the lips was drawn as a thin black line, after which the lower lip was painted wet into wet in vertical strokes.

Chronological summary of the picture's production

After the first underdrawing, which included at least the figures and the transfer of the portrait drawing by means of pouncing, the imprimatura was applied. Then the architectural perspective was constructed and the areas to be gilded were marked with incised lines, followed by the application of gold leaf.

At this point the first underpaintings were applied in tones of red, and the painting was further developed. Fouquet began with the background, followed by the flesh tones of the heads and the praying hands of the donor. The red glazes on the robe and book, and probably also the red ornamentation of the gold edging and the light daubs of the fabric texture, were next, followed at last by the blue of the robe. Only at this late stage was the head of Étienne Chevalier moved from its original position. The hands of St. Stephen and a slight enlargement of the stone toward the left were likewise executed very late and in a similar manner.

The history and condition of the Berlin panel since its acquisition

In 1937, the painting was lent to the world exposition in Paris along with other works from Berlin museums. During World War II, it was initially transported to the air-raid shelter on the Museumsinsel along with most of the collection,[18] but was later evacuated to the Merkers Mine in Thuringia. In 1945, the works stored there found their way to Wiesbaden, to the Central Art Collecting Point of the U. S. Army. In 1946, Fouquet's panel was brought to Washington in a mixed lot of 202 paintings from Berlin museums; there, the works were deposited, X-rayed, and finally exhibited in March 1948. The exhibition traveled to an additional thirteen cities in the United States; Fouquet's painting, however, only went as far as Boston, where it was withdrawn in August 1948 due to acute blistering.[19]

In 1982/83, the painting was subjected to comprehensive restoration, including complete removal of the varnish and of large areas of overpainting. The strongly abraded paint on the back of the donor's head and the front edge of his face was reconstructed by retouching. The right half of St. Stephen's white stole and large areas of his blue robe, along with the gilding, were likewise comprehensively retouched; the ornamental red pattern on the gilding was heavily retraced. The inscription on the frieze in the right half of the picture is more clearly legible in a photograph from 1969.[20]

1   Critical catalogue of 15th-century Netherlandish and French painting; project under the direction of Katrin Dyballa, funded by the DFG and the Ernst von Siemens-Stiftung.

2   The technical images were prepared by Christoph Schmidt, technical photographer, Gemäldegalerie SMB.

3   The analyses were conducted on June 22, 2017, in collaboration with Sabine Schwerdtfeger of the Rathgen Research Laboratory.

4   The Antwerp painting was not subjected to the same technical analysis, but observations in this essay will be based on the individual findings published in Vandenbroecke and Guislain-Wittermann 1996, unless otherwise noted.

5   Report of dendrochronological analysis by Peter Klein on September 19, 1990, measurement from December 2, 1981.

6   Avril in Cat. Paris 2003, p. 127.

7   On the evidence for a panel splitting, see Schiessl 1998.

8   On the history of this technique, see Stehr, Dubois 2014; Oberthaler 1998.

9   A similar dark underdrawing in a fluid medium was also observed on the priming of the *Portrait of Jouvenel des Ursins* (fig. 123); Cat. Paris 2003, p. 116.

10   See Reynaud 1983, pp. 97-99, and Cat. Paris 2003, pp. 108-109.

11   μ-XRF performed by the Rathgen Research Laboratory on June 22, 2017.

12   As observed by Stephan Kemperdick.

13   According to Bouleau 1963, pp. 72-73.

14   The results of the micro X-ray fluorescence analysis (μ-XRF) performed by the Rathgen Research Laboratory on June 22, 2017, show varying proportions of iron and mercury in Chevalier's red garment. A particularly high level of mercury was identified in the book, indicating a strong admixture of sinopia. The underpainting of the blue robe consisted exclusively of iron with no mercury, so that here, apparently, earth pigments were used without any admixture of sinopia.

15   Vandenbroeck and Guislain-Wittermann 1996, p. 61.

16   In addition to silicon and some aluminum, which point to the use of lapis lazuli, at some measuring points the μ-XRF consistently revealed significant levels of copper from an admixture or preparation with a copper-bearing blue pigment such as azurite. Thus the expensive pigment ultramarine was not the only one used.

17   Since no phosphorus was detected by the μ-XRF in any of the black areas, we may assume that Fouquet did not use bone black, but worked exclusively with non-detectable carbon compounds such as lampblack or vegetable black. In the *chaperon* draped over Chevalier's shoulder, the presence of copper suggests an admixture of blue pigment, possibly azurite, probably added in order to achieve an especially deep black tone.

18   As documented in a note attached to the prewar frame.

19   Report in Birkmeyer 1949.

20   The obviously heavily and incorrectly retraced letters read SRNIREST-PHRNUIPIE(...).

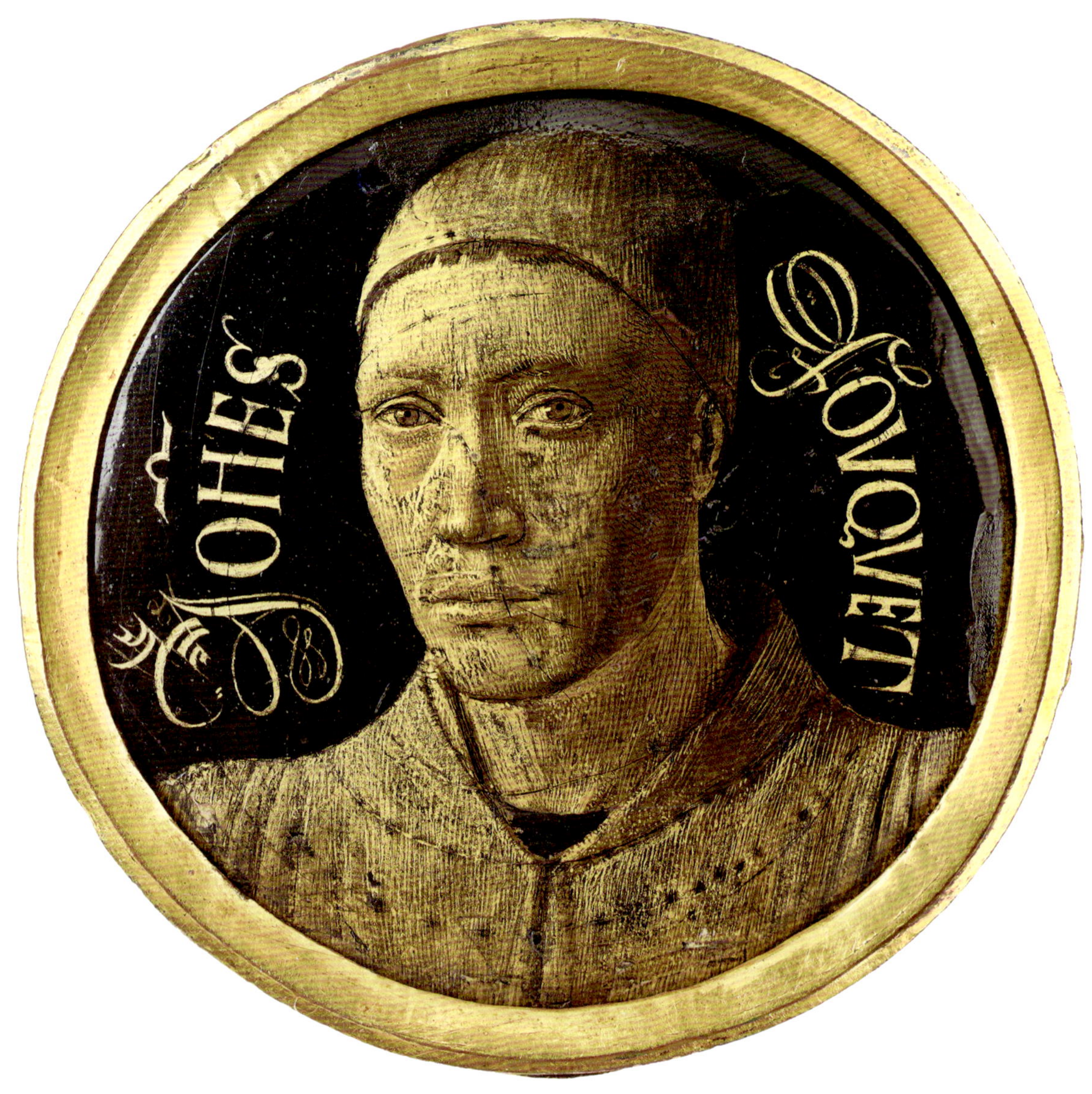

CAT. 2
Jean Fouquet

SELF-PORTRAIT

after 1452
Enamel and gold on copper
Diameter with edging 7.5 cm; without edging 7.2 cm
Inscription: JOH(ANN)ES FOUQUET
Provenance: Gift of Comte Hippolyte de Janzé, 1860
Paris, Musée du Louvre, Département des Objets d'art,
Inv. Nr. OA 56

Selected bibliography: Chennevières 1853 – Curmer 1864, pp. 127-129 – Marquet de Vasselot 1904 – Schaefer 1967, pp. 195-196, no. 27-30, p. 210 – Gauthier 1972, pp. 306-308, 419 – Schaefer 1975, pp. 54-58 – Reynaud 1981, no. 6, pp. 22-27 – Schaefer 1994, pp. 139, 292 – Schaefer 2000, pp. 297f., 300 – Thiébaut in Cat. Paris 2003, pp. 131-137 – Förstel 2008, pp. 4-7

Élisabeth Antoine-König and Béatrice Beillard

REFLECTIONS IN A GOLDEN EYE –
JEAN FOUQUET'S ENIGMATIC SELF-PORTRAIT

The rediscovery of the self-portrait in the second half of the 19th century

In 1853, Fouquet's self-portrait (fig. 109)[1] was introduced to the public—or at least to a small circle of aficionados of French art—in an engraving published by Philippe de Chennevières in his *Portraits inédits d'artistes français*.[2] At the time, the work was in the collection of the Vicomte Hippolyte de Janzé (Rennes 1790–Paris 1865), who was to donate it to the Louvre seven years later.

The engraving created by Frédéric Legrip (Rouen 1817–Paris 1871) for Chennevières does not accurately render Fouquet's work and serves the artist ill (fig. 110): the portrait is reversed, the artfully composed inscription is cut off, and the subtle modeling of the face in the gold monochrome of the original is lost in the graphic reproduction. As François Avril has pointed out, the form of the cap is slightly different as well,[3] likely a result of the engraver's lack of skill rather than a later alteration of the original. In addition, although the enamel was reproduced in its original size, the framing was entirely the product of Legrip's imagination.

Handwritten notes by the scholar Auguste Vallet de Viriville (Paris 1815–Paris 1868)—probably compiled in preparation for his books on Charles VII from 1859 to 1865[4]—shed an interesting light on the condition of the work during those years.[5] These documents include a page with a pen drawing of the back side of the medallion, seemingly traced from the outline of the object itself (fig. 111). The sketch is not dated, nor is there any indication of the location of the artifact at the time; yet in order to make the drawing, Vallet de Viriville would have to have held the medallion in his own hand at Janzé's before 1860. He notes that the upper portion of

the head is damaged, and he depicts a ring of metal inside a hole at the upper edge of the medallion. Most likely the enamel was damaged when this hole was drilled, causing the large break in the upper portion of the cap. When the medallion arrived at the Louvre in 1860, a note was made in the inventory that the cap had been chipped and the damaged spot filled in with

Fig. 109. Jean Fouquet, *Self-Portrait*, after restoration in 2009

Fig. 110. Jean Fouquet, *Self-Portrait*, engraving by Frédéric Legrip for Philippe de Chennevières, *Portraits inédits d'artistes français*, Paris 1853

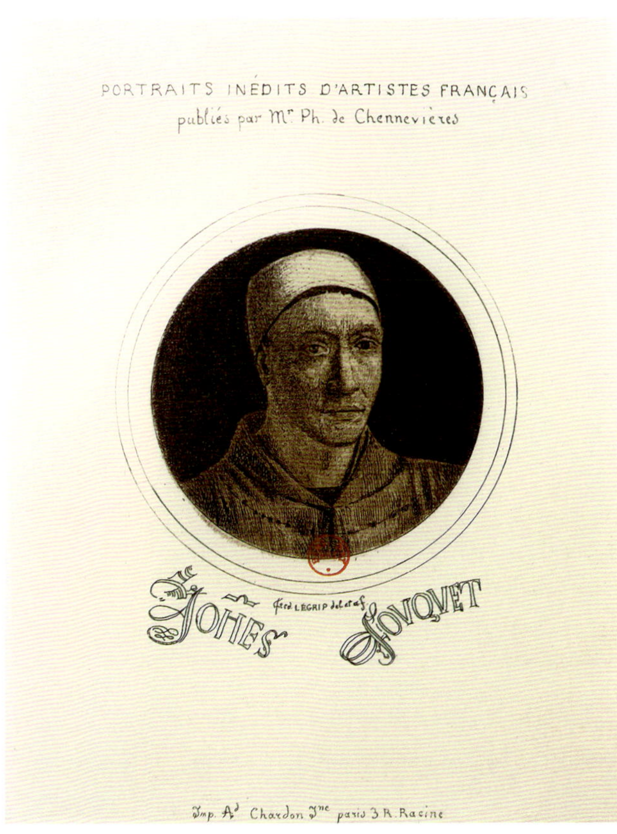

black wax.[6] This procedure had probably been performed earlier, even if the wording leaves open the possibility that it occurred when the piece was acquired by the Louvre. One thing, however, is proven beyond doubt: in the course of the enamel's restoration, the drilled hole was filled in and the copper tab that is still visible there today was soldered onto the back with tin (fig. 112).

Although Chennevières' publication, as well as the subsequent transfer of the medallion to the Louvre, attracted much attention and inspired further study of Fouquet's oeuvre, it is still surprising that the connection between the self-portrait and the *Melun Diptych* was not recognized until fifty years later, in 1904. Thus it will be useful to briefly discuss the stages that led to this realization, though without rehearsing in detail the history of the ensemble, which has already been thoroughly researched.[7]

The Vicomte de Janzé, an officer of the cavalry, was a collector of antiquities, a benefactor of the present-day Bibliothèque nationale, a member of the Commission consultative des Musées Impériaux, and an amateur photographer.[8] In 1856, Vallet de Viriville wrote that the Vicomte, enamored of the quality of the work, had acquired the medallion about twenty years earlier at an auction in Paris—that is, at a point in time when little was known about Fouquet.[9] Only later, when studies on Fouquet began to proliferate, did Janzé's interest awaken to the medallion in his possession. Since in 1853, Philippe de Chennevières had considered the self-portrait a curiosity and had viewed it with a certain bewilderment,[10] he did not inspect it in detail. Thus Vallet de Viriville was the first to thoroughly examine it, as his sketch shows, and he was also the first—in 1856,[11] and again in his study of enamel art in 1857—to associate the work with the *Melun Diptych*. By comparing the self-portrait both formally and technically with the medallions from the diptych, he established a connection to the painted medallions described by Godefroy,[12] though without claiming that the portrait itself had once belonged to the diptych. The motivic con-

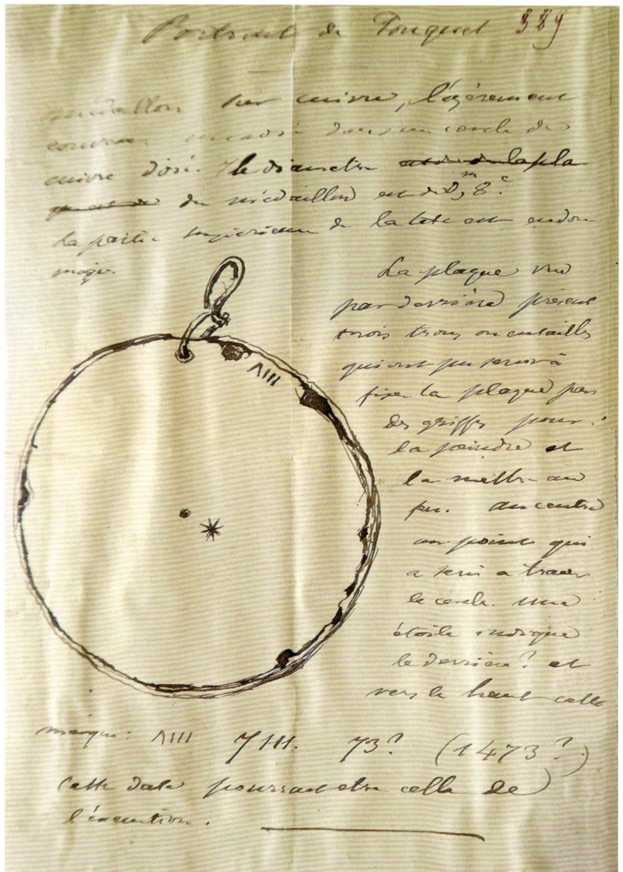

Fig. 111. Sketch of reverse of Fouquet's self-portrait, Auguste Vallet de Viriville, Paris, BNF, N.a.fr. 5086, f. 103 v, pièce n 389

Fig. 112. Reverse of Fouquet's self-portrait (without frame)

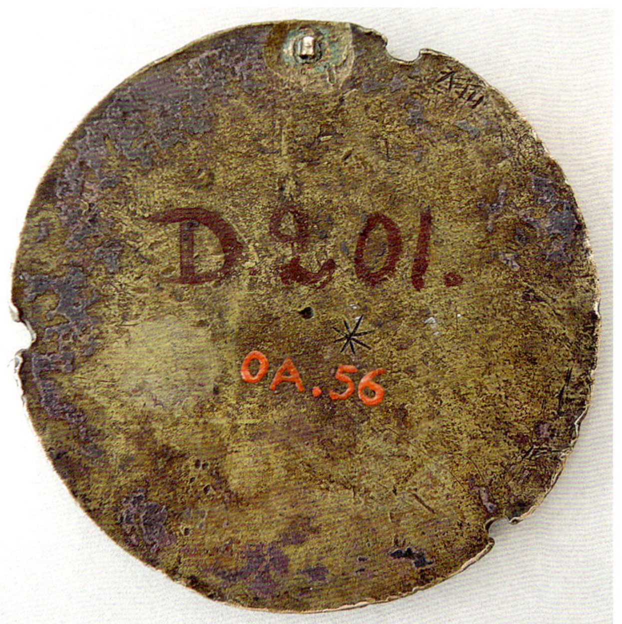

nection established by Vallet de Viriville was then repeated in numerous studies of Fouquet throughout the second half of the 19th century.[13]

The decoration of the frame of the *Melun Diptych* with enamels is confirmed by the description provided by Denys Godefroy in his 1661 book on Charles VII.[14] Significantly, he refers to the frame as "bordures"; according to him, its blue velvet covering was decorated with evenly-spaced love-knots ("lacs d'amours") embroidered in silver and gold and flanked by the letter "E" set with fine pearls. Mounted between the love-knots were medium-sized medallions of gilt silver, which represented sacred scenes and whose figures were admirably painted.[15] A source from the late 17th century, not precisely dated, augments Godefroy with a reference to enamel borders.[16]

There is no surviving depiction of the diptych in its original condition, that is, before its dismantling and the removal of the frame. The first attempt at reconstruction was that of Eugène Grésy in 1845 (fig. 113), when the panels were already divided between Antwerp and Frankfurt. Since he was unable to view the diptych, Grésy used an older print for the Madonna—which also explains why his rendering is now oriented correctly—and noted in the caption: *d'après un graveur anonyme de la fin du XVIIIe siècle*.[17] For the wing showing Étienne Chevalier, which he incorrectly positioned on the right-hand side, only Godefroy's description was available to him. He depicted the medallions in quatrefoils; with regard to their iconography, he remained as vague as Godefroy, who nonetheless was the only one to mention depictions of saints.

The hypothesis that the self-portrait had belonged to the diptych was first formulated by Henri Bouchot in connection with the major exhibition *Les Primitifs français* at the Louvre and the Bibliothèque nationale in 1904.[18] Here the diptych was reunited for the first time since it had been taken apart in the 18th century,[19] and on this occasion Bouchot showed the Louvre self-portrait as an enamel on the frame. In addition, he surmised that as a protegé of the king's mistress, Jean Fouquet had painted this enamel to express his gratitude and devotion to her.[20] Bouchot's attribution produced a snowball effect: the same year, Marquet de Vasselot published his study "Deux émaux de Jean Fouquet," and while he hesitated to asso-

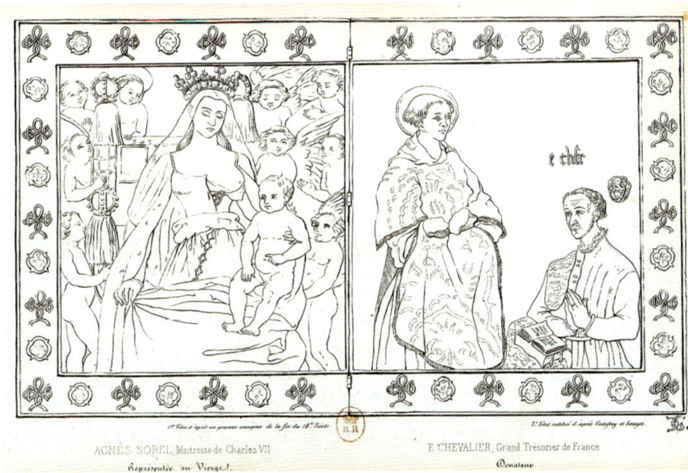

Fig. 113. Proposed reconstruction of the *Melun Diptych*, Eugène Grésy, 1845

ciate the self-portrait (fig. 115) with the *Melun Diptych*, he nonetheless ascribed to the diptych a hitherto unknown enamel (fig. 114) that had recently been acquired by the Kunstgewerbemuseum in Berlin.[21]

The history of the Berlin medallion between the late 18th and the late 19th century is as obscure as the fate of the self-portrait. According to Netzer,[22] it had belonged to the London art dealer and collector Isaac Falcke (1819–1909), who supposedly left part of his collection to the industrialist Alfred Beit (1853–1906) in 1891 through the friendly mediation of Wilhelm Bode. In 1891, the company Wernher, Beit & Co. donated the enamel to the Kunstgewerbemuseum, perhaps in honor of Bode. We know as little about how the medallion had found its way to London as we do about how, where, or from whom Falcke acquired it.

While at first the medallion was interpreted as representing the *Descent of the Holy Spirit*, Marie-Madeleine Gauthier and, following her, Claude Schaefer demonstrated that it depicts a scene from the story of St. Stephen: the choosing of the Seven Deacons from the host of the faithful, along with the Jews.[23] The attribution of the Berlin medallion to Fouquet strengthened the hypothesis that the Berlin donor panel had been framed by scenes from the life of St. Stephen, while the Madonna was surrounded by images from the life of Christ. In addition, Michel Hérold found a reference to a journey by the painter Gaultier de Campes to Melun

153

in 1503, where he admired a panel with scenes from the life of St. Stephen.[24]

The first portrait tondo in French painting

While there is no longer any doubt that Fouquet's self-portrait belonged to the frame of the diptych painted for Étienne Chevalier, the extraordinarily ambitious character of the image still provokes astonishment in the viewer. As the first round painted portrait in Western art since antiquity, the work is exceptional not only for its technique, which we will discuss further below, but also for its level of quality and its significance.

The artist depicted himself as a bust, his face turned toward the viewer or praying onlooker in a three-quarter view. His clothing and hairstyle reflect the fashions of the mid-15th century: he wears a simple felt cap and a doublet with padded shoulders (*jaquette*), like that of Charles VII in his portrait of the latter. His hair is trimmed short over his forehead, while his full, soft face is that of a man still young. Unmoving, he gazes at the viewer with a pensive, slightly melancholy expression. In his silent meditation, is Jean Fouquet gazing at his patron Étienne Chevalier, or at himself as he looks in the mirror?

In her analysis of Fouquet and the art of geometry, Marie-Thérèse Gousset has analyzed the meticulous geometric conception underlying this portrait, which places the artist's gaze at the center of the composition.[25] The bright gold of the inscription JOH(ANN)ES FOUQUET, which frames his countenance and extends to the level of the eyebrows, also helps illumine the artist's serious gaze and lends him dignity. Moreover, Fouquet presents himself as an artist of intellect by Latinizing his first name and using antique epigraphy for all but the initials.

Scholars have rightly emphasized the Italian influences in this self-portrait, which can probably be traced back to Fouquet's journey to Italy. His models likely included examples of antique epigraphy, artist portraits like that of Filarete on the doors of St. Peter's or Ghiberti's portrait busts on the Gates of Paradise of the Baptistery in Florence, and painting on glass, above all Sienese works of the Trecento.[26]

Though all these elements are clearly recognizable, Fouquet nonetheless occupies an artistic middle ground between Italy and the Netherlands. The basic scheme of the medallion as a self-portrait reveals the inspiration of Jan van Eyck: the beautiful Gothic initials, for example, recall Jan's signature on the Arnolfini portrait beneath the convex mirror, which serves as the vanishing point

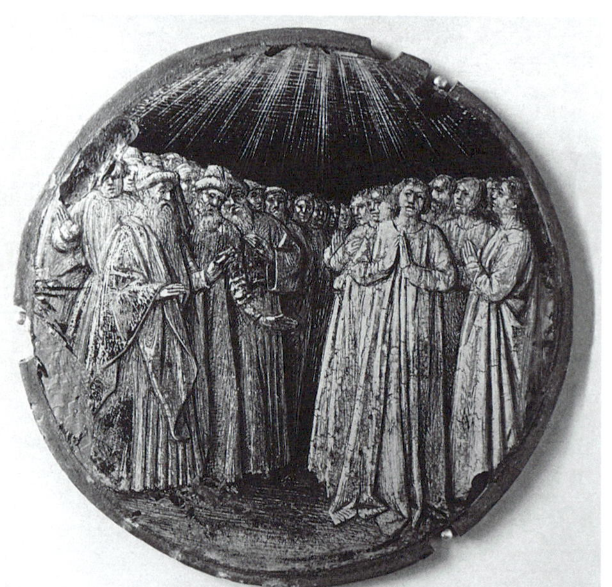

Fig. 114. Jean Fouquet, *Scene from the Life of St. Stephen: The Choosing of the Seven Deacons*, enamel and gold on copper, formerly Berlin, Kunstgewerbemuseum (lost 1945)

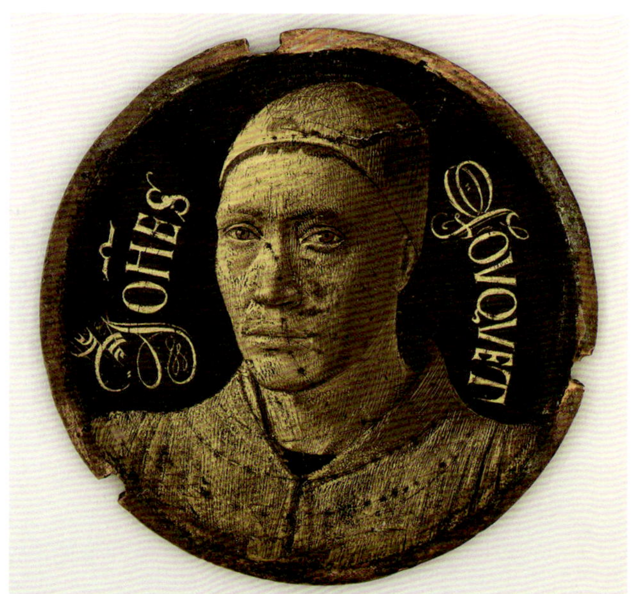

Fig. 115. Jean Fouquet, *Self-Portrait*, before restoration in 2009, without frame

for the entire composition.[27] Other aspects of the *Melun Diptych* likewise seem indebted to Eyckian themes of reflection and effects of light—for example the reflections of a window in the stone knobs of the Virgin's throne, or the slightly convex form of the self-portrait, reminiscent of the convex mirror in the Arnolfini portrait. Finally, the idea of framing the diptych with historiated medallions recalls the similarly decorated frame of the Arnolfini mirror, though in the latter the scenes from the life of Christ appear much simpler. Fouquet's masterful rendering of the vitality of his own countenance and the intensity of his gaze is matched by his fascination with the compressed space of the mirror. In a beautiful and apt turn of phrase, Marie-Madeleine Gauthier described the surface of the dark enamel in the self-portrait as "deep and brilliant, like that of a magic mirror."[28]

In his self-portrait Fouquet also displayed consummate skill in a technique that he frequently used in manuscript illumination: gold monochrome painting. Around the same time as the diptych or a little later, Fouquet painted highly unusual gold accents in the *Hours of Étienne Chevalier*. There he used gold monochrome not only to model the figures, but also for entire scenes in the bas-de-page of illuminated pages. In an echo of the enamels surrounding the *Melun Diptych*, two out of the three medallions with scenes from the martyrdom of St. Catherine appear on a ground of lapis-lazuli blue.[29] The artist also tended to paint the initials in the book of hours with scenes in gold monochrome on a purple or blue ground. An especially wide range of motifs appear on pages whose layout preserved the traditional field for inscriptions; here he even varied the decorative principle by placing a diptych beneath the Incipit on the page with St. Martin of Tours.[30] In such cases, the primary scene is accompanied by episodes in gold monochrome in much the same way that the image of Étienne Chevalier and his patron saint was surrounded by medallions with scenes from the life of St. Stephen, or, very likely, the Virgin and Child on the right wing of the diptych with scenes from the life of Christ.

Viewed under magnification, Fouquet's Paris self-portrait reveals the characteristic marks of this greatest of all 15th-century French painters (fig. 116): freedom of the hand in the gold hatching as well as firmness and

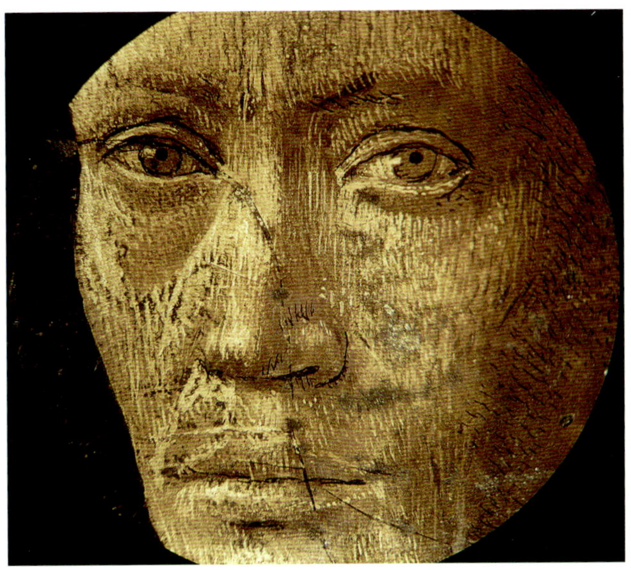

Fig. 116. Jean Fouquet, *Self-Portrait*, detail of face

precision of stroke wherever the gold was removed with the needle to indicate contours, for example in the eyes, nose, and mouth. Fouquet seems to have brought the full range of his talent as a portraitist to bear in this medallion, and as the earliest known autonomous self-portrait by a painter, it also bears witness to the artist's own self-awareness. Yet the question arises: is this self-portrait, signed by Fouquet, really his first one, or had

Fig. 117. Orvieto Cathedral, vault painting, detail

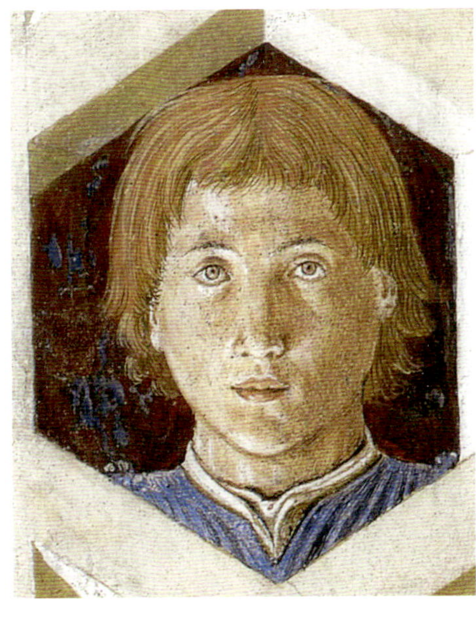

he perhaps already used his own image previously to indicate his presence and participation in a work?

In her essay "Jean Fouquet en Italie," Fiorella Sricchia Santoro has convincingly argued that the assistant of Fra Angelico who painted a series of youthful heads in the hexagons of the chapel of San Brizio in Orvieto in the summer of 1447 could only have been Jean Fouquet.[31] Her attribution to Fouquet of three drawings that previously had been attributed to Gozzoli (cat. 10) is equally persuasive.[32] Two of these drawings are closely related to works created for Étienne Chevalier: here, too, we see putti and festoons like those in the double-page illumination of the Office of the Virgin,[33] as well as white highlights that strongly resemble the gold monochrome painting in the book of hours. Furthermore, the head of the man in one of the drawings is closely related to the St. Stephen of the diptych.

According to Sricchia Santoro, the surprising natural vitality of the frontal head of a blond youth in Orvieto unequivocally bears the handwriting of Fouquet (fig. 117);[34] however, I am inclined to carry her observation even further and identify this young man—the only one in the series who looks at the viewer—as the young Fouquet himself. Indeed, this youthful countenance has the same nasal bridge with a small bump, the same fleshy nostrils, and the same full-lipped mouth as the enamel in the Louvre. Furthermore, just as in the latter, the amber-colored gaze of the young man in the hexagon occupies the center of the composition, and the face likewise stands out against

a dark ground, illuminated by the white of the trompe-l'oeil frame. In the Louvre self-portrait, Fouquet is certainly older; the oval of his face is a little longer and his hair appears better groomed. Yet the artist's gaze, both proud and earnest, is still the same as in the Orvieto hexagon.[35]

In his enamel self-portrait, Fouquet placed a drop of light at the edge of his golden eye, thus imbuing his own gaze—as fascinating as it is impenetrable—with an enigmatic intensity (fig. 118).

The technical analysis of Jean Fouquet's self-portrait

As extraordinary as Fouquet's self-portrait is in its boldness of composition and meaning, the complex process by which it was created is equally astonishing. The analyses performed in 2009 and again in 2017 by conservator Béatrice Beillard, together with Isabelle Biron, Ingénieur d'études at the Centre de Recherche et de Restauration des Musées de France (C2RMF),[36] give us a better understanding of the process used by Fouquet to achieve such masterful results, though as we will see, much still remains unclear.

The copper plate on which the artist created his portrait is a fairly thick circular disk, 7.2 cm in diameter and 2.6 mm in thickness, slightly convex in the center. Contrary to customary practice, the back of the plate was not enameled. Its light, almost yellow color (the copper is not oxidized) suggests a rather high firing temperature (fig. 112).[37] Fine dark traces of the plate on which the work was heated during the firing process produce a slight relief around the edge.

In addition, three marks are visible on the back side of the medallion: an engraved star in the middle, an indentation embossed with a punch, and the letters IIIV on the upper right edge next to one of three notches. These notches were meant to accommodate the wooden dowels that would fasten the medallion to the frame of the diptych before being covered by the metal ring. The copper is somewhat abraded on the top to allow an eyelet to be soldered on with tin. As mentioned previously, this eyelet was clearly a later addition; it covered the hole visible in the drawing by Vallet de Viriville (fig. 111), and thus

Fig. 118. Jean Fouquet, *Self-Portrait*, detail of right eye

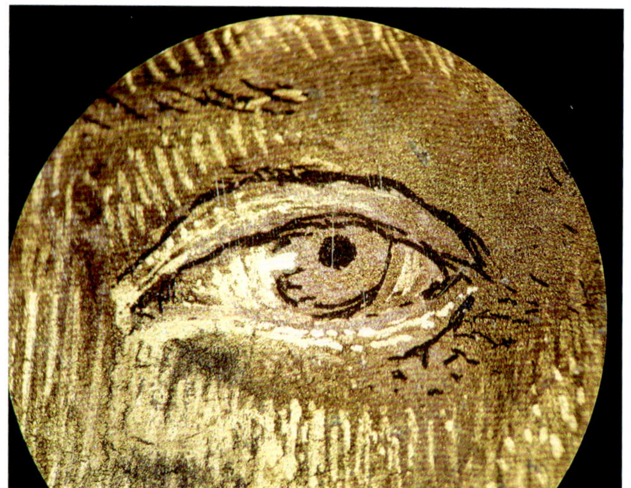

could only have been added in the second half of the 19th century.

First, a layer of blackish glass powder was laid down on the copper plate. The color of this glass is discernable only under heavy magnification and only in certain areas, depending on the play of light on the transparent glass material. In actual fact, the glass is blue, as confirmed by chemical analysis of the elements with ion beams, performed by Isabelle Biron of C2RMF.[38]

After this first layer was fired, the drawing was applied in gold, probably in two stages. First, the portrait was established as a large area in granular, rose-toned gold;[39] then, a needle was used to draw into this layer of gold, exposing the smooth, glossy surface of the bluish-black enamel. In this stage, the image emerged with all of its gradations of shadow. After another firing process, a second layer of gold, now yellow-toned, was applied in small vertical strokes of varying thickness, depending on how the light was supposed to fall on the form and the modeling effect desired. Finally, the medallion was fired one last time.

Thus at least three firing processes were involved in the production of this image: one for the dark-colored glass, and two subsequent ones for the portrait in gold. An enlargement of the right eye reveals the care the painter took to give his gaze a vital, lively quality (fig. 118): the eye was first drawn with parallel strokes using the needle in the layer of rose-toned gold, and then heightened with yellow gold, creating a three-dimensional effect. Finally, the iris received a fleck of yellow gold, brightening the gaze from the midst of the rose gold ground.

Certain irregularities reveal additional interventions in the work in the modeling of the face and garment, and at the same time call attention to a technical aspect aptly described by Dominique Thiébaut in 2003:[40] certain areas of gold show stronger relief than others, especially in the area of the garment. In addition, magnification reveals that in those places where vertical defects were smoothed with a blade after firing, the surface of the enamel seems not smooth, but slightly grainy (fig. 119).

In addition, the portrait is marked by a number of curving lines. Three of them are concentric, but the fourth crosses the lips, ascends the nose, and intersects the left eye before ending outside the face (fig. 120). The lines are punctuated with tiny bumps resulting from air bubbles, which occur

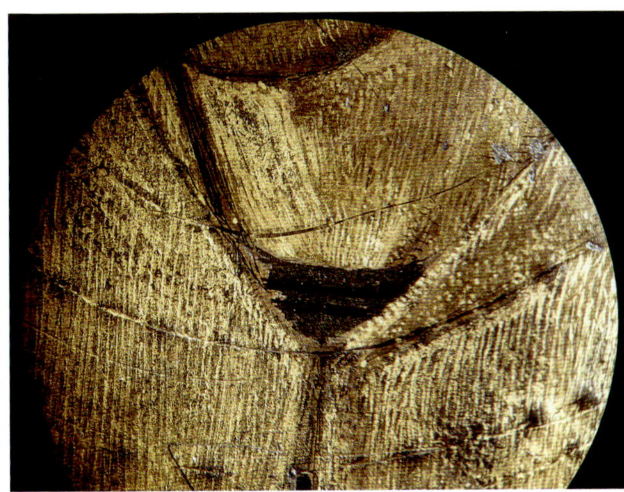

Fig. 119. Jean Fouquet, *Self-Portrait*, detail of garment

at regular intervals and are thicker where the lines end. By no means were these bumps considered desirable; otherwise they would not have been abraded before the application of the second layer of gold, which partially covers them.

The first of these lines forms a circle outside the inscription, the second runs through the middle of the letters, and the third passes beneath them. The last curve veers away and passes over the face. The circular lines must be clearly distinguished from the incised strokes of the drawing in the layer of gold, as described above for example in the area of the eyes. In view of their almost perfect geometric arrangement, these lines could not have appeared by chance; rather, Isabelle Biron believes they were intentionally placed. Marie-Thérèse Gousset has argued in a similar manner[41] and has convincingly interpreted them as guidelines constructed with the compass to ensure precise placement of the signature. But why, then, does one of them intersect the right eye?

Contrary to what one might at first assume, this line was not caused by a technical defect; for in fact the radiography performed by Elsa Lambert at C2RMF shows that the copper plate is preserved in very good condition, undamaged and with no cracks. Nor is the enamel itself cracked, but rather has been intentionally scratched. Theoretically, copper that was not enameled on the back could be damaged by tension from the enameled front, but in this case the plate is too thick for that to happen. Apparently, the garlands of small air bubbles resulted from the firing after the first layer of gold was applied, when the portrait was already in place and before the area of the garment was smoothed out. Since the lines lie on the dark enamel beneath the gold and not on the surface, they cannot be due to vandalism or iconoclasm at a later time.

Thus it would seem that although he had fully mastered his technique, Jean Fouquet still had to accept certain defects in the portrait that arose during the course of the work. If the lines on the dark enamel were intentionally drawn, the air bubbles abraded by the artist certainly were not. More numerous on the outer lines, these bubbles were caused by excessive heat when the drawing was first applied in gold.

The placement of the central line, however, remains puzzling: could it have been accidental, occurring when the lines framing the inscription were drawn? The third line, intended to run beneath the letters, should have passed below the artist's hairline. Did Fouquet's hand slip as he was drawing the third circle? Indeed, it is difficult to imagine that with all the care the artist took— and even all the pride with which he conceived his own portrait—he would have voluntarily "injured" himself in this way, even damaging his own golden eye. Passing through his countenance, the third line keeps its secrets.

The medallion was lightly restored by Béatrice Beillard for the 2010 exhibition *France 1500* in Paris. At that time, she noted that the head itself was in good condition, but that the bluish-black enamel at the edge of the medallion showed a number of cracks that had been filled earlier in its history. The largest of these was the area above the cap which, as mentioned before, had broken off when the copper was drilled. A smaller crack was found behind the "T" in the signature "Fouquet," as well as a number of restored fissures in the lower garment area. These older, very skillful repairs were kept. But the disintegration of the most extensive restoration of an older defect, where the patch was raised, had become visible as a black ridge, since the varnish applied over it had broken off. This restoration—which, as mentioned earlier, was undertaken when the medallion was given to the Louvre in 1860 or a little earlier—consisted of a resin varnish on a nonsoluble black ground. Gold powder was applied in small parallel strokes between the two varnishes, and after the raised

area had once again been affixed, the crack between the original enamel and the older restoration was closed. Finally, the modeling of the cap was corrected with a little gold powder.

During this restoration, the medallion was removed from its beveled edging, which is made of gilt copper and shows an irregular curvature (fig. 121).[42] This edging may or may not be original to the medallion; in 1845, Grésy showed the medallions in quatrefoils, perhaps working entirely from his imagination, but perhaps relying on the lost print.[43] Either way, the edging of the medallion is very old and shows numerous tool marks on the interior as well as evidence of mounting and thick gilding on the outside. An empty margin about 5 mm wide runs around the entire perimeter of the medallion's enameled surface. This margin is punctuated by three evenly-spaced notches; the medallion in Berlin also showed this feature (figs. 114, 115).

The engraved marks on the edging correspond to the notches on the enameled plate, although the incised number is different: while the edging reads "+ II" (fig. 121), the back side of the medallion, as mentioned earlier, is inscribed "IIIV." Thus if the edging was made at the same time as the enamel portrait, it may have been intended for another medallion and may have been switched during the process of assembly.

Unresolved questions

Despite this thorough analysis of Fouquet's self-portrait, many questions still remain unanswered. It would be ideal if the Berlin medallion could be investigated in exactly the same way, in order to compare the processes by which the objects were made and potentially arrive at further insights. Who knows whether the Berlin medallion, which has been lost since 1945, might not someday appear again, to the delight of art enthusiasts? Perhaps someday we will even find another enameled medallion from the *Melun Diptych*; these small, precious objects may have been spared the ravages of time and may still be awaiting rediscovery in a drawer or an attic.

Yet none of these possible finds would tell us exactly when they disappeared from Melun. Significantly, a postscript by Godefroy, found by Claude Schaefer in

Godefroy's preparatory manuscript but missing from the printed edition of 1661, states that the "border" of the diptych showed places where a number of medallions had already been stolen.[44] This circumstance may also explain why Godefroy says nothing of Jean Fouquet, for surely he would have recorded the inscription from the self-portrait. Apparently all the medallions had disappeared by the 18th century, as Martin Gauthier, a scholar from Melun, reports in his *Notes pour servir à l'histoire de Melun* of 1768.[45] This author is probably the same Gauthier who also inscribed the back of the Antwerp Madonna panel (fig. 95).

The possible provenance of Fouquet's self-portrait thus becomes even more intriguing and enigmatic. Also unresolved is the question of which part of the diptych's frame the self-portrait adorned. Marquet de Vasselot and others may have been right to reject the notion that a self-portrait like this could have smuggled its way into the ranks of images of St. Stephen and Christ on the open diptych. It seems possible to me that it was mounted on the painted back side of the Berlin panel, which is now lost and about whose design we know nothing. In the closed position, this panel would have appeared as the front of the diptych. Yet the painter could also have immortalized himself with his medallion on the lower frame of the Madonna picture. In this way, the Mother of God would have looked directly down at him, while he himself gazed at his patron and all those who offered their prayers before the image of the Virgin.

The first color reproduction of the medallion appeared in Léon Curmer's groundbreaking study *Oeuvre de Jehan Foucquet* in 1866–1867;[46] even before its publication, however, the most effusive admirer of the portrait medallion, Vallet de Viriville, had offered to send one copy each of Curmer's work to two important enamelists of the time, Alfred Meyer (1832–1904) and Claudius Popelin (1825–1892), so that they could make a replica.[47] It is not known whether this project was ever realized; no copies of Fouquet's self-portrait have ever been found. Yet it is certain that both enamelists were fascinated by Fouquet's use of gold monochrome painting and were responsible for a revival of the technique in the enamel art of the late 19th century. In 1895 Alfred Meyer, a painter at the Sèvres porcelain factory, analyzed the technique used in the self-portrait, which at that time was exhibited

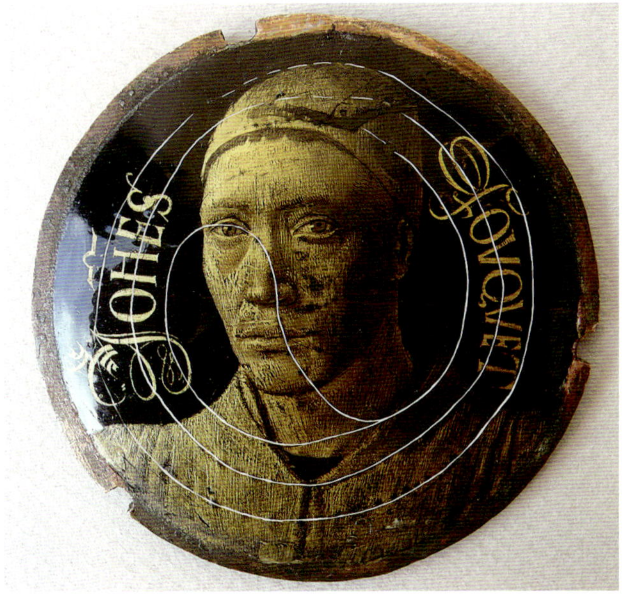

Fig. 120. Jean Fouquet, *Self-Portrait*, diagram of lines scratched into enamel, drawing by Béatrice Beillard

in the Galerie d'Apollon of the Louvre. He wrote that after applying a wash of gold with the brush as in a watercolor, gold powder should be dissolved in slightly gummed and sugared water and allowed to dry. Then, all the halftones and shadow areas should be engraved with a sharp instrument as in an aquatint, leaving the enameled plate untouched.[48] This technique using gold powder was called "émail en sgraffiti d'or" and was tirelessly employed by Claudius Popelin.[49]

The late 19th-century fascination with Fouquet seems like a distant echo of the enthusiastic pronouncement made by the Dominican Francesco Florio in a letter to his friend Jacopo Tarlato in 1477: "Doubt not, I tell you the truth: this Fouquet veritably has the power to create living figures with his brush, and thus is nearly the equal

Fig. 121. Detail of frame of self-portrait, with mark for assembly: "+ II"

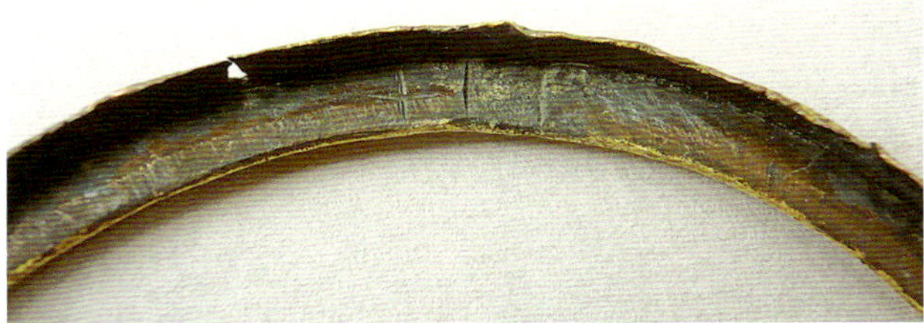

of Prometheus".[50] Doubtless Fouquet's efforts to breathe life into the gaze of his figures so impressed the artist's contemporary that he invested him with Promethean status. In the self-portrait, is it the "sacred fire" that shines forth from the "reflection in a golden eye"? The point of light in Fouquet's eye is virtually unique in painting, for it is positioned not on the iris, but in the orb of the eye itself, overlapping the edge of the iris. Only one other face shows this reflection: the one angel who gazes directly at the viewer in the Antwerp *Virgin and Child*, the seraph to the right above the head of the Christ Child.

1   The title of this essay alludes to the book by Carson McCullers, *Reflections in a Golden Eye*, Boston 1941, filmed by John Huston in 1967.

2   Chennevières 1853, unpaginated.

3   Avril's observation is reported by Thiébaut in her essay on the self-portrait in Cat. Paris 2003, p. 132.

4   Auguste Vallet de Viriville 1859. As a professor at the École des Chartes and a specialist in the history of the Hundred Years' War, Vallet de Viriville was especially known as the biographer of King Charles VII and Joan of Arc; his publications included *Chronique de la Pucelle* (1859) and *Procès de condamnation de Jeanne d'Arc* (1867).

5   Bibliothèque nationale de France, Département des manuscrits, N.a.fr. 5086 (Notes historiques sur le règne de Charles VII), f. 103 v, pièce n 389. I am grateful to François Avril for informing the Département des Objets d'art of the Louvre of these documents during the preparation for his major Fouquet exhibition in 2003.

6   "Le sommet de la tête est écaillé, et l'écaillure a été remplie par de la cire noire."

7   In the extensive bibliography on the *Melun Diptych* and the self-portrait, the work of two scholars, in particular, should be emphasized: Nicole Reynaud 1981, no. 4-6, pp. 18-27, and François Avril in Cat. Paris 2003, no. 7-8, pp. 121-137.

8   At his death in 1865, Janzé bequeathed the finest objects in his collection of antiquities (169 bronzes and ceramics) to the Cabinet des Médailles of the Bibliothèque nationale; the remainder of his collection was sold at auction in Paris on April 16, 1866. On his role as benefactor, see Cat. Paris 1989, p. 237. I am grateful to my colleagues Inès Villela-Petit, Mathilde Avisseau, and Florence Codine from the Cabinet des Médailles, who very generously provided me with access to information on this important donor to the Bibliothèque nationale. The catalogue of antiquities bequeathed by Janzé can be accessed on the internet at: http://gallica.bnf.fr/ark:/12148/btv1b53085310z.r=Janz%C3%A9?rk=21459;2. A catalogue from the auction of his graphic collection is found at: http://gallica.bnf.fr/ark:/12148/bpt6k380248j.r=Janz%C3%A9?rk=107296;4.

9   Vallet de Viriville, 1856, p. 475.

10   As he expressed it in his unpaginated book of 1857: "avec une extrême défiance et un certain embarras."

11   In an unpublished lecture for the Société des Antiquaires de France; lectures for the latter were published in the *Bulletin* beginning in 1857, and in the *Journal* in 1856.

12   Vallet de Viriville, in *Revue archéologique* 1857, p. 289: "On peut y joindre les médaillons peints en émail par le même artiste, et dont parle Étienne [sic] Godefroy. Ces médaillons décoraient le diptyque offert par Étienne Chevalier à Notre-Dame de Melun, et qui se conserva dans cette église jusqu' à l' époque de la révolution française." In 1856 he had written: "Je citerai un autre terme de comparaison plus direct. Il existait jadis dans l'église Notre-Dame de Melun un admirable diptyque entièrement peint par Jean Fouquet et que Denis Godefroy décrivait au XVIIe siècle: (...) Ces médaillons, évidemment, n'étaient autre que des camaïeux d'or, peints exactement, sauf la différence du fond, dans le même procédé que le médaillon appartenant à M. le vicomte de Janzé."

13   For example in Friedländer 1896.

14   Godefroy, who according to Vallet de Viriville 1857, p. 425, was a distant descendant of Étienne Chevalier, also records an epitaph inscribed in Gothic letters on a large panel on the wall and tells the ongoing history of the mass donated by Chevalier, which was said at 6:00 a.m. both summer and winter. According to Godefroy, the mass was no longer said at the altar of the burial chapel behind the choir, but rather in the chapel of St. Barbara, due to the large number of the faithful who usually attended; Schaefer 1975, p. 99, citing the manuscript, fol. 384v.

15   Godefroy 1661, pp. 885-886: "... les bordures desditz tableaux sont couvertes en dedans de velours bleu, orné et enrichy tout autour de quantité de grands lacs d'amour à l'antique, séparés d'un esgale distance l'un de l'autre; et tissus d'une petite broderie d'or et d'argent; dans chaque coste desquels lacs, est un grand E (Estienne) aussi à l'antique, tout couvert de petites perles fines; et entre ces lacs d'amour, sont les médailles d'argent doré, de moyenne grandeur, représentans quelque histoire saincte, dont les personnages sont peints admirablement bien."

16   *Recueil d'épitaphes de Paris et de ses environs*; BnF, fr. 8224, pièce 663 v.

17   Illustration in Grésy 1845, not numbered. Vallet de Viriville 1857, p. 426, saw this print in Grésy and asserted that it had been created in 1805 for Alexandre Lenoir (1761–1839), specifically for the latter's *Musée des monuments français. Recueil de portraits inédits des hommes et des femmes qui ont illustré la France sous différents règnes, dont les originaux sont conservés dans ledit musée* (Paris 1809); supposedly, however, it was not reproduced there since the original was not or was no longer in Lenoir's possession. Vallet de Viriville attributed the print to a certain Pourvoyeur ("né vers 1780, mort vers 1840"). Unfortunately, the page is not identified, and there is no trace of it in the file of Jean Baptiste François Pourvoyeur (1784–1851) in the Bibliothèque nationale in Paris. According to this account, the Madonna panel was known to Lenoir in 1805 when the print was made, but was definitely not in his possession in 1809. It is uncertain whether the painting was still in its original frame at that time. Although it is unlikely that Lenoir would own the panel only to let it go again, we can still assume that in 1805 it was on the market in Paris or in a private collection, which accords with what we know about its history between 1775 and 1841. The precision and erudition that usually characterized Vallet de Viriville's work are a good argument for trusting him.

18   Cat. Paris 1904, no. 42; L'émail de la bordure, p. 19: "On suppose que Jean Fouquet favori de la maîtresse royale a peint cet émail pour consacrer son souvenir et sa gratitude."

19   On the financial considerations related to the restoration of the collegiate church, which presumably motivated the canons to sell the famous diptych in 1773–75, see Förstel 2008.

20   Aside from this observation, however, Bouchot says nothing about the connection between the diptych and the self-portrait in the book accompanying the 1904 exhibition; he mentions the medallion only in connection with the orthography of Fouquet's name, which he derives from it (p. 271).

21   Marquet de Vasselot 1904, p. 147: "... d'où provient cet émail? Peut-être, bien que ce soit là une hypothèse purement gratuite, du cadre même du diptyque de Melun. Ne serait-il pas tentant d'imaginer que nous avons là un fragment de ce somptueux ensemble?"

22   Netzer 1999, no. 64, p. 163.

23   Gauthier 1972, pp. 306-308; Schaefer 1975, pp. 54-57.

24   Hérold 1998, p. 51: "pour visiter ung beau tableau qui est en l'église dud. Meleng, ouquel est partie du martire, invention et translation de ms. Sainct Étienne."

25   Gousset in Cat. Paris 2003, pp. 80-81.

26   As noted already by Reynaud 1981, pp. 24-26, and Dominique Thiébaut in Cat. Paris 2003, pp. 132-135.

27 The initials represent a decorative script that emerged in princely chancelleries beginning in the 1430s and which is developed in the so-called Alphabet of Mary of Burgundy, probably derived from a lost examplar for Charles the Bold; König 2015.

28 Gauthier 1972, p. 306.

29 Cat. Paris 2003, no. 24.43, fig. p. 214; Reynaud 2006.

30 The diptych appears beneath St. Martin, the medallions below St. Nicholas, panels with ogee arches on the page with St. John the Baptist, and square or rectangular reliefs on a marble ground for St. John the Evangelist and St. James; Cat. Paris 2003, no. 24, fig. 38, 39, 31, 32, 36; Reynaud 2006, fig. pp. 183, 189, 151, 157, 173.

31 Sricchia Santoro 2003.

32 Ibid., pp. 60-61, fig. 13, 14 and 15.

33 Cat. Paris 2003, no. 24.4-5, fig. pp. 196-7; Reynaud 2006, fig. 40-41.

34 Sricchia Santoro 2003, p. 59: "dont la surprenante vitalité naturelle … semble ne tolérer que le nom de Fouquet," and fig. 8.

35 The *Lit de Justice de Vendôme* added as a frontispiece at the beginning of the Munich Boccaccio shows a head among the spectators that is sometimes interpreted as a self-portrait by the artist; here, however, I do not recognize Fouquet's features and thus cannot endorse Erik Inglis's ambitious argument for "Fouquet's self-portraits"; Inglis 2011, pp. 19-35.

36 With the assistance of Thierry Borel (†) and Elsa Lambert for radiography.

37 Speel 2002, p. 35.

38 In her *Rapport d'examen* of December 2009, Isabelle Biron writes: "Il s'agit d'un silicate alcalin coloré au cobalt. Ce verre contient de relativement fortes teneurs en calcium et de faibles teneurs en plomb et en étain."

39 This granular impression is produced by the firing of gold powder, which then penetrates into the glass.

40 Dominique Thiébaut in Cat. Paris 2003, p. 131.

41 Marie-Thérèse Gousset in Cat. Paris 2003, pp. 79-81 and fig. 3.

42 Performed by the conservator Marie-Emmanuelle Meyohas.

43 See n. 17 above.

44 Paris, Bibl. de l'Institut de France, fonds Godefroy, Ms. 241, fol. 358: "… on voit dans ladite Bordure les places de plusieurs médailles qui ont été derobéz" (as quoted in Schaefer 1975, p. 99).

45 Quoted in Förstel 2008, p. 7 of the reprint: "autour de ce tableau estoient plusieurs belles médailles que l'on y voit plus."

46 As early as June 1864, Vallet de Viriville was anticipating Curmer's work on Fouquet, even before the preceding publication of Curmer's *Les Evangiles*. The latter contains an initial mention of "Jehan Foucquet," but does not include the chromolithograph by Émile Daumont, which first appears in Curmer II, 1867, unpaginated, accompanied by a text by Vallet de Viriville.

47 Paris, BnF, N.a.fr. 5086 (Notes historiques sur le règne de Charles VII), f. 99v, pièces n 344 (juin 1864) and n 346. Once again I would like to thank François Avril for making these very interesting documents on the history of the medallion available to the Département des Objets d'art.

48 Meyer 1895, p. 38: "Après avoir massé au pinceau avec de l'or employé en lavis, à l'instar de l'aquarelle, la poudre d'or délayée dans de l'eau légèrement gommée et sucrée, et après avoir laissé séché, on grave avec une pointe comme pour la gravure à l'eau forte toutes les parties qui produiront les demi-teintes et les ombres, laissant à nu le fond de la plaque émaillée pour obtenir son effet."

49 Popelin 1868, p. 45.

50 Salmon 1855, p. 105.

CAT. 3
Jean Fouquet

PORTRAIT STUDY OF GUILLAUME JOUVENEL DES URSINS

ca. 1460/70
Black, red, white, and ochre chalks, heightened with brush in pink, on gray primed paper; old backing laminated around the edges
26.7 x 19.6 cm
Inscription on verso, pen in brown: dit is van d[ei]ghen hant van meester rogier/ t – st/ 2-10 gelde (added later, probably by a collector of the 17th century, Fig. 129)[1]
Provenance: Collection of Carl von Rumohr, acquired in 1846 (as Hans Holbein)
Kupferstichkabinett, Staatliche Museen zu Berlin, KdZ 5578
Selected bibliography: Friedländer 1910 – Arnolds 1947, pp. 5-6 – Reynaud 1981, no. 8, pp. 29-31 – Cat. Berlin 1994, no. VI.4, pp. 307-309 (Sigrid Achenbach) – Cat. Paris 2003, no. 6, pp. 118-120 (Dominique Thiebaut; with older bibliography) – Brahms 2016, pp. 193-195

Without question, the portrait of the French chancellor Guillaume Jouvenel des Ursins is one of the finest pieces in the world-famous collection of the Kupferstichkabinett in Berlin. It is also the only surviving drawing that can be attributed with certainty to Jean Fouquet. In 1910, Max J. Friedländer discovered the previously anonymous drawing among the Netherlandish works in the Kupferstichkabinett and recognized its connection to Fouquet's portrait painting of the chancellor in the Louvre (Fig. 123). Guillaume Jouvenel des Ursins, Baron of Trainel (1401–1472), was a member of one of the most powerful families in France; as chancellor from 1445 to 1461, and from 1465 until his death, he was also the most important official in France under Charles VII and Louis XI.
The extraordinary degree of realism and the close-up view of the subject's face, which turns to the right in a three-quarter view, suggest that Fouquet created the drawing directly from life. He focused his entire attention on the countenance of his sitter, documenting all of its irregularities and wrinkles, and depicted the clothing only incidentally in the form of a mantle collar. In this respect, the drawing differs significantly from the painting, as well as in its directness and greater naturalism. These differences may indicate that the drawing preceded the painting and was not executed as a later copy or study. The obvious divergences also explain why neither the drawing nor the painting show any evidence of direct mechanical transfer of the motif.
The unusual technique of the drawing inspired Friedländer to describe it as an "incunabulum of pastel painting." Today, after extensive visual analysis, it presents itself as a complex mixture of media. Fouquet used colored chalks, but supplemented them with pink gouache applied with a brush. In addition, he primed the paper in gray as a midtone, which not only enabled him to create forms and shadows with dark chalks and place highlights with light ones, but also, in combination with delicate red and pink tonalities, to evoke the natural color of human skin. With its sophisticated color accents, almost life-size format, and early date, the portrait study is unquestionably unique for its epoch, from both an artistic and a technical standpoint. Nothing comparable exists from the period before it, either from south or north of the Alps.

Georg Josef Dietz and Dagmar Korbacher

---

1   We are most grateful to Stephan Kemperdick, Bas Dudok van Heel, Peter Schatborn, and Holm Bevers for assistance with the transcription and interpretation.

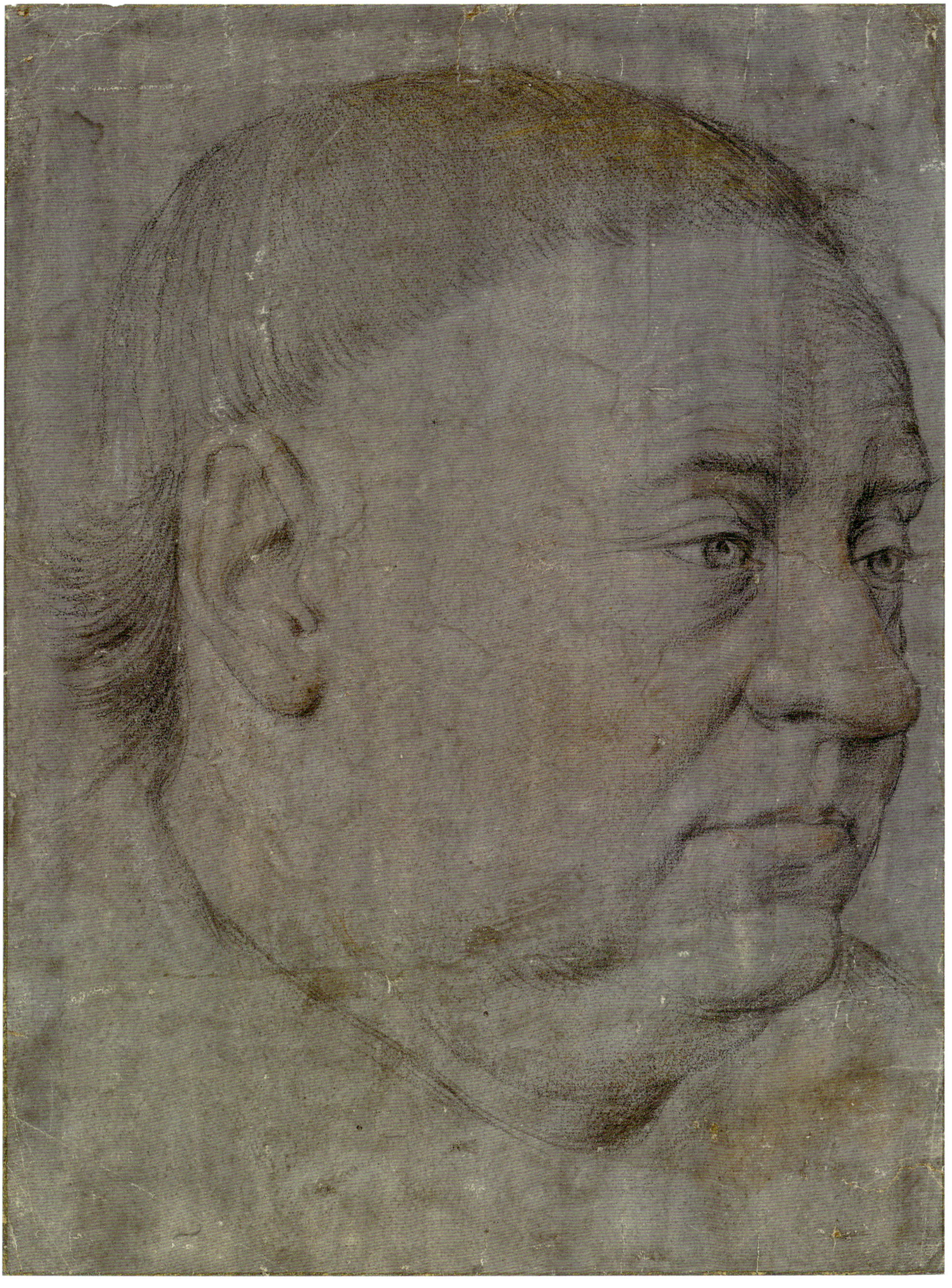

Georg Josef Dietz and Dagmar Korbacher

PIONEER ON PAPER:
JEAN FOUQUET'S PORTRAIT DRAWING OF GUILLAUME JOUVENEL DES URSINS IN THE KUPFERSTICHKABINETT IN BERLIN

Without a doubt, Jean Fouquet's portrait study of Guillaume Jouvenel des Ursins is one of the finest drawings in the Kupferstichkabinett in Berlin (cat. 3). It was acquired in 1846 as a work by Hans Holbein the Younger, an attribution that did not prove tenable.[1] Max J. Friedländer discovered the work among the anonymous Netherlandish drawings, associated it for the first time with the painted portrait of the French chancellor in the Louvre dated to around 1460 (fig. 123), and published an essay in 1910 attributing the drawing to Jean Fouquet. To this day, it is one of only three drawings—the others are in St. Petersburg (fig. 124) and New York (fig. 125)—attributed to the artist;[2] only the drawing in the Kupferstichkabinett, however, is uncontested in its attribution to Fouquet. According to Friedländer, "the Berlin drawing reveals itself as a creation of the French master even more clearly than the other two,"[3] a fact that establishes it as a reference point for Fouquet's graphic oeuvre. The portrait is especially significant, however, for its delicate and variously colored accents: Friedländer described it as an "incunabulum of pastel painting,"[4] an assessment that has often been quoted ever since and has persisted to the present day with greater or lesser sophistication.[5] There is no question that on account of its early date, its nearly life-size format (26.7 x 19.6 cm), and its nuanced accents of color, the portrait study must be considered unique for its epoch. Nothing comparable exists from the previous period, either from south or north of the Alps. It is therefore worthwhile taking a closer look at the portrait of Guillaume Jouvenel.

Technical questions and observations

The artist drew the portrait on paper that was primed on one side with a thin gray coat.[6] With this surface functioning as the midtone, he developed the portrait study using at least two black chalks in varying degrees of hardness. A firm black chalk allowed him to draw more precise, continuous lines and thus lent itself to contours and the basic linear structure of the head and neckline. A second, more variable and somewhat softer chalk abraded only on the tooth of the paper when used with light pressure, producing strokes that were broader, open, and more textured, particularly suitable for rapid shading as well as for the rendering of the hair. With stronger pressure, it could also be used to produce deep black lines. The artist probably used a dry white chalk to create the highlights, particularly in the whites of the eyes, but also in the reflections of light on the hair at the back of the head and the collar near the back of the neck. Highlights also appear somewhat less clearly in the outer corner of the right eye and the eyelid above it, in the nasolabial area, and on the cheek where it meets the ear.[7] The palette is significantly enriched by two red chalks: one, of a firmer consistency, left a rather brownish, sometimes rough, barely pigmented mark, while the other produced a brighter red-orange color. The darker chalk was used, for example, in the lower lip and on the contour of the nose, while the brighter one appears in the upper lip and the middle of the forehead.

Fig. 123. Jean Fouquet, *Guillaume Jouvenel des Ursins*, ca. 1460/65, oak, 96 x 73.2 cm, Paris, Musée du Louvre

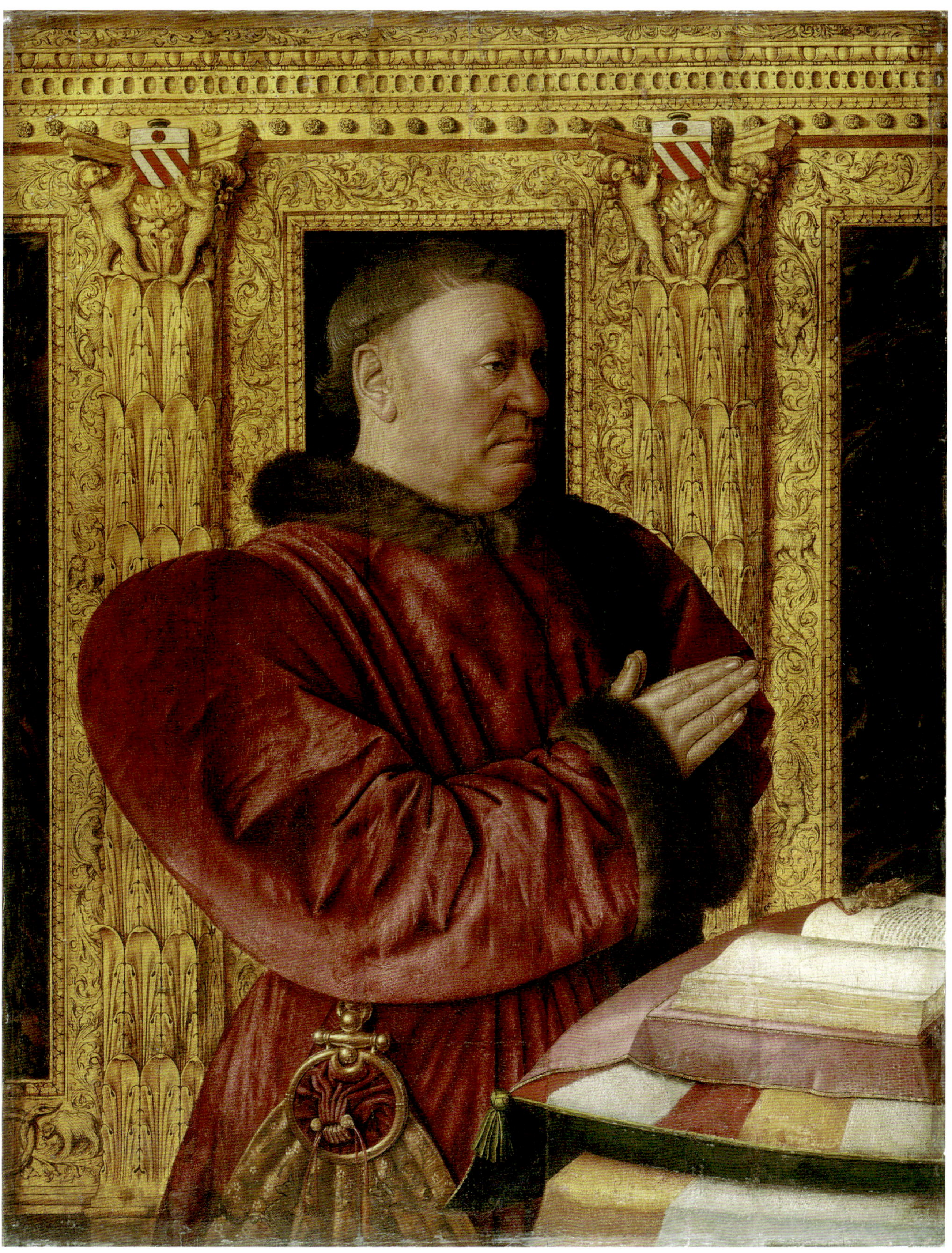

The hair, in turn, was colored primarily at the front of the head using yellow ochre chalk applied in horizontal hatch marks that were partially blended by the artist. Most unusual are the delicate pink highlights found above all on the forehead and next to the eye toward the temples, as well as on the bridge of the nose, the nasal wing, and in the ear area. Though they are very subtle, it was precisely these pink accents that in recent years constituted the primary reason for associating this drawing with pastel painting.[8] Unlike black, white, red, brown, yellow, or even blue chalk (fig. 129a), it is virtually inconceivable that pink-colored chalk could be obtained directly from nature by the extraction and shaping of natural occurrences of colored earths or minerals.[9] This fact may have persuaded earlier viewers that Fouquet was obviously using drawing chalks that had been artificially produced.

The results of visual analysis of the drawing materials with the help of a reflected light microscope[10] offer further insight into the means by which the drawing was created. The analysis evaluated the traces of the media left behind on the paper and the morphology of the abrasions. According to the results, the harder black marks were most likely made with a natural black chalk, a carbon-rich clay shale (fig. 126).[11] The softer chalk, on the other hand, could have been artificially produced from soot and a binding agent.[12] The extremely homogenous and extremely fine-particle pigmentation of the two red chalks and the ochre-colored chalk suggests two different natural variants of red chalk, iron oxide as well as natural ochre with hydrated iron oxide. Both occur in multiple gradations of color. The situation is quite different with the pink-colored marks: here the enlargement clearly shows a mixture of red and white pigments. In addition, the very compact accretion, along

Fig. 125. Jean Fouquet (attributed), *Portrait of an Ecclesiastic*, ca. 1455/65, metalpoint and black chalk on white primed paper, 19.8 x 13.5 cm, New York, Metropolitan Museum, Acc. No. 49.38

Fig. 124. Jean Fouquet, *Portrait of an Elderly Man (King Louis XI?)*, ca. 1475 (?), brush with black and gray, charcoal, and red chalk on gray primed paper, 27.8 x 20.6 cm, St. Petersburg, Hermitage, Inv. OP-3895

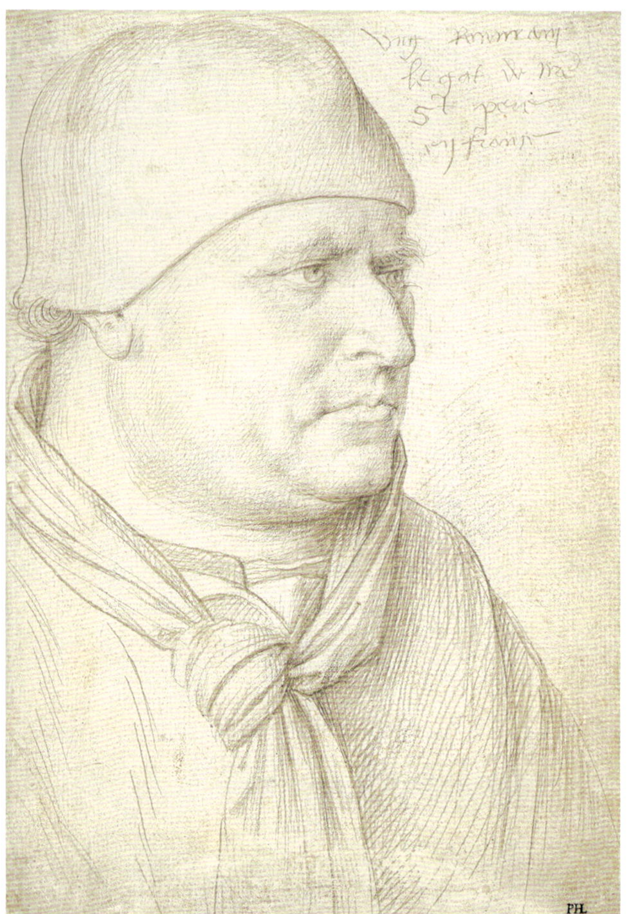

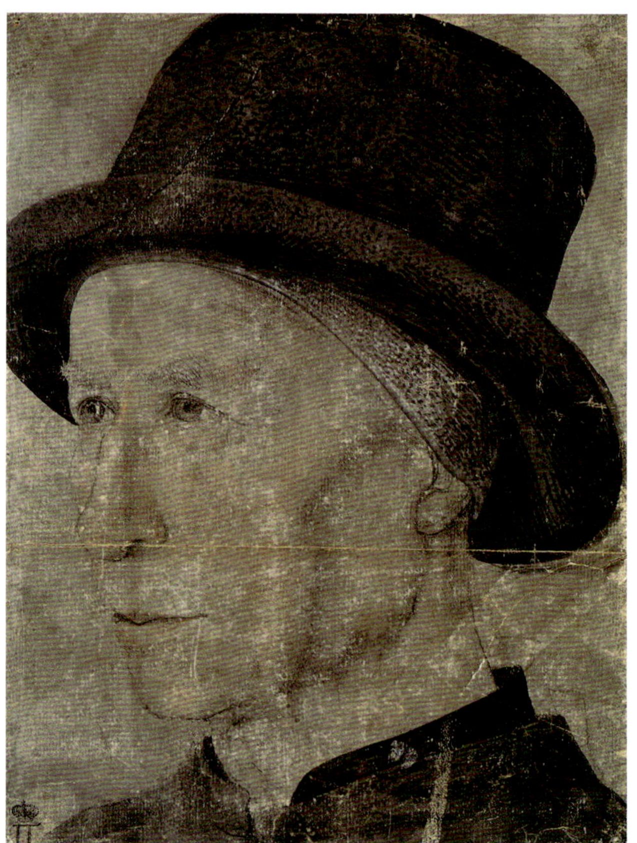

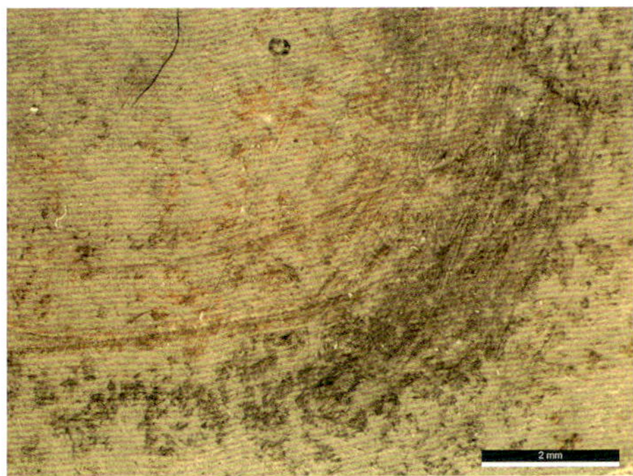

Fig. 126. Microscopic image of black and red chalk with rough abrasion

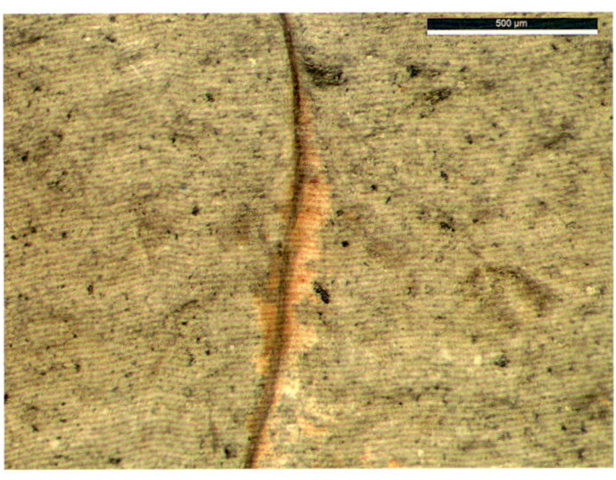

Fig. 127. Microscopic image of pink color with red and white pigment and a brush hair

with a brush hair that has dried in the color, proves that we are dealing here not with dry chalk, but rather with color applied in a fluid medium (fig. 127). Thus the theory that Fouquet was the first pastel painter is not tenable, especially since it appears that he used only natural colored chalks, perhaps with the exception of the one black chalk.[13] Yet even if these findings seem for the moment to demystify, as it were, the Berlin drawing, and even though Fouquet now can no longer be considered the "inventor of pastel painting," more recent art technical studies have already separated the tradition of colored chalk drawing from what we now call pastel painting. We now know that the latter developed independently in the late 17th century with the development of specially manufactured pastel sticks with pigments, fillers, and binding agents, produced in extensive sets in various tonal gradations. Homogenous abrasion and consistency of texture were the prerequisite for the creation of vibrantly colored works in which the entire picture surface was covered with colored chalk.[14] The word "pastello," up to now assumed to be the origin of our term for the medium, occurs in the writings of Leonardo; his instructions for the production of "pastelli" in the Codex Madrid I is usually interpreted as the first reference to artificially produced colored chalks or pastel sticks. The technique he describes may well have lent itself to that purpose as well, but in the original context there is no reference whatsoever to color, but only to a sticky mass.[15] In the Codex Forster II², on the other hand, Leonardo actually describes a process for the production of colored chalks.[16]

The function of the drawing

The function of the drawing was first identified by Friedländer: it documents an important stage in the production of an official portrait. Thus, as far as we know, the panel with the portrait of Jouvenel des Ursins is the only 15th-century French painting for which a preparatory drawing survives.[17] It is highly probable that the drawing was created from life, since it constitutes a very direct, immediate, almost life-size portrait representation. The artist produced a close-up image of the face of an older man, turned toward the right in a three-quarter view; the face is rendered with remarkable, indeed nearly documentary precision in all of its irregularities and wrinkles. The subject's clothing, suggested only by the collar of his mantle, is simple and only incidentally sketched. Only in the painted version do we see a high fur collar which, like the rest of the robe, clearly indicates the high social standing of the chancellor and the official character of the portrait (fig. 123). As is often the case in the transition from drawn to painted portraits, the facial features were changed and corrected when the drawing was rendered in painted form. In the drawing, the chancellor's face seems more immediate, somewhat younger, and less grave than in the painting—perhaps due to the painting's stronger emphasis on the forehead wrinkles and the more obviously downward orientation of these lines and the corners of the mouth, as well as the significantly fleshier nose. The dimensions of the drawn and painted portrait heads correspond to each other, though they do not agree in every detail. It is hardly surprising, therefore, that neither the painting[18] nor the drawing[19] show signs of direct transfer, such as *spolvero* (pounce) marks or traces of the stylus.[20] It has frequently been noted that the dimensions of the paper on which the drawing was made, as well as the relation between the picture area and the drawn head, correspond to those of the painted head and the dark field behind it in the gold-framed paneling.[21] This correspondence, however, could also have occurred by chance: while the size relationship in the painting does agree with the drawing, the exact position of the head within the rectangle does not match the *mise-en-page* of the drawn head, and we do not know whether the paper was cut.[22]

Up to this point, it has generally been assumed that the application of color to the drawing was primarily intended to serve the artist as a mnemonic aid, with a view to the later execution of the painting.[23] In this context, reference has often been made to van Eyck's famous portrait drawing of an old man, now in Dresden; in this work, although the artist did not use colored chalk to differentiate the physiognomy, he made notes of various colors in silverpoint in the margin.[24] In our opinion,

however, this comparison is not entirely fair, for it suggests that the delicate coloration in Fouquet's portrait of Jouvenel des Ursins served only to remind the artist of the color of the model's hair and complexion for later use in the painting. For such a purpose, the use of two different blacks along with red, brown, yellow, and white chalk, as well as pink gouache applied with the brush, seems rather elaborate; furthermore, the colors indicated in these areas were hardly so complex as to require notation, but instead seem downright trivial: pink for the lips, white for the eyeballs, etc. In addition, the blond tones of the hair in the drawing significantly differ from the painted portrait, where the subject is depicted with dark brown hair. Much more important in this context are the lighting effects which connect the drawing to the painting and which to some extent are exactly copied in the latter, in particular the striking reflection of light on the back of the head, as well as the overall impression of spotlight illumination from the left, leaving much of the face in shadow as it turns away. Moreover, the color also acquires a compositional function in its interaction with the black chalks, particularly in the modeled areas.[25] Here Fouquet was clearly experimenting with a specific color scheme in order to intensify the sense of realism and indeed the vitality of the portrait. In any case, the level of abstraction in the drawing is considerably less than what is produced by monochromatic and more linear techniques, as seen for example in the comparison with the silverpoint drawing in New York (fig. 125). In the Berlin drawing, the observed subject matter is not translated into a monochromatic system of lines, but is modeled in areas of chiaroscuro and color; even aside from the greater degree of mimesis, this approach may also have made it easier for the artist to later translate the image into a colored painting.[26] It also may have served to impress the patron with its remarkable realism and to convince him of Fouquet's artistic abilities. The use of primed paper, a technique Fouquet could have learned during his stay in Italy, points in the same direction:[27] in 15th-century Florence, drawings on this kind of elaborately prepared surface often served as "presentation and contract drawings."[28] The use of *carta tinta* as a drawing surface may often have been associated with the intended execution of the work as a painting.[29] Furthermore, the rendering of a portrait in colored chalks on a blue or

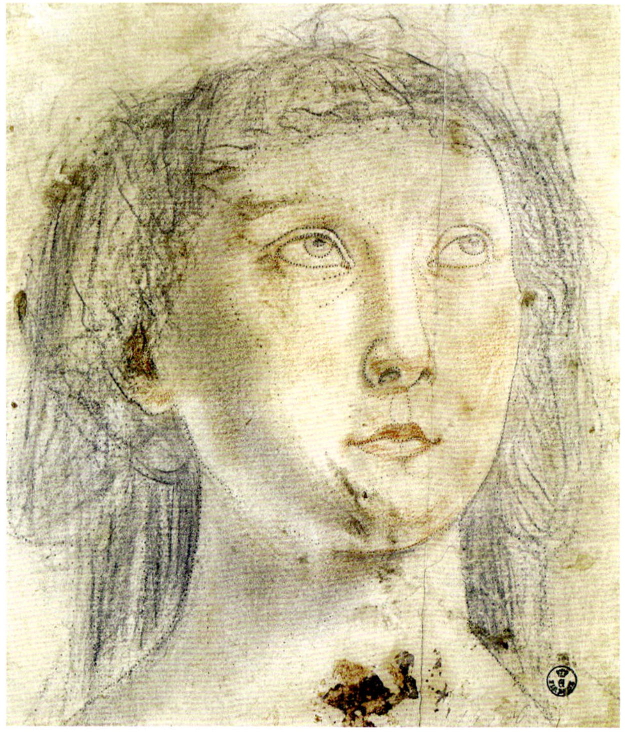

Fig. 128. Pietro del Pollaiolo, *Personification of Faith*, ca. 1470, black, red, and white chalk, 21.1 x 18.2 cm, Florence, Gabinetto Disegni e Stampe degli Uffizi, Inv. Nr.14506 F

Fig. 129. Inscription on verso of drawing (pen in brown), montage of backlit and UV image (blue)

green ground accords surprisingly well with the natural coloration of skin, where veins show through everywhere in a delicate pale blue.[30] Finally, in the present instance the priming was probably also a technical necessity, in order to obtain better abrasion of the rough natural chalk and to avoid potential damage to an unprimed paper surface.[31]

There are no other examples from this period of portraits in red, ochre, black, and white chalk, let alone in combination with a brush, on primed paper.[32] A relatively early drawing in which red, white, and black chalk are used to accentuate and enliven facial features is the study for the head of the personification of Faith by Pietro del Pollaiolo in the Uffizi, dated to around 1470 (fig. 128);[33] here, however, the artist did not prime the paper before using it as a drawing surface. Other works which—for lack of contemporaneous examples—are often mentioned as comparative material are Leonardo's portrait of Isabella d'Este in the Louvre, Boltraffio's portrait drawings, and even the delicate portraits by the hand of Jean Clouet; all of these, however, are more than a generation later, and all likewise were executed on unprimed paper. The same is true of the portrait drawings of Agnès Sorel in the "trois crayons" technique,[34] copied from a prototype by Jean Fouquet and dated to the 16th century (cat. 5).[35] All in all, there is considerable evidence that the technique known as "colorire asseccho"[36] actually originated in France, and that Leonardo, long considered its inventor, learned it from the French artist Jean de Perréal.[37]

The inscription on the verso

The portrait study of Guillaume Jouvenel des Ursins seems to have been a coveted collector's item by the 17[th] century at the latest. An inscription on the verso, until now considered illegible, was recently brought to light in its entirety and deciphered (fig. 129).[38] Written in Dutch, it states: "dit is van d[ei]ghen hant van meester rogier/ t – st/ 2-10 gelde." Apparently, the owner at the time considered the drawing to be a work by Rogier van der Weyden and wanted to emphasize its authenticity.[39] Among 17[th]-century collectors of Old Master drawings, the practice had become increasingly common of using an inscription to emphasize the work's status as an authentic original by a great master and not a copy or an imitation.[40] Since Fouquet had already been forgotten as an artist, it was logical for a 17th-century collector to identify the creator of the drawing as Rogier van der Weyden, who had remained very well-known as an Early Netherlandish artist of that epoch. Although the information on Rogier reported by a writer like Karel van Mander in his *Schilder-Boeck* of 1604 was relatively vague and anecdotal, van Mander still celebrated him as an outstanding artist, indeed as a genius.[41] Certainly the inscription on our drawing does not represent the attribution of a connoisseur based, for example, on stylistic similarity to other drawings by Rogier;[42] rather, it probably arose from a perceived general resemblance to the especially lifelike panel portraits by Rogier and his milieu, such as the portrait of a fat man in the Gemäldegalerie in Berlin (cat. 7).

Conclusion

While the true identity of both artist and portrait subject were rediscovered only centuries later, the outstanding quality of the drawing has always been recognized. Its technique, which led Friedländer to call it an "incunabulum of pastel painting," is today revealed as a complex mixture of media. Although the drawing has little to do with "pastel" in the contemporary meaning and usage of the term, its status as a drawing in colored chalk, even with gouache accents, indisputably characterizes it as a

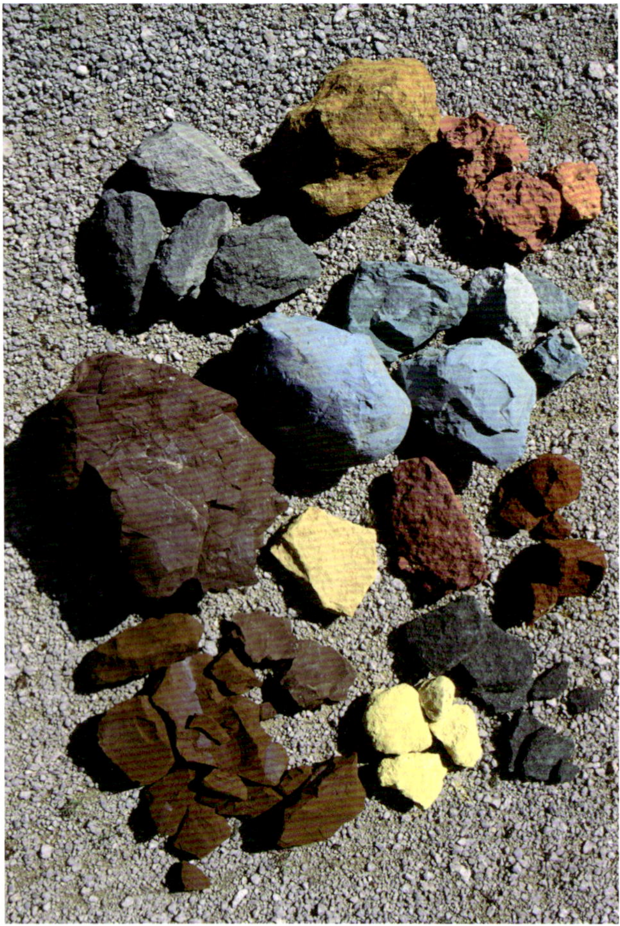

Fig. 129a. Colored Chalks, Sollection Félicien Carli, Paris

preliminary form of the pastel technique that would later emerge. Even the choice of a gray midtone as the drawing's ground is a pioneering development in portrait art.[43] Thus, while Friedländer's oft-quoted dictum cannot be interpreted to mean that the Berlin portrait drawing of Guillaume Jouvenel des Ursins by Fouquet is a "prototype" of pastel painting, it may still be considered a graphic "precursor" of the later medium.[44] This work, utterly unique and groundbreaking in so many respects, distinguishes Jean Fouquet as a 15th-century pioneer on paper.

1   The auction catalogue of the von Rumohr collection emphasized the extraordinary quality of the drawing (Frenzel 1846, p. 314, no. 3388a). In Cat. Berlin 1910, no. 97, it was still listed as the work of an early 16th-century Netherlandish artist, but with a note that it was by Jean Fouquet and was associated with the portrait of the chancellor Ursins (p. XVI).

2   The attribution of the New York silverpoint drawing to Fouquet (cf. Cat. Paris 2003, cat. 13, pp. 147-148) is somewhat disputed; for the St. Petersburg head, see Cat. Paris 2003, cat. 12, pp. 142-146.

3   Friedländer 1910, p. 230.

4   Ibid., p. 228.

5   For example, Cat. Berlin 1994, no. VI.4, pp. 307-309 (Sigrid Achenbach); Cat. Paris 2003, no. 6 (Dominique Thiebaut); Reynaud 1981, no. 8.

6   The color was applied in vertical strokes with a broad brush or sponge. The reflected light microscope (cf. n. 10) shows the following color components in a matrix that cannot be precisely defined visually: numerous black particles, also transparent red (probably a red lacquer) in lesser quantity as well as blue and blue-green pigments. Today the verso of the paper is largely obscured by laminations; when backlit, the paper shows a ribbed texture with laid lines and chain lines running vertically at intervals of ca. 3.2 to 3.9 cm. There is no watermark.

7   The condition of the surface has naturally deteriorated with age, and the reduction of the colored medium through abrasion of the surface makes it difficult to determine whether the white highlights were applied with a dry stick or in opaque white applied with a brush, which however was kept quite dry. The existing traces, however, seem to indicate a stick, since they do not appear compact anywhere, but rather loose and irregular.

8   For example, in Cat. Berlin 1994, cat. VI.4, p. 309 (Sigrid Achenbach); Reynaud 1981, p. 29, also mentions "pastel rose" in addition to the chalks, apparently on the basis of information from Peter Dreyer (p. 82, n. 86); explicitly in Cat. Paris 2003, p. 118 (Dominique Thiebaut). Friedländer (1910, p. 227) mentions only "four chalks," specifically "black, brownish-red, white, and yellowish-brown in the hair."

9   On natural colored chalks, see the extensive discussion in Burns 2007, pp. 8ff, with reference to Cennino Cennini's treatise on painting from ca. 1400, in which he mentions the occurrence of yellow ochre, light and dark red, blue, and white earths in the surroundings of Siena (cf. Cennini 1871, Cap. 45, pp. 29-30).

10 Reflected light microscope Leica MZ8 (enlargement up to 100x), light source Schott KL2500 LCD.

11 Cennini mentions this material around 1400; Cennini 1871, Cap. 34, p. 23.

12 Charcoal can probably be ruled out; cf. Dietz 2008, esp. pp. 39-43.

13 The question of whether these chalks were ground, and the pigments then purified and artificially formed into sticks with the addition of binding agent, could only be answered through analysis of the binding agent, which, however, would require a test sample from the original.

14 Burns 2007, pp. XVII-XX.

15 Cf. Nova 2008, p. 159. The passage could also be describing the production of glue sticks.

16 London, Victoria & Albert Museum; fol. 159r, Bambach 2008, pp. 186-189.

17 Cf. Cat. Paris 2003, at cat. 5, p. 114 (Dominique Thiebaut).

18 Ibid.

19 Based on examination of the front and back side under incident light, a microscope, and extreme oblique light.

20 The *spolvero* or pouncing technique is a method of transfer in which the contour lines of an initial drawing are perforated with a needle. The prototype is then laid on a new picture surface and the perforations daubed with a small bag of charcoal dust, transferring the so- called pounce marks to the new surface; Bambach 1999, pp. 56-62. On tracing with the stylus, cf. ibid., pp. 335-338.

21 Reynaud 1981, p. 31; Cat. Paris 2003, at cat. 5, p. 114 (Dominique Thiebaut).

22 The ca. 3 mm-wide line framing the image is drawn with gold on a green ground and is probably the addition of a later collector. The size of the drawing, 26.7 x 19.6 cm, could indicate that it was a half-sheet of the 32 x 46 cm format customary in France in the 14th and 15th centuries (cf. Tschudin 2007, p. 259), so that some degree of cutting may certainly be assumed.

23 Brahms 2016, p. 194.

24 Dresden 2005, cat. 11, pp. 62-67, especially pp. 62-63 (Thomas Ketelsen); Brahms 2016, p. 194.

25 Some of the black in the hair lies on top of the yellow, and in the nose, red chalk is superimposed on white. This integration of media definitively rules out the possibility, at first perhaps conceivable, that the drawing was reworked or colored by a later hand.

26 Brahms 2016, pp. 194-195.

27 Reynaud 1981, p. 29, and the essay by Rowley in this volume.

28 Graul 2008, p. 12. Significantly, many of the drawings executed on paper primed with color in mid-15th-century Florence were studies of heads (cf. ibid., p. 11).

29 Cf. Graul 2008, p. 10. Cennini himself viewed "drawing on colored paper as a decisive step on the way to colored rendering."

30 Moreover, blank areas do not stand out in glaring white (cf. n. 46 and Dietz/Röhrs 2013, p. 285).

31 Cf. similar observations and considerations for the combination of natural black chalk and primed paper in the work of Albrecht Dürer (Dietz 2012, p. 348) and Ottavio Leoni (Dietz, Röhrs 2013, p. 285).

32 Zvereva 2002, pp. 19-20.

33 Nova 2008, p. 174, n. 23, Cat. London, no. 33, p. 164 (Hugo Chapman), and Brahms 2016, p. 196; the drawing is executed in black chalk (or charcoal?) as well as red and white chalk and measures 211 x 182 mm (Florence, Gabinetto Disegni e Stampe degli Uffizi, Inv. Nr.14506 F).

34 Drawn with a combination of black, white, and red chalk.

35 Florence (cat. 5); Paris, BNF, département des Estampes, Inv. Rés. Na. 21, f. 28; Cat. Paris 2003, no. 14, 15. The close-up view, as well as the lively characterization of the individual physiognomy of the portrait subject, recalls the portrait drawing of an older man by Francesco Bonsignori (Albertina, Cat. Berlin/New York 2001, no. 154).

36 "Dry coloring"; Leonardo in his so-called Ligny Memorandum of ca. 1499-1500; Bambach 2008, p. 181; Zvereva 2002, p. 19.

37 Discussed in detail in Bambach 2008, pp. 177-181.

38 The inscription is only perceptible when backlit and in part under UV radiation. We are most grateful to Stephan Kemperdick, Bas Dudok van Heel, Peter Schatborn, and Holm Bevers for assistance with the transcription and interpretation.

39 The significance of the price of 2 Gulden, 10 Stuiver remains unclear.

40 Held 1963, especially p. 93.

41 Van Mander (trans. Floerke) 1906, vol. 1, pp. 73-77.

42 Only a very few drawings are considered authentic works by Rogier, including perhaps the silverpoint portrait of a young woman in the British Museum (Inv. 1874,0808.2266).

43 The idea of choosing toned papers for chalk drawings or pastel painting eventually developed into a tradition. One of the oldest reported formulas is that of de Mayerne; it is said to have come from a young Flemish painter named Leonhard, assistant to the painter Clary, a pupil of Van Dyck, and to have been noted on July 31, 1634: "The paper for painting should have some color, in order to deaden the white of the paper, if that is what you use. For this purpose, dissolve soot from the oven in water and pass the paper through it, let it dry, and paint on it. Otherwise take blue or gray paper." (quoted in Berger 1901, p. 347).

44 Carmen C. Bambach on Fouquet's role in the history of pastel painting: "(…) in general, it seems demonstrable that the techniques of mimetic combinations of black chalk with red chalk, especially to render portraits and head studies (though not exclusively), appear to have been first explored by French artists, as early as the mid-1450s, if not before, and Jean Fouquet was among its pioneers." Bambach 2008, p. 177; Nova 2008, passim; Brahms 2016, p. 193.

CAT. 4
Jean Fouquet (?)

THE JESTER GONELLA

ca. 1435/40 (?)
Oak, 36.3 x 25.9 x 0.4 cm, painted surface ca. 34.2 x 23.3 cm
On the reverse, remains of green-black marbling (fig. 131)
The panel was restored in 2017.
Provenance: Inventory of the collection of Archduke Leopold Wilhelm of Austria, No. 343, 1659
Vienna, Kunsthistorisches Museum, Inv. 1840
Selected bibliography: Engerth 1882, p. 395, no. 561 – Gonse 1891, vol. 2, pp. 122ff. – Baldass 1938, no. 720 – Brockwell 1949 – Baldass 1952, p. 61, n. 6, no. 66 – Begeer 1952 – Panofsky 1953, p. 440, n. 4 – Cat. Vienna 1963, no. 265 – Pächt 1974 – Pächt, Kreidl 1981 – Reynaud 1981, pp. 6-8, 90, no. 1 – Lombardi 1983, pp. 45-48, 61ff. – Sterling 1987, pp. 35-41 – Campbell 1990, p. 94 – Ginzburg 1996 – Schaefer 1994, pp. 21-23, 289 – Châtelet 1997 – Evans 1998, pp. 168ff. – Cat. Paris 2003, pp. 94-96, no. 1 (F. Avril) – Thiébaut 2003, pp. 32-34 – Inglis 2011, p. 15, 114

The Vienna panel shows the figure of an old man, squeezed into a tall vertical format as if into a narrow window. Bent forward, his posture appears almost brashly assertive, while his strange, upturned gaze seems to search the viewer: the jester grins impudently, as if he had been watching us for a long time and had caught us off guard, in keeping with his role as the mocker at court. The traditional identification of the figure as a jester is doubtless correct and is manifested in his rustic, ill-groomed appearance, striped clothing, and especially the bell on his collar at the left. His extremely short arms are probably not owed to the depiction but mark him as a dwarf—recalling Velázquez' later jester portraits.
Few paintings can boast an attribution history as varied as this one. In its first known inventory listing, it was described as a work by Giovanni Bellini in the manner of Dürer; in 1882, Engerth cited it as a Venetian work, but noted aptly that it was more reminiscent of van Eyck. Three years later, Gonse claimed to recognize in it the hand of Pieter Bruegel the Elder (ca. 1525–1569). A date of about a hundred years earlier, however, became more

widely accepted, and sometimes this was coupled with an attribution to Jan van Eyck. The case for the latter was first made by Renders in 1947;[1] it was accepted by Brockwell and further developed by Begeer in 1952. Baldass and Panofsky, on the other hand, explicitly rejected it; instead Baldass proposed that the work might have been created by a Flemish painter active in the south of France. Then in 1974, in a major study of the panel that represented a masterpiece of stylistic analysis, Otto Pächt attributed the painting to Jean Fouquet for the first time; since then, his argumentation has been accepted by the majority of scholars.[2] Yet despite Pächt's magisterial analysis, which was further developed by Reynaud in 1981, doubts still remained, and the attribution has been rejected in particular by Albert Châtelet and François Avril.[3]
The name Gonella—which appears not only in the inventory of 1659, but also on a modest painted copy from the 17th century—was associated with three jesters at the 15th-century court of the Este in Ferrara.[4] Pächt therefore surmised that Fouquet had painted the portrait there during his Italian journey. However, the panel is fashioned of oak from the Baltic region, a fact that decisively speaks against an origin in Italy, where poplar was usually employed as a picture support.[5] Skepticism regarding the traditional identification thus seems appropriate; it seems more likely, as Panofsky and Reynaud suggested,[6] that the painting depicts a jester from a court north of the Alps, but found its way to Italy early on and thus came to be identified with one of the famous jesters named Gonella. Yet one might also wonder, along with Baldass, whether the painting should even be considered a true portrait at all, and does not instead exemplify a single-figure genre image like those created by Quinten Massys and his followers.[7] In that case, the painting would embody the type of the shrewd, mocking jester, intended to amuse an aristocratic audience with his ugliness, scruffy beard, and inflamed little eyes.
The question of Fouquet's authorship remains a thorny problem. Pächt identified numerous formal parallels with

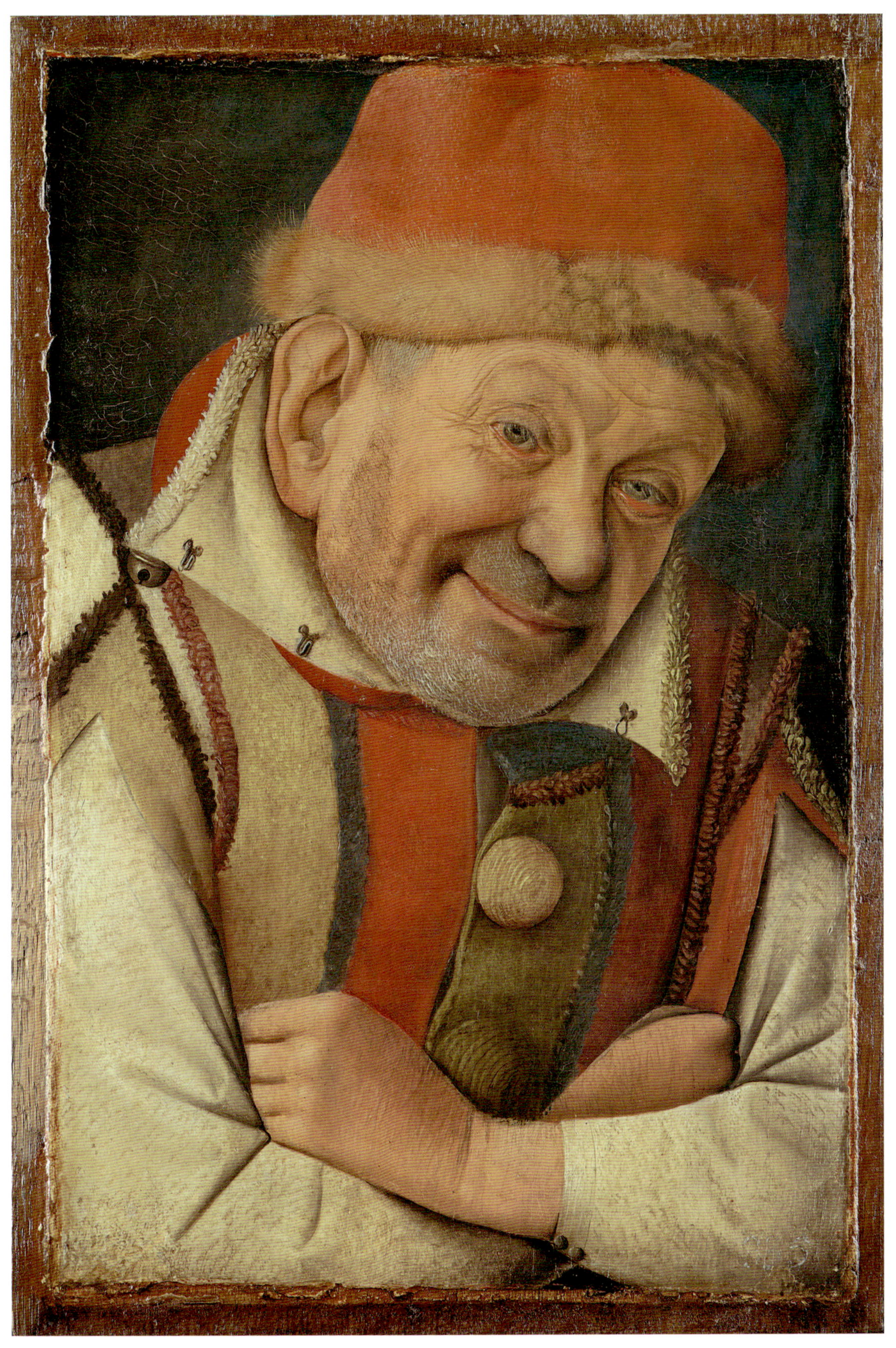

the work of the Touronese painter, beginning with the prominent, bulbous nose that strongly recalls the noses in portraits securely attributed to Fouquet, especially the nose of Charles VII with its black shadow along the edge turned away from the viewer (fig. 11). The ornamental pattern of parallel wrinkles on the jester's forehead also recalls Fouquet's portraits of Chevalier (fig. 41) and Jouvenel des Ursins (fig. 132); the pattern of forehead wrinkles in the latter, especially, is very similar indeed. Pächt also cleverly compares the wrinkled, grinning character with the face of an onlooker in the foreground of Fouquet's *Lit de justice*,[8] and finds echoes of the star-shaped folds of the sleeves in many of Fouquet's miniatures. He further sees a parallel approach to color in the rendering of distinct chromatic areas in details such as the podium with the pillow and book in the portrait of Jouvenel des Ursins (fig. 123). Finally, Pächt identifies precedents for

Fig. 131. Reverse of Cat. 4

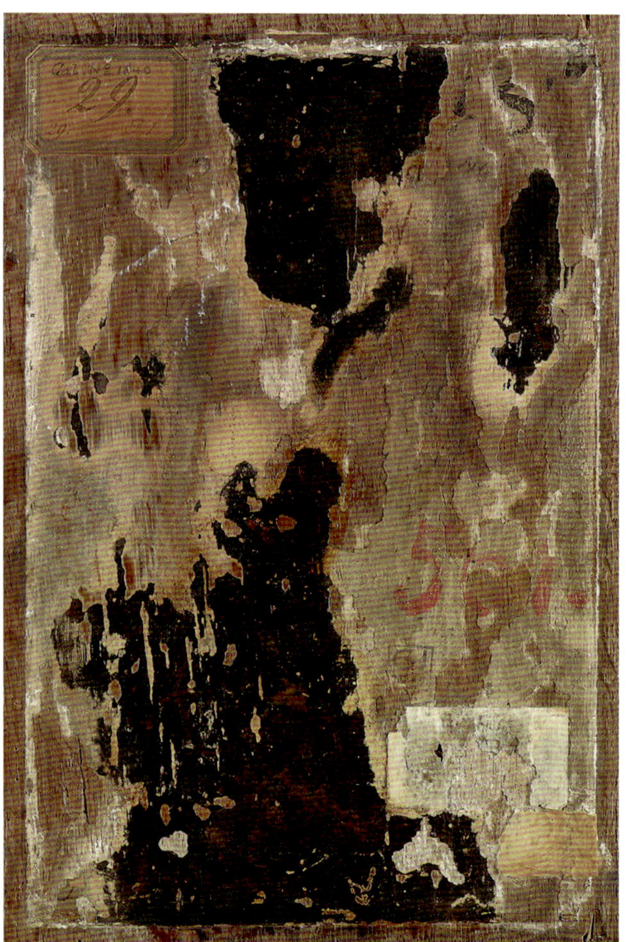

the unusual pose with crossed arms and the motif of a figure leaning out of a narrow window in other works by Fouquet.[9]

Yet at the same time, the detailed—though not Eyckian—rendering of the face differs from the heads in the panels securely attributed to Fouquet. The tiny strokes of the beard would hardly be conceivable in his other pictures, not only because of fashion, and in their execution the stubble seems quite unusual for the 15th century. The shapeless hands of *Gonella*, which are not entirely reconcilable with an artist of Fouquet's stature, were attributed by Pächt to overpainting, yet they appear even more shapeless in the underdrawing on the panel. The underdrawing as a whole is surprising:[10] executed with various tools, it shows a vast number of tiny check marks drawn with a fine pen indicating forms and shades on the side of the face turned away from the viewer; the ear, too, is underdrawn in a detailed, but not very skillful manner. Squiggled lines at the edge of the collar to the right could indicate either a zone of shadow or an intended fur lining. The jacket is otherwise rendered primarily in broad strokes, with quick slashes of the brush indicating the folds of the sleeves. No comparable underdrawings appear on the panels securely attributed to Fouquet: at most, the fold lines drawn rapidly with the brush and the loose, parallel hatch marks applied here and there, for example on the Berlin donor panel (fig. 96), could be compared with a few areas of the *Gonella*. At the same time, it is important to remember that the paintings securely attributed to Fouquet were underdrawn using cartoons on a scale of 1:1, which was clearly not the case with the Vienna panel; this does not rule out that the same artist could have used differing procedures. On the other hand, the dense hatching with fine strokes of the pen seems a unique instance in a painting of the mid-15th century, and nothing comparable appears even among drawings on paper; the closest correspondence might be found in certain drawings made around 1500 by followers of Hugo van der Goes.[11]

The color notations in French in the underdrawing of the Vienna panel—"rouge" is clearly legible beneath the red stripe in the middle, while "blanc" appears beneath the right sleeve and is abbreviated "b" in the collar and on the shoulder—bear witness to a Francophone painter.[12] Such an artist, however, could just as well have come from the

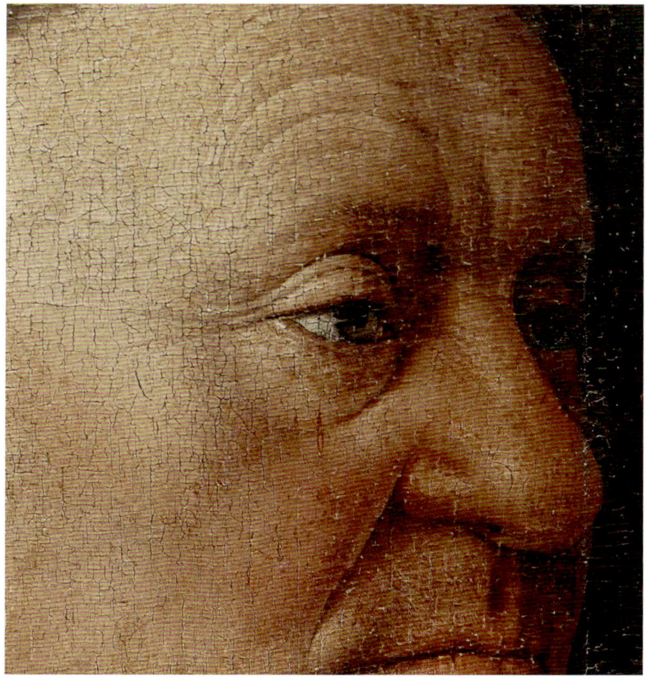 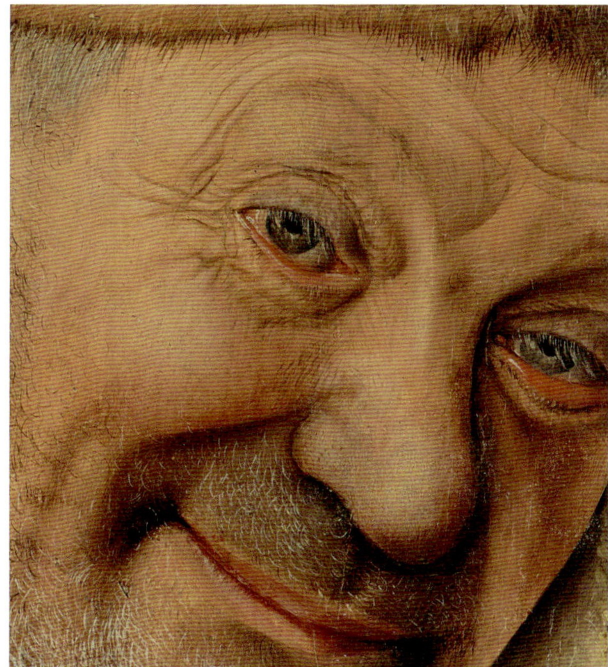

Fig. 132. Forehead of Guillaume Jouvenel (fig. 123) - Gonella

southern Netherlands—Tournai, Valenciennes, Liège, etc.—as from the heartland of the crown. Even apart from the question of language, however, the use of Baltic oak wood makes it unlikely that the panel originated in the Loire region around Tours, since the panels securely attributed to Fouquet are fashioned of local oak, cut in France. The wood speaks rather for an origin in the Netherlands, where Baltic oak was the standard material for painted panels.

As a work by Fouquet, the *Gonella* could only be a very early piece, whose obviously Netherlandish character left its mark in the history of the scholarship on the painting in the form of attributions to Bruegel and van Eyck. Analysis of the wood indicates that Fouquet would have to have executed the painting in the North, i.e., during his presumed stay in the Netherlands. The date suggested by dendrochronology – at or around the mid-1430s – would accord well with this supposition.[13] Yet the painterly execution, which is not very reminiscent of Fouquet, and the entirely different style of underdrawing suggest that the piece could have been painted by another French-speaking artist in the southern Netherlands. It is also not inconceivable that the work was made significantly later than the mid-15th century, even as late as the 16th century.

Perhaps the unprecedented opportunity to view the Vienna panel alongside works securely attributed to Jean Fouquet in this exhibition will shed further light on the question of its authorship.

Stephan Kemperdick

1 In the Brussels journal *Le Soir* of July 10, 1947, cited in Baldass 1952, p. 61, n. 6.
2 Sterling 1987, Schaefer 1994, Reynaud 1981, Campbell 1990, Ginzburg 1996, Thiébaut 2003, Evans 1998, Inglis 2011.
3 Châtelet 1997, who also convincingly refutes the attempt by Ginzburg 1996 to identify Fouquet with a Frenchman mentioned in Ferrara in 1441, apparently an artilleryman. Avril in Cat. Paris 2003, p. 96.
4 Begeer 1952, pp. 129-131, 135ff.; the copy is lost.
5 See the essay by Klein in this volume.
6 Panofsky 1953, p. 440, n. 4; Reynaud 1981, p. 8; Evans 1998, p. 169, suggests that Fouquet himself took the picture with him to Italy.
7 Cf. Cat. Rotterdam 2015, fig. 87-89, 92, 155, 157, 158.
8 Pächt 1974, p. 55, fig. 48. The *Lit de justice* was added to the beginning of the Munich *Boccaccio*; see Cat. Paris 2003, no. 32, fig. p. 273.
9 Pächt 1974. The latter motif appears in almost exactly the same form in the work of Fouquet's pupil Jean Colombe; ibid., fig. 35, 36.
10 Investigated in 2017 by the Kunsthistorisches Museum; the KHM intends to publish the results in the context of a planned exhibition focusing on the *Gonella*.
11 For example the St. Luke by a southern Netherlandish artist, ca. 1500, now in the Kupferstichkabinett in Berlin, KdZ 2405, Buck 2001, p. 253.
12 Pächt, Kreidl 1981.
13 See the essay by Klein in the present volume.

CAT. 5
French, after Jean Fouquet

PORTRAIT OF AGNES SOREL

2nd quarter of the 16th century
Red, gray, and black chalk on paper, 26.8 x 19.6 cm
Provenance: Collection of Catherine de Medici
Florence, Galleria degli Uffizi, Gabinetto Disegni e Stampe,
Inv. No. 3925 F.
Bibliography: Cat. Paris 2003, no. 14, pp. 150-152 (François
Avril); Moreau-Néalton 1910, p. 33

The portrait drawing is striking for its clear contours, with very few interior details and little to no modeling in the face. Only the most delicate shading appears on the temples and throat as well as in the chin and cheek areas, imbuing the half-profile face with a noble bearing that is further intensified by a few colored accents on the eyes, mouth, and ear. In addition to the portrait drawing in Florence, two others also exist which are nearly identical to the one presented here, even in their dimensions, but which to some extent are significantly inferior in execution. These versions reveal the identity of the portrait subject, since each includes an inscription designating the lady as "La belle Agnés".[1] The facial features immortalized in the drawings do in fact correspond to Jean Fouquet's *Virgin* from the *Melun Diptych* and show the same heart-shaped face, high forehead, slender, slightly curving nose, small mouth, and delicate chin. The fashionable accessory of the ribbon across the forehead, emerging from beneath the bonnet, likewise appears on both the Melun *Virgin* and the tomb figure of Agnès Sorel (fig. 58). Since this same ribbon is misunderstood in the Paris drawing and is represented as a kind of pearl-studded diadem, we may assume that only the drawing in Florence is a direct copy of the lost portrait study by Jean Fouquet. The latter, in turn, was probably a preliminary study for a now-lost panel painting, like Fouquet's surviving study for the portrait of Guillaume Jouvenel (cat. 3). Both in the latter and in the drawing of Agnès Sorel, the heads are depicted nearly life size in a closely cropped composition, on pages of almost exactly the same size. In addition, both drawings have colored accents in red that give the portraits a more lifelike appearance. The most striking feature in all three drawings of Agnés Sorel, however, is the emphasis on line. Thus it seems likely that Fouquet's original drawing was likewise conceived in linear form, probably in order to serve as a cartoon for a painting. Fouquet did in fact use cartoons, as proven by the infrared images of the *Melun Diptych* (figs. 96 and 97), which reveal pounce marks for the figure of the donor Étienne Chevalier, as well as one of the angels.

As a collector, Catherine de Medici embraced the long-standing tradition of portrait galleries. She not only furnished her palace in Paris with a gallery of French kings beginning with Francis I, but also collected portrait drawings of personalities from the latter's courtly milieu, works created for the most part by François Clouet. The drawing now in Florence and a few others constitute exceptions to this rule, and prove that Catherine was also interested in including personalities from earlier generations, such as the mistress of King Charles VII.

Katrin Dyballa

---

1   Cf. Cat. Paris 2003, no. 15, pp. 151-153 (François Avril); Aix-en-Provence, Bibliothèque Méjanes, ms. 442, pl. XXVIII, and BnF, Département des Estampes, Rés. Na 21, f. 28.

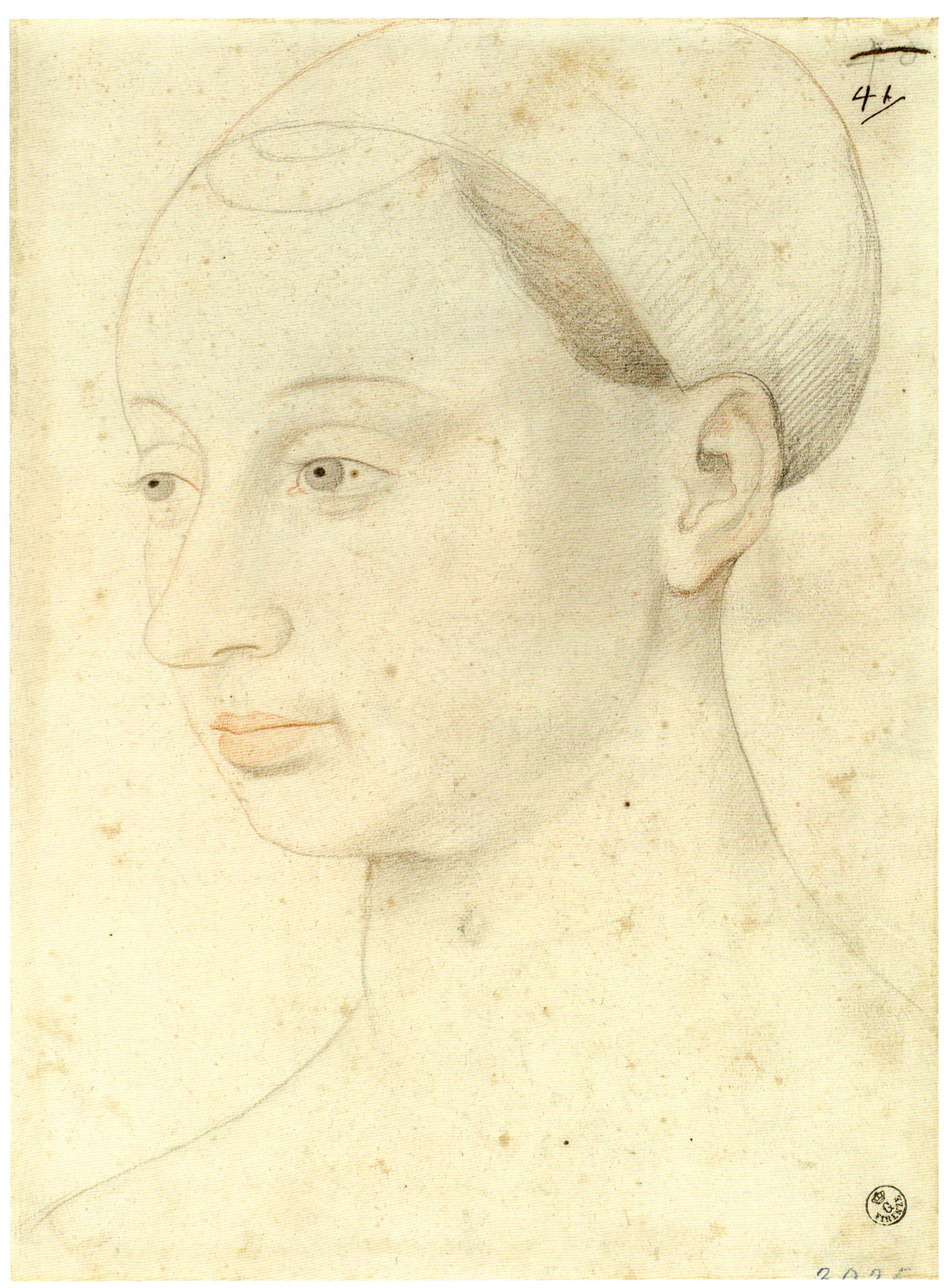

CAT. 6
Jan van Eyck

PORTRAIT OF A MAN WITH RED CHAPERON

ca. 1438/40
Oak, 30 x 21.7 cm, thickness 1.1 cm; on the reverse, remains
of red bole and wax seal of Ranuccio Farnese
Painted surface 28.8 x 20.6 cm
Provenance: Collection of Ranuccio Farnese (1569–1622), Parma; Palazzo del Giardino di Parma, 1680; Galleria del Duca di
Parma, 1708; Collection of the Earl of Shrewsbury, 1857; acquired for the museum at the auction of the Nieuwenhuys Collection at Christie's, 1886
Gemäldegalerie, Staatliche Museen zu Berlin, Cat. No. 523 A
Selected bibliography: von Tschudi 1887, pp. 172-174; Panofksy
1953, vol. 1, p. 172; Dhanens 1980, pp. 333-336; Campbell
1988, pp. 192-193, 198, 207; Thiébaut 2003, p. 33; Wedekind
2007, p. 235

When this painting was acquired for the Gemäldegalerie
in 1886, the museum was clearly proud to add another
Jan van Eyck to what was already the most extensive collection of Flemish works for its time. The description of
the portrait subject penned by Hugo von Tschudi, however, was less than flattering: "But what is most memorable
of all is the expressive ugliness of the features. An oblong,
completely beardless countenance […] is dominated by a
nose, not ignoble in form but of extravagant length, that
descends from the flat forehead […] down to the broad
cartilaginous point […]. At first glance his small eyes
seem to convey an expression of impish weakness; upon
closer examination, however, the finer features of a reserved, shrewd, and coolly calculating character are unmistakable."[1]
At the time of the panel's acquisition, the portrait subject
was already identified with the same gentleman depicted
in van Eyck's double portrait of 1434 in London, identified with the merchant Giovanni Arnolfini of Lucca. This
identification, however, is by no means secure, and is in

fact unlikely.[2] Jan van Eyck's authorship, on the other
hand, is beyond doubt, and the old, Italian attribution of
the work to Albrecht Dürer had already been rejected in
the 19th century. In contrast to his negative characterization of the portrait subject, Hugo von Tschudi had nothing but effusive praise for the painterly art of Jan van
Eyck: "a shimmering enchantment of light and color has
been poured out […] upon the drawing".[3] From the beginning, the paintings of Jan van Eyck had inspired fascination with their glowing flesh tones and evocation of
light and shadow as well as their veristic materiality and
sensitive tactility of surfaces and colors. Van Eyck used
light and shadow in a subtle manner, not only to model
forms, but above all to lend his pictures atmospheric expression.[4] Accordingly, as Erwin Panofsky aptly observed,
his portraits show a peculiarity that also characterizes the
Berlin panel: the half of the subject's face turned toward
the viewer is partially veiled in shade, while the averted
side is illuminated by a source of light[5]—exactly the opposite of what is seen in portraits by the Master of Flémalle, Rogier van der Weyden, and Jean Fouquet (cat. 1,
6). As an innovator in the art of painting, Jan van Eyck's
fame spread all the way to Italy, even in his own lifetime.
Filarete described him as a masterful painter; yet he also
mentioned the Frenchman, Fouquet, noting that he was
highly experienced in the representation of nature. In this
case, Filarete's claim was based on first-hand evidence,
since he encountered Fouquet in Rome.

Katrin Dyballa

1   Von Tschudi 1887, pp. 172-73.
2   Campbell 1998, pp. 192-93, 198; Wedekind 2007, p. 235.
3   Von Tschudi 1887, p. 173.
4   Friedländer 1924, vol. 1, p. 137.
5   Panofksy 1953, vol. 1, p. 172; cf. also Thiébaut 2003, p. 33.

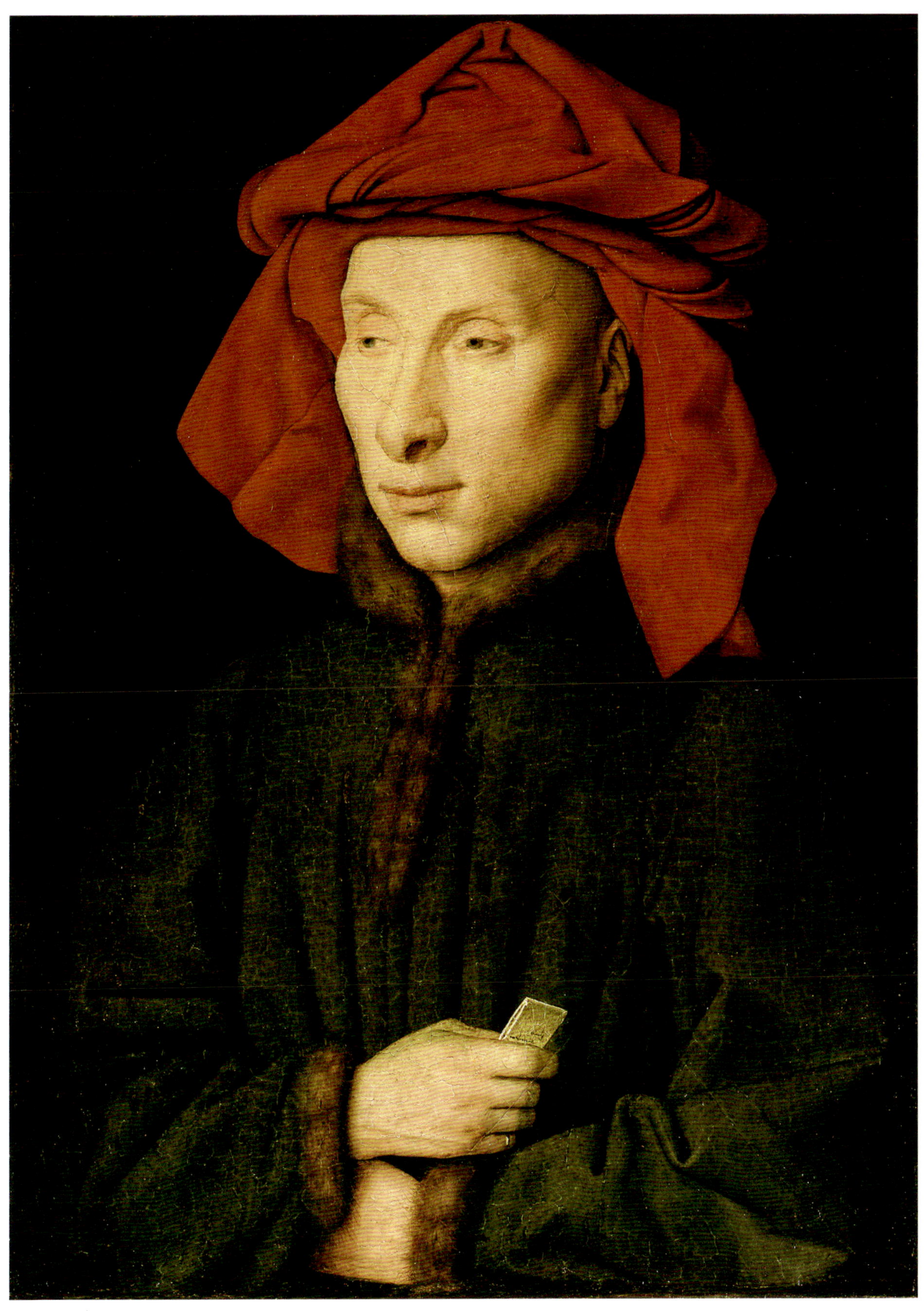

CAT. 7

Group of Master of Flémalle / Rogier van der Weyden (?)

PORTRAIT OF A STOUT MAN

ca. 1435/40

Oak with remains of integrated frame, 30.3 x 18.7 cm, thickness 0.7 cm

Painted surface 29.3 x 17.8 cm

The panel was restored in 1901.

Gemäldegalerie, Staatliche Museen zu Berlin, Cat. No. 537A

Provenance: Private collection, England; acquired for the KFMV from P. & D. Colnaghi & Co. at Christie's, London, 1901

Selected bibliography: Friedländer 1902, pp. 17-19 – Friedländer 1924, vol. 2, p. 111, no. 61 – Friedländer 1931, pp. 353-55 – Friedländer 1933, p. 12 – de Tolnay 1939, p. 60, no. 10 – Panofsky 1953, p. 426 n. 8 – Frinta 1966, p. 55 – Campbell 1996, p. 126 – Cat. Frankfurt/ Berlin 2008/09, no. 16 (Stephan Kemperdick)

The striking portrait of a middle-aged man stands out against an unusually light ground. The closely cropped view shows him turning slightly toward the left; gazing into the distance; he looks past the viewer with a concentrated expression. The dark-haired man is distinguished by his short haircut, prominent nose, and wide-eyed gaze, but above all by his protruding lower lip and fleshy chin. The painting was acquired on the English art market in 1901. Up to that point, it had been considered a "Portrait of Van Eyck by Van Eyck" in keeping with the inscription on the back of the panel. Max J. Friedländer, however, who published it the following year, corrected this identification and suggested that it was an anonymous portrait by the "Master of Flémalle".[1] Later, he came to view it as a work by Rogier van der Weyden,[2] but the attribution to the Master of Flémalle (or Robert Campin), continued to prevail for the most part—some even claimed the picture was a copy of a work by the Flémalle Master.[3] The discussion of the picture's attribution gained momentum in 1957 when a twin showed up in a private collection, a work that is now in the Thyssen-Bornemisza collection in Madrid. When the two paintings were compared, for the most part the newly-discovered one was given preference

and considered the original. In the end, however, it was proven that exactly the opposite was true: the Madrid picture was copied from the Berlin one.[4] But who painted it? The answer remains unclear, but features such as the portrait's similarity to the figure of Nicodemus from Rogier's *Descent from the Cross* from before 1443 may mark it as an early work by that artist.[5] The painter of the Berlin portrait shows a gift for precise observation, which is skillfully employed in this picture. The shadow of the beard has a realistic appearance, the skin seems to breathe, and the right half of the picture is carefully shaded with individually accentuated hairs. The depiction of the fur and wool of the garment likewise displays a subtle rendering of texture.

On closer observation, however, an inconsistency also becomes apparent: the right eye in the shaded half of the face is not accurately foreshortened. This phenomenon also occurs in other portraits by Rogier: it is especially visible, for example, in the portrait of a young woman (fig. 5), where the subject's eyes are in fact positioned frontally with respect to the viewer. Fouquet adopts a similar approach in his *Portrait of Étienne Chevalier*: here, as in the *Stout Man*, the side of the face turned away from the viewer is heavily shaded and the receding half of the face is foreshortened, but not the eye: only the darker values suggest optical foreshortening. This high-contrast approach to light, which generally suppresses subtle reflections and heightening in favor of a stronger chiaroscuro and plasticity, is common to both portraits.

Katrin Dyballa

1   Friedländer 1902, pp. 17-19. .

2   Friedländer 1924, vol. 2, p. 111, no. 61; idem 1933, p. 12.

3   De Tolnay 1939, p. 60, no. 10; Panofsky 1953, vol. 1, p. 426 n. 8.

4   Frinta 1966, p. 55, made reference to the pentimento visible in the IRR, but still viewed the Madrid picture as the original one; Campbell 1996, p. 126; Cat. Frankfurt, Berlin 2008/09 (Kemperdick), no. 16, p. 268.

5   Cf. Friedländer 1931, pp. 353-55; Cat. Frankfurt, Berlin 2008/09, p. 268 (Stephan Kemperdick).

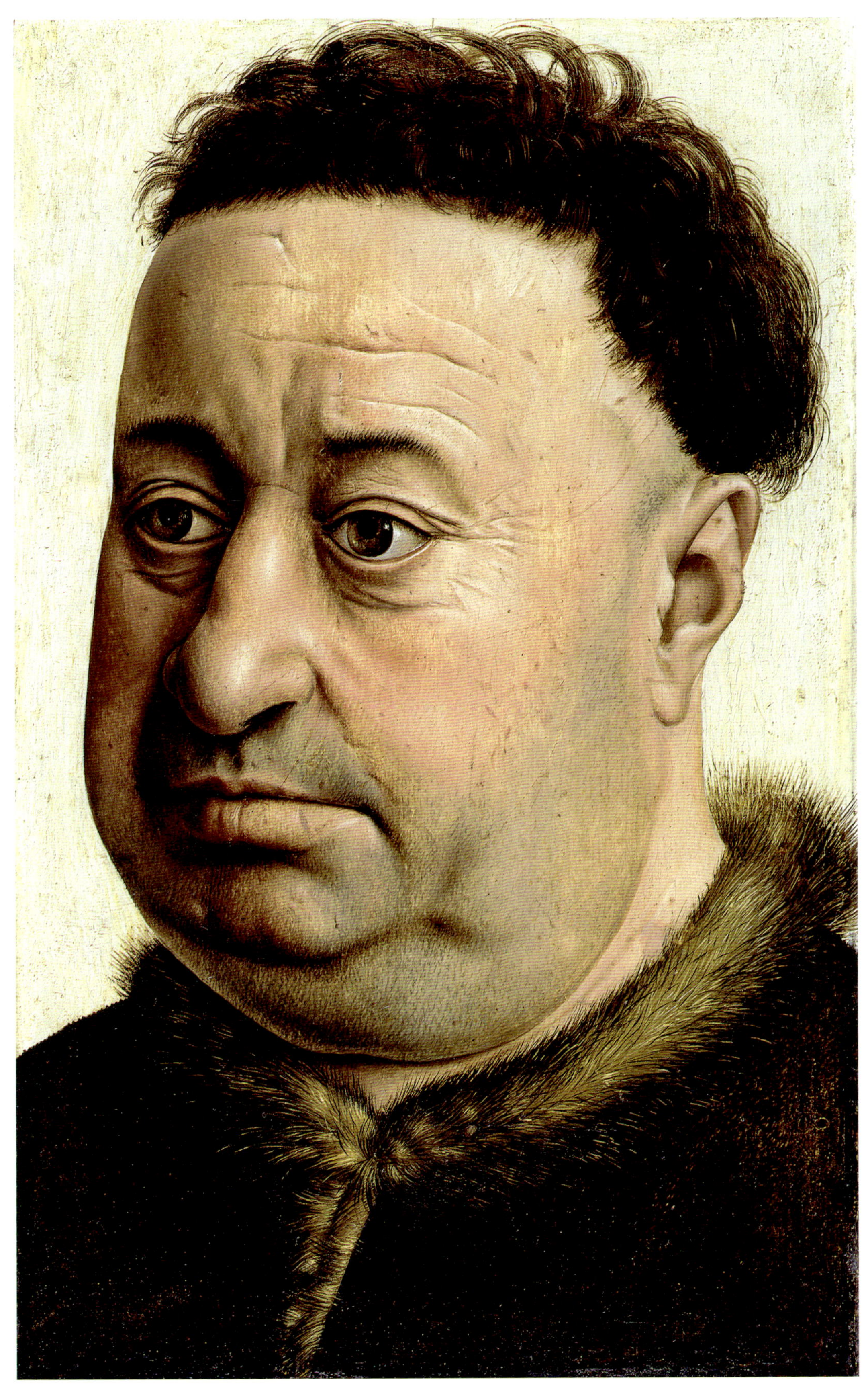

CAT. 8
Petrus Christus

PORTRAIT OF A YOUNG WOMAN

ca. 1470
Oak, 29 x 22.5 cm
Acquired with the Solly Collection, 1821
Gemäldegalerie, Staatliche Museen zu Berlin, Cat. No. 532
Selected bibliography: Waagen 1824 – Passavant 1833, p. 424
– Bode 1887, p. 217 – Weale 1909, p. 101 – Friedländer 1924,
p. 95 – Panofsky 1953, p. 313 – Upton 1990 – Cat. New York
1994, no. 19 – Cat. Berlin 2010, p. 124

In front of a grayish wall with wooden wainscoting, a young woman – or rather, a girl – clothed in a sumptuous blue velvet dress with a fur-trimmed neckline gazes solemnly at the viewer. Her throat is adorned with a three-tiered necklace, covered by a nearly transparent veil whose edges appear along the contours of her bare shoulders. Her face, subtly illuminated from the left, is framed by the black band of her tall bonnet as it passes beneath her chin; a dark velvet ribbon lies on her high forehead over her tightly pulled-back, dark blond hair.

The refined play of light on the young woman's white skin, her severe appearance—almost jewel-like against the dark wainscoting with her rich jewelry and the intense color of her luxurious dress—and the distance and reserve with which she directs her slightly angled gaze toward the viewer lend this portrait an enigmatic, yet noble effect.

In keeping with Netherlandish tradition, the painter uses a closely cropped composition and a small format to establish a direct connection between the portrait subject and the viewer. This proximity is intensified by the suggestion of the secular interior space within which the young lady is seated. The painter emphasizes the material quality of her clothing and the sumptuous details of her jewelry with meticulous precision; the dark colors serve to focus our attention on the girl's unusual physiognomy, which is stylized in accord with the ideals of beauty of that time.

Today, we can only speculate as to the portrait subject's identity: when Waagen described the picture shortly after its purchase, it apparently possessed a frame signed by "Petrus Christophori" with an inscription identifying the girl as a "niece of the famous Talbot" (probably John Talbot, 1st Earl of Shrewsbury, commander of the English in the Hundred Years' War).[1] It has been suggested that it might instead represent one of the latter's granddaughters, who could have visited Bruges in 1468 for the wedding of Charles the Bold to his third wife Margaret of York.[2] The combination of finery emphasizing the young girl's rank and the emphasis on her youthful beauty could indicate that the portrait was made for purposes of courtship and marriage. The stylized features of the young woman, her high forehead, and her flawless white complexion reflect late medieval ideals of feminine beauty to which Fouquet's Melun *Virgin*, created about 15 years earlier, is also indebted.

Christine Seidel

---

1   Maryan W. Ainsworth in Cat. New York 1994, pp. 166ff., with reference to Waagen 1824 (for the first mention of the signed frame) and Waagen 1862, vol. 1, p. 94.
2   The two girls' aunt, Margaret Talbot, was present at the wedding in Bruges; Upton 1990, pp. 29ff.; Cat. New York 1994, p. 168.

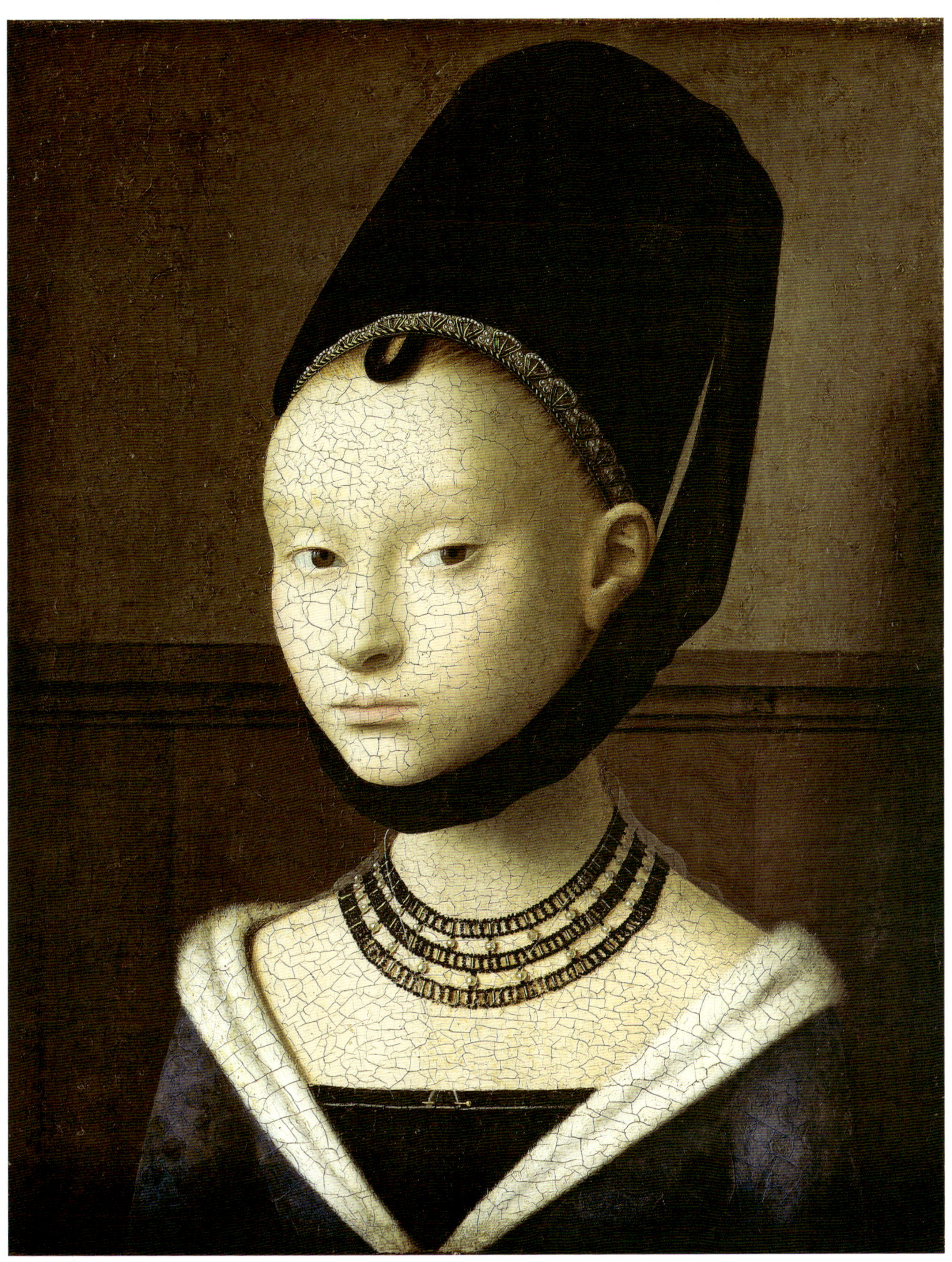

CAT. 9
Barthélemy d'Eyck (attributed)

PAGE FROM THE SO-CALLED *COCKERELL CHRONICLE*

ca. 1440

Pen in brown and black, coloring applied with brush in red, pink, brown, gray, and green over a preliminary drawing in black, on vellum, 30.8 x 19.6 cm

Inscriptions: Pindarus poeta; fuit ho tempore. Artaxerses; fuit anno iijm°CCCCIXXXXViij (3498). Corgias, fuit ho tempore.- Socrates philosophus; fuit ho tempore. Esdras qui legem reparavit; fuit ho tempore. Empledocles philosophus; fuit ho tempore.- Zenon philosophus; fuit ... (illegible). Nermias;...(illegible). Genutius vecturius/ Julius manilius. Sul/ pitius. Sextius. Cura/tius. Appius claudius.

Provenance: acquired on the London art market, 1960

Kupferstichkabinett, Staatliche Museen zu Berlin, KdZ 24599

Bibliography: Cat. Berlin 1973, no. 27 – Schulze Altcappenberg 1995, no. A.13 – Elen 1995, no. 20 – Evans 1998, p. 169 – Cat. Madrid 2001, no. 53 (Dominique Thiébaut) – Cat. Angers 2009, no. 18 (Nicole Reynaud; with older bibliography)

Eight *Uomini famosi*, or great personages of antiquity, are depicted in three registers. At the top are the Greek poet Pindar, the Persian king Artaxerxes, and the Greek philosopher Gorgias; beneath them are Socrates and the Old Testament priest Ezra, as well as Empedocles, a Greek philosopher like Zeno of Elea, who appears in the lower register to the left; finally, to the right is Nehemiah, who rebuilt the walls of Jerusalem after the Babylonian exile. All are historical figures from the fifth century before Christ. This page, along with eight others, was part of a series which (apart from the Berlin piece) had belonged to the collection of Sir Sidney Cockerell since 1919 and was auctioned off in 1958.[1] Originally, the pages were part of a chronicle in book form—the so-called *Cockerell Chronicle*[2]—which narrated the history of the world from its beginnings to the time of the book's creation. Its imagery is ultimately derived from a fresco cycle of *Uomini famosi*, painted in the Casa Orsini in Rome by Masolino and completed in 1432. The *Cockerell Chronicle* follows this cycle only indirectly, however, for it was copied from another manuscript, the *Crespi Chronicle* illuminated by Leonardo da Besozzo,[3] a Lombard painter who had apparently made drawings directly from Masolino's fresco cycle in the late 1430s. The *Crespi Chronicle* originated in the milieu of King René d'Anjou in Naples, as evidenced by the inclusion of Charles I of Anjou in the illustrious circle of figures represented. It served to legitimate the ruler by establishing the house of Anjou as a climax and apogee of world history. A similar function may also be assumed for the *Cockerell Chronicle*.

The pages of the *Cockerell Chronicle* are striking for the extraordinary quality of their delicate brush drawings, which clearly surpass those of the *Crespi Chronicle*. The faces are expressive and highly varied, modeled in tiny brushstrokes; along with some of the details of clothing, they point to an artist from the North. Today, the attribution to Barthélemy d'Eyck,[4] who is known to have later worked for René d'Anjou, is widely accepted; it has never been proven, however, and so it is worth remembering that the Cockerell pages also show an affinity to Jean Fouquet. Ever since Ilaria Toesca first attributed the drawings to him in 1952, Fouquet has been considered as a possible candidate for their creator, most recently by Mark Evans in 1998. Fedja Anzelewsky conceded that there is "a similarity of type between Fouquet's heads and those of the Cockerell pages." If the theory of Fouquet's authorship of the *Cockerell Chronicle* is at all tenable, the manuscript could only represent an early work from the 1440s. Particular types and postures still appear in similar form in the miniatures of the *Hours of Étienne Chevalier*; nonetheless, there is no substantive proof either for or against Fouquet's authorship.

Dagmar Korbacher

1   Amsterdam, Rijksmuseum; New York, Metropolitan Museum; Washington, National Gallery; Ottawa, National Gallery of Canada; London, Koerner Collection; The Netherlands, private collection; Zurich, Buchholz Collection; Melbourne, National Gallery of Victoria.

2   Dismantled at an unknown point in time, probably before its addition to the Cockerell collection.

3   Crespi Collection, Milan.

4   Reynaud 1989, pp. 25-32.

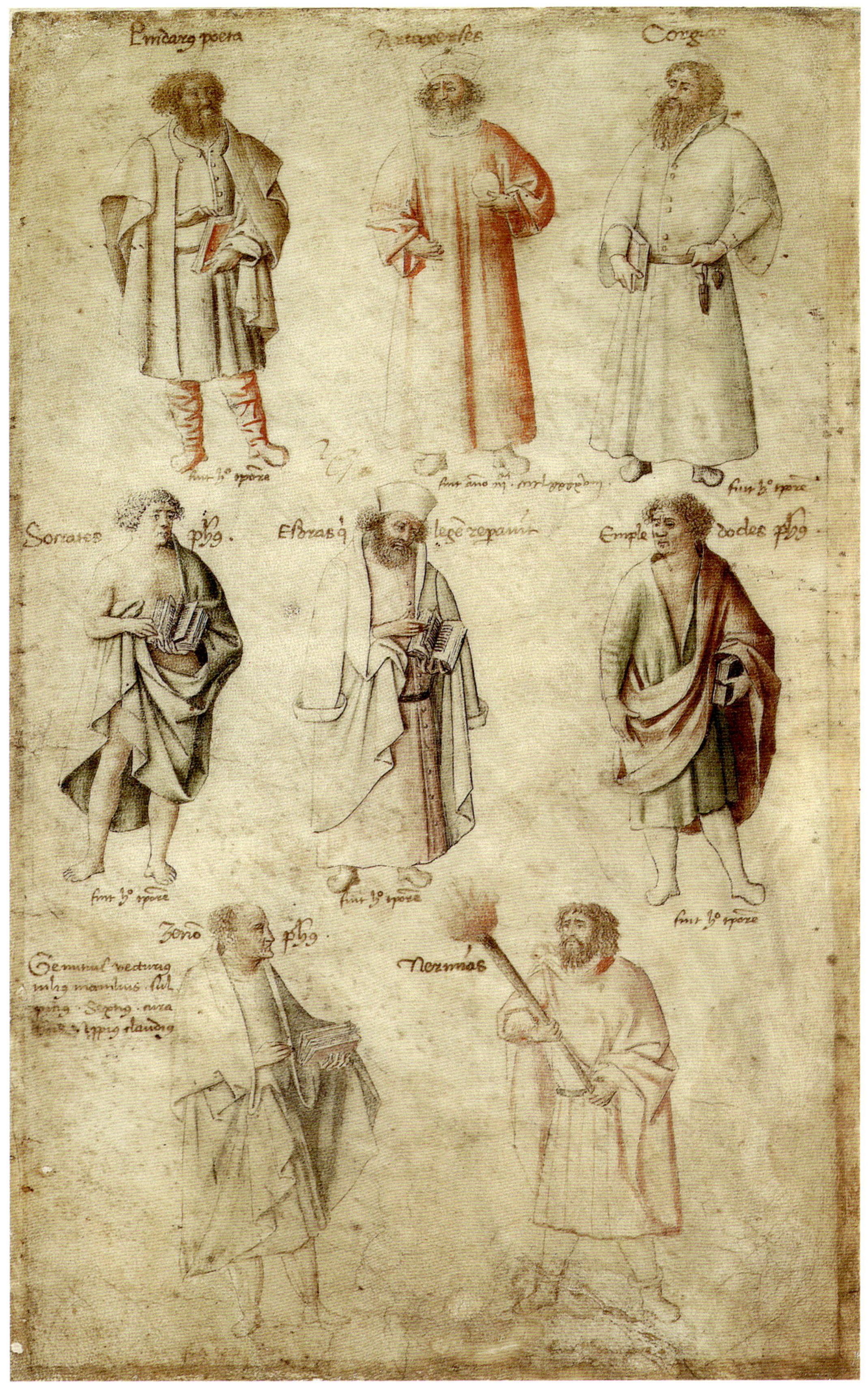
Pindarus poeta
Artaxerses
Gorgias
Sorates phs
Esdras q lege reparauit
Empedocles phs
Zeno phs
Nerinas

ST. LAWRENCE, WOMAN HOLDING A CHILD, AND TWO PUTTI (AFTER FRA ANGELICO)

ca. 1450

Verso: a wild boar (pen and brush in grayish brown over a preliminary drawing in black chalk)

Pen and brush in brown over a preliminary drawing in black chalk, 22.8 x 16.9 cm (large damaged area in lower right, borders added)

Provenance: Collection of Adolf von Beckerath, acquired 1902 Kupferstichkabinett, Staatliche Museen zu Berlin, KdZ 5578 recto

Bibliography: Schulze Altcappenberg 1995, no. 63r (with bibliography) – Cat. Montefalco 2002, no. 16, p. 194 (Patrizia Di Benedetti) – Sricchia Santoro 2003, p. 61 – Cat. Rom 2009, no. 40 (Lorenza Melli)

This page, which depicts various individual figures unconnected to each other, probably came from a pattern book belonging to the Florentine artist Benozzo Gozzoli.[1] The book comprised a group of drawings that could be used by the master himself, as well as by other members of his workshop, as artistic and iconographic prototypes for their own works. In this drawing, Gozzoli focuses on two figures from Fra Angelico's fresco of St. Lawrence distributing alms in the Cappella Niccolina of the Vatican, painted around 1447-1449, and renders them individually without reference to the original pictorial composition: he shows the saint himself, distributing alms from a purse, as well as a woman holding a child who also appears in the scene. The drawing was probably not made directly from the fresco, but rather from another drawing of these same figures, executed in the workshop of Fra Angelico (perhaps even by the artist himself) and now in Windsor

Castle.[2] Gozzoli himself was a member of this workshop and assisted Fra Angelico in the decoration of the Cappella Niccolina. Particularly interesting in the present context are the putti holding garlands in the upper third of the page, probably derived from an antique model. Although they do not appear in this form in the fresco decoration of the Cappella Niccolina, as Lorenza Melli has shown they nonetheless belong to the decorative repertoire used by Fra Angelico's workshop for this purpose: they are closely related to the garlands of fruits and flowers alternating with putti heads that subdivide the individual registers of the fresco cycle, and may represent an alternative design that was not executed. Like Benozzo Gozzoli, Jean Fouquet could also have had opportunity to study designs or pattern book drawings of this type in the circle of Fra Angelico. The Frenchman employed the same putti with garlands almost verbatim in the *Hours of Étienne Chevalier*: in the scene showing St. Stephen presenting his protégé to the Madonna (fig. 43), they appear at the top of a wall. Here, in keeping with the religious context, they are transformed into angels and supplied with wings, and hold not only garlands of leaves and fruit but also shields with the patron's coat of arms.

Dagmar Korbacher

---

1   Perhaps the pattern book now in Rotterdam; cf. Elen 1995, cat. no. 23, pp. 222-225. Although Elen does not mention the Berlin drawing, it is possible that it belonged to this book, particularly since it shows the same technique and dimensions as several other of the book's pages.

2   Cf. Cat. Rome 2009, no. 40, p. 244 (Lorenza Melli): Windsor, Royal Collection, Inv. 12812v.

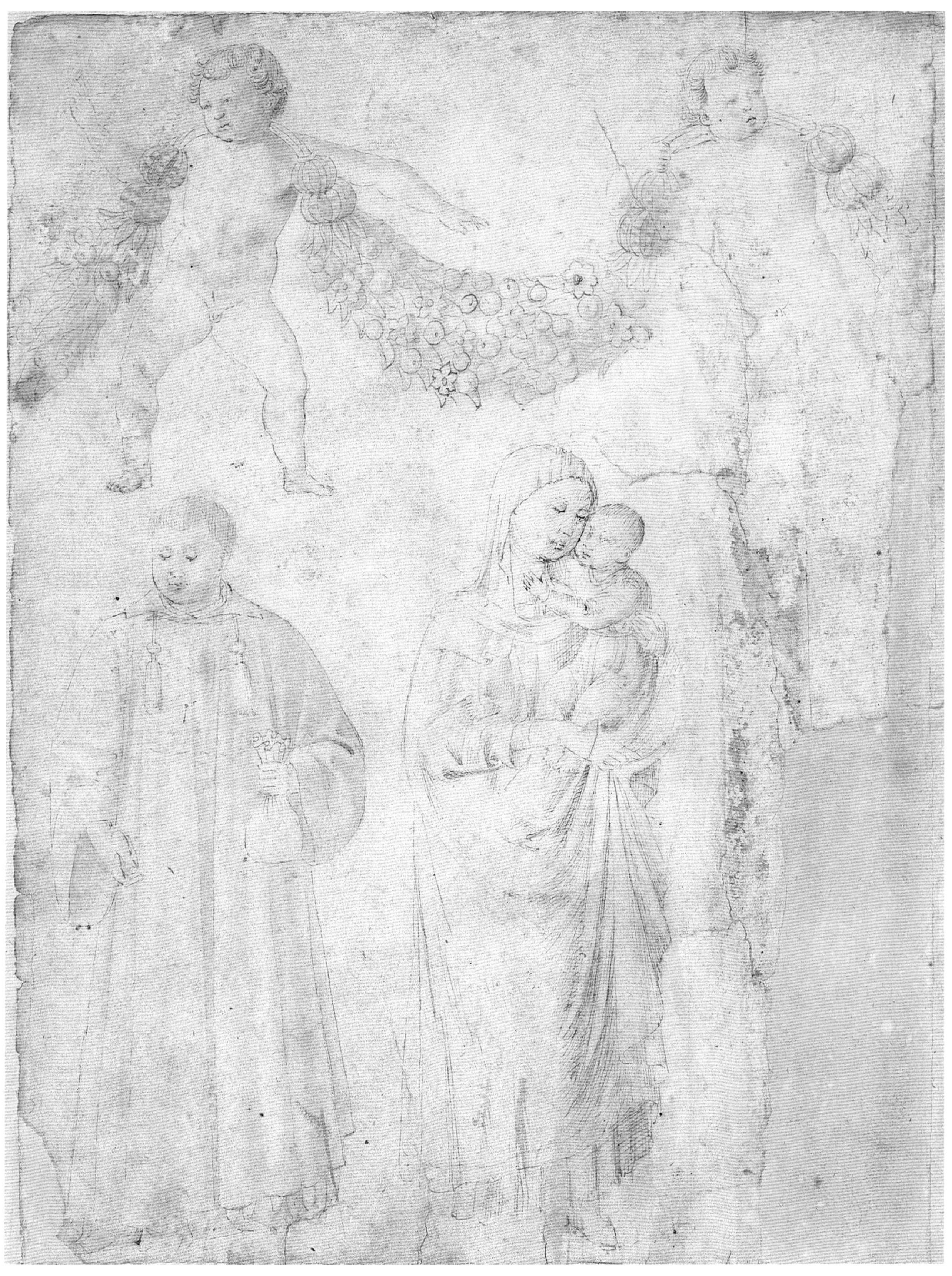

CAT. 11

School of Benozzo Gozzoli (Master Esiguo?)

STUDY OF A MONK KNEELING IN PRAYER
(AFTER PERUGINO), WITH REPEATED HEAD
AND PRAYING WOMAN

After 1495/1496
Pen and brush in brown with white heightening applied with brush, over preliminary drawing in black chalk, paper probably brown-toned on one side, 20.4 x 25.8 cm
Provenance: old collection, acquired before 1879
Kupferstichkabinett, Staatliche Museen zu Berlin, KdZ 4199
Bibliography: Schulze Altcappenberg 1995, cat. no. 88, p. 226 (with older bibliography) – Sricchia Santoro 2003, p. 55

In this drawing, a late 15th-century artist, probably a pupil of Benozzo Gozzoli, depicted two separate kneeling figures with folded hands, deep in prayer. While the female figure to the right is a less developed study after an unknown model (and was not necessarily drawn by the same hand as the other figure on the page), the monk on the left, depicted on a much larger scale, is derived from the crucifixion fresco by Perugino in the church of Santa Maria Maddalena dei Pazzi in Florence, painted around 1494-1496. At the left edge of the fresco, which is subdivided into arch-shaped sections, St. Bernard kneels in adoration, contemplating the crucified Christ. The creator of the drawing seems to have been especially fascinated by the head of the saint, shown from below at a steep angle, and repeated the motif in enlarged form to the right of the full figure. In this way, he could more precisely study the reflections of light on the left half of the face and more clearly model the

distinctive head using brushstrokes of varying length. In the fresco, the view from below corresponds to the real observer's vantage point, since the painting is somewhat elevated on the wall; at the same time, however, it also implies a spiritual looking up to the saint and, together with him, to the crucified Christ. In its effect, the perspective of this representation of a saint is reminiscent of a *Sacra Conversazione* in which the central Madonna with the child has been replaced with the crucified Christ.

The drawing illustrates a development in early Florentine Renaissance art, since in his figure of St. Bernard, Perugino himself made reference to a predecessor: Fra Angelico's head of St. Francis in the large crucifixion in the chapter house of the cloister of San Marco in Florence (fig. 34). Fouquet, too, who may have spent time in Florence in the 1440s, could have seen this head of a saint rapt in worship, viewed from below; in any case he was especially receptive to the work of Fra Angelico. Fouquet's head of St. Stephen on the panel of the *Melun Diptych* (cat. 1) is clearly reminiscent of the head of St. Francis;[1] its slight tilt and the view from below lend this saint, too, an inward-looking expression.

Dagmar Korbacher

---

1   Cf. Sricchia Santoro 2003, p. 55.

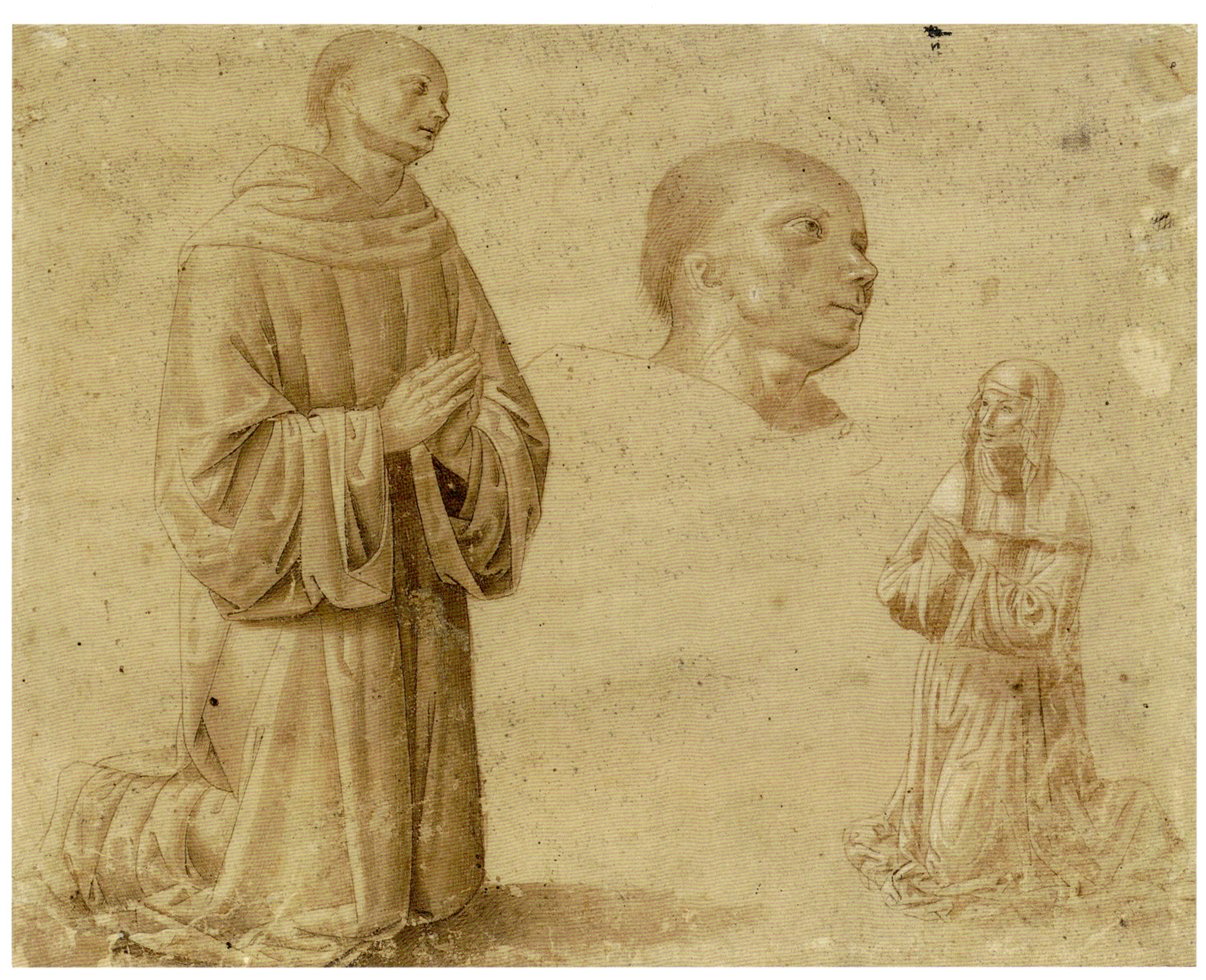

Peter Klein

DENDROCHRONOLOGICAL EXAMINATION
OF JEAN FOUQUET'S PANEL PAINTINGS

Dendrochonology enables us to determine the felling date of a tree and thus to obtain an indication for the dating of paintings on wood. Its principle is to measure the width of the growth rings and to compare their sequence to a standard chronology. For the production of oak wood supports for paintings, panel makers would use boards that were cut from the tree trunks with a radial orientation. The bark and in most cases also the sapwood would be removed. In consequence, it is no longer possible to determine the exact year of the felling of a tree, but only the exact date of the youngest growth ring. The number of the trimmed rings of the sapwood and the length of seasoning of the wood can be derived from collected statistics. They provide a probability for the examined group. In individual cases, discrepancies from this data can occur. The origin of the oaks needs to be taken into account, since different amounts of sapwood can occur depending on the geographical origin. In general, the number of sap-

wood rings decreases in Europe from east to west. Wood from Eastern Europe has a so-called median (average) of 15 sapwood rings. 50% of all collected data show between 13 and 19 growth rings, but the extremes are a minimum of 9 and a maximum of 36 rings. When it comes to oak wood from France, a minimum of 7 and a median (average) of 17 sapwood rings can be assumed, with 50% of all collected data ranking in a margin of 13 to 23 years.

The following chart lists the number of boards of the individual paintings, the number of the growth rings of the individual boards and the youngest growth ring of each board. From this, the earliest possible and the most probable felling date can be concluded. In order to determine the earliest possible felling date – the painting cannot have been made before that date – one needs to add at least 9 or 7 sapwood rings respectively to the youngest detectable growth ring of the heartwood. The probable felling date can be attained by adding the median of 15

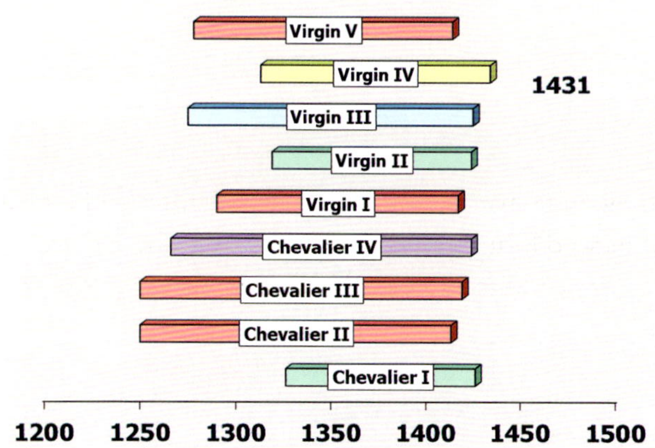

Diagram 1: Dendrochronological dating of the Virgin and Child and of Étienne Chevalier; the youngest growth ring dates from 1431. Boards from the same tree are represented in the same color. Several boards from the panels of the Virgin and Étienne Chevalier come from the same tree.

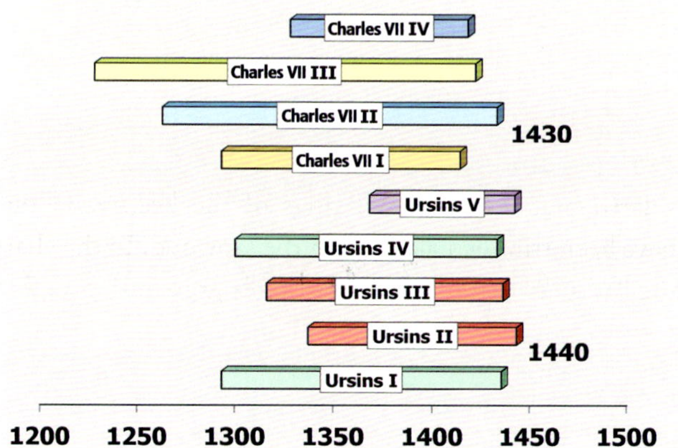

Diagram 2: Dendrochronological dating of Charles VII and Guillaume Jouvenel; 1430 and 1440 indicating the youngest growth rings

WORK	TYPE OF WOOD	NUMBER OF GROWTH RINGS	YOUNGEST HEARTWOOD RING	ESTIMATED DATE, ASSUMING 17 SAPWOOD RINGS AND 2 YEARS OF SEASONING	ORIGIN OF THE WOOD
Étienne Chevalier Berlin	oak	I= 100 II=163 III=169 IV=158	1423 1410 1416 1421	1450	France
Virgin and Child Antwerp	oak	I=127 II=105 III=150 IV=121 V=136	1414 1421 1422 1431 1411	1450	France
Guillaume Jouvenel des Ursins Paris	oak	I=142 II=106 III=120 IV=133 V=74	1432 1440 1433 1430 1439	1459	France
Charles VII Paris	oak	I=121 II=170 III=194 IV=90	1411 1430 1419 1415	1449	France
Jean Jouvenel des Ursins Indianapolis	oak	I=135	1429	1448	France
Gonella Vienna	oak	I=151	1417	1434 (median of 15 sapwood rings)	Baltic

Chart 1: List of paintings ascribed to Jean Fouquet

or 17 growth rings respectively. However, it must be considered that some growth rings of the heartwood may have been trimmed along with the sapwood. In the chart, the dating of the youngest detectable growth ring is exact as well as the earliest possible felling date, while the probable felling date is an estimation. Another uncertainty lies in the time span between the felling of a tree and the use of its wood. In regards to paintings from the 15th to 17th century empirical values suggest a usual storage time between two and eight years.

BIBLIOGRAPHY

Adams 2013 Tracy Adams, "Isabeau of Bavaria, Anne of France, and the History of Female Regency in France," in: Early Modern Women. An Interdisciplinary Journal 8, 2013, pp. 119-147

Ades 1996 Dawn Ades, "Paris 1937. Kunst und nationale Macht," in: Cat. London/Barcelona/Berlin 1996, p. 58-62

Aikema 2007 Bernard Aikema, "Netherlandish painting and early Rennaissance Italy. Artistic rapports in a historiographical perspective," in: Hermann Roodenburg (ed.), *Cultural Exchange in Early Modern Europe, vol. IV: Forging European Identities, 1400-1700*, Cambridge, UK, pp.100-137

Alberti 2000 Leon Battista Alberti, *Das Standbild, die Malkunst, Grundlagen der Malerei*, ed. by Oskar Bätschmann, Christoph Schäublin in collaboration with Kristine Patz, Darmstadt 2000

Andrault-Schmitt 2010 Claude Andrault-Schmitt, *La cathédrale de Tours*, La Crèche 2010

Armstrong 1983 Lillian Armstrong, "The Illustration of Pliny's Historia Naturalis. Manuscripts before 1430," in: Journal of the Warburg and Courtauld Institutes 46, 1983, pp. 29-35

Arnolds 1947 Günter Arnolds, *Französische Zeichnungen. Zeichnungen des Kupferstichkabinetts in Berlin*, Berlin 1947

Aurea Roma 2000 *Aurea Roma. Dalla città pagana alla città cristiana*, exh. cat. Rome, December 22, 2000 – April 20, 2001, Rome 2000

Avril 1977 François Avril, "Pour l'enluminure provençale: Enguerrand Quarton peintre de manuscrits?," in: Revue de l'art, 35, 1977, pp. 9-36

Avril 1985 François Avril, "Le destinataire des Heures Vie à mon désir: Simon de Varie," in: Revue de l'art, 67, 1985, pp. 33-44

Avril 2013 François Avril, "Les Heures de Jeanne de France, duchesse de Bourbon: un chef-d'œuvre du Maître de Jouvenel retrouvé," in: Art de l'enluminure, no. 47, 2013, pp. 4-28

Avril, Gousset, Guenée 1987 François Avril, Marie-Thérèse Gousset, Bernard Guenée, *Jean Fouquet. Die Bilder der Grandes Chroniques de France*, Graz 1987

Baedeker 1888 Karl Baedeker, *Belgique et Hollande y compris le Luxembourg: manuel du voyageur*, 13th ed., Leipzig 1888

Baldass 1938 Ludwig von Baldass, *Katalog der Gemälde-Galerie*, Vienna 1938

Baldass 1952 Ludwig von Baldass, *Jan van Eyck*, Cologne 1952

Baldini 1985 Umberto Baldini, Bruno Nardini (ed.), *Santa Croce. Kirche, Kapellen, Kloster, Museum*, Stutttgart 1985

Bambach 1999 Carmen C. Bambach, *Drawing and Painting in the Italian Renaissance Workshop. Theory and Practice, 1300-1600*, Cambridge 1999

Bambach 2008 Carmen C. Bambach, "Leonardo's notes on pastel drawing," in: *Le tecniche del disegno rinascimentale: dai materiali allo stile; atti del convegno internazionale (Firenze, 22-23 settembre 2008)*, ed. by Marzia Faietti,

Lorenza Melli, Alessandro Nova (= Mitteilungen des Kunsthistorischen Institutes in Florenz 52, 2008), Florence 2008, pp. 176-204

Barker 2003 Michael Barker, "International Exhibitions at Paris culminating with the Exposition Internationale des Arts et Techniques dans la vie moderne – Paris 1937," in: The Journal of the Decorative Arts Society 1850 – The Present, 27, 2003, pp. 6-21

Barr 1966 Alfred H. Barr, Jr., *Picasso: Fifty Years of His Art*, New York, The Museum of Modern Art, Reprint edition, 1966

Basin 1933 Thomas Basin, *Histoire de Charles VII*, ed. by Charles Samaran, vol. I-II, Paris 1933

Baumstark 1995 Reinhold Baumstark (ed.), *Das Goldene Rößl. Ein Meisterwerk der Pariser Hofkunst um 1400, Katalog der Ausstellung des Bayerischen Nationalmuseums*, Munich 1995

Baxandall 1984 Michael Baxandall, *Die Kunst der Bildschnitzer*, Munich 1984

Bazin 1937 Germain Bazin, in: René Huyghe, *Cent trente Chefs-d'oeuvre de l'art français du moyen âge au 20. siècle; Précédés d'une introduction: L'art français par René Huyghe, conservat., d'une étude sur le moyen âge et la renaissance par Germain Bazin, conservat., d'une étude sur le 17me et 18me siècles par Jacques Combe et d'une étude sur le 19me siècle par Maurice Raynal*, Paris 1937

Beaucourt 1891 Gaston Du Fresne de Beaucourt, *Histoire de Charles VII*, vol. 6, Paris 1891

Becksmann 2010 Rüdiger Becksmann, *Die mittelalterlichen Glasmalereien in Freiburg im Breisgau, Münster Unserer Lieben Frau (Corpus Vitrearum Medii Aevi Deutschland, Baden und Pfalz, Teil 2)*, 2 vols., Berlin 2010

Begeer 1952 R.J.M. Begeer, "Le buffon Gonella peint par Jan van Eyck," in: Oud Holland 67, 1952, pp. 125-143

Bellosi 1992 Luciano Bellosi, "Sulla formazione fiorentina di Piero della Francesca," in idem (ed.), *Una scuola per Piero. Luce, colore e prospetiva nella formazione fiorentina di Piero della Francesca*, exh. cat. Florence, Uffizi 1992/93, Venice 1992, pp. 17-54

Bellosi 1998 Luciano Bellosi, *Cimabue*, Milan 1998

Belting 1994 Hans Belting, *Likeness and Presence: A History of the Image before the Era of Art*, trans. E. Jephcott, Chicago and London, 1994

Beltramini, Collareta 2012 Maria Beltramini, Marco Collareta, "Fouquetiana," in: Maria Monica Donato, Massimo Ferretti (ed.), *"Conosco un ottimo storico dell'arte". Per Enrico Castelnuovo. Scritti di allievi e amici pisani*, Pisa 2012, pp. 181-188

Benedetti 1549 Alessandro Benedetti, *Il fatto di arme del Tarro fra i principi italiani e Carlo ottavo re di francia*, Venice 1549

Benjamin 1968 Walter Benjamin, "The Work of Art in the Age of Mechanical Reproduction," in Walter Benjamin, *Illuminations*, ed. by Hannah Arendt, New York 1968

Berger 1901 Ernst Berger, *Quellen für Maltechnik während der Renaissance und deren Folgezeit*

(XVI.-XVIII. Jahrhundert) in Italien, Spanien, den Niederlanden, Deutschland, Frankreich und England, Munich 1901

Białostocki 1970 Jan Białostocki, "The Eye and the Window. Realism and Symbolism of Light-Reflections in the Art of Albrecht Dürer and His Predecessors," in: *Festschrift für Gert von der Osten*, Cologne 1970, pp. 159-176

Birkmeyer 1949 Karl M. Birkmeyer, "Bericht über 202 Bilder aus Berliner Museen in den Vereinigten Staaten von Amerika," New York, 22 April, 1949

Bitterer 2013 Thomas Bitterer, *Marmorverkleidungen stadtrömischer Architektur. Öffentliche Bauten aus dem 1. Jahrhundert v. Chr. bis 7. Jahrhundert n. Chr.*, Munich 2013

Blake McHam 2013 Sarah Blake McHam, *Pliny and the Artistic Culture of the Italian Renaissance. The Legacy of the Natural History*, New Haven/London 2013

Bode 1887 Wilhelm Bode, "La Renaissance au musée de Berlin," in: Gazette des beaux-arts 35, 1887, pp. 204-220

Bode 1896 Wilhelm Bode, "Der Berliner Museums-Verein. Bericht über die Erwerbungen 1894 und 1895," Berlin 1896

Bode 1902 Wilhelm Bode, "Königliche Museen – A. Gemäldegalerie," in: Amtliche Berichte aus den königlichen Kunstsammlungen 23, 1902, p. 1

Boisserée 1978-1995 Sulpiz Boisserée, *Tagebücher 1808-1854, im Auftrag der Stadt Köln herausgegeben von Hans-J. Weitz*, 5 vols., Darmstadt 1978-1995

Bouchot 1904 Henry Bouchot, *L'Exposition des primitifs français. La peinture sous les Valois*, Paris [1904]

Bouleau 1963 Charles Bouleau, *The Painters Secret Geometry*, London 1963

Bourin 1970 Jeanne Bourin, *La Dame de Beauté*, Paris 1970

Bouyer 1937 Raymond Bouyer, "L'Art à l'Exposition de 1937," in: Revue de l'Art 71, 1937, pp. 160-17

Brahms 2016 Iris Brahms, *Zwischen Licht und Schatten. Zur Tradition der Farbgrundzeichnung bis Albrecht Dürer*, Paderborn 2016

Brockwell 1949 Maurice Brockwell, "A New Van Eyck," in: The Connoisseur 124, 1949, pp. 79ff.

Brown 1989 D. Catherine Brown, *Pastor and Laity in the Theology of Jean Gerson*, Cambridge, 1989

Brucher 1987 Günter Brucher, *Die sakrale Baukunst Italiens im 11. und 12. Jahrhundert*, Cologne 1987

Bruderer Eichberg 1998 Barbara Bruderer Eichberg, *Les neuf choeurs angéliques. Origines et évolution du thème dans l'art du Moyen Âge (Civilisation Médiévale 6, Collection dirigée par Gabriel Bianciotto, Robert Favreau, Piotr Scubiszewski)*, Poitiers 1998

Bryant 1986 Lawrence M. Bryant, *The King and the City in the Parisian Royal Entry Ceremony. Politics, Ritual and Art in the Renaissance*, Geneva 1986

Buck 2001 Stephanie Buck, *Die niederländischen Zeichnungen des 15. Jahrhunderts im Berliner Kupferstichkabinett. Kritischer Katalog*, Turnhout 2001

Buck 2009 Stephanie Buck, "Die Zeichnungen des 14. und 15. Jahrhunderts in der Universitätsbibliothek Erlangen," in: Hans Dickel (ed.), Zeichnen vor Dürer, Petersberg 2009, pp. 64-67

Buranelli 2001 Francesco Buranelli (ed.), *Il Beato Angelico e la capella Niccolina*, Novara 2001

Burnard 1937a Robert Burnard , "Dans les Musées d'Art Moderne. La Rétrospective de l'Art Français," in: special issue of L'Illustration, August 1937, 7 pages, unpaginated

Burnard 1937b Robert Burnard, "Rétrospective de l'Art Français," in: Le Livre d'or officiel de l'Exposition internationale des arts et des techniques, Paris 1937, pp. 64-67

Burns 2007 Thea Burns, *The Invention of Pastel Painting*, London 2007

Bushart 1985 Magdalena Bushart, "Bauplastik im Dritten Reich," in: *Entmachtung der Kunst. Architektur, Bildhauerei und ihre Institutionalisierung 1920 1960*, ed. by Magdalena Bushart, Bernd Nicolai, and Wolfgang Schuster, Berlin 1985, pp. 104 113

Caglioti 2015 Francesco Caglioti, "A Spiritello Rediscovered," in Andrew Butterfield (ed.), *Donatello in Motion. A Spiritello Rediscovered*, New York 2015, pp. 14-43

Camille 2001 Michael Camille, "'For Our Devotion and Pleasure': The sexual objects of Jean, Duc de Berry," in: Art History 24, 2001, pp. 7-32

Campbell 1990 Lorne Campbell, *Renaissance Portraits*, New Haven/London 1990

Campbell 1996 Lorne Campbell, "Campin's Portraits," in: *The National Gallery. Robert Campin New Directions in Scholarship*, ed. by Susan Foister and Susie Nash, Turnhout 1996, pp. 123-135

Campbell 1998 Lorne Campbell, *National Gallery Catalogues. The Fifteenth Century Netherlandish School*, London 1998

Castelfranchi Vegas 1966 Liana Castelfranchi Vegas, I rapporti Italia Fiandra (II), in: Paragone Arte XVII, 1966, pp. 42-69

Cat. Angers 2009 *Splendeur de l'enluminure. Le Roi René et les livres*, ed. by Marc-Édouard Gautier, exh. cat. Angers, Château, Angers 2009

Cat. Antwerp 1845 *Catalogue du Musée d'Anvers. Publié par le Conseil d'administration de l'académie Royale des Beaux-Arts*, Antwerp 1845

Cat. Antwerp 1857 *Catalogue du Musée d'Anvers. Publié par le Conseil d'administration de l'académie Royale des Beaux-Arts*, 1857

Cat. Basel 2006 Stephan Kemperdick (ed.), *Das frühe Porträt. Aus den Sammlungen des Fürsten von und zu Liechtenstein und dem Kunstmuseum Basel*, exh. cat. Basel, Kunstmuseum, 2006

Cat. Basel 2011 Bodo Brinkmann, Katharina Georgi, Stephan Kemperdick (ed.), *Konrad Witz*, exh. cat. Basel, Kunstmuseum, Ostfildern 2011

Cat. Berlin 1910 *Katalog der Zeichnungen Alter Meister im Kupferstichkabinett, vol. 1: Italien, Frankreich, Spanien*, Berlin 1910

Cat. Berlin 1973 Fedja Anzelewsky, *Vom späten Mittelalter bis zu Jacques Louis David. Neuerworbene und neubestimmte Zeichnungen im Berliner Kupferstichkabinett*, Berlin 1973

Cat. Berlin 1994 *Das Berliner Kupferstichkabinett. Ein Handbuch zur Sammlung*, ed. by Alexander Dückers, 2nd edition, Berlin 1994

Cat. Berlin 2010 *Gemäldegalerie Berlin. 200 Meisterwerke der europäischen Malerei*, Berlin 2010

Cat. Berlin 2014 Stephan Kemperdick, Johannes Rößler (ed.), *Der Genter Altar der Brüder van Eyck in Berlin. 1820-1920*, Gemäldegalerie der Staatlichen Museen – Preußischer Kulturbesitz, Berlin 2014

Cat. Berlin/New York 2011 Keith Christiansen, Stefan Weppelmann (ed.), *Gesichter der Renaissance. Meisterwerke italienischer Portraitkunst*, Berlin 2011

Cat. Bern 1963 Florens Deuchler, *Die Burgunderbeute*, exh. cat. Bern, Historisches Museum 1963

Cat. Bern/Bruges/Vienna 2008/09 *Karl der Kühne (1433-1477)*, ed. by Susan Marti, Till-Holger Borchert, Gabriele Keck, exh. cat. Bern, Bruges, Vienna 2008/09

Cat. Boston 2016 *Beyond Words. Illuminated Manuscripts in Boston Collections*, ed. by Jeffrey F. Hamburger, William P. Stoneman, Anne-Marie Eze, Lisa Fagin Davis and Nancy Netzer, exh. cat. Boston, Houghton Library, Isabella Stewart Gardner Museum and McMullen Museum of Art, Chicago 2016

Cat. Bourges 2004 *Une fondation disparue de Jean de France, duc de Berry. La Sainte-Chapelle de Bourges*, exh. cat. Bourges, Musée du Berry, Paris 2004

Cat. Dresden 2005 Thomas Ketelsen, Uta Neidhardt (ed.), *Das Geheimnis des Jan van Eyck. Die frühen niederländischen Zeichnungen und Gemälde in Dresden*, Munich et al. 2005

Cat. Frankfurt/Berlin 2008/09 Stephan Kemperdick, Jochen Sander (ed.), *Der Meister von Flémalle und Rogier van der Weyden*, exh. cat. Frankfurt a.M., Städel Museum, Berlin, Gemäldegalerie SMB, 2008/09

Cat. London 2010 Hugo Chapman, Marzia Faietti (ed.), *Fra Angelico to Leonardo. Italian Renaissance Drawings*, London 2010

Cat. London/Barcelona/Berlin 1996 *Kunst und Macht im Europa der Diktatoren 1930 bis 1945. XXIII. Kunstausstellung des Europarates*, Munich 1996

Cat. Los Angeles 2003 Thomas Kren, Scot McKendrick (ed.), *Illuminating the Renaissance: The Triumph of Flemish Manuscript Painting in Europe*, exh. cat. The J. Paul Getty Museum, Los Angeles, 2003

Cat. Madrid 2001 Mauro Natale (ed.), *El Renacimiento Mediterráneo*, exh. cat. Madrid, Museo Thyssen-Bornemisza, 2001

Cat. Montefalco 2002 Bruno Toscano (ed.), *Benozzo Gozzoli. Allievo a Roma, maestro in Umbria*, exh. cat. Montefalco (Perugia), Chiesa-Museo di San Francesco, 2002, Milan 2002

Cat. New York 1982 *The Last Flowering. French painting in manuscripts, 1420-1530*, ed. by John Plummer in collaboration with Gregory T. Clark, exh. cat. New York, The Pierpont Morgan Library, New York/London 1982

Cat. New York 1994 Maryan W. Ainsworth (ed.), *Petrus Christus. Renaissance Master in Bruges*, exh. cat. New York, Metropolitan Museum of Art, 1994

Cat. New York 2005 Laurence Kanter, Pia Palladino (ed.), *Fra Angelico*, exh. cat. New York, Metropolitan Museum of Art, 2005

Cat. New York 2011 Anne van Buren et al., *Illuminating Fashion: Dress in the Art of Medieval France and the Netherlands 1325-1515*, exh. cat. The Morgan Library & Museum, New York 2011

Cat. Paris 1904 Henri Bouchot, *Les Primitifs français exposés au Pavillon de Marsan et à la Bibliothèque Nationale*, Paris 1904

Cat. Paris 1937a *Chefs-d'œuvre de l'Art français*, préface de Léon Blum, avant-propos de Jean Zay, introduction par Henri Focillon, Édition Palais National des Arts Paris, 2 vols., Paris 1937

Cat. Paris 1937b *Chefs-d'œuvre de l'Art français*, préface de Georges Huisman, Édition des Musées nationaux, 2 vols., Paris 1937

Cat. Paris 1987 *Paris 1937. L'art indépendant. Exposition présentée dans le cadre du cinquantenaire de l'Exposition Internationale des arts et des techniques dans la vie moderne*, Paris 1987

Cat. Paris 1989 *Les donateurs du Louvre*, exh. cat. Paris, Musée du Louvre, 1989

Cat. Paris 1993 François Avril, Nicole Reynaud (ed.), *Les manuscrits à peinture en France 1450-1520*, exh. cat. Paris, Bibliothèque Nationale, 1993

Cat. Paris 2003 François Avril (ed.), *Jean Fouquet. Peintre et enlumineur du XVe siècle*, exh. cat. Paris, Bibliothèque nationale de France, Paris 2003

Cat. Paris 2004a *Paris 1400. Les arts sous Charles VI.*, exh. cat. Paris, Musée du Louvre 2004

Cat. Paris 2004b Dominique Thiébaut, Philippe Lorentz, François-René Martin (ed.), *Primitifs français. Découvertes et redécouvertes*, exh. cat. Paris, Musée du Louvre 2004

Cat. Prague 2006 Jiri Fajt (ed.), *Karl IV. Kaiser von Gottes Gnaden. Kunst und Repräsentation des Hauses Luxemburg 1310-1437*, exh. cat. Prague, Castle, Munich 2006

Cat. Rome 2009 *Beato Angelico. L'alba del Rinascimento*, ed. by Alessandro Zuccari, exh. cat. Rome, Musei Capitolini, 2009

Cat. Rotterdam 2012 Stephan Kemperdick, Friso Lammertse (ed.), *The Road to van Eyck*, exh. cat. Rotterdam, Museum Boijmans-Van Beuningen, 2012

Cat. Rotterdam 2015 Peter van der Coelen, Friso Lammertse (ed.), *De ontdekking van het dagelijks leven van Bosch tot Bruegel*, exh. cat. Rotterdam, Museum Boijmans-Van Beuningen, 2015

Cat. Washington/Antwerp 2006/07 *Prayers and Portraits. Unfolding the Netherlandish Diptych*, ed. by John Oliver Hand et al., Washington/Antwerp 2006/07, New Haven et al. 2006.

Cat. Vienna 1963 *Katalog der Gemäldegalerie. II. Teil, Vlamen, Holländer, Deutsche, Franzosen*, Vienna 1963

Causa 1954 Raffaello Causa, "Sagrera, Laurana e l'arco di Castelnuovo," in: Paragone Arte V, 1954, pp. 3-23

Cennini 1871 Cennino Cennini, *Das Buch von der Kunst oder Tractat der Malerei*, ed. by Albert Ilg (Quellenschriften für Kunstgeschichte und Kunsttechnik des Mittelalters und der Renaissance, 1), 1871, Reprint Osnabrück 1970

Champeaux, Gauchery 1894 Alfred de Champeaux, Paul Gauchery, *Les travaux d'art exécutés pour Jean de France, Duc de Berry, avec une étude biographique sur les artistes employés par ce prince*, Paris 1894

Champion 1931 Pierre Champion, *Agnès Sorel. La Dame de Beauté*, Paris 1931

Chapuis 2004 Julien Chapuis, *Stefan Lochner. Image Making in Fifteenth-Century Cologne*, Turnhout 2004

Chartier 1858 Jean Chartier, *Chroniques de Charles VII*, vol. II, ed. by Vallet de Viriville, Paris, 1858

Chastellain 1864 *Œuvres de Georges Chastellain*, ed. by Kervyn de Lettenhove, vol. IV: Chronique 1461-64, Paris 1864

Châtelet 1975 Albert Châtelet, „„La Reine Blanche" de Jean Fouquet. Remarques sur le „Diptyque de Melun"", in: *Études d'art français offertes à Charles Sterling*, ed. by Albert Châtelet, Nicole Reynaud, Paris 1975, pp. 127-138

Châtelet 1996 Albert Châtelet, "Jacob de Littemont," in: *En Berry, du Moyen-âge à la Renaissance*, ed. by Philippe Goldman and Christian-E. Roth, Bourges 1996, pp. 79-86

Châtelet 1997 Albert Châtelet, "Le portrait de Gonella peut-il- être attribué à Fouquet?," in: Bulletin monumental, 155, 1997, pp. 154-55

Châtelet 2000 Albert Châtelet, *L'Age d'or du manuscrit à peintures en France au temps de Charles VI et Les Heures du Maréchal Boucicaut*, Dijon 2000

Châtelet 2008 Albert Châtelet, "Les Heures Dunois conservées à la British Library," in: L'Art de l'enluminure 25, 2008, pp. 2-73.

Châtelet 2009 Albert Châtelet, "Portrait et dévotion," in: Olariu 2009, pp. 153-165

Chennevières 1853 Philippe de Chennevières, *Portraits inédits d'artistes français*, Paris 1853

Christiansen 1982 Keith Christiansen, *Gentile da Fabriano*, London 1982

Cianfarini 1997 Angela Cianfarini, "Consensus filaretiano per Jean Fouquet: un Fiorentino e un Oltremontano alla corte romana di Eugenio IV," in: Sergio Rossi, Stefano Valeri (ed.), *Le due Rome del Quattrocento*, symposium papers (Rome, Università La Sapienza, 21-24 February, 1996), Rome 1997, pp. 213-224

Cianfarini 2000 Angela Cianfarini, "Riflessi del soggiorno romano sotto Niccolo V nell'arte di Jean Fouquet e dei suoi seguaci," in: Franco Bonati (ed.), *Niccolo V nel sesto centenario della nascita*, symposium papers (Sarzana, 8-10 October, 1998), Biblioteca Apostolica Vaticana 2000, pp. 383-398

Clancy 1988 Stephen C. Clancy, "Books of Hours in the „Fouquet style": The relationship of Jean Fouquet and the „Hours of Etienne Chevalier" to French manuscript illumination of the fifteenth century," Ph.D., Cornell University 1988

Clancy 1993a Stephen C. Clancy, "The Illusion of a „Fouquet Workshop": The „Hours of Charles de France," the „Hours of Diane de Croy," and the „Hours of Adelaïde de Savoie"," in: Zeitschrift für Kunstgeschichte, 56, 1993, pp. 207-233

Clancy 1993b Stephen C. Clancy, "Historiated initials in search of a manuscript: Jean Fouquet and the Hours of Charles de Bourbon," in: Gazette des Beaux-Arts, 122, 1993, pp. 17-20

Clouzot 2007 Martine Clouzot, *Images de musiciens (1350-1500). Typologie, figurations et pratiques sociales*, Turnhout 2007

Cole Ahl 1996 Diane Cole Ahl, *Benozzo Gozzoli*, New Haven/London 1996

Contamine 2017 Philippe Contamine, *Charles VII. Une vie, une politique*, Paris 2017

Contamine, Tesnière 2013 Philippe Contamine, Marie-Hélène Tesnière, "Jeanne de France, duchesse de Bourbon, et son livre d'heures," in: Monuments et mémoires de la Fondation Eugène Piot, 92, 2013, pp. 5-65

Contensou 1987 Bernadette Contensou, "Autour de l'exposition des Maîtres de l'art indépendant en 1937," in: Cat. Paris 1987, pp. 11-18

Corio 1503 Bernardino Corio, *Historia continente da l'origine di Milano tutti li gesti, fatti, e detti preclari*, Milan 1503

Cornette 1938 Arthur Henry Cornette, *Een Antwerpsch Maeceen Ridder Florent Van Ertborn 1784-1840*, Antwerp 1938

Cornette 1939 Arthur Henry Cornette, *Introduction aux maîtres anciens du Museé Royal d'Anvers*, Antwerp 1939

Cornette 1941 Arthur Henry Cornette, *Drie uren in het Koninklijk Museum voor Schoone Kunsten van Antwerpen*, Antwerp 1941

Courcelles 1824 Jean-Baptiste-Pierre Jullien de Courcelles, *Histoire généalogique et héraldique des pairs de France, des grandes dignitaires de la couronne, des principales familles nobles de royaume, et des maisons princières de l'Europe*, Paris 1824

Curmer 1864 Léon Curmer, *Jehan Fouquet (notice extraite du volume d'appendices des Évangiles publiés par Léon Curmer)*, Paris 1864

Curmer 1867 Léon Curmer, *La Vie et les œuvres de Jehan Fouquet*, Paris 1867

de Laborde 1855 Léon de Laborde, *La Renaissance des arts à la cour de France, Additions au tome premier. Peinture*, Paris 1855

De Man 1950 Henrik de Man, *Jacques Cœur. Der königliche Kaufmann*, Bern 1950

De Mont 1914 Pol De Mont, *De oude meesters der schilderkunst in het Koninklijk Muzeum van Schoone Kunsten te Antwerpen*, Antwerp 1914

De Rynck 2017 Patrick De Rynck, "Gesprek: Historisch weerzien," in: Zaal Z, Koninklijk Museum voor Schone Kunsten Antwerpen 6, no. 22, 2017, pp. 6-12

De Simone 2002 Gerardo de Simone, "L'ultimo Angelico. Le Meditationes del cardinal Torquemada e il ciclo perduto nel chiostro di S. Maria sopra Minerva," in: Ricerche di storia dell'arte. 76. Presenze cancellate. Capolavori perduti della pittura romana di metà Quattrocento, 2002, pp. 41-87

De Simone 2009 Gerardo de Simone, "Velut alter Apelles. Il decennio romano del Beato Angelico," in: Alessandro Zuccari, Giovanni Morello, Gerardo de Simone (ed.), *Beato Angelico. L'alba del Rinascimento*, exh. cat. Rome, Musei Capitolini 2009, Milan 2009, pp. 129-143

De Simone 2017 Gerardo de Simone, *Il Beato Angelico a Roma 1445-1455*, Florence 2017

de Tolnay 1939 Charles de Tolnay, *Le maître de Flémalle, et les frères van Eyck*, Brussels 1939

De Vos 1999 Dirk De Vos, *Rogier van der Weyden. Das Gesamtwerk*, Munich 1999

Delaporte 1965 Yves Delaporte, *Les trois Notre-Dame de la cathédrale de Chartres*, Chartres 1965

Denis 1939 Maurice Denis, *Histoire de l'Art religieux*, Paris 1939

Dervieu 1910 Lieutenant-Colonel Dervieu, "Les chaises et les sièges au Moyen Âge," in: Bulletin monumental 74, 1910, pp. 207-241

Dhanens 1980 Elisabeth Dhanens, *Hubert und Jan van Eyck*, Königstein im Taunus 1980

Dhanens 1998 Elisabeth Dhanens, *Hugo van der Goes*, Antwerp 1998

Di Lorenzo 2004 Andrea Di Lorenzo, "Regesto fiorentino," in Matteo Ceriana et al. (ed.), *Fra Carnevale. Un artista rinascimentale da Filippo Lippi a Piero della Francesca*, exhibition. cat. Milan, Pinacoteca di Brera, New York, Metropolitan Museum of Art 2004/05, Milan 2004, pp. 290-302

Didi-Huberman 1995 Georges Didi-Huberman, *Fra Angelico. Unähnlichkeit und Figuration*, Munich 1995

Dietz 2008 Georg Josef Dietz, *Die Zeichentechnik Matthias Grünewalds. Untersuchung am Bestand des Kupferstichkabinetts Berlin*, ed. by Gerhard Banik and Volker Schaible, (Weiße Reihe des Instituts für Museumskunde an der Staatlichen Akademie der Bildenden Künste Stuttgart), vol. 24, Munich 2008

Dietz 2012 Georg Josef Dietz, "Zur Technik der Zeichnung, ihrer Aufgabe und Verwendung im Werk Albrecht Dürers," in: Peter Strieder, *Dürer*, 3. überarbeitete und erweiterte Ausgabe, Königstein i. Ts. 2012, pp. 342-349

Dietz, Röhrs 2013 Georg Josef Dietz, Stephan Röhrs, "Analyses et recherches scientifiques de dessins d'Ottavio Leoni au Kupferstichkabinett de Berlin," in: Francesco Solinas (ed.), *Ottavio Leoni*, Paris 2013, pp. 273-288

Dimier 1938 Louis Dimier, "Les Œuvres des Ecoles des Pays-Bas en France. L'Exposition des chefs-d'œuvre de l'art français," in: Oud Holland 55, 1938, pp. 171-174

Driver 2012 Martha Driver, "Uncovering the Meanings of Nudity in the Belles heures of Jean, Duke of Berry," in: *The Meanings of Nudity in Medieval Art*, Farnham, Surrey/ Burlington, VT, 2012, pp. 149-182

Du Fresne de Beaucourt 1882-91 Gaston du Fresne de Beaucourt, *Histoire de Charles VII*, 4 vols., Paris 1882-91

Dunlop 2015 Anne Dunlop, *Andrea del Castagno and the Limit of Painting*, London/Turnhout 2015

Durrieu 1904a Paul Durrieu, *La Peinture à l'Exposition des Primitifs Français*, Paris 1904

Durrieu 1904b Paul Durrieu, "La question des œuvres de jeunesse de Jean Fouquet," in: *Recueil des mémoires publiés par la Société nationale des antiquaires de France à l'occasion de son centenaire*, Paris 1904, pp. 111-119

Durrieu 1906 Paul Durrieu, "Le livre d'heures peint par Jean Fouquet pour Philippe de Commynes," in: Comptes rendus des séances de l'Académie des Inscriptions et Belles-Lettres, 50, no. 4, 1906, p. 257

Durrieu 1907 Paul Durrieu, "La légende et l'histoire de Jean Foucquet," in: Annuaire-bulletin de la société de l'histoire de France, 44, 1907, pp. 111-128

Durrieu 1911 Paul Durrieu, "La peinture française depuis l'avènement de Charles VII jusqu'à la fin des Valois (1422-1589)," in: André Michel, *Histoire de l'art*, vol. 4, 2. part, Paris 1911, pp. 701-751

Eikelmann 1995a Renate Eikelmann, "Goldemail um 1400," in: Baumstark 1995, pp. 106-130

Eikelmann 1995b Renate Eikelmann, "Zur Geschichte des Marienbildes, genannt Goldenes Rössl," in: Baumstark 1995, pp. 52-57

Elen 1995 Albert Jan Elen, *Italian late-medieval and renaissance drawing-books from Giovannino de'Grassi to Palma Giovane: a codicological approach*, Utrecht 1995

Endemann 2009 Klaus Endemann, "Das Kultbild des Bischofs. Zur Imad-Madonna des Paderborner Doms," in: Westfalen 87, 2009, pp. 121-148

Engerth 1882 Eduard R. von Engerth, *Kunsthistorische Sammlungen des Allerhöchsten Kaiserhauses. Gemäldegalerie. Beschreibendes Verzeichnis*, vol. 1, Vienna 1882

Esch 1978 Arnold Esch, Doris Esch, "Die Grabplatte Martinus V. und andere Importstücke in den römischen Zollregistern der Frührenaissance," in: Römisches Jahrbuch für Kunstgeschichte XVII, 1978, pp. 211-217

Evans 1985 Mark L. Evans, "Un motif italianisant dans le Boccace de Munich de Fouquet," in: Revue de l'art 67, 1985, pp. 45-48

Evans 1998 Mark Evans, "Jean Fouquet and Italy. '... buono maestro, maxime a ritrarre del naturale'," in: *Illuminating the Book. Makers and Interpreters. Essays in Honour of Janet Backhouse*, London 1998, pp. 163-189

Favier 2001 Jean Favier, *Louis XI*, Paris 2001

Ferré 2008 Rose-Marie Ferré, "La commande artistique à la cour de René d'Anjou" (thèse de doctorat, université de Paris-Sorbonne, 2008

Fircks 2016 Juliane von Fircks, "Islamic Striped Brocades in Europe: The „Heinrichsgewänder" in Regensburg from a Transcultural Perspective," in: Juliane von Fircks and Regula Schorta, *Oriental Silks in Medieval Europe. Riggisberger Berichte 21*, Riggisberg 2016, pp. 266-287

Flores D'Arcais 1995 Francesca Flores D'Arcais, *Giotto*, New York/London/Paris 1995

Focillon 1936 Henri Focillon, "Le style monumental dans l'art de Jean Fouquet," in: Gazette des Beaux-Arts XV, 1936, pp. 17-32

Focillon 1950 Henri Focillon, *Le peintre des Miracles Notre Dame*, Paris 1950

Förstel 2008 Judith Förstel, "Etienne Chevalier, Jean Fouquet et Melun," in: *Présence royale et aristocratique dans l'Est parisien à la fin du Moyen Âge*, Nogent-sur-Marne 2008, pp. 96-107

online: patrimoine.iledefrance.fr/sites/default/files/medias/2015/etienne_chevalier.pdf

Forsyth 1972 Ilene H. Forsyth, *The Throne of Wisdom. Wood Sculpture of the Madonna in Romanesque France*, Princeton New Jersey 1972

Fortelle 1843 Bernard de la Fortelle, *Histoire et description de Nôtre-Dame de Melun*, Melun 1843

Fournier 1973 Gabriel Fournier, *Châteaux, villages et villes d'Auvergne au XVe siècle d'après l'Armorial de Guillaume Revel*, Genève/Paris 1973 (Bibliothèque de la Société française d'archéologie 4)

Frenzel 1846 J. Gottlieb Abraham Frenzel, *Die Kunstsammlung des Freiherrn C.F.L.F. von Rumohr*, Lübeck 1846

Fricke 2007 Beate Fricke, *Ecce Fides: die Statue von Conques, Götzendienst und Bildkultur im Westen*, Munich 2007

Friedländer 1896 Max J. Friedländer, "Die Votivtafel des Estienne Chevalier von Fouquet," in: Jahrbuch der Königlich Preußischen Kunstsammlungen 17, 1896, pp. 206-214

Friedländer 1902 Max J. Friedländer, "Ein Bildnis des Meisters von Flémalle," in: Jahrbuch der Königlich Preußischen Kunstsammlungen 23, 1902, pp. 17-19

Friedländer 1910 Max J. Friedländer, "Eine Bildnisstudie Jean Fouquets," in: Jahrbuch der Königlich Preußischen Kunstsammlungen 31, 1910, pp. 227-230

Friedländer 1924-37 Max Friedländer, *Die altniederländische Malerei, Bd. 1-14*, Berlin and Leiden 1924-1937

Friedländer 1931 Max J. Friedländer, "Flémalle-Meister-Dämmerung," in: Pantheon 8, 1931, pp. 353-355

Friedländer 1933 Max J. Friedländer, "Der Rogier-Altar aus Turin," in: Pantheon 11, 1933, pp. 7-13

Frinta 1966 Mojmir S. Frinta, *The Genius of Robert Campin*, Den Haag and Paris 1966

Frommel, Wolf 2016 Sabine Frommel, Gerhard Wolf (ed.). *Architectura picta nell'arte italiana da Giotto a Veronese*, Modena 2016

Fulton 2002 Rachel Fulton, *From Judgment to Passion. Devotion to Christ and the Virgin Mary, 800-1200*, New York 2002

Gaborit 2013 Jean-René Gaborit, "Le trône de la Vierge: essai de typologie," in: Subes-Picot, Manchot 2013, pp. 147-162

Ganz 2010 David Ganz, "Weder eins noch zwei. Jan van Eycks Madonna in der Kirche und die Scharnierlogik spätmittelalterlicher Diptychen," in: David Ganz, Felix Thürlemann (ed.), *Das Bild im Plural, Mehrteilige Bildformen zwischen Mittelalter und Gegenwart*, Berlin 2010, pp. 41-65.

Gaussin 1982 Pierre-Roger Gaussin, "Les conseillers de Charles VII (1418-1461)," in: Francia 10, 1982, pp. 67-130

Gauthier 1972 Marie-Madeleine Gauthier, *Émaux du moyen-âge occidental*, Fribourg 1972

Gerbron 2012a Cyril Gerbron, "Le Christ est une page: exégèse et mémoire dans l'armadio degli argenti de Fra Angelico," in: Histoire de l'art 71, 2012, pp. 51-62

Gerbron 2012b Cyril Gerbron, "Le cas Fra Angelico. Georges Didi-Huberman contre la tradition," in: Francesca Alberti et al. (ed.), *Penser l'étrangeté*, Rennes 2012, pp. 195-214

Gerson 1973 Jean Gerson, *Œuvres complètes de Jean Gerson*, ed. by P. Glorieux, vol. X, Paris 1973

Ginzburg 1996 Carlo Ginzburg, *Jean Fouquet. Ritratto del buffone Gonella*, Modena 1996

Godefroy 1661 Denis Godefroy, *Histoire de Charles VII, Roy de France (...)*, Paris 1661

Gonse 1891/92 Louis Gonse, "Le nouveau palais des Musées à Vienne," in: Gazette des Beaux-Arts 1, 1891, p. 403, ibid. 2, 1892, pp. 122-23

Göttler 1990 Christine Göttler, "Die Disziplinierung des Heiligenbildes durch altgläubige Theologen nach der Reformation. Ein Beitrag zur Theorie des Sakralbildes im Übergang vom Mittelalter zur Frühen Neuzeit," in: *Bilder und Bildersturm im Spätmittelalter und in der frühen Neuzeit*, ed. by Bob Scribner (Wolfenbütteler Forschungen 46), Wiesbaden 1990, pp. 263-297

Gousset 2003 Marie-Thérèse Gousset, "Fouquet et l'art de géometrie," in: Cat. Paris 2003, pp. 76-86

Graf 1997 Johannes Graf, „Verbindung von französischer Tradition mit sachlicher Modernität". Gustav René Hocke berichtet über die Weltausstellung 1937 in Paris," in: Reisekultur in Deutschland. Von der Weimarer Republik zum „Dritten Reich", ed. by Peter J. Brenner, Tübingen 1997, pp. 101-126

Grant 2005 Lindy Grant, *Architecture and Society in Normandy 1120-1270*, New Haven/London 2005

Gras 2015 Samuel Gras, "The Master of Jeanne de France, duchesse de Bourbon. A bridge between Jean Fouquet and the artists of the Jouvenel Group," in: *Re-inventing traditions. On the transmission of artistic patterns in late medieval manuscript illumination*, ed. by Joris C. Heyder and Christine Seidel, Bern et al. 2015, pp. 145-169

Graul 2008 Jana Graul, "Farbige Fonds in der Florentiner Zeichnung," in: *Le tecniche del disegno rinascimentale: dai materiali allo stile; atti del convegno internazionale; [Firenze, 22 - 23 settembre 2008], ed. by Marzia Faietti; Lorenza Melli; Alessandro Nova (= Mitteilungen des Kunsthistorischen Institutes in Florenz 52 2008)*, Florence 2008, pp. 6-22

Gréber 1937 Jacques Gréber, *Exposition 1937, Pavillon Français. Introduction de Jacque Gréber, presentation de Henri Martin*, Paris 1937

Gresch 2004 Diethelm Gresch, "Das „e" in der Wenzelsbibel," in: Kunstchronik 2004, pp. 131-137

Grésy 1845 Eugène Grésy, *Recherches sur les sépultures récemment découvertes en l'église Notre-Dame de Melun, suivies d'une dissertation sur les prétendues amours d'Agnès Sorel et Étienne Chevallier*, Melun 1845

Grosshans 1991 Rainald Grosshans, "Simon Marmion. Das Retabel von Saint-Bertin zu Saint-Omer. Zur Rekonstruktion und Entstehungsgeschichte des Altares," in: Jahrbuch der Berliner Museen 1991, pp. 63-98

Guiffrey 1896 J. Guiffrey, *Inventaires de Jean duc de Berry (1401-1416)*, vol. II, Paris 1896

Guillouët 2013 Jean-Marie Guillouët, "La cathédrale des ducs de Bretagne. XVe siècle," in: Jean-

Paul James (ed.), *Nantes. La grâce d'une cathédrale*, Strasbourg 2013, pp. 41-59

H.B. 1937 H.B., "Weltausstellung 1937," in: Der Morgen. Monatszeitschrift der Juden in Deutschland. Begründet von Professor Dr. Julius Goldstein, 13, 1937, pp. 137-142

Hamburger 2000 Jeffrey F. Hamburger, "Seeing and Believing. The Suspicion of Sight and the Authentication of Vision in Late Medieval Art and Devotion," in: *Imagination und Wirklichkeit. Zum Verhältnis von mentalen und realen Bildern in der Kunst der frühen Neuzeit*, ed. by Klaus Krüger, Alessandro Nova, Mainz 2000, pp. 47-69

Harbers 1937 Guido Harbers, "Streifzug durch die Pariser Weltausstellung 1937. Mit Lichtbildaufnahmen des Verfassers," in: Der Baumeister 35, 1937, pp. 269-278

Hediger, Kurmann-Schwarz 2014 Christine Hediger, Brigitte Kurmann-Schwarz, "Reliquie und Skulptur im Glasfenster. Intermediale Auratisierung am Beispiel von Notre-Dame la Belle-Verrière," in: *Auratisierung. Mediologische Perspektiven im Anschluss an Walter Benjamin*, ed. by Ulrich Johannes Beil, Cornelia Herberichs, Marcus Sandl (Medienwandel – Medienwechsel – Medienwissen, vol. 27), Zürich 2014, pp. 136-160

Hegner 2015 Kristina Hegner, *Aus Mecklenburgs Kirchen und Klöstern. Der Mittelalterbestand des Staatlichen Museum Schwerin*, Petersberg 2015

Held 1963 Julius Samuel Held, "The Early Appreciation of Drawings," in: *Studies in Western Art. Acts of the Twentieth International Congress of the History of Art*, vol. 3, Princeton 1963, pp. 72-95

Henzler 2012 Christine Juliane Henzler, *Die Frauen Karls VII. und Ludwigs XI. Rolle und Position der Königinnen und Mätressen am französischen Hof (1422-1483)*, Cologne, Weimar, Vienna 2012

Herman 2014 Nicholas Herman, "A newly discovered portrait of Louis XII by Jean Bourdichon," in: The Burlington Magazine, 156, 2014, pp. 507-509

Héroard 1868 *Journal de Jean Héroard sur l'enfance et la jeunesse de Louis XIII, 1601-1610*, ed. by E. Sachiè, E. de Barthélemy, Paris 1868

Hérold 1998 Michel Hérold, "Aux sources de l'invention: Gaultier de Campes, peintre à Paris au début du XVIᵉ siècle," in: Revue de l'art 120, 1998, pp. 49-57

Hirschbiegel 2003 Jan Hirschbiegel, *Étrennes. Untersuchungen zum höfischen Geschenkverkehr im spätmittelalterlichen Frankreich zur Zeit König Karls VI. (1380 – 1422)*, Munich 2003

Hocke 1937 Gustav Rainer Hocke, *Das geistige Paris*, Leipzig-Markkleeberg 1937

Hoffmann 1937 Heinrich Hoffmann (ed.), *Deutschland in Paris. Ein Bild-Buch von Heinrich Hoffmann*, Munich 1937

Hoffmann 2004 Volker Hoffmann, "Le "Trône de Dagobert" au Cabinet des Médailles de la Bibliothèque nationale," in: Bulletin de la Société de l'histoire de l'Art français 2004, pp. 9-19

Hofmann 2004 Mara Hofmann, *Jean Poyer. Das Gesamtwerk*, Turnhout 2004

Hofmann 2007 Mara Hofmann, "Jean Poyer et Jean Bourdichon. Peintres de retables à Tours vers la fin du XVe siècle," in: Art sacré, 24, 2007, pp. 190-205

Holmes 1997 Megan Holmes, "Disrobing the Virgin: The Madonna lactans in Fifteenth-Century Florentine Art," in: *Picturing Women in Renaissance and Baroque Italy*, ed. by Geraldine A. Johnson, Sarah F. Matthews-Grieco, Cambridge 1997, pp. 167-195

Houtard 1906 Maurice Houtard, *Jacques Daret, peintre du XVe siècle*, Tournai 1906

Huizinga 1924 (1999) Johan Huizinga, *The Waning of the Middle Ages*, New York 1924 (reprint 1999)

Huyghe 1937 René Huyghe, *Cent trente Chefs-d'œuvre de l'art français du moyen âge au 20me siècle; Précédés d'une introduction: L'art français par René Huyghe, conservat., d'une étude sur le moyen âge et la renaissance par Germain Bazin, conservat., d'une étude sur les 17me et 18me siècles par Jacques Combe et d'une étude sur le 19me siècle par Maurice Raynal*, Paris 1937

Huyghe 1937a René Huyghe, "La peinture française du XIVme au XVIIme siècle. - Figures et portraits - Les chefs-d'œuvre de l'art français à l'exposition internationale de 1937", in: Huyghe 1937

Huyghe 1937b René Huyghe, *La peinture française du XIVme au XVIIme siècle. - Figures et portraits - Les chefs-d'oeuvre de l'art français à l'exposition internationale de 1937*, Paris 1937

Inglis 2011 Erik Inglis, *Jean Fouquet and the Invention of France. Art and Nation after the Hundred Years War*, New Haven/London 2011

Jalabert 1963 Denise Jalabert, *Notre-Dame de Paris*, Paris 1963

Janssen 2002 Sandra Janssens, "The catalogue of Ridder Florent van Ertborn," in: Koninklijk Museum voor Schone Kunsten Antwerpen, Jaarboek 2002, pp. 85-112

Jantzen 1910 Hans Jantzen, *Das niederländische Architekturbild*, Leipzig 1910

Jenni, Theisen 2014 Ulrike Jenni and Maria Theisen, *Mitteleuropäische Schulen. IV (ca. 1380–1400): Hofwerkstätten König Wenzels IV. und deren Umkreis* (= Denkschriften der Österreichischen Akademie der Wissenschaften, phil.-hist. Klasse. Band 458 (Veröffentlichungen zum Schrift- und Buchwesen des Mittelalters. Band I,13), 2 vols., Vienna 2014

Jezler 1994a Peter Jezler, "Jenseitsmodelle und Jenseitsvorsorge - Eine Einführung," in: idem. 1994b, pp. 13-26

Jezler 1994b Peter Jezler (ed.), *Himmel, Hölle, Fegefeuer, Das Jenseits im Mittelalter, Katalog der Ausstellung im Schweizerischen Landesmuseum*, Zurich 1994

**Journal d`un bourgeois 2009** *Le Journal d`un Bourgeois de Paris: tenu pendant les règnes de Charles VI et Charles VII*, transl. by Nathalie Desgrugillers-Billard, vol. I-III, Clermont-Ferrand 2009

Journal d'un bourgeois 1963 *Journal d'un bourgeois de Paris à la fin de la guerre de Cent Ans (1405-1449)*, ed. by Jean Thiellay, Paris 1963

Kahsnitz 1995 Rainer Kahsnitz, "Kleinod und Andachtsbild. Zum Bildprogramm des Goldenen Rössls," in: Baumstark 1995, pp. 58-89

Kangaslahti 2011 Kate C. Kangaslahti, "Making the Cosmopolitan National. The Politics of Assimilation and the Foreign Artist in Interwar France," in: *Im Dienst der Nation. Identitätsstiftungen und Identitätsbrüche in Werken der bildenden Kunst*, ed. by Matthias Krüger and Isabella Woldt, Berlin 2011, pp. 119-139

Kemp 1996 Wolfgang Kemp, *Die Räume der Maler. Zur Bilderzählung seit Giotto*, Munich 1996

Kemperdick 1999 Stephan Kemperdick, *Rogier van der Weyden 1399/1400-1464*, Cologne 1999

Kemperdick 2010 Kemperdick, Stephan, *Deutsche und böhmische Gemälde 1230-1430*, Gemäldegalerie Berlin 2010

Kemperdick 2014 Stephan Kemperdick, "Der Totentanz auf Simon Marmions Altarflügeln aus Saint-Omer in der Berliner Gemäldegalerie," in: Maria Deiters, Jan Raue, Claudia Rückert (ed.), *Der Berliner Totentanz. Geschichte, Restaurierung, Öffentlichkeit*, Berlin 2014, pp. 145-155

Klein 1986 Peter Klein, "Dendrochronologische Untersuchungen an Gemäldetafeln und Musikinstrumenten," in: Dendrochronologia 3, 1986, pp. 25-44

König 1974 Eberhard König, "Jean Fouquet. Das Stundenbuch des Étienne Chevalier" (Review of Sterling, Schaefer 1971), in: Zeitschrift für Kunstgeschichte 36, 1974, pp. 164-179

König 1982 Eberhard König, *Französische Buchmalerei um 1450. Der Jouvenel-Maler, der Maler des Genfer Boccaccio und die Anfänge Jean Fouquets*, Berlin 1982

König 1987 Eberhard König, "The History of Art and the History of the Book at the Time of the Transition from Manuscript to Print," in: Bibliography and the Study of 15ᵗʰ Century Civilization (British Library Occasional Papers 5), ed. by Lotte Hellinga, John Goldfinch, London, Warburg Institute and British Library, 1987, pp. 151-184

König 1996 Eberhard König, *Das liebentbrannte Herz. Der Wiener Codex und der Maler Barthélmy d'Eyck*, Vienna/Graz 1996

König 2007 Eberhard König, *Die Bedford Hours*, Stuttgart 2007

König 2009 Eberhard König, "La réalité du portrait dans les manuscrits enluminés," in: Olariu 2009, pp. 167-189

König 2012 Eberhard König, *Devotion from Dawn to Dusk. The Office of the Virgin in Books of Hours of the Koninklijke Bibliotheek in The Hague*, Leiden 2012

König 2013 Eberhard König, *Tour de France. 32 Manuskripte aus den Regionen Frankreichs, ohne Paris und die Normandie. 13. bis 16. Jahrhundert, Antiquariat Heribert Tenschert*, 2 vols., Ramsen 2013

König 2013b Eberhard König, "Charles the Bold and the Mary of Burgundy Style: or Who Said "Voustre Demeure"?," in: *Staging the Court of Burgundy. Proceedings of the Conference "The Splendour of Burgundy"*, ed. by Wim Blockmans et al., Turnhout 2013, pp. 287-299

König 2015 Eberhard König, *Das Kalligraphiebuch von Maria von Burgund. Brüssel, Bibliothèque royale de Belgique, Ms. II 845*, Lucerne 2015

König 2017 Eberhard König, *Paris mon amour*, Bibermühle 2017

Kren 2005 Thomas Kren, "Looking at Louis XII's Bathsheba," in: *A Masterpiece Reconstructed: The Hours of Louis XII*, ed. by Thomas Kren mit Mark L. Evans, Los Angeles 2005, pp. 50-51

Kren 2010 Thomas Kren, "Bathsheba Imagery in French Books of Hours Made for Women, ca. 1470-1500," in: *The Medieval Book Glosses from Friends & Colleagues of Christopher de Hamel*, ed. by James H. Marrow, Richard A. Linenthal, William Noel, Houten 2010, pp. 169-170

Kretzenbacher 1981 Leopold Kretzenbacher, *Schutz- und Bittgebärden der Gottesmutter. Zu Vorbedingungen, Auftreten und Nachleben mittelalterlicher Fürbitte-Gesten zwischen Hochkunst, Legende und Volksglauben*, Munich 1981

Künstler 1975 Karl Künstler, "Jean Fouquet als Bildnismaler," in: Wiener Jahrbuch für Kunstgeschichte 28, 1975, pp. 9-38

Kurmann 2004 Peter Kurmann, "Eine fiktive "Kathedrale" des 15. Jahrhunderts," in: Sylvia Claus et al. (ed.), *Architektur weiterdenken. Werner Oechslin zum 60. Geburtstag*, Zurich 2004, pp. 128-141.

Kurmann 2010 Peter Kurmann, "Herbst der Kathedrale. Die niederländische Sakralbaukunst zur Zeit Karls des Kühnen und ihre mediale Spiegelung in der "Kirchenmadonna" des Jan van Eyck," in: Klaus Oschema and Rainer C. Schwinges (ed.), *Karl der Kühne von Burgund. Fürst zwischen europäischem Adel und der Eidgenossenschaft*, Zurich 2010, pp. 248-271.

Kurmann-Schwarz 1988 Brigitte Kurmann-Schwarz, *Französische Glasmalereien um 1450. Ein Atelier in Bourges und Riom*, Bern 1988

Kurmann-Schwarz 1999 Brigitte Kurmann-Schwarz, "Les verriers à Bourges dans la première moitié du XVe siècle et leurs modèles: tradition et renouveau," in: *Vitrail et arts graphiques, Table ronde coordonnée par Michel Hérold et Claude Mignot* (Les cahiers de l'École nationale du patrimoine 4), Paris 1999, pp. 137-149

Kurmann-Schwarz 2014 Brigitte Kurmann-Schwarz, "Construction d'un mythe au Moyen Âge et à l'époque moderne. Nouvelles études sur la cathédrale de Chartres au XIIᵉ siècle," in: Francia 41, 2014, pp. 239-253

Kurmann-Schwarz 2017 Brigitte Kurmann-Schwarz, "La Vierge de la chapelle Notre-Dame de la cathédrale de Sens. Une reine des anges donnée par le chanoine Manuel de Jaune (de Jauna ou de Pelavicinis) en 1334," in: *La métropolitaine sénonaise: la première cathédrale gothique dans son contexte (1164-2014), Actes du Colloque organisé en l'honneur du 850ᵉ anniversaire de la consécration de la cathédrale Saint-Étienne de Sens*, pp. 303-323 (in print)

Kwastek 2001 Katja Kwastek, *Camera. Gemalter und realer Raum der italienischen Frührenaissance*, Weimar 2001

Labarte 1879 Jules Labarte, *Inventaire du Mobilier de Charles V, Roi de France*, Paris 1879

Labbé 1937 Edmond Labbé, "Les leçons de l'Exposition," in: *Le Livre d'or officiel de l'Exposition internationale des arts et des techniques*, Paris 1937, pp. 19-26

Laclotte 1967 Michel Laclotte, "Rencontres franco-italiennes au milieu du XVe siècle," in: Acta Historiae Artium Academiae Scientiarum Hungaricae, XIII, 1967, pp. 33-41

Laclotte 1995 Michel Laclotte, "À propos de Fouquet: des putti et un boeuf," in: Francesco Abate and Fiorella Sricchia Santoro (ed.), *Napoli, l'Europa. Ricerche di storia dell'arte in onore di Ferdinando Bologna*, Catanzaro 1995, pp. 95-100

Laclotte 2003 Michel Laclotte, *Histoires de musées. Souvenirs d'un conservateur*, Paris 2003

Laclotte, Thiebaut 1983 Michel Laclotte, Dominique Thiebaut, *L'École d'Avignon*, Paris 1983

Langhanke 2013 Birgit Langhanke, "Die Madonnenreliefs im Werk von Antonio Rossellino," Diss. Ludwig-Maximilian-Universität München, 2013, edoc.ub.uni-muenchen.de

Le Bouvier 1979 Gilles le Bouvier dit le Héraut Berry, *Les Chroniques du Roi Charles VII*, ed. by Henri Courteault and Léonce Celier, Paris 1979

Le Glay 1839 A. Le Glay, *Correspondance de l'Empereur Maximilien Ier et de Marguerite d'Autriche sa fille*, Paris 1839

Le Pogam 2013 Pierre-Yves Le Pogam, "Les Vierges assises gothiques: un héritage passéiste ou une typologie signifiante?," in: Subes-Picot, Mathon 2013, pp. 131-145

Le Roux de Lincy 1855 Guillebert de Metz, *Description de la Ville de Paris au XVe siècle*, ed. by Antoine Le Roux de Lincy, Paris 1855

Legenda Aurea 1978 *Die Legenda Aurea des Jacobus de Voragine*, transl. by R. Benz, 9. edition, Heidelberg 1978

Leprieur 1897 P. Leprieur, "Jean Fouquet," in: Revue de l'art ancien et moderne 1897, vol. 1, pp. 25-41; vol 2, pp. 15-30, 147-160, 347-359

Lindquist 2017 Sherry M.C. Lindquist, "Masculinist Devotion: Flaying and Flagellation in the Belles heures," in: *Down to the Skin: Images of Flaying in the Middle Ages*, ed. by Larissa Tracy, New York 2017, pp. 173-207

Livre d'Or 1937 République Française, Ministère du Commerce et de l'Industrie (ed.), *Livre d'Or officiel de l'Exposition Internationale des Arts et Techniques dans la Vie Moderne*, Paris 1937

Lombardi 1978 Alessandro Lombardi, "Il Dittico di Melun," in: Antichità viva XVII, 1978, pp. 5-10

Lombardi 1983 Sandro Lombardi, *Jean Fouquet*, Florence 1983

Longhi 1914 Roberto Longhi, "Piero dei Franceschi e lo sviluppo della pittura veneziana," in: L'Arte XVII, 1914, pp. 198-221 and 241-256, also in: *Opere complete. I. Scritti giovanili. 1912-1922*, Florence 1961, vol. I, pp. 61-106

Longhi 1927 Roberto Longhi, *Piero della Francesca*, Rome (Valori Plastici, 1927), now in *Opere complet.e III. Piero della Francesca, 1927. Con aggiunte fino al 1962*, Florence 1963

Longhi 1952a Roberto Longhi, "Ancora sulla cultura di Fouquet," in: Paragone Arte III, 1952, pp. 56-57, also in *Opere complete. IX. Arte italiana e arte tedesca, con altre congiunture fra Italia e Europa*, Florenz 1979, pp. 39-40

Longhi 1952b Roberto Longhi, "I fiamminghi e l'Italia," in: Paragone Arte III, 1952, pp. 47-50, also in: *Opere complete. IX. Arte italiana e arte tedesca, con altre congiunture fra Italia e Europa*, Florence 1979, pp. 23-25

Longhi 1952c Roberto Longhi, "Presenza di Masaccio nel Trittico della neve," in: Paragone Arte III, 1952, pp. 8-16, also in: *Opere complete. VIII/1. 'Fatti di Masolino e di Masaccio' e altri studi sul Quattrocento 1910-1967*, Florence 1975, pp. 77-84

Longhi 1955 Roberto Longhi, "Una 'Crocefissione' di Colantonio," now in *Opere complete.*

IX. Arte italiana e arte tedesca, con altre congiunture fra Italia e Europa, Florence 1979, pp. 27-33

Longhi 1995 Roberto Longhi, *Il palazzo non finito. Saggi inediti 1910-1926*, Milan 1995

Longnon, Cazelles 1969 Jean Longnon, Raymond Cazelles, *The Très riches Heures of Jean, Duke of Berry*, Musée Condé, Chantilly, New York 1969

Lord 1937 Douglas Lord, "Chefs-d'Œuvre de L'Art Français," in: The Burlington Magazine for Connoisseurs, no. 413, 71, 1937, p. 93

Lorentz 2003 Philippe Lorentz, "Jean Fouquet et les peintres des anciens Pays-Bas," in: Cat. Paris 2003, pp. 38-49

Lorentz 2004a Philippe Lorentz, *La crucifixion du Parlement de Paris (Musée du Louvre, collection Solo)*, Paris 2004

Lorentz 2004b Philippe Lorentz, "Les peintres de Philippe le Hardi et de Jean sans Peur à Dijon," in: *L'art à la cour de Bourgogne. Le mécenat de Philippe le Hardi et de Jean sans Peur (1364-1419)*, ed. by Stephen Fliegel, Sophie Jugie, exh. cat. Dijon, Paris 2004, pp. 95-99

Lorentz 2013 Philippe Lorentz, "De Bruges à Bourges: un peintre eyckien en France au milieu du XVe siècle: le „Maître de Jacques Cœur" (Jacob de Litemont?)," in: *Kunst und Kulturtransfer zur Zeit Karls des Kühnen*, ed. by Norberto Gramaccini and Marc Carel Schurr, Bern 2013, pp. 177-202

Marchand 2003 Eckart Marchand, "Una mensa fighure d'apostoli e del nostro signiore. Ghirlandaios Abendmahlsdarstellungen," in: Michael Rohmann (ed.), *Domenico Ghirlandaio. Künstlerische Konstruktion von Identität im Florenz der Renaissance*, Weimar 2003, pp. 89-128.

Marquet de Vasselot 1904 Jean-Joseph Marquet de Vasselot, "Deux émaux de Jean Fouquet," in: Gazette des beaux-arts, 32, 1904, pp. 140-148

Marrow 1985 James H. Marrow, "Miniatures inédites de Jean Fouquet. Les Heures de Simon de Varie," in: Revue de l'art, 67, 1985, pp. 7-32

Marrow, Avril 1994 James H. Marrow, François Avril et al., *The Hours of Simon de Varie*, Los Angeles 1994

Marti, Mondini 1994 Susan Marti, Daniela Mondini, "„Ich manen dich der Brüsten min, Das du dem Sünder wellest milte sin". Marienbrüste und Marienmilch im Heilsgeschehen," in: Jezler 1994, pp. 79-90

Martin 2003 François-René Martin, "L'ancêtre, l'artisan, le primitif, Jean Fouquet dans l'Art du XXe siècle," in: Cat. Paris 2003, pp. 87-93

Martin 2004 François-René Martin, "Les Primitifs français au XIXe siècle. De l'érudition dispersée aux synthèses conflictuelles," in: Cat. Paris 2004a, pp. 47-57

McKendrick 2007 Scot McKendrick, "The Earliest Reproduction of the Crucifixion of the Parlement de Paris," in: Caroline Zöhl, Mara Hofmann (ed.), *Von Kunst und Temperament. Festschrift für Eberhard König*, Turnhout 2007, pp. 176-182

Meiss 1967-1974 Millard Meiss, *French Painting in the Time of Jean de Berry*: vol. 1 *The Late 14th Century and the Patronage of the Duke*, (London/New York 1967); vol. 2 *The Boucicaut Master*, (London/New York 1968); vol. 3 *The Limbourgs and Their Contemporaries*, (London/New York 1974)

Meiss, Eisler 1960 Millard Meiss, Colin Eisler, "A New French Primitive," in: The Burlington Magazine 102, 1960, pp. 233-240

Meyer 1895 Alfred Meyer, *L'art de l'émail de Limoges ancien et moderne, traité pratique et scientifique*, Paris 1895

Miles 2008 Margaret R. Miles, *A Complex Delight. The Secularization of the Breast, 1350-1750*, Berkeley Calif. 2008

Mills 2015 Robert Mills, *Seeing Sodomy in the Middle Ages*, Chicago/ London 2015

Milnes 1982 Eric C. Milnes, "From Rags to Riches: A New Look at an Old Chair," in: Furniture History 17, 1981, pp. 61-64

Mollat 1991 Michel Mollat, *Der königliche Kaufmann. Jaques Coeur oder der Geist des Unternehmertums*, Munich 1991

Monnas 2012 Lisa Monnas, *Renaissance Velvets*, London 2012

Moreau-Néalton 1910 Étienne Moreau-Néalton, *Chantilly. Crayons français du XVIe siècle*, Paris 1910

Müller 2000 Matthias Müller, "Das irdische Territorium als Abbild eines himmlischen: Überlegungen zu den Monatsbildern in den Très Riches Heures des Herzogs Jean de Berry," in: Andreas Beyer (ed.), *Bildnis, Fürst und Territorium*, Munich 2000, pp. 11-29.

Nagel, Wood 2010 Alexander Nagel, Christopher Wood, *Anachronic Renaissance*, New York 2010

Nash 2008 Susie Nash, *Northern Renaissance Art* (Oxford History of Art), Oxford 2008

Netzer 1999 Susanne Netzer, *Maleremails aus Limoges. Der Bestand des Berliner Kunstgewerbemuseums*, Berlin 1999

Niebaum 2016 Jens Niebaum, *Der kirchliche Zentralbau der Renaissance in Italien. Studien zur Karriere eines Baugedankens im Quattro- und frühen Cinquecento*, 2 vols., Munich 2016

Niessen 2005 Willy Niessen, Pieter Roelofs, and Mieke van Veen-Liefrink, "The Limbourg Brothers in Nijmegen, Bourges, and Paris," in: *The Limbourg Brothers: Nijmegen Masters at the French Court, 1400-1416*, ed. by Rob Dückers, Pieter Roelofs, exh. cat. Njjmegen, Museum Het Valkhof, 2005. pp. 20-22

Nouvelle biographie 1866 *Nouvelle biographie générale depuis les temps les plus reculés jusqu'à nos jours, publiée par MM. Firmin Didot frères*, vol. 5: Beaumarchais - Biccius, Paris 1866

Nova 2008 Alessandro Nova, "Pietre naturali, gessi colorati, pastelli e il problema del ritratto," in: *Le tecniche del disegno rinascimentale: dai materiali allo stile; atti del convegno internazionale* (Firenze, 22 - 23 settembre 2008), ed. by Marzia Faietti, Lorenza Melli, Alessandro Nova (= Mitteilungen des Kunsthistorischen Institutes in Florenz vol. 52.2008,2/3, Florence 2008, pp. 158-175

Oberthaler 1998 Elke Oberthaler, "Tafelbildbehandlungen im kunsthistorischen Museum," in: Manfred Koller (ed.) *Restauratorenblätter (19), Gemälde auf Holz und Metall*, ed. by the Austrian Section of the IIC, 1998, pp. 45-54

Olariu 2009 Dominic Olariu (ed.), *Le portrait individuel. Reflexions autour d'une forme de représentation. XIIe-XVe siècles, Actes du colloque sur le portrait au Moyen Age*, Paris 2004, Bern et al. 2009

Oledzka 2016 Eva Oledzka, *Medieval and Renaissance Interiors in Illuminated Manuscripts*, London 2016

Olivier de la Marche 1884 *Mémoires d'Olivier de la Marche*, ed. by Henri Beaune, J. d'Arbaumont, vol. II, Paris 1884

Ortheil 1995 Hanns-Josef Ortheil, "Detektiv erkennt die Kleckse, Review of Didi-Huberman 1995," in: Frankfurter Allgemeine Zeitung, Feuilleton of 10 October, 1995

Ozenfant 1937 Amédée Ozenfant, "Notes d'un Tourisme à l'Exposition," in: Cahiers d'Art 12 (1937), pp. 241-247

Pächt 1941 Otto Pächt, "Jean Fouquet. A Study of His Style," in: The Journal of the Warburg and Courtauld Institutes, 4, 1941, pp. 85-102

Pächt 1974 Otto Pächt, "Die Autorschaft des Gonella-Bildnisses," in: Jahrbuch der Kunsthistorischen Sammlungen in Wien, 79, 1974, pp. 39-88

Pächt, Kreidl 1981 Otto Pächt, Detlev Kreidl, "Le portrait de Gonella," in: Gazette de Beaux-Arts, VIme pér. 97, 1981, pp. 2-8

Panofsky 1953 Erwin Panofsky, *Early Netherlandish Painting: its Origins and Character*, Cambridge/Mass. 1953

Paolucci 2010 Antonio Paolucci (ed.), *Il Tempio Malatestiano a Rimini*, Modena 2010

Passavant 1833 Johann David Passavant, *Kunstreise durch England und Belgien*, Frankfurt a.M. 1833

Pastoureau 2006 Michel Pastoureau, "Les couleurs de la Vierge," in: *Images de la Vierge dans l'art du vitrail, Actes du Colloque de Bourges 2003*, in: Art sacré, Cahiers de Rencontre au Patrimoine religieux 21, 2006, pp. 7-19

Pélicier 1882 Paul Pélicier, *Essai sur le gouvernement de la Dame de Beaujeu 1483–1491*, Chartres 1882

Perkinson 2009 Stephen Perkinson, *The Likeness of the King. A prehistory of portraiture in late medieval France*, Chicago/London 2009

Perls 1940 Klaus Perls, *Jean Fouquet*, London 1940

Peter (in print) Michael Peter (ed.), *Velvets of the Fifteenth Century*, Riggisberger Berichte 24 (in print)

Pfisterer 2011 Ulrich Pfisterer, "Eyes Wide Shut or the Renaissance of Sex," in: Oxford Art Journal 34, 2011, pp. 480-483

Pfisterer 2016 Ulrich Pfisterer, "Die Erotik der Macht: Visualisierte Herrscher-Potenz in der Renaissance," in: *Menschen und Politische Ordnung*, ed. by Andreas Höfele, Beate Kellner, Paderborn 2016, pp. 181-184

Philippe 1983, Robert Philippe, *Agnès Sorel*, Paris 1983

Piaget, Picot 1908 Arthur Piaget and Émile Picot, *Oeuvres poétiques de Guillaume Alexis, prieur de Bucy*, vol. 3, Paris 1908

Pinelli 2002 Antonio Pinelli, "Esercizi di metodo: Piero e Benozzo a Roma, tra cronologia relativa e cronologia assoluta," in: Ricerche di storia dell'arte. 76. Presenze cancellate. Capolavori perduti della pittura romana di metà Quattrocento, 2002, pp. 7-30

Plagnieux 2010 Philippe Plagnieux, *L'art du Moyen Âge en France*, Paris 2010

Plagnieux 2013a Philippe Plagnieux, "La Vierge à l'enfant du prieuré parisien de Saint-Martin-des-Champs: son insertion dans le contexte architectural et liturgique," in: Subes-Picot, Mathon 2013 pp. 118-128

Plagnieux 2013b Philippe Plagnieux, "D'une chapelle de la Vierge l'autre: l'exemple du prieuré clunisien de Saint-Martin-des-Champs à Paris," in: Bulletin du Centre d'études médiévales d'Auxerre, BUCEMA [online], hors-série 6, 2013, URL: http://cem.revues.org/12726

Poeschke 1990 Joachim Poeschke, *Die Skulptur der Renaissance in Italien, vol. 1, Donatello und seine Zeit*, Munich 1990

Popelin 1868 Claudius Popelin, *L'Art de l'émail, leçon faite à l'Union Centrale des Beaux Arts*, Paris 1868

Potin 2017 Yann Potin, "1420. La France aux Anglais?," in: *Histoire Mondiale de la France*, ed. by Patrick Boucheron, Paris 2017, pp. 228-230

Pradel 1986 Pierre Pradel, *Anne de France (1461-1521)*, Paris 1986

Rakint 1937 Wladimir Rakint, "Allemagne," in: Revue de l'Art 71, 1937, pp. 196-198

Rapp-Buri, Stucky-Schürer 2001 Anna Rapp-Buri, Monica Stucky-Schürer, *Burgundische Tapisserien*, Munich 2001

Reynaud 1981 Nicole Reynaud, *Jean Fouquet, Les dossier du département des peinture, exposition présentée au Louvre*, Paris 1981

Reynaud 1982 Nicole Reynaud, "Un nouveau manuscrit attribué à Enguerrand Quarton," in: Revue de l'art, 57, 1982, pp. 61-66

Reynaud 1983 Nicole Reynaud, "La radiographie du 'Portrait de Charles VII par Fouquet'," in: Revue du Louvre 33, 1983, pp. 97-99

Reynaud 1989 Nicole Reynaud, "Barthélémy d'Eyck avant 1450," in: Revue de l'art 84, 1989, pp. 22-43

Reynaud 2006 Nicole Reynaud, *Jean Fouquet. Les Heures d'Etienne Chevalier*, Dijon 2006

Richards 2007 John Richards, "Fouquet and the Trecento," in: Zeitschrift für Kunstgeschichte 70, 2007, pp. 449-472

Ring 1949 Grete Ring, *A Century of French Painting. 1400-1500*, London 1949

Ringbom 1964 Sixten Ringbom, *Icon to Narrative. The rise of the dramatic close-up in fifteenth-century devotional painting*, Åbo 1964 (Reprint Dornspijk 1984)

Roelofs 2005 Pieter Roelofs, "Johan Maelwael, Hofmaler in Geldern und Burgund," in: Rob Dückers, Pieter Roelofs, *Die Brüder van Limburg. Nijmegener Meister am französischen Hof (1400-1416)*, Stuttgart 2005, pp. 35-53

Roettgen 1996 Steffi Roettgen, *Wandmalerei der Frührenaissance in Italien, vol. 1, Anfänge und Entfaltung, 1400-1470*, Munich 1996

Roettgen 1997 Steffi Roettgen, *Wandmalerei der Frührenaissance in Italien, vol. 2, Die Blütezeit, 1470-1510*, Munich 1997

Rouse, Rouse 2000 Richard Rouse, Mary Rouse, *Manuscripts and Their Makers: Commercial Book Producers in Medieval Paris 1200-1500*, Turnhout 2000

Rowley 2014 Neville Rowley, "Introduction. Roberto Longhi, fragments de masques," in: Predella 36, 2014, pp. 7-11

Rumohr 1822 Carl von Rumohr, "Schreiben an den Herausgeber," in: Kunst-Blatt, 28 November, 1822, pp. 377-379

Russo 1996 Daniel Russo, "Les représentations mariales dans l'art d'Occident du Moyen Âge. Essai sur la formation d'une tradition iconographique," in: *Marie. Le culte de la Vierge dans la Société médiévale*, ed. by Dominique Iogna-Prat, Éric Palazzo and Daniel Russo, Paris 1996, pp. 173-291

Salmon 1855 A. Salmon, "Description de la ville de Tours sous le règne de Louis XI par F. Florio," in: Mémoires de la société archéologique de Touraine VII, 1855, pp. 82 ff.

Salzer 1898 Anselm Salzer, *Die Sinnbilder und Beiworte Mariens*, Linz 1898

Sauerländer 1994 Willibald Sauerländer, "Gedanken über das Nachleben des gotischen Kirchenraums im Spiegel der Malerei," in: Münchner Jahrbuch der bildenden Kunst 45, 1994, pp. 165-182.

Scaillérez 2015 Cécile Scailliérez, "Quelques propositions pour Jean Perréal et le portrait français autour de 1515," in: *La France et l'Europe autour de 1500*, ed. by Geneviève Bresc-Bautier, Thierry Crépin-Leblond and Élisabeth Taburet-Delahaye, Paris 2015, pp. 179-192

Schaefer 1967 Claude Schaefer, "Fouquet 'le jeune' en Italie," in: Gazette des beaux-arts 70, 1967, pp. 189-212

Schaefer 1971 Claude Schaefer, "Recherches sur l'iconologie et la stylistique de l'art de Jean Fouquet," Thèse présentée devant Université de Paris IV le 24 février 1971 (ms.)

Schaefer 1975 Claude Schaefer, "Le Diptyque de Melun de Jean Fouquet conservé à Anvers et à Berlin," in: Jaarboek van het Koninklijke Museum voor Schone Kunsten Antwerpen 1975, pp. 7-100

Schaefer 1994 Claude Schaefer, *Jean Fouquet. An der Schwelle zur Renaissance*, Dresden/Basel 1994

Schaefer 2000 Claude Schaefer, "L'art et l'histoire. Etienne Chevalier commande au peintre Jean Fouquet le Diptyque de Melun," in: Yves Gallet (ed.), *Art et architecture à Melun au Moyen Âge, Actes du colloque d'histoire de l'art et d'archéologie tenu à Melun les 28 et 29 novembre 1998*, Paris 2000, pp. 293-300

Schaefer, de Hamel 1981 Claude Schaefer, Christopher de Hamel, "Du nouveau sur les Heures d'Étienne Chevalier illustrées par Fouquet," in: Gazette des beaux-arts 98, 1981, pp. 193-199

Schiessl 1998 Ulrich Schiessl, "History of Structural Panel Painting Conservation in Austria, Germany and Switzerland," in: Kathleen Dardes, Andrea Rothe (ed.), *The Structural Conservation of Panel Paintings. Proceedings of a symposium at the J. Paul Getty Museum, 24-28 April 1995*, Los Angeles 1998, pp.200-236

Schiller 1966 Gertrud Schiller, *Ikonographie der christlichen Kunst, vol. 1, Inkarnation – Kindheit – Taufe – Versuchung – Verklärung – Wirken und Wunder Christi*, Gütersloh 1966

Schindler 2016 Robert Schindler, *Die bebilderte Enea Silvio Piccolomini Handschrift des Charles de France. Ein Beitrag zur Buchmalerei in Bourges und zum Humanismus in Frankreich*, Turnhout 2016

Schmidt 2003 Dagmar Schmidt, *Der Freskenzyklus von Ambrogio Lorenzetti über die gute und die schlechte Regierung. Eine danteske Vision im Palazzo Pubblico von Siena* (Diss. Univ. St. Gallen), Bamberg 2003

Schmidt 2006 Victor M. Schmidt, "Precedents and Contexts of Fifteenth-Century Devotional Diptychs," in: *Essays in Context. Unfolding the Netherlandish Diptych*, ed. by John Oliver Hand and Ron Spronk, New Haven / London 2006, pp. 15-31

Schmidt 2008 Victor M. Schmidt, "Johan Maelwael and the Beginnings of Netherlandish Canvas Painting," in: *Invention. Northern Renaissance Studies in Honor of Molly Faries*, ed. by Julien Chapuis, Turnhout 2008, pp. 20-29

Schramm 1954 Percy Ernst Schramm, "Die Throne und Bischofsstühle des frühen Mittelalters," in: *Herrschaftszeichen und Staatssymbolik. Beiträge zu ihrer Geschichte vom dritten bis zum sechzehnten Jahrhundert*, vol. 1, Stuttgart 1954, pp. 316-335

Schreiner 2011 Klaus Schreiner, "Deine Brüste sind süßer als Wein. Ikonographie, religiöse Bedeutung und soziale Funktion eines Mariensymbols," in: *Rituale, Zeichen, Bilder. Formen und Funktionen symbolischer Kommunikation im Mittelalter*, ed. by Ulrich Meier, Gabriela Signori, Gerd Schwerhoff, Cologne, Weimar, Vienna 2011, pp. 207-241

Schrempf 1938 Claus Schrempf, "Das geistige Paris. Bemerkungen zu einer Schrift von Gustav R. Hocke," in: Kultur und Leben. Beilage zu den Leipziger Neuesten Nachrichten no. 39. 8 February, 1938, p. 7

Schulze Altcappenberg 1995 Hein-Th. Schulze Altcappenberg, *Die italienischen Zeichnungen des 14. und 15. Jahrhunderts im Berliner Kupferstichkabinett. Kritischer Katalog*, Berlin 1995

Schwager 1970 Klaus Schwager, "Über Jean Fouquet in Italien und sein verlorenes Porträt Papst Eugen IV." in: *Argo. Festschrift für Kurt Badt*, Cologne 1970, pp. 206-234

Scott 1980 Margaret Scott, *Late Gothic Europe 1400-1500 (History of Dress Series)*, Sydney/Toronto 1980

Seidel 1977 Max Seidel, "Ubera Matris. Die vielschichtige Bedeutung eines Symbols in der mittelalterlichen Kunst," in: Städel-Jahrbuch 6, 1977, pp. 41-98

Seidel 2014 Christine Seidel, "Tradition and Innovation in the work of Jean Colombe. The usage of models in late 15th century French manuscript illumination," in: *The Use of Models in Medieval Book Painting*, ed. by Monika Müller, Newcastle upon Tyne 2014, pp. 137-166

Seidel 2017 Christine Seidel, *Zwischen Tradition und Innovation. Die Anfänge des Buchmalers Jean Colombe und die Kunst in Bourges zur Zeit Karls VII. von Frankreich*, Simbach am Inn 2017

Signori 2014 Gabriela Signori, "Das innere Gespräch mit Gott. Repräsentation und Imaginatio in der spätmittelalterlichen Theologie bzw. Theorie des Bildes und der Bilder," in: *Den Himmel öffnen … Bild, Raum und Klang in der mittelalterlichen Sakralkultur*, ed. by Therese Bruggisser-Lanker (Publikationen der Schweizerischen Musikforschenden Gesellschaft, Serie II, 56), Bern 2014, pp. 35-65

Smital, Winkler 1926 Otto Smital, E. Winkler, *Livre du cuer d'amours espris*, Vienna 1926

Sonet 1956 Pierre Sonet, *Répertoire d'incipit de prières en ancien français*, Geneva 1956

Sorel 1640 Charles Sorel, *La Solitude et l'Amour philosophique de Cléomède, premier sujet des exercices moraux*, Paris 1640

Speel 2002 Erika Speel, "Limoges School painted enamels: the processes and their technical aspects," in: I. Müsch (ed.), *Maleremail des 16. und 17. Jahrhunderts aus Limoges*, Braunschweig, Herzog Anton Ulrich-Museum 2002, pp. 27-37

Speer 1969 Albert Speer, *Erinnerungen*, Frankfurt am Main 1969

Spencer 1963 Eleanor P. Spencer, "L'Horloge de Sapience (Bruxelles, Bibliothèque royale, ms. IV 111)," in: Scriptorium XVII, 1963, pp. 277-299

Spies 2003 Werner Spies, *Kontinent Picasso*, Munich 2003

Spike 1997 John T. Spike, *Fra Angelico*, Munich 1997

Sricchia Santoro 1978 Fiorella Sricchia Santoro, "Arte italiana e arte straniera," in Giovanni Previtali (ed.) *Storia dell'arte italiana. Parte prima: materiali e problemi. Volume terzo: L'esperienza dell'antico, dell'Europa, della religiosità*, Turin 1978, pp. 71-171

Sricchia Santoro 2003 Fiorella Sricchia Santoro, "Jean Fouquet en Italie," in: Cat. Paris, 2003, pp. 50-63

Stange 1967 Alfred Stange, *Kritisches Verzeichnis der deutschen Tafelbilder vor Dürer*, vol. 1, Munich 1967

Steh, Dubois 2014 Ute Stehr, Hélène Dubois, "Über die Spaltung und die Restaurierungsgeschichte der sechs Flügel des Genter Altares in Berlin," in: Cat. Berlin 2014, pp.122-137

Sterling 1971 Charles Sterling, "Jean Fouquet et l'Italie," in: idem, Claude Schaefer, *Les Heures d'Étienne Chevalier*, Paris 1971, pp. 7-19

Sterling 1976 Charles Sterling, "Jan van Eyck avant 1432," Revue de l'art 33, 1976, pp. 7-82

Sterling 1987a Charles Sterling, "Charles VII vue par Jean Fouquet," in: L'Œil 389, December 1987, pp. 34-41

Sterling 1987b Charles Sterling, *La peinture médiévale à Paris 1300-1500*, vol. 1, Paris 1987

Sterling 1988 Charles Sterling, "Fouquet en Italie," in: L'Œil 392, March 1988, pp. 22-31

Sterling 1990 Charles Sterling, *La peinture médiévale à Paris 1300-1500*, vol. 2, Paris 1990

Sterling, Schaefer 1971 Charles Sterling, Claude Schaefer, *Das Stundenbuch des Étienne Chevalier*, Munich 1971

Stirnemann 2005 Patricia Stirnemann, *Les Heures d`Étienne Chevalier par Jean Fouquet*, Paris 2005

Stockhausen 1997 Tilmann von Stockhausen, "Wilhelm von Bode und die Gründung des Kaiser-Friedrich-Museums-Vereins," in: *100 Jahre Mäzenatentum. Die Kunstwerke des Kaiser-Friedrich-Museums-Vereins Berlin*, Berlin 1997, pp. 21-30

Stratford 1993 Jenny Stratford, *The Bedford Inventories. The Worldly Goods of John, Duke of Bedford, Regent of France (1389–1435)*, London 1993

Subes-Picot, Mathon 2013 Marie-Pasquine Subes-Picot, Jean-Bernard Mathon (ed.), *Vierges à l'Enfant médiévales de Catalogne: mises en perspectives*, Perpignan, 2013

Syndikus 1996 Candida Syndikus, *Leon Battista Alberti. Das Bauornament*, Münster 1996

Taburet-Delahaye 2004 Elisabeth Taburet-Delahaye, *Paris 1400. Les arts sous Charles VI*, exh. cat. Louvre, Paris 2004

Tesnière 2015 Marie-Hélène Tesnière, *Le livre d'heures de Jeanne de France*, Paris 2015

Thiébaut 2003 Dominique Thiébaut, "Fouquet portraitiste," in: Cat. Paris 2003, pp. 29-37

Thiébaut 2006 Dominique Thiébaut, "Antonello, Barthélemy d'Eyck, Enguerrand Quarton e altri: contatti, influenze reciproche o coincidenze artistiche?," in Mauro Lucco (ed.), *Antonello da Messina. L'opera completa*, exh. cat. Rome, Scuderie del Quirinale 2006, Cinisello Balsamo 2006, pp. 43-63

Toesca 1952 Ilaria Toesca, "Gli 'Uomini famosi' della biblioteca Cockerell," in: Paragone Arte III, 1952, pp. 16-20

Tolnay 1939 Charles de Tolnay, *Le maître de Flémalle, et les frères van Eyck*, Brussels 1939

Tschudi 1887 Hugo von Tschudi, "Ein männliches Bildnis des Jan van Eyck," in: Jahrbuch der Königlich Preußischen Kunstsammlungen 8, 1887, pp. 172-174

Tschudin 2007 Peter F. Tschudin, *Grundzüge der Papiergeschichte*, ed. by Stephan Füssel, Bibliothek des Buchwesens, vol. 12, Stuttgart 2007

Turner 2005 Nancy Turner, "The Manuscript Painting Techniques of Jean Bourdichon," in: *A Masterpiece reconstructed. The Hours of Louis XII*, ed. by Thomas Kren, Mark Evans, Los Angeles 2005, pp. 63-79

Upton 1990 Joel M. Upton, *Petrus Christus: his place in Fifteenth-Century Flemish Painting*, University Park 1990

Vaesen, Charavay 1895 Joseph Vaesen, *Étienne Charavay, Lettres de Louis XI*, vol. V, Paris 1895

Vale 1968 M. G. A. Vale, "Jean Fouquet's portrait of Charles VII," in: Gazette des Beaux-Arts 71, 1968, pp. 243-248

Vale 1974 M.G.A. Vale, *Charles VII*, Berkeley/Los Angeles 1974

Vallet de Viriville 1856 Auguste Vallet de Viriville, "Découverte d'un portrait de Jean Fouquet, peint par lui-même," in: Journal général de l'instruction publique et des cultes 25, no. 77, 24 September 1856, p. 475

Vallet de Viriville 1857 Auguste Vallet de Viriville, "Jean Fouquet, peintre français du XVe siècle," in: Revue de Paris, 1 August , 1857, pp. 409-437, 1 November, 1857, pp. 141-145 (reprint in Curmer 1864, pp. 96-124)

Vallet de Viriville 1857b Auguste Vallet de Viriville, "Observations sur l'émaillerie et sur quelques monuments émaillés de l'Antiquité ainsi que du Moyen Âge," in: Revue archéologique 1857, pp. 277-291

Vallet de Viriville 1859 Auguste Vallet de Viriville, *Charles VII, roi de France et ses conseillers*, Paris 1859

Vallet de Viriville 1863 Auguste Vallet de Viriville, *Histoire de Charles VII roi de France et de son époque. 1403-1461*, Paris 1863

Van der Velden 2006 Hugo van der Velden, "Diptych Altarpieces and the Principle of Dextrality," in: John O. Hand, Ron Spronk (ed.), *Essays in Context: Unfolding the Netherlandish Diptych*, Cambridge/Mass.2006, pp. 124-155

Van Lerius 1851 Théodore Van Lerius, *Notice sur le catalogue du Musée d'Anvers, rédigé par M. Jean-Alfred De Laet, professeur, agrégé à l'université de Gand*, Ghent 1851

Van Mander 1906 Karel van Mander, *Das Leben der niederländischen und deutschen Maler* (vol. 1), transl. by Hans Floerke, Munich 1906

Vanbeselaere 1959 Walther Vanbeselaere, in: *Musea van België. Koninklijk Museum voor Schone Kunsten te Antwerpen. Oude meesters*, Antwerp 1959

Vanbeselaere 1966 Walther Vanbeselaere, in: Fernsehsendung "Openbaar Kunstbezit Vlaanderen" 1966

Vandenbroeck 2014 Paul Vandenbroeck, *De eeuw der Vlaamse Primitieven*, Antwerp 2014

Vandenbroeck, Guislain-Wittermann 1996 Paul Vandenbroeck, Regine Guislain-Wittermann, "Le Madone de D'Etienne Chevalier, Examen Technologique et Traitment," in: *S.O.S Peintures Anciennes. Sauvegarde de 20 Oeuvres sur Panneau, 4 Octobre - 8 Decembre 1996, Museum voor Oude Kunst*, Brussels 1996, pp. 55-63

Vasari 1568 Giorgio Vasari, *Le Vite de' più eccellenti pittori scultori e architettori nelle redazioni del 1550 e 1568*, Rosanna Bettarini, Paola Barocchi (ed.), vol. III, Testo, Florence 1971

Vaughn 2002 Richard Vaughn, *Philip the Bold. The Apogee of Burgundy*, Woodbridge 2002

Villela-Petit 2003 Inès Villela-Petit, *Le Bréviaire de Châteauroux*, Paris (et al.) 2003

Waagen 1824 Gustav Friedrich Waagen, "Extrait d'une lettre de M. le docteur Waagen, au secrétaire de la société des beaux-arts à Gand. Berlin, 8 Janvier 1825," in: Messager des sciences et des arts, Ghent 1824, pp. 438-450

Waagen 1839 Gustav Friedrich Waagen, *Kunstwerke und Künstler in England und Paris*, vol. 3, Berlin 1839

Waagen 1851 Gustav Friedrich Waagen, in: Kunstblatt, 2, no. 12, 1851, pp. 91-94

Waagen 1862 Gustav Friedrich Waagen, *Handbuch der deutschen und niederländischen Sammlungen*, Stuttgart 1862

Waddel 2008 Gene Waddel, *Creating the Pantheon. Design, Materials and Construction*, Rome 2008

Wappers 1923 Jacques Wappers, *Le Musée d'Anvers en une heure. Ce qu'il faut voir. Ce qu'il faut savoir. Les Maîtres anciens*, 1923

Weale 1909 William H. James Weale, "Les Christus," in: Annales de la Société d'Emulation de Bruges 59, 1909, pp. 97-120, pp. 363-64

Wedekind 2007 Gregor Wedekind, "Wie in einem Spiegel. Porträt und Wirklichkeit in Jan van Eycks „Arnolfinihochzeit"," in: Zeitschrift für Kunstgeschichte 70, 2007, pp. 325-346

Wellmann 2013 Kathleen Wellman, *Queens and Mistresses of Renaissance France*, New Haven/London 2013

Wescher 1947 Paul Wescher, *Jean Fouquet und seine Zeit*, Basel 1947

Wescher 1948 Paul Wescher, "Jean Perréal, the „Master of Charles VIII"," in: The Art Quarterly 11, 1948, pp. 352-357

Westheim 1937 Paul Westheim, „Die Meisterwerke der französischen Kunst. Im neuen Palais des Beaux-Arts," in: Pariser Tageszeitung, 27. July 1937, vol. 2, no. 409, p. 4

Wetter 2015 Evelin Wetter, *Liturgische Gewänder in der Schwarzen Kirche zu Kronstadt in Siebenbürgen*, Riggisberg 2015

Willet 1996 Johan Willet, *Zeitzeugnisse. Aus dem Notizbuch eines Touristen auf der Weltausstellung von 1937*, Amédée Ozenfant, in: Cat. London/Barcelona/Berlin 1996, pp. 115-118

Winkler 1959 Friedrich Winkler, "Ein frühfranzösisches Marienbild," in: Jahrbuch der Berliner Museen 1, 1959, pp. 179-189

Wolfthal 2011 Diane Wolfthal, "Religious Devotion, Aristocratic Status, and Crusading Fervour in Rogier van der Weyden's Diptych of Pilippe de Croÿ," in: *Essays in Renaissance Art in Honour of Colin Eisler*, ed. by John Garton, Diane Wolfthal, Toronto 2011, pp. 105-123

Zay 1937 Jean Zay, "L'Education National à l'Exposition," in: Le Livre d'or officiel de l'Exposition internationale des arts et des techniques, Paris 1937, pp. 79-84

Zervas 1987 Diane Finiello Zervas, *The Parte Guelfa, Brunelleschi e Donatello*, Locust Valley/N.Y. 1987

Zervos 1936 Christian Zervos, "Réflexions sur la tentative d'esthétique dirigée du IIIe Reich," in: Cahiers d'Art 11, 1936, pp. 209-212

Zink 2004 Michel Zink, *Le Moyen Âge à la lettre. Un Abécedaire médiéval*, Paris 2004

Zvereva 2002 Alexandra Zvereva, *Les Clouet de Catherine de Médicis. Chefs-d'œuvre graphiques du Musée Condé*, Paris 2002